Baldrige Award Winning Quality

Sixth Edition

How to Interpret the Malcolm Baldrige Award Criteria

Mark Graham Brown

QUALITY RESOURCES ®
A Division of The Kraus Organization Limited
New York, New York

ASQC
Quality Press
Milwaukee, Wisconsin

This text is independently produced by Quality Resources and is not an official document created by or endorsed by the Secretary of Commerce nor the National Institute of Standards and Technology or any other organization, governmental or private, having official recognition and/or association with the Malcolm Baldrige National Quality Award.

Printed in the United States of America

00 99 98 97 96   10 9 8 7 6 5 4 3 2 1

Quality Resources
A Division of The Kraus Organization Limited
902 Broadway, New York, New York 10010

ASQC Quality Press
611 East Wisconsin Avenue
Milwaukee, Wisconsin 53202

Library of Congress Cataloging-in-Publication Data

Brown, Mark Graham.
    Baldrige award winning quality : how to interpret the Malcolm
Baldrige Award criteria / Mark Graham Brown.—6th ed.
        p.   cm.
    Includes bibliographical references.
    ISBN 0-527-76318-7
    1. Malcolm Baldrige National Quality Award. 2. Total quality
management—United States—Awards. I. Title.
HD62. 15.B76   1995
658.5'62'07973—dc20   94-2795
                                                       CIP

ISBN 0-527-76318-7

CONTENTS

INTRODUCTION

The Malcolm Baldrige Award is nine years old in 1996. By now, just about every company in the United States has heard something about the award and is at least somewhat familiar with this approach to running a company, called total quality management, or TQM. Since 1988, there have been literally hundreds of articles published on the Baldrige Award and how companies are using the award criteria to improve their operations. When the first edition of this book was published in 1991, it was the only one of its kind on the market. Now there are at least six others, and chapters in many quality management books, that address the award.

The Growth and Decline of the Quality Movement

The Malcolm Baldrige National Quality Award began in 1988 to promote total quality management, or TQM, as an increasingly important approach for improving the competitiveness of American companies. In the past seven years, what started out as an add-on approach consisting of some statistical analyses of quality, training, and the formation of groups of employees working in teams to solve problems has gone through some major changes. More than two thirds of the companies that begin a TQM initiative end up failing or dropping the initiative before it can really take hold. If TQM has failed it is because of errors in implementation rather than the approach itself being flawed. Implementing TQM as a program will doom you to eventual failure. A program has a beginning and end, and does not change the basic approach to running a business. For TQM to succeed, an organization needs to integrate its philosophies and practices into its day-to-day approach of running the business.

Baldrige winners all have this characteristic in common, even though their approaches to delighting their customers are often vastly different. TQM is far from dead. It has gone through some major changes in recent years, however. Most companies now call TQM something like "continuous improvement" or "re-engineering," or many other phrases. The basic philosophies and practices of the TQM movement are still valid, and still being used by successful companies like AT&T, Xerox, and others. As you will see when you read Chapter 2, the Baldrige Award no longer asks for a TQM effort. In fact, even the word "quality" has been mostly removed from the criteria. Quality is just one of many measures a successful organization needs to concern itself with. The new Baldrige standards now call for balance among customer satisfaction, employee satisfaction, and business results.

One of the reasons the 1996 Baldrige criteria focus more strongly on a balance between business results and customer satisfaction is that some companies have gone out of business or at least gotten into financial trouble even though they had exceptional levels of customer satisfaction and quality. MGM Airlines used to offer the best quality service on flights between New York and Los Angeles of any airline. Their coach was like first class on other airlines, and first class was like going to heaven without dying. The airline no longer operates its route from New York to L.A., however. It now flies only charter flights. Even though quality was exceptional, many customers were not willing to pay MGM's higher prices and deal with a limited number of flights per day.

Baldrige Winner Files for Chapter 11

In recent years, stories have arisen about problems that Baldrige winners have faced subsequent to winning the award. The first and most serious story concerns the Wallace Company, a 1990 Baldrige winner. Wallace is a Houston-based distributor of pipes, valves, and related equipment and parts for oil and chemical plants. The newspaper and business magazine stories presented dire headlines sounding like:

> *Baldrige winner goes in toilet while executives make speeches about quality.*

The newspaper stories explain that the company got into financial trouble because no one was minding the store while the executives traveled all over making speeches, and the folks back home were too busy conducting tours for and talking to the thousands of companies who wanted to know how they too could win the Baldrige Award. In January, 1992, the Wallace Company's troubles became so bad that they filed for Chapter 11.

When, however, you talk to the people at the Wallace Company you get a very different story than the one in the newspapers. Their side of the story is that in mid-1991, a large bank bought the bank that Wallace had done business with for many years. Consequently, Wallace was assigned a new loan officer. Wallace is a highly leveraged business, so they had had a close relationship with their previous banker. During 1991, a couple of Wallace's biggest competitors filed for bankruptcy because the recession had caused business to drop off so severely that sufficient cash was not coming in to allow them to stay in business. Good news for Wallace, right? Unfortunately, Wallace's new banker looked at what happened to these other companies and decided that Wallace might be next. Wallace was losing business because their customers were buying up inventory from the two bankrupt competitors at greatly reduced prices. Wallace's customers said, "We like you people and will continue to buy from you in the future, but the company down the street's going out of business, and has the same parts for half what you want for them."

Observing this, Wallace's new banker decided to call their loan. By the end of 1991, Wallace had temporarily lost much of its business due to the misfortune of its competitors, and then had to pay off a huge loan all at once. Since they didn't have the cash to pay off the loan or the resources to keep afloat until the customers bought all of the competitors' inventory and came back to Wallace, there was only one solution. In January, 1992, Wallace filed for bankruptcy. Since then, Wallace has been purchased by a larger company who is willing to infuse the necessary cash to get the business going again.

According to Wallace officials, to suggest that their winning the Malcolm Baldrige Award, or their total quality effort more generally, had anything to do with their financial troubles is ridiculous. As quoted in the January, 1992, issue of *The Quality Observer*, former CEO Michael Spiess puts it this way:

> *To be real blunt, winning the Malcolm Baldrige National Quality Award had absolutely nothing to do with the position that Wallace finds itself in today. In fact, had it not been for the fact that we embraced total quality management, we wouldn't be around . . . to enjoy the '91 recession. (p. 12)*

Problems of Other Baldrige Winners

Other Baldrige winners have also experienced troubles. IBM, whose Rochester, Minnesota, plant won the award in 1991, had a very bad year in 1992. Yet, under new CEO Gerster, IBM is still using the Baldrige criteria to assess and improve the organization. The company has come back strong in 1994 and has become profitable again. General Motors, whose Cadillac Division won in 1990, closed many of its plants in 1992 and 1993 due to sluggish sales and excessive labor and overhead costs. Both of these companies had one division or plant of their organizations win the Baldrige Award. When the entire parent company is having trouble, though, people forget that it wasn't IBM or General Motors as such that won the Baldrige Award. The IBM plant that won continues to be successful despite its troubles, as does the Cadillac division of General Motors. Cadillac's 1992 Seville STS won most of the major annual automotive awards, and levels of Cadillac's customer satisfaction and sales continue to improve.

Other Controversies Surrounding the Baldrige

In an October 14, 1992, *Wall Street Journal* headline, the process used to select winners was questioned by a unit of Westinghouse that felt it should have won the award, but did not for political reasons:

> *In an action never previously reported, the Commerce Department blocked a recommendation by the contest's expert judges to award a Baldrige to Westinghouse Idaho Nuclear Co., a unit of Westinghouse Electric Corp. that processes nuclear material for the federal government. The veto appears to mark the first time since the competition began in 1988 that the department, which administers the award, has rejected the advice of the nine-member judging panel. (p. B1)*

The Commerce Department has always had the final say on the selection of winners, but since this is the first time the Department has ever overruled the judges' recommendations it raises questions about the credibility of the entire process. Prior to selecting winners, a thorough investigation of the finalists is conducted, looking at records from the police, the FBI, the IRS, and other regulatory agencies. The purpose of this review is to make sure that the company does not have any skeletons in its closet that might come out after the company won the award. As I understand it, the Westinghouse facility had received several safety violations from the Nuclear Regulatory Commission, and the Commerce Department did not feel that a company that received such violations would be a good role model for other businesses in the country.

Another controversy arose in late 1992 when the winners were announced. One 1992 winner was AT&T Universal Card Services, a company that won in the service category. Cries of protest arose because this company has only been in business since 1990. Baldrige Examiners are generally taught to look for at least three to five years' worth of data in the sections that call for results. Three to five data points are important for several reasons. First, one cannot determine whether a trend exists by looking at two data points only. Statisticians generally believe that seven data points are the minimum necessary to establish any kind of trend in data. The second reason is that the criteria call for evidence of *sustained positive results*. Critics argue that AT&T Universal Card Services had only two years' worth of data at the most, which is hardly enough to establish any kind of trend, and certainly not a sufficient time period to suggest that results can be sustained.

In responding to these concerns about how a two-year-old company could possibly win the award, Baldrige officials explain that while trends and ability to sustain results are important, so are the levels of performance as depicted on graphs. AT&T's results were so powerful and at such high levels, officials explain, that this offset the fact that the company could provide only two years' worth of data. While this response sounds reasonable, and is consistent with the scoring scale, it doesn't satisfy many of the critics.

Beyond the Headlines—The Real Payoff of Using the Baldrige Criteria

The bad news about Baldrige winners and finalists seems to make it to the front page, whereas the good news ends up in small print in the back of the paper. The real test of whether or not the Baldrige criteria are a road map for running a better company is whether companies that win the award are better off financially than those that do not apply for the award.

Business executives who dismiss the Baldrige Award as a trophy whose acquisition is more driven by CEOs' egos than by a desire for improved performance need to take a look at the business results of Baldrige winners. The National Institute of Standards and Technology, which administers the Baldrige, reports that of the publicly traded companies that won the award between 1988 and 1993 they returned a collective 92% in the stock market. The S&P index during the same time period showed a 33% return. If you separate out the organizations where the entire company won the Baldrige Award, their stocks have increased in price by an amazing 188%. That means that $100,000 invested in the eight companies that received Baldrige Awards for their entire organizations would have resulted in $288,000. The same $100,000 invested in the S&P Index would have brought in $133,000. Among the companies who won the award is stellar performer Solectron, whose stock has increased over 1000% since going public, and 527% since winning the Baldrige Award in 1991. Solectron used the Baldrige criteria as a road map for designing their company, which they originally purchased for about $150,000.

More Evidence That Following Baldrige Leads to Business Success

Armstrong, the Lancaster, Pennsylvania, firm that manufactures flooring, furniture, and related items has been doing Baldrige assessments of its business units for the past several years. Quality V.P. Bo McBee, who serves as a Senior Examiner for Baldrige, reports on research in his company that shows a clear correlation between scores on Baldrige assessments and the profitability of a business. In other words, units that do well on Baldrige, tend to also do well on their business results. Armstrong's Building Products Operations became one of 2 companies to win a Baldrige Award in 1995.

AT&T is another organization that has had a great deal of success using Baldrige as an assessment and improvement tool. AT&T is the only company to have won three Baldrige Awards, and the prestigious Deming Award. Using the Baldrige criteria to evaluate and improve all of its business units, AT&T under the leadership of CEO Bob Allen has transformed itself from a slow, plodding, and heavily bureaucratic organization to a lean, customer-focused, profitable business that every competitor is having a hard time beating. The October 19, 1994, edition of *USA Today* reports:

> *Analysts say that it is no wonder AT&T's trophy case is sagging under the weight of quality awards. "AT&T is a lean mean fighting machine" says Danil Briere, president of Telechoice Consultants. After cutting 140,000 jobs, taking $25 million in restructuring charges, and re-shaping its bureaucratic culture, AT&T has emerged as the player to beat in telecommunications. (p. 2-B)*

The Baldrige Award Has Served its Purpose Well

In spite of all the criticism about fairness in judging, and whether or not meeting the criteria predicts financial success, the Baldrige has done more to improve the quality of U.S. products and services than anything that has come before it. Quality is now something that almost every company in America is working on. The biggest benefit of the Baldrige criteria is that we now have a common framework for making sense out of all of the theories, tools, and approaches that are part of the quality movement. We have a common language and a common way of understanding where to apply all of these theories and techniques. Another benefit of the Baldrige has been that companies are now sharing and talking to one another to help one another get better. This sharing and helping almost never occurred five years ago—companies kept to themselves, and shared only those practices that they were certain would not help a competitor. The Baldrige Award has been successful beyond the greatest expectations of its founders. It has given rise to 18 similar awards in other countries, 5 of which are modeled exactly on the Baldrige criteria. Thirty-eight states in the U.S. have either established their own quality awards or have an effort underway. Through these "baby Baldriges," quality is being deployed even more pervasively than through the Baldrige by itself. In fact, the existence of state-level quality awards is one of the primary reasons why Baldrige applicants dropped from around 100 in previous years to 71 in 1994 and 47 applicants in 1995.

Interpreting the Baldrige Criteria

One problem for users of the Baldrige Award criteria is that they can be difficult to interpret. The criteria are written to be very general, because they must apply equally to both service and manufacturing organizations, and they must apply to organizations ranging in size from a few hundred employees to many thousands. Because the criteria are so general, they are difficult to interpret. The other thing that makes the criteria hard to use for assessment is that they are non-prescriptive. In other words, they don't tell you how you should run your organization. In my work as a management consultant and as a Baldrige Examiner, I've encountered many instances where people had difficulty interpreting the Baldrige criteria. Other examiners and quality improvement consultants I've spoken to report similar observations.

The purpose of this text, then, is to provide readers with a better understanding of the 52 Areas to Address that make up the Baldrige Award criteria. The book is designed to aid organizations that are actually preparing an application for the Baldrige Award, as well as the many organizations that will be using the award criteria as a way of improving their quality improvement efforts.

How to Use This Book

Generally, there are two types of uses for this book:

1.   As a guide for individuals who are responsible for coordinating or actually writing a Baldrige Award application.

2.   As a tool for individuals who wish to audit or assess their organization using the Baldrige Award criteria, or who wish to apply for an internal award based upon the criteria. Individuals who are responsible for developing assessment and improvement plans based upon the Baldrige criteria will also find the book useful.

The specifics of the book are directed primarily toward the individuals of the first category, with information provided on how to write various sections of the Baldrige Award application. Chapters 1 and 2 provide general information on understanding the 1996 Award criteria. Chapter 3 explains how to write an application. Chapter 4 explains how the seven categories of criteria work together as a system, and covers the overall themes carried throughout the criteria. Chapter 5 includes information on the scoring scale. The next seven chapters cover the seven main categories in the Baldrige criteria. Each of these chapters includes an overall explanation of the main category and definitions of the Examination Items and the Areas to Address. Also provided are sections entitled "What They're Looking For Here," which describe the criteria as seen by the Examiners. This section is followed by a listing of "Key Indicators," or evaluation factors, provided to further assist you with the interpretation of the criteria. Naturally, I assume that those companies seriously considering challenging for the Award have had a quality system in place for several years and that their use of this text is to help them best represent their quality systems and demonstrate compliance with the Baldrige criteria.

This information is also helpful to individuals using the criteria for the second purpose. For this second type of user, the various "indicators" that are listed for each of the 52 Areas to Address are helpful in devising Baldrige-based audit instruments and in developing plans rooted in each of the seven categories in the Baldrige criteria. Chapter 12 explains how to plan and conduct an organization audit using the Baldrige criteria as a baseline. The final chapter outlines alternative assessment approaches and how to use such assessments as an input to your strategic planning process.

Complete copies of the 1996 Award Criteria and Application Forms and Instructions are included in Appendices A and B, respectively. If you are not already familiar with the criteria, I suggest that you quickly review them as a means of preparing for reading and working with this text. If you are interested in actually applying for the award, you might want to obtain the *original* 1996 Award Criteria and the Application (two separate documents) so that you can work with the original entry forms. For the purpose of actually applying for the award, you should familiarize yourself with *all* the information in both forms. These two documents are available free of charge through the National Institute of Standards and Technology, Route 270 and Quince Orchard Road, Administration Bldg., Room A537, Gaithersburg, MD 20899-0001.

How the Information For This Book Was Compiled

The information in this book was compiled on the basis of my experience as a Baldrige Award Examiner from 1990 through 1992. My experience as an examiner enabled me to review actual applications, discuss the examination process and award criteria with numerous other examiners, and participate in the Examiner Training Workshop in which examiners are trained to interpret the criteria. I also served as the lead judge for the California version of the Baldrige Award in 1994 and 1995. The text is not an official publication of the National Institute of Standards and Technology, and the suggestions and opinions in it are my own.

The information in this book also draws upon my consulting experience, in which I help companies develop their own quality improvement processes based upon the Baldrige criteria.

Additional Notes to The Reader

Because the Baldrige Examiners are not allowed to disclose any information contained in award applications, all of the examples used in this text are fictitious. Some are based upon actual applications but are thoroughly disguised so as to protect the anonymity of the applicants. Some companies have volunteered or have made public specific information about their experiences in challenging for the Award. These companies have been mentioned by name.

Future Volumes

Revised and updated editions of this work are planned for each year, assuming that the Baldrige Award criteria continue to be revised and improved each year. Suggestions on how we might improve the 1997 version of this book are welcome, and should be directed to:

Mark Graham Brown
c/o Quality Resources
A Division of The Kraus Organization Limited
902 Broadway
New York, NY 10010

Chapter 1

Understanding the
Malcolm Baldrige
National Quality Award

To help encourage U.S. companies and reward them for providing high quality products and services, the Malcolm Baldrige Award was created in 1987 through an act of Congress. According to the 1996 Award Criteria, the award is designed to promote:

- *understanding of the requirements for performance excellence and competitiveness improvement*
- *sharing of information on successful performance strategies and the benefits derived from implementation of these strategies (p. 1)*

According to Harvard professor, David A. Garvin:

In just four years, the Malcolm Baldrige National Quality Award has become the most important catalyst for transforming American business. More than any other initiative, public or private, it has reshaped managers' thinking and behavior. (1991, p. 80)

With the changes they have made to the 1995 and 1996 Baldrige criteria, the standards will become more of a road map to running a successful business. The 1996 criteria will force even former Baldrige winners to stretch to reach the new standards.

The existence of the Baldrige Award is based upon Public Law 100-107, which creates a public-private partnership designed to encourage quality from American companies. The Findings and Purposes sections of Public Law 100-107 state that:

1. The leadership of the United States in product and process quality has been challenged strongly (and sometimes successfully) by foreign competition, and our Nation's productivity growth has improved less than our competitors' over the last two decades.

2. American business and industry are beginning to understand that poor quality costs companies as much as 20 percent of sales revenues nationally and that improved quality of goods and services goes hand in hand with improved productivity, lower costs, and increased profitability.

3. Strategic planning for quality and quality improvement programs, through a commitment to excellence in manufacturing and services, are becoming more and more essential to the well-being of our Nation's economy and our ability to compete effectively in the global marketplace.

4. Improved management understanding of the factory floor, worker involvement in quality, and greater emphasis on statistical process control can lead to dramatic improvements in the cost and quality of manufactured products.

5. The concept of quality improvement is directly applicable to small companies as well as large, to service industries as well as manufacturing, and to the public sector as well as private enterprise.

6. In order to be successful, quality improvement programs must be management-led and customer-oriented, and this may require fundamental changes in the way companies and agencies do business.

7. Several major industrial nations have successfully coupled rigorous private-sector quality audits with national awards giving special recognition to those enterprises the audits identify as the very best; and

8. A national quality award program of this kind in the United States would help improve quality and productivity by:

   A. Helping to stimulate American companies to improve quality and productivity for the pride of recognition while obtaining a competitive edge through increased profits;

   B. Recognizing the achievements of those companies that improve the quality of their goods and services and providing an example to others;

   C. Establishing guidelines and criteria that can be used by business, industrial, governmental, and other organizations in evaluating their own quality improvement efforts; and

   D. Providing specific guidance for other American organizations that wish to learn how to manage for high quality by making available detailed information on how winning organizations were able to change their cultures and achieve eminence.

The Award is managed by the National Institute for Standards and Technology (NIST), which is part of the Department of Commerce and is named for Malcolm Baldrige, who served as Secretary of Commerce from 1981 until his tragic death in a rodeo accident in 1987. His managerial excellence contributed to long-term improvement in efficiency and effectiveness of government.

The actual award is quite impressive. It is a three-part Steuben Glass crystal stele, standing 14 inches tall, with a 22 karat gold-plated medal embedded in the middle of the central crystal. This prestigious award is presented to winners by the president of the United States at a special ceremony in Washington, D.C.

So what happens to the thousands of sets of criteria that get sent to companies that don't end up applying for the Baldrige Award? Some get thrown in the trash, but from my experience and conversations with clients and colleagues most become dog-eared and are photocopied many times over. They are being used by all types and sizes of companies as the standards by which their own quality improvement efforts and activities are assessed.

Robert Galvin, former chairman of Motorola (1988 Baldrige Award winner), is quoted in the April 23, 1990, issue of *Fortune* as saying:

> *If all eligible companies in the U.S. went for the Baldrige, the natural growth rate of the GNP would rise by an extra half a percentage point. (p. 101)*

So, the value isn't necessarily in winning the award as much as in providing a common set of standards for implementing total quality management.

WHO CAN WIN THE AWARD?

The award program is set up so there can be a maximum of six winners each year—two large manufacturing companies, two large service companies, and two small businesses, which may be either manufacturing or service. In the seven years that the award has been given out, the maximum number of winners has been five, in 1992. In 1989, only two companies won the award, both being large manufacturing companies. The winners from the past seven years are listed in the box on the next page.

One thing that has happened during the past few years is that an increasing number of service companies and small companies have applied for the Baldrige Award. One of the indicators that TQM is being further deployed across the U.S. is the number of small companies that apply for the award. In 1994, many of the 71 applicants were small companies. The winners in 1991 were all fairly small companies. This fact encouraged a number of small businesses across the country, who realized that you don't have to be a Xerox or IBM to win the award. In fact, it is probably easier for a small company to implement an approach like TQM. Many companies were scared off when Xerox reported that it took them 800,000 labor hours to prepare their winning Baldrige application in 1989. Ronald Schmidt, CEO of 1991 award winner Zytec Corporation, reports that they spent a total of $8,900.00 on their application. They did not hire any consultants to help them, and the executives completed the application themselves. Ames Rubber, a 1993 small business winner, figures it spent a total of around $25,000 on their application effort, including the on-site visit time.

AWARD WINNERS: 1988 to 1995

1995 Award Winners

Manufacturing
Corning Telecommunications
Products Division
Armstrong Building Products
Operations
Lancaster, PA

1994 Award Winners

Service
AT&T Consumer Communications
Basking Ridge, NJ
GTE Directories
Dallas/Ft. Worth, TX

Small Business
Wainwright Industries
St. Peters, MO

1993 Award Winners

Manufacturing
Eastman Chemical Company
Kingsport, TN

Small Business
Ames Rubber Corp.
Hamburg, NJ

1992 Award Winners

Manufacturing
AT&T Network Systems Group
Transmission Systems Business Unit
Morristown, NJ
Texas Instruments, Inc.
Defense Systems & Electronics
Group
Dallas, TX

Service
AT&T Universal Card Services
Jacksonville, FL
The Ritz-Carlton Hotel Company
Atlanta, GA

Small Business
Granite Rock Company
Watsonville, CA

1991 Award Winners

Manufacturing
Solectron Corp.
San Jose, CA
Zytec Corp.
Eden Prairie, MN

Small Business
Marlow Industries
Dallas, TX

1990 Award Winners

Manufacturing
Cadillac Motor Car Company
Detroit, MI
IBM Rochester
Rochester, MN

Service
Federal Express Corp.
Memphis, TN

Small Business
Wallace Co., Inc.
Houston, TX

1989 Award Winners

Manufacturing
Milliken & Company
Spartanburg, SC
Xerox Business Products and
Systems
Stamford, CT

1988 Award Winners

Manufacturing
Motorola, Inc.
Schaumburg, IL
Westinghouse Commercial
Nuclear Fuel Division
Pittsburgh, PA

Small Business
Globe Metallurgical, Inc.
Cleveland, OH

APPLICATION AND EVALUATION PROCESS

Applicants for the Baldrige Award must write up to a 70-page application (down from the 85 pages allowed in 1994) that explains how they have implemented total quality in their organization and the results they have achieved. The report is divided into seven sections, corresponding to the seven categories of criteria for the award:

1. Leadership	(9%)
2. Information and Analysis	(7.5%)
3. Strategic Planning	(5.5%)
4. Human Resource Development and Management	(14%)
5. Process Management	(14%)
6. Business Results	(25%)
7. Customer Focus and Satisfaction	(25%)

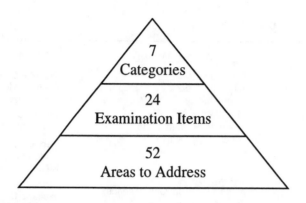

Figure 1.1: Hierarchy of Award Criteria

Each category is weighted according to its importance in the overall evaluation. As you can see, the last two categories are worth half the points, whereas category 3, Strategic Planning, is worth only 5.5%.

Each of these seven categories is further broken down into 24 Examination Items, which are themselves broken down into 52 Areas to Address; see Figure 1.1.

The application report needs to address each of the 52 Areas to Address separately. All Areas to Address should be covered by all organizations. However, an applicant does not lose credit if one or more Areas to Address do not pertain to his/her business. If an item is not relevant, the applicant must explain why, however. Chapters 6 through 12 of this book explain each of the criteria in detail, so that you can better understand what the examiners are looking for.

Evaluation

Figure 1.2 depicts the four-stage review process that occurs once an organization has submitted an application.

In Stage 1, all applications are reviewed by at least five members of the Board of Examiners. The board is composed of approximately 250 examiners selected from business, professional and trade associations, universities, and government. All members are recognized experts in the quality and performance improvement fields. When assigning board members to review applications, the experience and industry background of the examiner are matched to the applicant, provided that there is no conflict of interest. Examiners with manufacturing backgrounds receive applications from manufacturing companies and examiners with service industry experience receive service company applications. Board members must follow strict rules regarding the confidentiality of

STAGE 1: INDEPENDENT REVIEW AND EVALUATION BY AT LEAST FIVE MEMBERS OF THE BOARD

STAGE 2: CONSENSUS REVIEW AND EVALUATION FOR APPLICATIONS THAT SCORE WELL IN STAGE 1

STAGE 3: SITE VISITS TO APPLICANTS THAT SCORE WELL IN STAGE 2

STAGE 4: JUDGES' REVIEW AND RECOMMENDATIONS

Figure 1.2: Four-Stage Review Process

applications, and must agree to abide by a code of ethics, which includes nondisclosure of information from applicants. Examiners are not even allowed to reveal the names of companies that have applied for the award.

In Stage 2, the scored applications are then submitted to a Senior Examiner who reviews the variability in scoring, identifies major discrepancies, and schedules a consensus meeting. Much like a jury, the examiners must reach consensus on your score. A consensus meeting is held via conference call or in person, and is led by a senior examiner. Senior examiners are responsible for supervising the team of examiners assigned to review each company. A recommendation is made as to whether or not a site visit is warranted. A panel of judges decides whether or not to accept the recommendation, or to have the application reviewed by other examiners.

Of the 1,000 points possible to earn on an application, the majority of applications receive scores of less than 500 points. As a general rule, if an application receives a score of 601 or above, the organization is considered to have made it to the semifinals, and might qualify for a site visit. The 600 or above points is not a hard rule about who receives a site visit, only a general guideline based on what's happened in the past. During a site visit, Stage 3, a team of five or more examiners spends approximately three to five days in your facilities touring, conducting interviews, and reviewing data and records. Applicants are asked to make introductory and concluding presentations. The site visit is similar to having an audit done. The purpose of the site visit is to verify and clarify the information included in your written application and to resolve any issues or uncertainties that came up in reviewing your written application. The examiners may have accepted what you said in your written application at face value, but now they want to see proof of your claims.

The findings of the site visit are summarized in a site visit report that goes to the Baldrige Award judges for the Stage 4 review. It is during this review that the judges decide which applicants they will recommend in each category to be award winners. The panel of judges makes its recommendations to the National Institute of Standards and Technology, which makes final recommendations to the U.S. Secretary of Commerce. Those serving as judges are known nationally for their expertise in the quality field and have typically served as examiners or senior examiners in the past.

At the end of the calendar year, feedback reports are sent out to all Baldrige Award applicants. Regardless of the score, each applicant receives a detailed feedback report that summarizes the strengths and weaknesses identified by the examiners in their review of the application. Feedback reports are probably the most valuable result of applying for the award because they provide very specific information on the areas in which you excel and the areas that you need to work on. In fact, the feedback report is probably the best bargain in consulting services that you could buy. It costs $4,500 for large companies to apply for the Baldrige Award and $1,500 for small businesses. For that fee, you get five to six highly trained quality experts to review your company and prepare a detailed analysis of its strengths and weaknesses. If you wanted to purchase this service from an outside consulting firm, it may cost between $10,000 and $25,000, depending upon the size of your organization and the number of consultants involved. So, for $4,000 you receive a wealth of valuable information. In fact, many organizations realize that they are far from being at the level required to win the Baldrige Award, but apply anyway. That way, they can find out exactly where they need to focus their improvement efforts in the next few years.

WHAT THE EXAMINERS ARE REALLY LOOKING FOR

The three factors (or "evaluation dimensions") that the Baldrige Examiners look for in each section of an application are your:

- Approach

- Deployment

- Results

Approach refers to the processes you use to achieve quality products or services. Clearly there are certain themes that the Baldrige people look for in your approach:

- The degree to which the approach is prevention-based

- Focus on continuous improvement

- The appropriateness and effectiveness of the methods, tools, and techniques to the requirements

- The degree to which the approach is systematic, integrated, and consistently applied

- The degree to which the approach embodies effective evaluation/improvement cycles

- The degree to which the approach is based upon quantitative information that is objective and reliable

- The degree to which the approach is based upon cooperation and participation of all levels of employees

- The indicators of unique and innovative approaches, including significant and effective new adaptations of tools and techniques used in other applications or types of businesses

Deployment refers to how well your approach has been executed. It is possible that an organization has an exceptional approach, but it has only been implemented in a few areas. Some of the overall indicators for assessing deployment are:

- The appropriate and effective application of the stated approach to all product and service features

- The appropriate and effective application of the stated approach by all work units to all processes and activities

- The appropriate and effective application of the stated approach to all transactions and interactions with customers, suppliers of goods and services, and the public

Results are clearly *not* asked for in most of the 52 Areas to Address or 24 Examination Items. In fact, one of the big changes in 1996 is that results are only asked for in the following items:

- 6.1 Product and Service Quality Results

- 6.2 Company Operational and Financial Results

- 6.3 Human Resource Results

- 6.4 Supplier Performance Results

- 7.4 Customer Satisfaction Results

Some specific factors that are examined when evaluating results are:

- Current and past overall quality and performance levels

- The demonstration of sustained improvement or sustained high-level performance

- Demonstration of cause/effect between quality improvement efforts and quality results

- The rate/speed of performance improvement

- The breadth and importance of performance improvements

- Significance of quality improvements to the company's business

- The quality and performance levels relative to appropriate comparisons and/or benchmarks

Each of the 52 Areas to Address that are described in Chapters 6–12 of this book are identified as to whether they pertain to approach, deployment, or results (see brackets [ ]).

THE BALDRIGE HAS GIVEN RISE TO INTERNAL AWARDS

Many organizations have been using the Baldrige criteria to evaluate and improve their own companies, without ever intending to apply for the award itself. Among some of the organizations that use the criteria for assessment are:

- Air Products & Chemicals
- Appleton Papers
- McDonnell Douglas
- Baxter Healthcare
- Bell Atlantic
- Pacific Bell
- Roadway Express
- Ericsson
- U.S. Air Force
- Sheraton Hotels
- AT&T
- Boise Cascade
- Northrop Grumman
- NYNEX
- Bell South
- IBM
- Kodak
- Cargill Corporation
- Westinghouse
- Department of Energy

A few of these organizations have made some changes to the Baldrige criteria to customize them for their own organizations, but most use the criteria as is.

RESPONSIBILITIES AND BENEFITS OF WINNING THE BALDRIGE AWARD

Winning the Baldrige Award may be the dream of a number of companies' CEOs and executives. However, winning brings with it a great deal of responsibility. One price of winning is that you must share your approach to quality with others. As an award winner, you will be inundated with requests for information, tours, etc. Everyone will want to know how you did it, how much money you spent implementing total quality management, how much time it takes, and how they can take what you have done and apply it to their own companies. According to an article in the April 23, 1990, issue of *Fortune,* Richard Beutow, Motorola's vice president for quality, made 352 speeches to conventions and corporations, and answered requests for information from over 1,000 companies (p. 109). All of the award winners report similar interest and responses. So if you win, you must be prepared to share your secrets of success with the world, and be prepared to devote several full-time people to the task of responding to requests for information on how you won the Baldrige Award. According to Janet Fit of *USA Today:*

> *For some companies the onslaught can be overwhelming. "We've traveled tens of thousands of miles and made thousands of presentations," says Winston Chen, president of Solectron until he retired in March. Solectron won in 1991. "It's actually quite a bit of a burden. We chose to only do what we could afford to do." (October 19, 1994, p. 4-B).*

The benefits of winning, however, far outweigh the costs. Winners are allowed to publicize the award as much as they want to their customers. Xerox, for example, includes the Baldrige logo on all of its correspondence and product literature. This does wonders for promoting their image as a quality company. Motorola has taken similar advantage of the opportunity to advertise its quality achievements. Winners receive a great deal of peer recognition from other executives, competitors, and the entire business community. Winning is probably the best thing that can happen to a company to promote a positive quality image. Another benefit of winning is the impact the award has upon employee morale. Employees of Motorola, Xerox, Ritz-Carlton, Federal Express, AT&T, and the other award winners have long known that they worked for a quality company. But did the world know? Winning the award tells their business relations, neighbors, relatives, friends, and competitors that they work for one of the best companies in the country.

Chapter 2

What's New in the 1996 Criteria?

I THOUGHT THEY WERE GOING TO LEAVE IT ALONE THIS YEAR!

Senior Baldrige Award Examiners told me that the 1995 criteria would remain in effect for two years, and that the National Institute of Standards and Technology (NIST) would be revising the criteria bi-yearly. The reasons given for this decision were that the 1995 criteria had become a very complete system, with effective linkages and almost no overlap, and that organizations who used the Baldrige criteria for improvement were tired of having to learn a new set of criteria each year. I thought that I would not have to write a new version of this book this year, and my editor at Quality Resources and I debated whether or not the changes warranted a new version of the book. The decision was that because of the many subtle changes to the criteria, it was indeed crucial to publish a 1996 edition of the book.

The changes made this year are nowhere near the magnitude of the changes made from 1994 to 1995 when almost every aspect of the criteria changed. Most of the changes were vast improvements over previous versions of the criteria. The changes they made this year are also important ones. A suggestion I made in last year's edition of this book was actually incorporated into the criteria this year—A new item in Category 6.0 asks for human resource results. Now, if they'd just add another item that asks for results in the areas of ethics, environment, public safety, and community involvement. . . . Perhaps next year!

The number of items in the Baldrige criteria is still 24 as it was last year. However, item 6.3 was added and item 7.5 was deleted. Item 7.5 asked for comparative customer satisfaction results, and results of hard measures of customer satisfaction like market share and gains and losses of customers. It did not make sense as a separate item because comparative data must be presented on all graphs for the examiner to assess levels of performance. Hence, the old 7.4 and 7.5 have been combined into the new 7.4 and called "Customer Satisfaction Results."

These are the major changes. The point system has remained the same, and a lot of wordsmithing has been done to the areas to address and accompanying notes. Two of last year's 54 Areas to Address have been eliminated, leaving 52 this year. However, as in the past, the information has not disappeared, it simply appears under a single Area to Address letter.

WHAT'S NEW IN CATEGORY 1.0: LEADERSHIP?

The wording to 1.1a has changed somewhat, as has the information that is requested in this Area to Address. The first portion of the Area to Address, 1.1a (1), asks about how the executives create and maintain a leadership system that promotes the company's values, and the expectations of the executives for high performance and continuous improvement. The wording of this portion of the criteria is slightly different than last year, but its requirements are basically the same. The second portion of 1.1a in the 1996 criteria is different. It now asks about how executives are involved in increasing future growth opportunities for the company and its stakeholders. This is an excellent addition to the criteria, and an important part of the job of senior executives. It also asks about how senior executives set direction for the company, and integrate various performance improvement goals through strategic planning. This part is about the same as last year. The third portion of 1.1a is about the same as last year, asking for how executives review company performance and capabilities.

Area to Address 1.1b is basically the same as last year. It asks about how executives evaluate and improve the leadership system. The new thing asked for in 1996 is that the Area to Address also asks about how executives evaluate and improve their own leadership skills. In other words, what have they done to obtain feedback on their own leadership approaches, and how have their leadership styles or behaviors changed or improved over the last few years?

1.2, Leadership System and Organization has undergone quite a bit of change this year. What used to be 1.2a and b last year, have been combined and added to to create the new version of 1.2a. This new area to address is long, difficult to understand, and was much clearer last year as two separate short sentences in 1.2a and b. The first portion of the new 1.2a asks about the company organization structure, and the allocation of roles and responsibilities of various levels of managers and employees. The criteria are a little more explicit this year, but this Area to Address now contains too much jargon and is more difficult to understand. The second portion of 1.2a (2) is the old 1.2b, which asks about how the company communicates its values to employees, and how they ensure that behavior consistent with the values is reinforced in the work place.

The focus of the new 1.2b is quite a bit different than it was last year. Last year, it simply asked for information on how and how often performance data are reviewed. It now asks for quite a bit of information on the specific performance measures on which you collect data, and how these measures are related to the needs of customers and other stakeholders. This information belongs in section 2.1, which is about measurement, and it is redundant with what is asked for there. You do need to respond to what is being asked for here, however, so you will need to include a list of your overall performance metrics, and indicate how each measure relates to the needs of key stakeholders. A simple matrix chart should suffice.

1.2b (2) asks about how you review performance on these performance measures, which is what the criteria asked for last year. 1.2b (3) is new. It asks about how performance relative to competitors is tracked. Again, I think this is in the wrong place. This information belongs in section 2.2 that asks about competitor data that is collected and how it is used. In this Area to Address, you can probably get by by indicating whether or not you collect competitor performance data on each of the metrics on your scorecard. The new 1.2b (4) asks specifically how asset productivity is tracked. Some organizations today have implemented new performance metrics like EVA (Economic Value-Added) and MVA (Market Value-Added) to help them do a better job of tracking how well they use the company's assets. It is not necessary that you use either of these metrics, however. Traditional measures like ROCE (Return on Capital Employed) and ROI (Return on Investment) may be fine. The last portion of this new Area to Address [1.2b (5)] asks about how review findings are used to set priorities for performance improvement, and to help decide on the most appropriate course of action. This is a good addition. Last year's criteria simply asked about how performance is reviewed, and not about how you decide on priorities and improvement strategies when performance is below desired levels.

In summary, the new 1.2 is much broader than it was last year. It now focuses on two major issues:

- Organization structure and management systems

- Performance measures and analysis of data on those measures.

Because of the amount of overlap in the new 1.2b with items 2.1, 2.2, and 2.3, it now is very important to compare these sections for consistency in your application.

Item 1.3 has had some minor wordsmithing done to the Areas to Address, but they ask for exactly the same information as was requested last year.

WHAT'S NEW IN CATEGORY 2.0: INFORMATION AND ANALYSIS?

Item 2.1 is still about what you measure and why these measures were selected. Area to Address 2.1a has been lengthened from last year, and asks for some additional information on how your performance measures are linked to your overall business strategy or business fundamentals, along with how the measures relate to key business drivers. This is a good change. Companies tend to measure many things that are important in running the business, but may not be directly linked to key business drivers. The new 2.1a suggests that performance measures should be linked to one or the other.

The new criteria also ask for more information that shows the linkage between the performance measures you have selected, and your overall business strategy. This is an important link, and it makes the connection between 2.1 and 3.2 (Strategy Deployment) even stronger than last year.

Area to Address 2.1b is the same as last year, except that it now asks specifically for information on how your evaluation of your performance measures and measurement system involves assessing the linkage between measures and key business drivers. The concept of key business drivers has become a central theme in Baldrige, and appears almost as often as the word "quality" used to appear in older versions of the criteria.

A very little bit of copy editing has been done to the two areas to address in 2.2, but they ask for the same information as last year. Item 2.3 is word for word the same as last year, and will probably remain just as confusing to Baldrige applicants. I find that the entire page of notes on this item does little to alleviate the confusion over what is being asked for here. This one could use some surgery next year. It essentially asks how you use the data you talked about in 2.1 and 2.2 to manage your business.

WHAT'S NEW IN CATEGORY 3.0: STRATEGIC PLANNING?

Item 3.1 is almost word-for-word the same as last year. The wording of 3.1b has been simplified from last year, but still asks about how strategies and plans are turned into key business drivers. Item 3.2 is also exactly that same as last year. The only change I noticed was that a new note was added that helps explain 3.2b, and the types of projections that are asked about in the criteria.

WHAT'S NEW IN CATEGORY 4.0: HUMAN RESOURCE DEVELOPMENT AND MANAGEMENT?

Not much has changed in this entire category, which underwent quite a bit of change last year. Item 4.1 is the same as last year, with some minor changes in the notes. 4.2 is exactly the same as last year. The 1996 criteria booklet do include a glossary, that includes a definition of the phrase: "high performance work." Some minor editing has been done to 4.3a, which now asks about how training relates to improving customer responsiveness, along with enhancing "high performance of work units." Item 4.4 is exactly the same as last year. The last note (5) now indicates that results for this item are now reported in the new item—6.3: Human Resource Results.

WHAT'S NEW IN CATEGORY 5.0: PROCESS MANAGEMENT?

Both the a and b portions of 5.1 are the same as last year. The words in Area to Address 5.1c are slightly different in 1996. Last year's criteria ask about how the design process has been evaluated and improved to improve quality and cycle time. The new criteria ask about how the design process has been improved to achieve better quality, improved time to market, and better production and delivery processes. In other words, the new criteria are more specific in asking for particular types of improvements that have taken place due to changes you have made in your product/service design process. Items 5.2, 5.3, and 5.4 are all exactly the same as last year.

WHAT'S NEW IN CATEGORY 6.0: BUSINESS RESULTS?

Item 6.1 is exactly the same as last year. One of the notes that has again been included this year is very confusing. The third bullet in note 2 says that data collected through surveys or follow-ups with customers are appropriate to include in this section. This section has historically been used to present internal measures of product/service quality, not customer satisfaction data. Customer satisfaction data is asked for in item 7.4, and need not be duplicated here. Another reason for putting it in section 7.4 is that the item is worth more than twice as many points as this one.

The criteria for item 6.2 are almost the same as last year, except that results relating to HR performance are no longer asked for here. This section is now limited to data on financial, operational, and corporate citizenship measures. The point value of this section has also been reduced from 130 to 100 points this year.

6.3 is the new item for 1996. The 35 points that this item is worth were taken from 6.2 (20 points) and from 5.4 (15 points). There is a direct linkage between this item and the four items in category 4.0. The previous section (4.0) should have listed key HR measures and goals. The results or levels and trends on these measures should be presented in this section. As with other result sections, the criteria ask for data over multiple years so that trends can be assessed, and the presentation of industry and competitive/benchmark data, so that levels may be evaluated.

6.4, which now asks for supplier results, is the same as the old 6.3 from last year. The words in the criteria are the same, but the points have been reduced from 45 to 30 this year.

WHAT'S NEW IN CATEGORY 7.0:
CUSTOMER FOCUS AND SATISFACTION?

The only change I could find in item 7.1 is that 7.1b now asks about how you determine future expectations of both existing and **potential** customers. A few of the notes that accompany 7.1 have changed slightly, but the meaning of the three Areas to Address is still the same as last year. The notes just do a better job of explaining the words in the criteria. The overall description of 7.2 has been amended to include information on how increased knowledge of customers and better relationships with them will help the company improve its products, and generate ideas for new products/services. The wording of 7.2b has changed slightly, but it still asks for almost the same information about complaint tracking and resolution that it did last year. Information in aggregation and analysis of complaint data that used to be asked for in 7.2d has been moved to 7.2b this year, where it makes more sense.

The criteria for 7.3 are essentially the same as last year. Some of the words have been changed, and sentences simplified, but ask for the same as last year. The new 7.4 is a combination of what used to be 7.4 and 7.5 last year. As I mentioned earlier, it never made sense to have two separate items that ask for customer satisfaction results, so now there is only one. The 7.4a portion of the criteria ask for data to be presented on measures of customer satisfaction and dissatisfaction. 7.4b asks for you to present how your customer satisfaction results compare with competitors and benchmark organizations. Chances are you will present information on 7.4a and 7.4b on the same graphs. It is important that you provide hard data on customer buying behavior like market share or gains and losses of customers, along with soft data from surveys and other methods of gathering opinion data. While market share are no longer specifically called for in the criteria, it is mentioned in the notes, and would be appropriate for inclusion for most organizations.

Chapter 3

Preparing an Application
for the Baldrige Award

Preparing the written application for the Baldrige Award is a great deal of work. In fact, Xerox, one of the 1989 winners, claims to have spent over 800,000 labor hours gathering data and developing their application. Don't be scared off by the time spent by Xerox. The president of Globe Metallurgical, the 1988 small business Baldrige Award winner, says that he did most of the work on their application over a long weekend (*Fortune,* April 23, 1990, p. 103). It is important to spend a fair amount of time completing the application report because it will be all the examiners have to evaluate your company. Most award applicants never receive a site visit, as you need to score in the high 600s or better before you are scheduled for a site visit. Therefore, your application needs to be written in a thorough and comprehensive enough manner to achieve a qualifying score for a site visit.

The quality level of Baldrige Award applications varies considerably. Some are expertly written, contain only pertinent information, and are printed in four colors, so they look like an annual report. Others are poorly written, are missing information, and are typed on an old typewriter. The quality of your company is being judged based upon the quality of this report, so it is crucial that the application report be complete, clear, and error-free. In this chapter, I outline some major issues on how the application should be written and provide guidelines concerning mistakes to avoid when preparing your application. Examples are provided to help illustrate what to do and what not to do.

As a special note to readers, I suggest that the information provided in this chapter be reviewed in conjunction with the information contained in the 1995 Criteria and Application Forms and Instructions for the Malcolm Baldrige National Quality Award. Reproductions of these documents appear in the back of this text. An original set is available free of charge from the National Institute of Standards and Technology (see Appendices A and B).

GENERAL OUTLINE OF THE MAJOR COMPONENTS OF THE APPLICATION PACKAGE

Your 1996 application package must contain all required forms including (1) the Eligibility Determination Form (which must already have been approved); (2) the Application Form; and (3) the Site Listing and Descriptors Form. These forms are available in the 1995 Application Forms and Instructions booklet, as are complete instructions on how to prepare them.

Your application package must also contain an application report. The application report consists of a four-page overview of your business and a 70-page document that is generally divided into seven major sections, corresponding to the seven categories of criteria. In this document you must respond to and address all of the Examination Items and Areas to Address as presented in the criteria. If you are in the small business category your written document is limited to 70 single-sided pages (the four-page overview is not counted as part of the page limit). This 70-page limit includes charts, graphs, tables, and any supporting materials you decide to attach to your application. The examiners are very strict on this guideline. If your application report contains 80 pages, the Baldrige administrators will probably tear off the last 10 pages before sending the application to the examiners to review.

You may also be required to submit Supplemental Sections as a part of your application report. According to the Award Criteria, these are required when the applicant is a unit within a company that is in many different businesses. The Award Criteria booklet at the back of this book provides more details on this.

The major components of your application package should be organized into logical and clearly defined sections, such as:

- Application and Other Forms
- Overview
- 1.0 Leadership
- 2.0 Information and Analysis
- 3.0 Strategic Planning
- 4.0 Human Resource Development and Management
- 5.0 Process Management
- 6.0 Business Results
- 7.0 Customer Focus and Satisfaction
- Supplementary Sections (if required)

HOW TO WRITE THE APPLICATION

The way most internal users and award applicants approach writing the application is to form seven teams to work on each of the seven sections in the application. A project manager oversees the effort and attempts to edit the final document to make it appear as if it were written by one person. Although by far the most common approach, it is also the reason why most internal users and award applicants receive such low scores. *Using seven teams and/or individuals to work on each of the seven sections in the application is a major mistake.*

The seven categories of Baldrige criteria work together as a *system*. They are not seven independent factors. One of the most common problems appearing in Baldrige applications is what I call "disconnects." Disconnects are inconsistencies between sections. For example, an applicant might report in section 2.1 that they collect data on three different measures of customer satisfaction, but include no goals for these measures in section 3.2 and no graphs of results in section 7.4. *All seven sections need to be consistent and work together as a system.*

So, how do you ensure that all sections work together effectively? One answer is to have one person write the entire application. While this is not feasible in many large and complex organizations, it has been done. Marty Smith, of New England Telephone was the primary author of that company's Baldrige application. Marty had a committee that assisted in gathering information in writing the application, but he did the majority of the project coordination and writing himself. Several small companies that have won Baldrige Awards submitted applications written primarily by the CEOs.

In most large complex organizations it simply is not practical to have a single person write the application, so some type of team must be formed. But if forming teams around each of the seven Baldrige categories is not the way to organize the effort, how should it be done? A recent client of mine put together an application for the award by forming teams as follows:

> TEAM A: Section 1.0 Leadership
> TEAM B: Sections 4.2–4.4 Human Resource Development and
>   Management
> TEAM C: Sections 2.0, 3.2, and 7.3 Measures and Goals
> TEAM D: Sections 3.1, 4.1, 5.1, and 7.1 Planning
> TEAM E: Sections 5.2–5.4 and 7.2 Process and Customer Relationship
>   Management
> TEAM F: Sections 6.0, and 7.4 Results

Sections 1.0 and 4.0 in the Baldrige system are the easiest ones to work on independently of the other sections. The approach of dividing up into the six teams as listed above worked fairly well in this case, but Teams C, D, E, and F had to work closely with one another. Team F (results) did not write its sections until the measurement team (C) finished its section.

Another organization I worked with organized two small teams and one large team to prepare their Baldrige Award application:

TEAM A: 1.0 Leadership
TEAM B: 4.0 Human Resource Development and Management
TEAM C: 2.0, 3.0, 5.0, 6.0, 7.0

This approach also worked well and helped to ensure that the seven sections flowed together well. Granted, the third team that had five sections had a lot of work to do, but it was a larger team than the other two and was prepared for the bigger effort.

MANAGING THE APPLICATION DEVELOPMENT PROJECT

Regardless of how you choose to put together teams to write the application, you will undoubtedly need a steering committee to oversee and approve the application, as well as a project manager to coordinate the effort. The steering committee should consist of 4–7 executives, including the CEO and his/her direct reports. These individuals may not have any involvement in writing the application, but they should provide access to any data needed by those writing each section and review the completed report. The steering committee members allocate resources to write the application and make any decisions regarding policies and the divulgence of confidential information. Steering committee members should plan on attending a minimum of two 4–8-hour meetings and spending an additional 6–8 hours reviewing various sections of the application.

Once the steering committee has been formed, select a project manager. In some organizations, the vice president of quality is chosen. In others, a function manager or director fills the position. The job this individual currently has is not important. What is important is that this individual have a good overall knowledge of the entire organization, know quality concepts, have good rapport with other managers, and pay great attention to detail. The project manager is responsible for seeing that the individuals working on various sections of the application meet their deadlines and adhere to key quality standards. The project manager serves as the liaison between the steering committee and a group of representatives from the teams who will make up an award application committee.

The number of people who participate on the award application committee will depend upon the size and complexity of your organization and how you decide to divide into

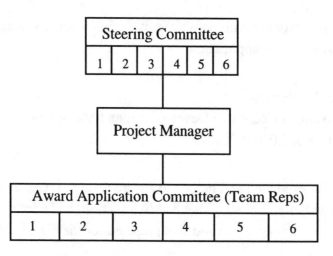

**Figure 3.1: Typical Organization Structure for
Baldrige Application Committee/Team**

teams. Figure 3.1 depicts a typical structure of the teams/committees that work on preparing the Baldrige application.

Select people to work on the award application committee who are knowledgeable of the area/category they have been assigned and possess excellent writing skills. This will consume a great deal of time over the months that it takes to polish the application, so it is important that their bosses release them from some of their other responsibilities.

It is also a good idea to form a team of individuals responsible for editing and formatting the various sections of the application, creating graphics, doing word processing, and coordinating the reproduction and binding of the application. These tasks are time consuming, yet important. And it is important that the application look good and be error free. The leader of the application production team should be a member of the award application committee and attend all key meetings.

The first task on the project manager's and the award application committee's agenda is to hold a meeting to create a project plan for the development and production of the application. A project plan is a detailed list of tasks, resources, estimates, and deadlines. It specifies the person(s) responsible and the amount of time allocated for performing each task. This serves as the basis from which a project can be built. The project plan can be created during a meeting facilitated by the project manager. An example of such a plan is shown in Figure 3.2. The numbers listed in the columns represent the time estimates (in days) for the various people who will work on the application. The plan presented is based upon using a seven-person award application committee. Time estimates apply to each person on the committees, and are based upon the assumption that quality assurance systems are already in place.

Project Plan
Baldrige Award Application

Tasks	Responsibilities & Time Requirements						Schedule
	PM	AAC	PROD	EDIT	SC	REV	
1. Project Planning Meeting							
a. Prepare for meeting	0.75	-	0.25	-	-	-	
b. Conduct/attend meeting	1.0	1.0	-	-	-	-	
c. Write Project Plan	1.0	-	1.0	0.25	-	-	
d. Review/Revise Project Plan	0.25	0.25	0.25	-	0.25	-	
2. Conduct Interviews and Gather Data	2.0	3.0	-	-	-	-	
3. Write First Drafts of Application Sections	2.0	2.5	5.0	4.0	-	-	
4. Review First Drafts	-	-	-	-	1.0	1.0	
5. Complete Mock Evaluations	0.5	-	-	-	-	2.0	
6. First Draft Feedback							
a. Assemble Reviewers' comments and evaluations	2.0	-	1.5	1.0	-	-	
b. Conduct/attend Feedback Meeting	2.0	2.0	-	-	-	-	
c. Document meeting outputs	1.0	-	2.0	-	-	-	
7. Write Second Drafts of Application Sections	1.5	1.5	-	3.0	-	-	
8. Production of Application Report							
a. Prepare and conduct/attend Production Planning Meeting	1.0	-	0.5	-	-	-	
b. Produce artwork, graphics, and printing specifications	1.5	-	4.0	0.5	-	-	
c. Printing of Final Award Applications	0.5	-	1.0	-	-	-	
9. Review Final Materials, Complete Forms, Prepare Overview, and Submit Application	1.5	0.5	1.5	0.5	0.5	-	4/3
TOTALS (days)	18.5	10.75	17.0	9.25	1.75	3.0	

KEY	PM	= Project Manager	EDIT	= Editors
	AAC	= Award Application Committee	SC	= Steering Committee
	PROD	= Production/Graphics	REV	= Reviewers

Figure 3.2: Project Workplan

As you can see in Figure 3.2, the plan includes a detailed list of tasks for each committee member or subcommittee. This plan is the project manager's tool for tracking the progress of the committee members. Many applicants don't bother to create such a plan and end up missing deadlines or having to race around at the last minute to complete the application in order to get it out by the April 3 deadline.

The best way to approach the application report is to look at each Examination Item and Area to Address separately. For each one, make a list of the data or resources needed for reference in order to prepare your response. For any Area to Address that asks for trends or data, you should also make a list of the graphs or charts you will need to prepare. This can be done in the committee meeting by listing the information on flipcharts, as demonstrated in Figure 3.3.

If you are working with several subcommittees, it may be necessary to assign information-gathering tasks to specific individuals. At the conclusion of the initial

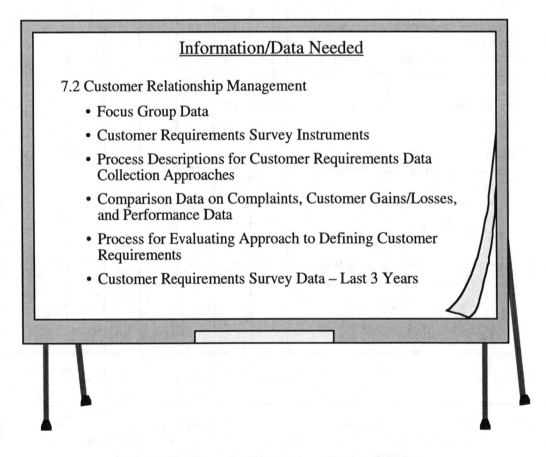

Figure 3.3: Example Flipchart from Planning Meeting

meeting, the project manager should formalize the project plan and distribute it to all award committee and steering committee members.

Gathering the information necessary to write the various sections of the Baldrige Award is the most difficult and time consuming task. Rarely will an organization have all the data needed readily at hand. Some data may not exist anywhere in the organization and may need to be collected. A number of departments and individuals within the organization may need to be contacted to collect all of the information needed to write each section of the application. The biggest problem experienced by committees working on the Baldrige application is lack of cooperation from other employees and managers who must dig up the information or data needed. This is one of the reasons that it is important to have high-level individuals on the steering committee. If the CEO or one of the vice presidents calls a manager to ask him or her where the data are that you requested in order to write your section of the award application, you can bet that the delinquent manager will get the information quickly.

All first drafts of sections of the application report should be turned in to the project manager, who will review them for accuracy, completeness, and clarity. He or she will return the edited copy of first drafts to the committee members who wrote them. The writers will then make the corrections suggested by the project manager and resubmit the application sections. If the project manager is satisfied that all of the necessary changes have been made, the material will be turned over to an editor who will edit the grammar, consistency, headings, readability, and other factors. After the sections have been edited, they will be turned over to production for word processing and preparation of graphics.

Once the report has been produced, internal copies should be prepared and distributed to the steering committee members and other key managers and technical professionals for their review. It is also a good idea to give the application to a few relatively new employees who have industry experience but little knowledge of the organization. These individuals can review the manuscript and the practices of your organization more objectively.

In addition to having many different people review the application and provide their feedback, it is also a good idea to train a group of people to actually evaluate the application against the Baldrige criteria. This might be a group of outside quality consultants or a group of your own employees. Whoever you select to perform this evaluation should be familiar with quality improvement concepts and tools, and be objective in their evaluation of the organization's application.

Feedback from reviewers and evaluations of the application should all be returned to the project manager by a specified date. After assembling and summarizing all of the comments, suggestions, and scores of the evaluators, the project manager should plan a two-day meeting with the award application committee to review the feedback and discuss changes and additions needed to each of their sections, as well as any overall comments that pertain to all sections. As each section is reviewed, the project manager should record the changes needed in each Area to Address to satisfy the reviewers' suggestions and to improve on the scores given during the mock evaluation.

Following the meeting, the committee members revise their assigned sections based upon the action items and suggestions outlined in the meeting. Final drafts are submitted to the project manager for review and to the editor for final editing. The entire application should then be given to production so that the layout, cover, tabs, and any other aspects of the final document can be designed. Some applicants custom-design a cover and special tabs for their applications, but this is definitely not necessary. In fact, an application that looks *too* slick may make the examiners suspect that the applicant is perhaps substituting flash for substance. Final artwork is then done, the materials are thoroughly proofread, and the application is printed and bound.

Then, the tough part comes—the waiting. Applications are due on April 3rd and you won't receive feedback for many months. This can be very frustrating, but the review process takes a long time.

Figure 3.4 provides a graphic representation of the major steps involved in completing an application. The exact process you use will no doubt vary somewhat from this. A mock evaluation by people trained on the Baldrige criteria is an important step that you should not leave out. Many organizations don't do this because they lack time or expertise. Lack of time shouldn't be a problem if you prepare the application far enough in advance. Lack of expertise is no excuse either. Universities and professional associations such as the American Society for Quality Control and the Association for Quality and Participation offer workshops on how to interpret the Baldrige criteria.

HOW TO WRITE THE APPLICATION REPORT

The main reason for writing this book is that many applicants and others using the Baldrige Award Criteria misinterpret what the Areas to Address are requesting. Reading Chapters 6–12 of this book and using them as a reference when writing your responses to each of the 52 Areas to Address should help you to interpret the criteria accurately. In writing your report, it is important that you don't make the same mistakes made by many of the previous Baldrige Award applicants.

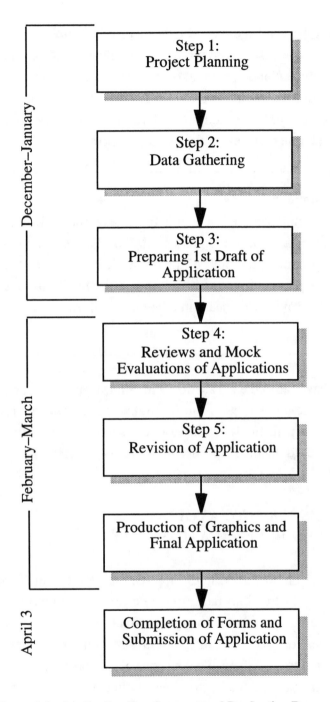

Figure 3.4: Application Development and Production Process

Pages 42–46 of the 1995 Baldrige Award Criteria provide some fairly specific instructions and advice about the best way to write your application. Make sure that you read these pages thoroughly and understand all of the guidelines. An important guideline that bears repeating is to make sure that you reference each section with the appropriate numbers and letters. It is helpful to the examiners if you include the Examination Items in your response, for reference. An example is shown below.

3.2 Strategy Deployment

3.2a(1). Anacon's long-term quality goal is to achieve 100% customer satisfaction. Some related long-term goals are to possess 40% of the domestic market for automated teller machines, and 60% of the domestic market for POS terminals. One of the requirements we must address is to improve the reliability of our products. We need to work on improving the mean time between failures as well as our overall product lifespans.

Several applicants have labeled each section with a number to correspond to the Examination Item (e.g., 4.2, 3.1, etc.). But when this is done without indicating *letters* for the Areas to Address, it is difficult for the examiners to find the information that pertains to each Area. You should denote responses to Areas by underscoring the Item/Area number and letter (e.g., 3.2a(1)).

TEN COMMON MISTAKES TO AVOID
WHEN WRITING YOUR APPLICATION

The general guidelines on how to write the application report (which appear in the Application Forms and Instructions package) are clear and well written. However, sometimes general guidelines are not enough to effectively guide performance. Judging by some of the applications received, many applicants either misunderstood the guidelines or chose not to read them. The purpose of this portion of the book is to list and explain some of the mistakes made by previous applicants. By reviewing this information, you should be able to avoid making some of the errors that others have made in the past. I have listed and discussed 10 of the most common mistakes in the pages that follow. Some of these are minor errors, but most are mistakes that may cost you a large percentage of the points which otherwise might have been earned for a particular item.

Some of the information in this section is based upon the Baldrige Award Criteria. Other information is based upon my own and other examiners' experience in reviewing applications.

Mistake #1: Reiteration of Words From the Criteria

This is a technique that can enhance your score only if the examiner is not paying much attention to what he/she is reading. Examiners all have other jobs, so frequently they must review the applications in the evenings, after a long day of work. If your response includes some of the same words from the criteria, at first glance, it sounds like your response meets the criteria well. An examiner who is tired might just skim your response and give it a high score because it "sounds good." However, you must remember that up to six different examiners review each application. For every one or two who give you a higher score because your response includes words from the criteria, there will be others who will take points away for this. Repeating the criteria in your response is unnecessary.

Mistake #2: Use of Examples Rather Than Descriptions of Processes

This commonly occurs when the applicant does not have a systematic process to describe. A typical response starts out with a general statement such as: "We identify customer requirements in a variety of different ways." This is then followed by a detailed example of one situation where customer requirements have been identified. The problem with responding this way is that it doesn't tell the examiners how you identify customer requirements. If you do not describe a well-defined process in your response, chances are that you do not have a process, and customer requirements are identified in a casual and unsystematic manner. Whenever the criteria ask about processes, respond with a fairly detailed description of a step-by-step process or with a detailed flowchart.

Mistake #3: No Examples When They Will Help to Illustrate a Process

This is just the opposite of Mistake #2, using an example as your response. Including an example or two helps to clarify a flowchart or process description. Examples add interest and credibility to your process descriptions; just be certain that you have adequately described the process(es) before the example is used. When you use examples, make sure that you label them as such, and explain whether or not the situations you described are typical. Remember that the examiners have never seen your company and may not even be very familiar with your industry. Examples help to paint a picture for the examiner, making it easier for him/her to understand how your processes and approaches work.

Mistake #4: Lack of Specificity

Of all the mistakes made by applicants, this is the most common and the most severe. Answering all of the 52 Areas to Address thoroughly within 70 pages is tough. It is obvious that many applications have been ruthlessly edited to include only the most necessary information. Often, too much information is eliminated. A vague and general description of a process will earn few points from the examiners. An example of a non-specific response is shown in the following box.

7.2c How the company follows up with customers on products, services, and recent transactions to determine satisfaction, resolve problems, to seek feedback for improvement, to build relationships, and develop ideas for new products and services.

We pride ourselves at MGB Industries at being proactive in our appraoch to managing relationships with our customers. With our own sales force and our field representatives, we are in almost constant contact with our various customers to ensure that we are consistently meeting or exceeding their expectations. This sometimes daily telephone or face-to-face contact has allowed us to forge strong bonds with our customers, making it likely that we will be their supplier of choice for years to come. One example of this is Willow Manufacturing, who has been a customer of ours for the last 21 years.

There is nothing particularly wrong with what is said in this example. The problem is that the response is vague and nonspecific. It also includes an example of an isolated incident, rather than describing a system or process. The response is about as long as the criteria, and not enough information is provided to adequately judge how well the applicant is doing on this Area to Address. When a response is vague or nonspecific, examiners are taught to assign a low score. You don't need to provide pages and pages of information in response to each area. However, a sentence or two is usually not enough.

Mistake #5: Presenting Data on Only a Few Quality Indices/Measures

This is also a very common occurrence, and one that will cause you to lose a significant number of points. If you collect data on over 40 different indices of quality and report on only five or six of them, the examiners might assume that you have chosen to report on only the measures for which your performance is good. Data not reported are often assumed to be negative. In one case study used to train the Baldrige Examiners, the applicant claims to have 160 indices that are used to measure quality. Yet, the application presents data on only three or four of these indices, and says nothing about performance levels for the other 150+ measures. While it may not be practical to present data for 160 indices, a great deal of information can be summarized in a table or chart. Examples of how to do this are presented in Chapter 11: Interpreting the Criteria for Business Results.

Mistake #6: Too Many Cross-References to Other Sections

According to the directions in the 1996 Award Criteria, you should:

Cross-reference when appropriate.

> *Applicants should try to make each Item response self-contained. However, there may be instances when responses to different Items are mutually reinforcing. It is then appropriate to reference responses to other Items, rather than to repeat information. In such cases, applicants should use Area designators (for example, "see 2.3a"). (p. 28)*

The criteria further explain that you should not repeat information included elsewhere. You can cross-reference information if it will help enhance your response to a particular Area to Address. Make sure that you cite the page number, the Examination Item (number), and the specific Area to Address (letter). For example:

> *"Additional information on our overall approach to human resource management is presented on page 28, in section 4.1a."*

You should minimize the amount of cross-referencing that you do, however. It is very frustrating to the examiners to have to constantly flip back and forth from section to section. Because each of the Areas to Address is designed to stand on its own, it should not be necessary to cross-reference very often.

Mistake #7:   Responding With Words When You Should Respond With Data

All of the Areas to Address in category 6, and one of the items in section 7 ask for trends and results. Any time you see the words "trends," "results," or "data" in the criteria, this should be your clue to make sure your response includes graphs and data. It is surprising that this is misinterpreted, but applicants sometimes describe a *process* when the criteria specifically ask for *trends (data)*. Or, they give a narrative summary of their results with no graphs or statistics. An example of a poor response follows.

6.2a Current levels and trends in key measures and/or indicators of company operational and financial performance. Graphs and tables should include appropriate comparative data.

We track many different indices that relate to operational performance factors used in our business. These measures have shown continuous improvements over the past five years, with significant improvements being demonstrated in the last year. We also track conformity of our support processes to quality standards. These measures, too, have shown improvement over the past few years.

Note that no graphs or statistics are included. Words and phrases such as "significant improvements" do not impress the examiners—they want to see the data. A narrative summary of the information included in graphs is good, but it is not a substitute for hard data.

Mistake #8: Responding With Information That is not Relevant to the Area to Address

This is also one of those mistakes that occurs quite frequently in the applications. It seems that either the applicants misunderstand some Areas to Address or that they understand them but have little to say in their response. Rather than admit something like: "We have not identified a process for tracking the degree to which customer requirements are met," applicants respond with some quality jargon that may seem good at first glance. But in reading it a second or third time one realizes that the response has nothing to do with what was asked for in the Area to Address.

An example of a response that is unrelated to the Area to Address is shown in box 7.3a (following).

7.3a How the company determines customer satisfaction. Include: (1) a brief description of processes, and measurement scales used; frequency of determination; and how objectivity and validity are assured. Indicate significant differences, if any, in processes and measurement scales for different customer groups or segments; and (2) how customer satisfaction measurements capture key information that reflects customers' likely future market behavior.

Customer satisfaction is our number one priority at Baker Industries. Every employee is expected to meet customer expectations for timely service and high quality products. We work in a collaborative fashion to systematically identify the ever-changing demands and expectations of our customers, and find ways of meeting those demands. Our quality and levels of customer satisfaction are unsurpassed in our industry, and continue to improve each year.

The Area to Address asks you to explain how the organization measures customer satisfaction. The example in the box does not discuss how customer satisfaction is measured. It only includes various "well written" phrases, which is typical of an application submitted by an organization that does not have the data to respond to an area. A response such as the one in the example would not earn any points, because there is no information that tells the reader how the company segments its customers and measures customer satisfaction.

Mistake #9: Use of Too Many Acronyms

I was once interviewing a man from AT&T on a consulting project, and I asked him to describe a particular process he was involved with, without using acronyms in his description. He just stuttered and couldn't explain the process without including a myriad of acronyms. Use of acronyms is very frustrating to the Baldrige Examiners. Everyone in your company may know what certain company-specific acronyms stand for, but the Baldrige Examiners won't. Spelling out what an acronym stands for the first time you use it will not solve the problem either. An examiner will forget and have to refer back to previous sections to recall what the CASE or AIP programs are. Avoid acronyms entirely if you can. This is tough for many large companies that have an acronym for every process, document, and program. An example of an acronym-laden response is shown in the following.

Our CEO, CIO, and CQO all strongly support the TQM effort at BMI through the initiation of a variety of programs such as the CCF (Customers Come First), AQP (Assessment of Quality Processes), and PTM (Participative Team Management). Our IIS and OEM Divisions have thoroughly implemented QFD using a variety of QITs (Quality Improvement Teams).

Mistake #10: Use of Too Much Industry, Quality, or Management Jargon

This irritates many of the Baldrige Examiners because it appears as though you are trying to impress them with your vocabulary. The application should be written at a fairly low reading level, about the same level used in an annual report to shareholders. It should not be written like a college textbook or a technical paper for a professional journal. Use of complicated words and jargon should be thoroughly discouraged. The Baldrige Examiners are probably as unfamiliar with your industry jargon as they are with your acronyms. To eliminate jargon, it is a good idea to have someone outside of your company, or new employees, review the application before it is finalized.

Even though the Baldrige Examiners may be familiar with quality jargon such as Quality Function Deployment or Taguchi Method, it is best not to overuse these terms either. Write the application as if it were to be read by shareholders or the general public. A tenth- to twelfth-grade reading level is appropriate. This is the same level as a magazine such as *U.S. News and World Report.*

Similarly, you may want to avoid using trendy management words and phrases such as

- Intrapreneuring
- Cross-functional management
- Participative team process
- De-layering

TEN RULES TO USE WHEN PREPARING GRAPHICS FOR YOUR APPLICATION

Up to this point we have been discussing the writing style of the application and common mistakes made when preparing the written response. Let's now turn our attention to graphics, which are also a big part of the application. So many of the applications contain poor and hard-to-read graphics that this subject warrants separate treatment and guidelines. I have outlined ten rules to keep in mind when preparing and discussing graphics in your application.

Rule #1: Explain Graphics in the Text

Some applicants have responded to an Area to Address that asks for data by simply including a graph, with no explanation of what the graph shows, or what kind of results are shown. A graph or chart should never be included without at least some explanation or reference in the text of your application. For example, you might say something like:

Figure 6.3 presents a summary of our major quality results compared to our foremost competitor: DMI. As you can see, we are superior to them in each of the six measures of quality results depicted in the bar graph.

Always explain what the graph represents and summarize the conclusions that can be drawn from the data depicted on the graph. Even though it may seem obvious, the examiner may miss the significance of certain data unless you call his/her attention to it.

For example:

The data in Figure 7.8 show that our levels of customer satisfaction have improved by over 80% in the last two years. We have shown steady improvements over each of the last five years.

Rule #2: Don't Duplicate Information from Graphics in the Text

This is just the flip side of the first rule. Graphics should be explained and referenced, but the information contained in them need not be duplicated in the text that accompanies them. This is simply a waste of valuable space and an insult to the examiner's intelligence. Figure 3.5 shows what *not* to do when explaining graphics.

As you can see in the graph below, the levels of customer satisfaction began at 78% satisfied in 1991, rose to 83% in 1992, dropped back to 79% in 1993, and rose again to 86% in 1994. In 1995, levels of customer satisfaction rose to 88% and to an all-time high of 92% so far in 1996.

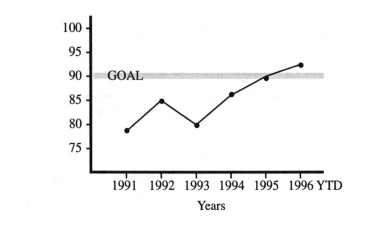

Figure 3.5 What *Not* to Do When Explaining Graphics

Rule #3: Don't Include More than Two Lines of Data on Any One Graph

In an attempt to conserve space, some applicants have tried putting four or more lines of data on a single graph. This is also done in an attempt to show interrelationships among different quality indices. You should never include more than two lines of data on a single graph. Figure 3.6 shows the right and wrong ways to present data graphically.

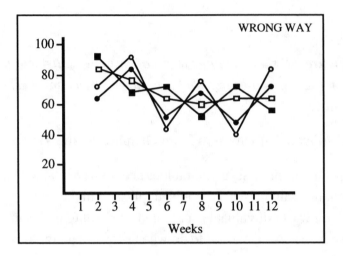

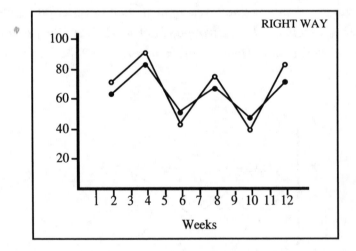

Figure 3.6: Put No More Than Two Lines of Data on a Graph

Rule #4: Graphs Should Depict Goals or Standards

A graph without a line to indicate a goal or standard is very difficult to interpret. Standard or goal lines should be drawn on all graphs to indicate how close actual performance is to desired performance. Figure 3.7 presents an example.

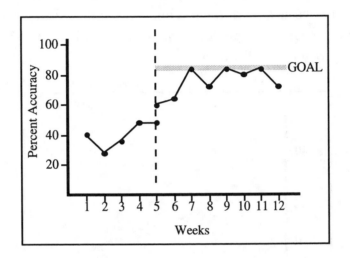

Figure 3.7: Goals Should Always Be Shown on Graphs

Rule #5:   Graphs of Performance Indices Should Show Improvement Using an Ascending Line

We are all taught that results are better when the line on a graph slopes up, representing an upward trend, and that a negative trend is indicated by a downward sloping line. Yet many applicants report positive quality results using negative indices such as number (or percent) of errors. Wherever possible, quality data should be presented in a positive fashion, so the line moves up as performance improves. Rather than graphing errors, graph the number or percentage of products *without* errors. Figure 3.8 shows the right way and wrong way to graph quality data.

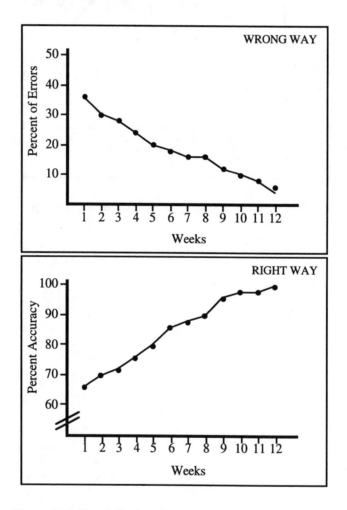

Figure 3.8: Graph Desired Performance So Improvements Appear as an Ascending Line

**Rule #6:   Scales on Graphs Should Be Set Up to Show Maximum Variability
              in the Data**

For your own benefit, it is important that you set up performance scales on graphs to show the maximum degree of change or variability in quality performance. For example, if customer satisfaction ratings are done on a percentage scale, you would not set up the scale from 0 to 100%, unless there were that much variability in the data. If scores over the last five years have ranged from 80% to 95%, you might set up the graph with a scale that goes from 70% to 100%. As you can see in the "Wrong Way" example in Figure 3.9, very little variability is seen in the data scale on the graph from 0 to 100%. The second graph with the smaller scale, however, shows a great deal of variability.

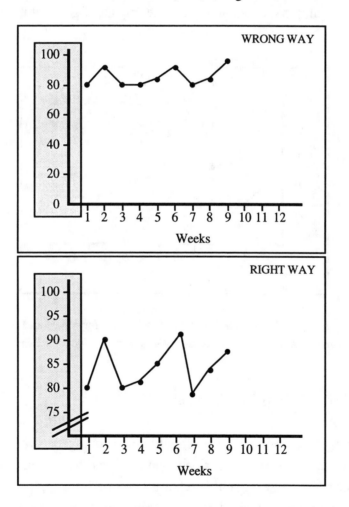

Figure 3.9: Setting Up the Scale for Performance on the Vertical Axis

Rule #7:   Separate Baseline Data From Post-Quality Improvement Data

Baseline data are data on levels of quality or other measures before a countermeasure or change has been introduced to improve performance. In many of the Areas to Address it is important that you demonstrate a cause–effect relationship between improvements in quality results and the introduction of quality improvement efforts or programs. In order to do this, you need to show quality levels both before and after you began your quality improvement effort. When depicting the data on a graph, separate the two phases using a dotted vertical line and do not connect the last baseline data point with the first post-improvement data point.

Figure 3.10 shows a sample graph that depicts the impact of goals and feedback on the percent accuracy.

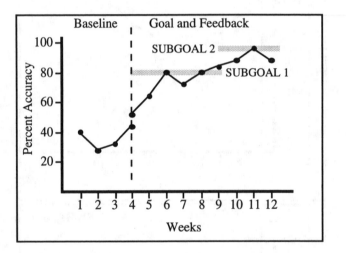

Figure 3.10: Graph Showing Baseline Performance and Percent Accuracy After Goals Were Set and Feedback Began

Rule #8: Use Standard Graphing Formats

Use of strange or exotic graphing formats should be discouraged. Several applicants included graphics that this examiner, for one, had trouble interpreting. Almost any type of quality data can be presented using either a bar graph or a line graph. Bar graphs are most effective when comparing summary data. Line graphs are most effective for showing trends and for showing data over time. Figure 3.11 shows a line graph that has been appropriately labeled.

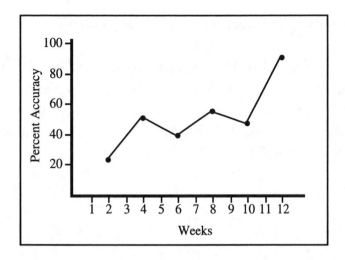

Figure 3.11: Line Graph Appropriately Labeled

Other acceptable formats include pie charts, cumulative line graphs, and scatter diagrams. Examples of these formats are shown in Figure 3.12.

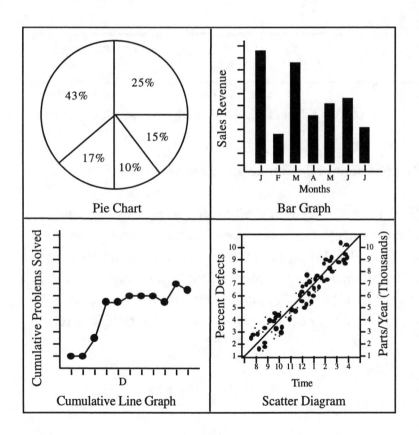

Figure 3.12: Various Ways of Graphing Performance

Rule #9: Graphs Should be Clearly and Specifically Labeled

Every aspect of the graphs included in your application should be appropriately and completely labeled. The two axes should indicate the quality dimension that is being depicted and the measure of time. Goals and subgoals should be labeled, along with the phases in your quality improvement efforts. An example of an appropriately labeled and easily read graph is shown in Figure 3.13.

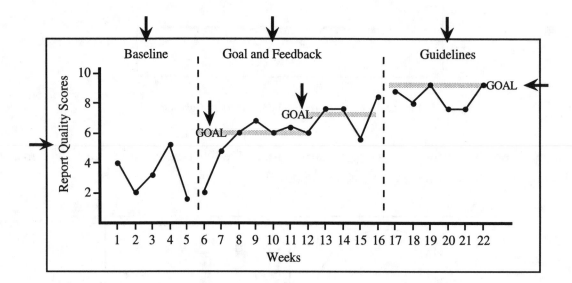

Figure 3.13: Graphs Should Be Clearly and Specifically Labeled

Rule #10: Graphs Should Be Simple and Free of Clutter

Some people tend to make a graph as informative as possible. Pointing out significant increases or improvements, indicating where key events have occurred that have impacted the data, and including other relevant information are thought to help the reader interpret the data better. This seems good in theory, but it often results in cluttered graphics that are difficult to read. A sample graph that includes a great deal of information is shown in Figure 3.14; it is cluttered and very hard to read.

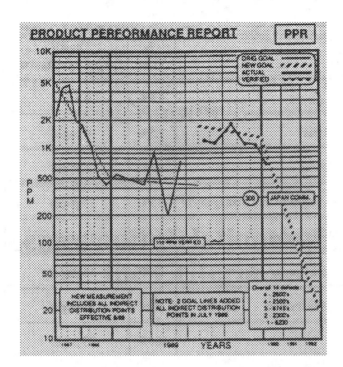

Figure 3.14: Graph is Cluttered and Very Hard to Read

This graph includes four different lines, too many notes, and scales that are very difficult to read. The spacing between years is unequal, as is the PPM scale on the vertical axis. Furthermore, we don't know what PPM means, nor whether the scale is number of defects, ratio of defects, or something else. In general, this graph represents a perfect example of what *not* to do when preparing your own. It violates at least four of the ten rules we have discussed.

LENGTH OF APPLICATION REPORT SECTIONS

You are allowed a maximum of 70 single-sided pages. These limits do not include the four page overview, the table of contents, tab dividers, and covers. Appendices and attachments are included in the 70-page limit, however. In deciding how much space to allocate for each of the seven sections of the report, you should keep in mind the weight given to each of the categories. The Business Results (6.0) and Customer Focus and Satisfaction categories (7.0) are worth 50% of the evaluation, so they should be allocated the most pages. The Strategic Planning category is worth only 5.5%, so relatively few pages are needed for this section. A suggested breakdown of the number of pages to allocate for each of the seven sections of the application report is as follows.

CATEGORY/SECTION	% Value	Suggested Length
1.0 Leadership	9%	7 pages
2.0 Information and Analysis	7.5%	6 pages
3.0 Strategic Planning	5.5%	5 pages
4.0 Human Resource Development and Management	14%	10 pages
5.0 Process Management	14%	10 pages
6.0 Business Results	25%	16 pages
7.0 Customer Focus and Satisfaction	25%	16 pages
TOTAL	100%	70 pages

PRODUCING THE FINAL COPY OF THE BALDRIGE APPLICATION

The appearance of the application is not formally one of the criteria by which it is evaluated, but appearance does give the examiners an overall impression of your organization. If the application is sloppy, poorly laid out, and includes typographical and other errors, this doesn't portray a positive image about the company's level of quality. The appearance of the applications ranges from corner-stapled applications that have been typed on old typewriters, to application reports that have been typeset, printed on expensive paper, and include four-color photos and graphics throughout.

It is certainly not necessary that the application include color photos or that it be typeset. Most laser printers and desktop publishing packages can produce written materials that look as good as those that have been typeset—for a fraction of the cost. The 1995 Application Forms and Instructions provide specifics on the type style and size that must be used in the application. Be sure to review this information before writing your application.

The Baldridge officials also discourage using 3-ring binders for your application. I suggest using a Cerlox plastic spiral binding. With this type of binding, the application can be opened flat on a desk and does not take up much space or hinder movement.

Be certain to include a table of contents, and to separate each of the seven main sections of the written report with tab dividers. I also suggest that pages be numbered sequentially within each tab, and that graphics and exhibits be integrated into the text and not placed at the end of each section or in appendices. Finally, material should be printed on both sides of each page to lessen the bulk and weight of the application.

Chapter 4

_____

Key Themes and Relationships Among the Criteria

THE BALDRIGE CRITERIA AS A SYSTEM

The Baldrige criteria are made up of seven Categories, which are further divided into 24 Examination Items and 52 Areas to Address. While each of the seven Categories is evaluated separately, there are relationships (or "linkages") between the seven and they function together as a system.

As you can see from Figure 4.1, the "driver," or beginning, of the Baldrige assessment is not Leadership, but customers and their requirements. Baldrige suggests that an

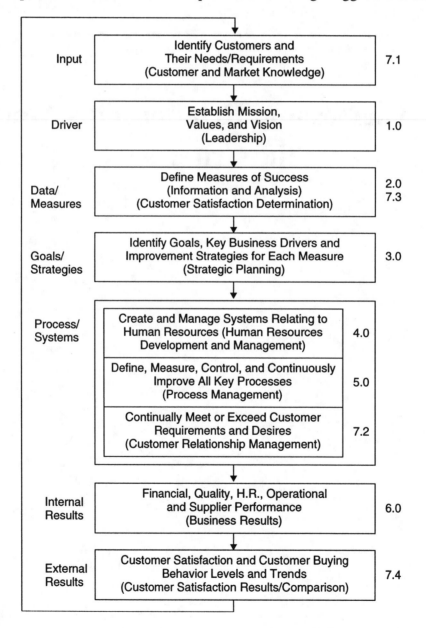

Figure 4.1: The Baldrige Criteria as a System

organization needs first to define its customers and markets, and then identify what is important to each of those groups of customers. Customers and their requirements are asked for in Item 7.1 of the Baldrige criteria. Once markets and needs have been identified, the company can develop its mission and direction, which is what is asked for in the Leadership (1.0) section. Once the mission and direction of the organization have been defined, you need to identify measures of success. Measures are asked for in Section 2.0, Information & Analysis, and Item 7.3, Customer Satisfaction Determination. Short- and long-term goals and strategies then need to be developed, relating to each of the performance measures. Planning is asked about in Section 3.0 of Baldrige. Based upon the goals and improvement strategies outlined in the organization's plans, you need to develop systems/processes: Section 4.0 asks about human resource systems; Section 5.0 asks about work processes in the direct and indirect areas of the organization; and item 7.2 asks about the processes used to manage relationships with customers. All of these systems/processes should work together to produce internal (6.0, Business Results) and external results for customers (7.4).

CORE VALUES IN THE BALDRIGE CRITERIA

Even though there are 52 different Areas to Address in the criteria, there are a few key themes or "core values" that underlie many of the items and categories. These recurring themes or values are:

Customer-Driven Quality

This is one of those concepts that every company today talks about but few actually follow in practice. Most companies assume that they can know what the customer wants and that they can define quality for the customer. Satisfying the real needs of customers is what this theme is about, as well as occasionally "delighting" customers with something they didn't ask for or expect. This theme runs throughout the criteria, involving the way executives set up the company's values and goals, as well as the method executives use to decide what data to collect, how to design new products/ services, and how to improve relationships with customers. This area involves an assessment of how well you really know what customers want and expect, and how you manage your organization so as to meet or exceed those expectations on an ongoing basis.

Leadership

Every single company that has won the Baldrige Award has a CEO, president, and often an entire team of senior executives that are completely committed to being customer-focused in both their heads and their hearts. For them, customer satisfaction and quality are regarded with as much, if not more, importance than other key measures of the company's operational and financial health. For example, AT&T Universal Card Systems, a winner in 1992, not only has top executives that are committed to customer satisfaction but has built its whole management approach and systems around the Baldrige criteria. In contrast, executives in most companies review financial and operational data at least once a month, if not every week. Quality and customer satisfaction data are often never reviewed by the senior executives unless there is a major problem that gets called to their attention.

Continuous Improvement and Learning

Back in 1991, the Baldrige criteria used to have a separate Examination Item that asked about continuous improvement. In 1992 this item was eliminated to reflect the fact that continuous improvement is not a separate activity. Instead, it is a theme that should run through every function and every process in an organization, and it should be integrated into all of the award criteria that ask for information on systems and processes. This is exactly what has been done with the Baldrige criteria from 1992 to 1995. Evidence of continuous improvement is asked for throughout all of the categories. Continuous improvement is also expected in those categories and items that ask for results. Standards are continually being raised in most industries. I read that the new Cadillacs are designed to go 100,000 miles before their first tune-up! No one would have believed this was possible even five years ago; it's the result of continuous improvement.

Employee Participation and Development

For a company to be truly customer-focused, every employee needs to be service-oriented. Karl Albrecht explains in his book, *Service Within:*

> *If you're not serving the customer, your job is to serve somebody who is. (p. 3)*

Companies that have been successful with their quality efforts have found that in order to get high levels of customer satisfaction, it is important to also have high levels of employee satisfaction. The 1995 Baldrige Award Criteria Booklet explains:

> *A company's success in improving performance depends increasingly on the skills and motivation of its workforce. (p. 3)*

Employee participation is often interpreted to mean that the Baldrige criteria require the use of teams. Teams are only one way of getting employees involved in improving quality and performance, and they often have been used inappropriately. I know of one organization that worked for five years to get to the point where 100% of its employees were on quality improvement teams. During this same five years overhead costs went up and quality went down. Teams should be used when they are appropriate, but they should not be viewed as a cure-all or the only way of getting employees involved. Employee development is also an important theme in the criteria. Employees are about the only asset an organization has that can't be copied by competitors.

Fast Response

When the quality movement first began to take hold in the U.S. in the early 1980's, quality meant an absence of defects. Companies began collecting statistics on the number of defects they found and then instituted new processes to improve the level of quality in their products and services. The problem that many found was that quality takes time. If quality was the priority rather than production or some other measure, deadlines were often missed. In 1992, the Baldrige criteria began to concentrate on cycle time or fast response as well as on quality and customer satisfaction. To customers in many businesses, timeliness is as important or more important than quality. Cycle time is also critical when introducing new products or services. Being the first one to introduce a new product can often make the difference in its success.

Design Quality and Prevention

Early efforts to implement quality improvement techniques usually focused on plant floor employees in manufacturing companies and customer contact employees in service businesses. The problem with this method is that most quality problems are caused during the design phase, not while in the factory or while interacting with customers. Designing quality in is the approach that is being encouraged with this theme, as opposed to fixing problems once they are uncovered down the road. This is a more preventive approach to quality.

Long-Range View of the Future

Companies that are the most successful today are those that anticipate trends in the economy, as well as customer preferences and demographics, and design their products and services to meet those future needs and demands. Many companies simply react to trends. The Baldrige criteria expect to see that a company predicts the trends accurately, using a more proactive approach. The term long range, in the sense that it is being used here, refers to 10 years or more in the future, not a year or two. A long-range outlook is also reflected in how the company manages its business. Investments in research, employee development, and cultivation of relationships with suppliers are all indicators of a long-range focus. Evidence that the company manages strictly according to quarterly financial results is the approach that the Baldrige Examiners do not want to see.

Management By Fact

The Baldrige criteria call for evidence of a scientific approach to management. What this means is that they want to see evidence that a company manages using data and analysis, rather than by following instincts. I once worked on a project for the newly opened Toyota plant in Georgetown, Kentucky. The project involved teaching U.S. workers and managers to solve problems and manage Japanese-style. When I talked to the Japanese people and asked them how they managed differently than we do, they explained that we both collect a lot of data. The difference is that Japanese managers make decisions based on analysis of the data. American managers make decisions with their "guts," or based on their feelings and instincts. This latter approach is the one that the Baldrige criteria discourage. Throughout many of the categories and examination items you will find that the criteria ask for evidence of a systematic, planned approach that has been based on the analysis of key data.

Partnership Development

Another theme that is characteristic of recent Baldrige Award winners is that they develop partnerships with various inside and outside groups and individuals. One way of doing this internally is the development of service pacts or agreements between a support function and its internal customers. The two groups get together and draw up an agreement regarding the levels of performance that the support department will adhere to, and the measures that the internal customer will use to evaluate the support function. The agreements also usually specify what the responsibilities of the customer are. The criteria also look for evidence of partnership development with outside groups such as suppliers, unions, and educational institutions. Many large corporations have adversarial relationships with employees, unions, suppliers, and essentially anyone from whom they buy goods or services. Suppliers are threatened so that the company will pay the lowest possible price, and employees are laid off whenever the company has a bad year. These companies have the attitude that suppliers and employees are a replaceable commodity. This is just the opposite of the attitude that the Baldrige Examiners are looking for in this theme.

Corporate Responsibility and Citizenship

The last theme that one sees in the criteria is evidence that the company is a good corporate citizen. Because Baldrige winners are held up to the world as role models of how to run a successful organization, it is important that they demonstrate exemplary performance in the areas of:

- Ethics
- Public health and safety
- Environment

Evidence is asked for that illustrates how the company develops improvement plans for these areas, as well as how it performs compared to other companies. Just contributing money to charities is not the essence of this theme. Rather, it is whether or not the company demonstrates concern for the community and the environment in everything it does. There are many large corporations, for example, that have terrible records in the areas of environmental protection and concern for public welfare that nevertheless donate millions to charities and educational institutions. A preventive approach is what is expected regarding this theme. Your responsiveness to problems when they occur is considered important, but so is what you did to prevent the problems from occurring in the first place.

Results Orientation

This is a new theme that has been added to the 1995 criteria. Based on the fact that business results are now worth 25% of the points in Baldrige, winners had better be results-oriented. The key to achieving good results is a balance between satisfying the needs of shareholders or owner, customers, and employees. Achieving high levels of customer satisfaction at the expense of financial performance will no longer result in a good Baldrige score. Two companies that I think are doing a good job of achieving this balance today are AT&T and IBM, both Baldrige winners. Both companies focus on achieving balance in their organizations' results, and have managed to be profitable, to be good places to work, and to achieve consistently high marks from customers. These organizations and many others have found that being results-oriented means much more than concentrating on this quarter's financial results. Longer-term measures such as customer satisfaction, employee satisfaction, and new product development must be part of the organization's overall scorecard.

An orientation toward specific types of results is also important. An analysis of the market, the economy, competition, and a number of other factors should help the company to decide its driving forces for success in the next 5–10 years. It might be increasing their market share, decreasing prices and operating expenses, or any number of things necessary to be a leader in the markets they serve. Results-oriented organizations need to show flexibility in pushing for different results from time to time, as situations change. One year, profits might be the most important index, and the next year it's safety and environmental performance.

KEY BUSINESS DRIVERS

A major theme in the 1995 and 1996 Baldrige Criteria is Key Business Drivers. Failing to do a good job identifying key business drivers or success factors for your organization will significantly impact your score on the entire Baldrige assessment. Key business drivers are the areas of performance that your organization needs to concentrate on to differentiate itself from its competitors. These are not generic things like quality, on-time delivery and competitive pricing. All organizations need to worry about these types of things. Key business drivers are specific to your organization and are the strengths you need to continue to exploit, or the weaknesses you need to correct to beat your competitors. For example, a cellular service provider listed multiple rate plans, and the highest transmission sound quality as two important success factors. A peanut company identified one key success factor: coming up with a genetically engineered low fat peanut. Key business drivers may come from customer inputs, market changes, or from the inability of key competitors to do something well. Key business drivers are the foundation of your strategic plan (3.2), should be used to develop performance metrics (2.1), identify important processes to benchmark (2.2), and may lead to the development of new products and/or services (5.1).

KEY RELATIONSHIPS AMONG THE SEVEN CATEGORIES

Although each of the 24 Examination Items is given a separate score and evaluated independently, performance on one item clearly affects performance on other items. Something that the Baldrige Examiners routinely do is to look for what I call "disconnects" or missed linkages among items in different categories. The more of these missed linkages that are found, the more likely it is that an applicant will receive a low score. A lack of consistency across the categories and items shows a system that is flawed, or at least an application that was not well planned and written. In the next few pages I will discuss the linkages that should be addressed for each of the seven categories, and the common "disconnects" that I have found in the Baldrige Award applications I've reviewed in the last few years.

1.0 Leadership—Key Relationships With Other Criteria

Compared to some of the other six categories, the Leadership category is fairly independent. However, there are a few things to check for in terms of overall consistency. Item 1.1, which asks about Senior Executive Leadership, should be consistent with information in Item 1.2, which asks about the company's organization structure and leadership system. In other words, what the Examiners are looking for is consistency between the management approach used by senior executives (1.1) and the approach to management defined in Item 1.2.

Item 1.1a(3) asks about how performance is reviewed. This item should be checked for consistency with 3.2, which asks about how plans are deployed. The processes described in these two sections of the application should be consistent with one another.

2.0 Information and Analysis—Key Relationships With Other Criteria

This is really the foundation of the entire application. Although this category is only worth 75 points, a low score here can affect your scores in categories 3.0, 5.0, 6.0, and 7.0. Item 2.1 asks for information on what you measure—what indices you have in your data base for tracking performance in the areas of:

- Customer satisfaction and retention
- Product/service performance
- Operational performance
- Supplier performance
- Cost and financial performance
- Employee-related measures

A linkage that is commonly missed is that between 2.1 and 3.2. Whatever indices you list in 2.1 should be the variables on which you set long- and short-term goals and develop improvement strategies, which is what is asked for in 3.2. I often see measures listed in 2.1 for which there are no goals in 3.2. Or, a more serious error, goals are listed in Item 3.2 for measurement indices that are not listed as part of the company's data base that is described in 2.1. Another common problem is a lack of consistency between the measurement indices listed in 2.1 and the data presented in Items 6.1, 6.2, 6.3, 6.4, and 7.4. In other words, Item 2.1 lists key measures for which there are no data presented in the items that ask for results. This is a warning sign for the Baldrige Examiner. It says that the company collects data on some important measures that it has neglected to present in sections 6.0 and 7.0. The implication is that performance must be poor or the data would have been included. Make sure that the performance indices that are listed in Item 2.1 all have goals in Item 3.2, and that you present results for all or at least most of these measures in sections 6.0 and 7.0. This is probably the most common type of error I see, and it can have a devastating effect on your score.

Another linkage to check for is that between Items 2.2 and 5.2 and 5.3. Item 2.2 asks about your competitive comparisons and benchmarking activities. What the Examiners want to see is that the processes that you have chosen to benchmark and report on in Item 2.2 are the same as the key processes that you have identified in Items 5.2 and 5.3. Often I see benchmarking done on processes that are not identified in category 5.0 as being the key processes that the organization needs to manage.

Item 2.3 is characterized as the "central intelligence item" within the Baldrige criteria. The importance of this item is demonstrated by the fact that almost an entire page in the 1996 Award Criteria booklet is devoted to explaining it. Item 2.3 asks for information on how you aggregate and analyze key data. You need to make sure that the aggregation of your data that you define here is consistent with the graphs and statistics you present in categories 6.0 and 7.0. For example, let's say that you describe in Item 2.3 how you aggregate eight different indices of customer satisfaction into a single customer satisfaction index. Yet, for Item 7.4 you don't present any aggregated customer satisfaction data. Similar relationships would be expected in your description of how financial, operational, and quality data are aggregated, and how the data are presented in category 6.0.

3.0 Strategic Planning—Key Relationships With Other Criteria

Category 3.0 asks for information on how you develop and deploy plans and strategies in your company. I've already mentioned that there should be a relationship between 1.1a(3), which asks about how performance is reviewed, and 3.2, which asks about how plans are deployed. Consistency should also be present between annual, or short-term, goals and strategies asked about in 3.2a and the longer-term goals and strategies. I often see completely different sets of goals for the short and the long term. Both sets of goals should be measured on the same indices, and these measurement indices should be the same ones that are mentioned in Item 2.1. In other words, if you list market share as a key measure, you should have both an annual and a long-term goal for market share.

Another relationship to check is that between 3.2b, which asks about projections of 2–5 year improvements in quality and operational performance, and 7.1b, which asks for information on how the company determines future requirements and expectations of customers. Both of these items ask for projections regarding the long-term future of the company and its customers. Information should be consistent for both sections.

Another commonly missed linkage I am always surprised to see is that between the goals listed in Item 3.2 and the goals presented on the graphs that appear in categories 6.0 and 7.0. For example, Item 3.2 might list the goal for product defects as .003, but the graphs in section 6.1 show the goal to be .005. This is a warning flag for the Baldrige Examiners.

4.0 Human Resource Development and Management—
Key Relationships With Other Criteria

Category 4.0 is more independent than any of the other six sections. However, there are a few key relationships to check for. Item 4.1 asks for information on your human resource plans, which should be derived from the goals and plans outlined in section 3.0. The Examiners will look for how your human resource goals are derived from your overall business goals. Often there is not a clear relationship between HR goals and business goals. HR goals often specify things such as: "All employees will receive a minimum of 20 hours of quality-related training in 1996." Your response for Item 4.1 should explain how this goal will help you achieve one or more overall business goals as listed in Item 3.2. There should also be consistency between the HR goals listed in Item 4.1 and the HR activities described in Items 4.2, 4.3, and 4.4.

Item 4.2 asks about how you design high performance work systems to promote excellent levels of organizational performance. The information in this section should be consistent with the information presented in Item 3.2a, which asks about efforts to reengineer work processes and improve productivity. Information in Item 4.2 also should be consistent with information presented in 1.2, which asks about organization structure and leadership systems. For example, if you describe self-directed work teams in section 4.2, this should also be mentioned in 1.2, where describing roles and responsibilities of different levels within the company (1.2a).

You might also draw attention to your strategies to link recognition and compensation to customer satisfaction and quality, on the one hand, and what you discuss in Item 1.1 when explaining approaches you have used to make sure that executives are committed to quality.

Item 4.4, which addresses employee satisfaction and morale, should be compared to Item 1.3, which asks for information on how you address public health and safety. The approach you take toward public safety should be compatible with your approach to employee safety, which is discussed in Item 4.4.

5.0 Process Management—Key Relationships With Other Criteria

Item 5.1 asks about how you design new products and services. Your response to this section should build upon and be consistent with your response to Item 7.1, which asks about how you determine customer requirements. Item 7.1 does not ask what you do with the requirements once you gather them, and Item 5.1 does not ask how you gather data on customer requirements. In Item 5.1 you should explain how you take the customer requirements data and translate them into product and service designs. Your response to 5.2 and 5.3 should identify your key processes and how you measure them. The processes identified in Items 5.2 and 5.3 should be consistent with the processes identified for benchmarking discussed in 2.2. The measures of the key processes described in Items 5.2 and 5.3 should also be consistent with the key measures identified in Item 2.1. Your answer to Item 2.1 need not list all of these process measures, but they should be consistent. For example, you might explain in Item 2.1 that one of your overall process measures is cycle time. More detail might be presented in Item 5.2 when discussing how cycle time is measured for specific processes.

There should also be a very close relationship between your responses for 5.2 and 5.3. These two Examination Items ask for essentially the same information. Item 5.2 asks about how you manage the process in the line organization, and Item 5.3 asks about managing processes in support functions. Both management approaches should be basically the same.

Categories 5.0 and 6.0 are fairly closely linked. Category 5.0 is strictly an approach and deployment category, and 6.0 asks for results only, relating to the approaches discussed in section 5.0. Item 5.2 asks about how you manage the key processes in producing your products or delivering your services, while Item 6.1 asks for results on the quality of your products or services, and Item 6.2 asks for operational and financial performance data. Similarly, Item 5.4 asks about how you manage suppliers' performance, and Item 6.4 asks for data on supplier performance. A summary of these linkages is shown in the box below.

Approach, Deployment	Results
5.2 ———————————→	6.1 and 6.2
5.3 ———————————→	6.2 and 6.3
5.4 ———————————→	6.4

6.0 Business Results—Key Relationships With Other Criteria

We've already discussed most of the relationships between category 6.0 and others, but some bear repeating here because of their importance. The most important link is between 2.1 and 6.0. The key measurement indices for the company that are presented in 2.1 should be the indices for which data are presented in sections 6.1–6.3. We also mentioned how goals described in Item 3.2 should be consistent with the goals presented on the graphs in category 6.0. Something else to check for is consistency between what you state in the overview regarding when your quality journey began and what you present as starting points in the data for category 6.0. If you explain that your performance improvement initiative began in 1989, and all of your graphs start with data from 1989, there is no way to evaluate the impact of the quality initiative. In other words, there is no baseline data against which to compare your current performance.

7.0 Customer Focus and Satisfaction—Key Relationships With Other Criteria

I've already explained the relationship between Items 7.1 and 5.1, which ask about determining customer requirements and about how those requirements are used to design products and services. There also should be a relationship between Area 7.1b, which asks about determining future customer requirements, and your response to 3.2b, which asks about two-to-five year projections on the future of the company. There may also be a relationship between Area 7.1c, which asks how you evaluate and improve your approach to determining customer requirements, and 7.3c, which addresses how you evaluate and improve your approaches to measuring customer satisfaction. Many companies use some of the same data to determine customer requirements as used to measure customer satisfaction.

Examination Item 7.2, which deals with how you manage relationships with customers, crosses over into a number of other areas to address.

Service standards, which are inquired about in 7.2a, should be consistent with goals that are outlined in Item 3.2. Sometimes a few macroservice standards are the same things as goals. For example, you might discuss in Item 3.2 that your 1995 goal is to receive an average rating of 4.75 on your 5-point customer satisfaction rating scale. Information in Area 7.2a should be consistent with this. I sometimes see customer-related goals in category 3.0 that are at different levels from the standards described in section 7.2.

Examination Item 7.3 asks about how the company measures customer satisfaction. The most important items to check this one against are 2.1 and 2.3. In Item 7.3 you need to identify the specific measurement instruments and methods used to collect data on customer satisfaction. Ideally, you will have a mix of soft measures such as surveys, and hard measures such as repeat business or gains/losses of customers. The measures that are described here should be the same as the measures of customer satisfaction that are defined in Item 2.1. You would be surprised at how many times different customer satisfaction indices are reported in these two sections. This is usually due to different individuals or teams writing the two sections and not bothering to talk to each other. The customer satisfaction measurement indices discussed in Item 7.3 should also be consistent with your description of how customer satisfaction data are aggregated in Item 2.3. If you discussed in detail how customer satisfaction data are aggregated in Item 2.3, you need only to refer back to that section, rather than repeating the information in Item 7.4.

The last Examination Item (7.4) asks for customer satisfaction results. First of all, make sure that you present data for the measurement indices that you list in sections 2.1 and 7.3. I often see a complete list of customer satisfaction measurement indices in section 7.3, but data on only a few of those measures presented in Item 7.4. This is such an obvious omission that you would think that it couldn't happen, but it does. Often the applicant is trying to get a good score in Item 7.3 by listing all of the different measures of customer satisfaction for which they collect data. Yet the data do not all show improvement, so the applicant either doesn't discuss the measures in Item 7.3 or fails to include the data covering those measures in Item 7.4. Sometimes linkages are missed on purpose. In general, it is better to present data for all the major indices that are discussed in section 7.3. The Examiners will be more lenient in scoring if a few of your graphs show downward or flat trends than they will if key data are completely missing.

It is also important to present points of comparison on the graphs that are included in section 7.4. The best graphs have three or four points of comparison. They show how your level of performance compares to:

- Your annual and long-term goals
- Key competitors
- Industry averages
- Benchmarks

Something to watch for in presenting these points of comparison is that they be consistent with information in other sections. Specifically, the goals in Item 3.2 should be the same goals that are depicted on your graphs. What sometimes happens is that performance doesn't look very outstanding compared to your own goals, so goals are simply adjusted. However, the writers of the applications sometimes forget to go back to change the goals and strategies that are outlined in Item 3.2. This is why it is so important to have many sources of comparison to use in evaluating your performance. Your own goals are completely arbitrary, and some companies set goals at levels they're sure they will be able to reach without much trouble.

The number of years for which data are presented is also important. If you began your quality initiative in 1987 and all graphs present data from 1990 on, the Examiners will wonder what happened to the missing years' data. They also won't be able to evaluate the impact of the quality movement, because there are no baseline data—no data from before 1987. The data you present in Items 7.3 and 7.4 should, moreover, be checked against the data presented in category 6.0. What I see happening in some service applications is that the data presented in Item 6.1 (Product and Service Quality Results) are the same as the data presented in Area 7.4b, which asks for data on key dissatisfaction indicators. For example, one company I worked with that ships cargo across the Pacific was confused as to where to put data on claims for damaged freight. This is a standard indicator for which they collect data, and it is clearly related to levels of customer satisfaction. Yet it is also a very strong indicator of customer dissatisfaction. So, does it go in 6.1 or 7.4b? The answer is that it goes in Item 6.1, because it is a measure on which the company itself collects data. If it had data on customer opinions of how the shipping company does in preventing freight damage, that data would go in Area 7.4b.

Similarly, market share and gains/losses of customers are sometimes thought to be operational or financial data that should be reported on in Item 6.2, not 7.5. The data need not go in both places, even though these are important measures. These data belong in section 7.5b.

SUMMARY OF KEY RELATIONSHIPS AMONG THE CRITERIA

When Reviewing These Criteria	Check For Correspondence With These Criteria
1.0 Senior Executive Leadership	
1.1	1.2, 7.1
1.2b	2.1, 2.2, 2.3
2.0 Information and Analysis	
2.1	3.2, 1.2
2.1	5.2, 5.3
2.1	6.1, 6.2, 6.3
2.1	7.4
2.2	1.1, 1.2, 2.1, 5.2, 5.3, 6.0, 7.4
2.3	1.2, 2.1, 2.2
2.3	6.1, 6.2, 6.3, 6.4, 7.4
3.0 Strategic Quality Planning	
3.1	1.1, 1.2, 7.1
3.2a	1.1, 1.2, 3.2b, 6.0, 7.1, 7.4
3.2b	3.2a, 7.1
4.0 Human Resource Development and Management	
4.1	3.1
4.1	3.2
4.1	4.2, 4.3, 4.4
4.2	1.1, 1.2
4.4	1.3

(continued)

SUMMARY OF KEY RELATIONSHIPS (continued)

When Reviewing These Criteria	Check For Correspondence With These Criteria
5.0 Management of Process Quality	
5.1	3.2, 7.1
5.2, 5.3	2.1, 3.2
5.2, 5.3	2.2
5.2	5.3
5.2	6.1, 6.2
5.3	6.3
5.4	6.4
6.0 Quality and Operational Results	
6.1, 6.2, 6.3, 6.4	2.1, 2.3
6.1, 6.2, 6.3, 6.4	3.2
6.1, 6.2, 6.3, 6.4	Overview
7.0 Customer Focus and Satisfaction	
7.1	1.1, 3.2, 5.1
7.1b	3.2b
7.1c	7.3c
7.2a	3.2, 5.2
7.3	2.1, 2.3, 7.4
7.4	2.1, 2.3, 7.3
7.4	3.2
7.4	6.1, 7.1
7.4	Overview
7.4	6.2

Chapter 5

Understanding the
Baldrige Award Scoring Scale

According to a major quality consultant's data base from a survey they conduct on the Baldrige criteria, "corporate America" rates 560 points out of the 1000 on the Baldrige scale. An organization I consulted with scored themselves at 700/1000 on a Baldrige self-assessment survey, and was shocked when they got knocked out of the first round upon actually applying for the Baldrige Award. The truth is that most companies think they rate much higher on the Baldrige scale than they really merit. If corporate America were really at an average level of 560 on the Baldrige scale, U.S. products and services would be beating everyone else's in quality.

THE TRUTH

The truth is that corporate America is nowhere near 560 points on the Baldrige scale. If we define corporate America as including small and large service and manufacturing companies, corporate America is really around 150 points or less. As a Baldrige Examiner, I evaluated a company once that received a score of 26 points out of 1000. Another Examiner gave an applicant 60 points out of 1000. These are companies that thought they had a chance at winning a Baldrige!

MISINFORMATION

One of the major reasons for this gap between where companies think they are and where they really stand on the Baldrige scale is the popularity of surveys as a means of self-assessment. I've written one myself that has been published for the last five years in the June issue of the *Journal for Quality and Participation*. If you review the advertisements in any of the quality journals, you can find ads for at least half a dozen companies with surveys that claim to tell you "where you really stand" on the Baldrige scale. The problem with all of these surveys, not excluding my own, is that they are all based upon internal company opinions and self-report data. Consequently, they are all questionable measures of your status on the Baldrige scale. Some of them look very scientific. They are computer scored and you receive a detailed report showing you a variety of different breakdowns of the data. But no matter how many computers are used or how many data comparisons are done, much of it is doubtful because it is based upon people's opinions of themselves and their work. People tend to think that they are further along applying the Baldrige principles than they really are.

Using one of these surveys to assess your Baldrige status is like filling out a questionnaire to determine your level of health and physical fitness, rather than going to a hospital or clinic and actually getting a physical. A survey is an inexpensive method of determining where you stand, but chances are you will not get an accurate assessment. Companies such as Northrop, Westinghouse, IBM, Cargill, AT&T, and Pacific Bell use a more thorough approach to evaluation against the Baldrige criteria by simulating the Baldrige Award process. Applications are prepared and scored just like they are in Baldrige, using internal and external Examiners that have been through several days of training. Some of these organizations even conduct site visits of the best scorers to validate the information contained in the written application. An approach like this is likely to give you a score that is within 10% of the score you would receive if you actually applied for the Baldrige Award.

HOW DO BALDRIGE APPLICANTS AND WINNERS SCORE?

When you look at the breakdown of scores over the last few years, you find that most of the Baldrige Award applicants score less than 600 points out of a possible 1000. In fact, about 80% of applicants score between 0 and 600 points. The rule used to be that you needed a score of 600 points or greater to receive a site visit, but this is not a hard rule. In the last few years, there were several organizations that received site visits that scored less than 600. Receiving a site visit with less than 600 points is still not common, but it is possible—especially if you are a small business. The Baldrige Examiners are taught to be less stringent in their scoring of small companies. Examiners learn not to expect as much evidence of a systematic approach to everything. Informal approaches sometimes work very well in small companies.

WHAT IT TAKES TO WIN

People I talk to at workshops I teach on the Baldrige criteria generally believe that it takes a score of 900 or better to win a Baldrige. Last year's distribution of scores indicates that this is far from the truth. Many companies that have won Baldrige Awards received scores that were less than 750. None of the applicants received scores in the eight or nine hundreds, as might be expected. When deciding on a winner, the nine Baldrige Judges look less at the scores than they do the comments on strengths and areas for improvement, and how these factors relate to the business the applicant is in.

UNDERSTANDING THE SCORING SCALE

Scoring for the Baldrige is done using a scoring scale of 0–100%. Scores are generally done in multiples of 10, using guidelines provided by the Baldrige Award Office. The chart below provides a summary of the scoring scale that appears on page 25 of the 1996 Award Criteria Booklet. Although some things changed from 1995 to 1996 in the award criteria, the scoring guidelines are exactly the same as last year. Because the criteria have changed, it will be even tougher to receive a high score, however.

SCORE	APPROACH/DEVELOPMENT	RESULTS
0%	■ no systematic approach evident; anecdotal information	■ no results or poor results in areas reported
10% to 30%	■ beginning of a systematic approach to the primary purposes of the Item ■ early stages of a transition from reacting to problems to a general improvement orientation ■ major gaps exist in deployment that would inhibit progress in achieving the primary purposes of the Item	■ early stages of developing trends; some improvements *and/or* early good performance levels in a few areas ■ results not reported for many to most areas of importance to the applicant's key business requirements
40% to 60%	■ a sound, systematic approach, responsive to the primary purposes of the Item ■ a fact-based improvement process in place in key areas; more emphasis is placed on improvement than on reaction to problems ■ no major gaps in deployment, though some areas or work units may be in very early stages of deployment	■ improvement trends *and/or* good performance levels reported for many to most areas of importance to the applicant's key business requirements ■ no pattern of adverse trends *and/or* poor performance levels in areas of importance to the applicant's key business requirements ■ some trends *and/or* current performance levels — evaluated against relevant comparisons and/or benchmarks — show areas of strength and/or good to very good relative performance levels
70% to 90%	■ a sound, systematic approach, responsive to the overall purposes of the Item ■ a fact-based improvement process is a key management tool; clear evidence of refinement and improved integration as a result of improvement cycles and analysis ■ approach is well-deployed, with no major gaps; deployment may vary in some areas or work units	■ current performance is good to excellent in most areas of importance to the applicant's key business requirements ■ most improvement trends *and/or* performance levels are sustained ■ many to most trends *and/or* current performance levels — evaluated against relevant comparisons *and/or* benchmarks — show areas of leadership and very good relative performance levels
100%	■ a sound, systematic approach, fully responsive to all the requirements of the Item ■ a very strong, fact-based improvement process is a key management tool; strong refinement and integration — backed by excellent analysis ■ approach is fully deployed without any significant weaknesses or gaps in any areas or work units	■ current performance is excellent in most areas of importance to the applicant's key business requirements ■ excellent improvement trends *and/or* sustained excellent performance levels in most areas ■ strong evidence of industry and benchmark leadership demonstrated in many areas

APPROACH, DEPLOYMENT, AND RESULTS

You will notice that three factors are assessed as part of the scoring scale. <u>Approach</u> refers to the systems you have in place to improve quality and customer satisfaction. Some of the factors Baldrige examiners look at when assessing your approach are the degree to which your approaches are:

- Systematic, planned, logical, and tailored to your key business factors
- Prevention-based versus inspection and correction-based
- Based upon thorough analyses of needs and constraints
- Systematically evaluated and improved over time
- Innovative and unique

<u>Deployment</u> essentially means the extent to which your approach has been implemented across the organization. Many companies have unsystematic approaches that are fully deployed. Obviously, this won't earn you a high score. What the Baldrige Examiners

would like to see is a sound approach that has been implemented in all parts of the organization. Simply having a sound approach by itself does not earn a high score. When assessing deployment, the Baldrige scale looks at implementation of your approaches across:

- All transactions with customers, suppliers, and the public
- All operations, facilities, and businesses
- All products and services
- All levels and functions of employees

Results are the third aspect of the Baldrige scoring scale. Results refer to data. Results are asked for and assessed in the following items and areas to address within the 1996 Baldrige criteria: 6.1, 6.2, 6.3, 6.4 and 7.4. These Areas/Items ask only for results—no information on approach or deployment is requested. When evaluating your results, the Baldrige Examiners look at:

- Your overall level of performance
- How your performance levels compare to competitors and to benchmarks
- Rate of improvement, or the slope of trends in your data
- The breadth of the data, whether improvements are shown on all key measures of performance
- The degree to which results have been sustained and show continuous improvement over time
- Absence of negative trends or flat performance at low levels.

If you refer back to the scoring scale, you will notice that scores are grouped into five bands, with descriptors for each of these bands, across the three factors: approach, deployment, and results. I will explain, below, what a Baldrige Examiner is likely to see in an organization when a score is assigned for each of the ten levels from 0% to 100%.

Scores of 0 on Approach /Deployment

Scores of zero are actually given out quite frequently by Baldrige Examiners when they evaluate each of the 24 Examination Items. Companies that assess themselves, however, rarely give zeros in any area. Part of this discrepancy stems from a lack of understanding of what constitutes a zero. The scoring scale uses the word "anecdotal" for the approach, deployment, and results factors when describing what a zero looks like. This means that the only evidence provided consists of stories, or anecdotes, illustrating how the company does in meeting the criteria. No matter how impressive, examples or stories are not worth anything on this scale.

Most of the items that ask about your approach are looking for a *system*. A score of zero would indicate that you probably have no system. Even a small business would be expected to have informal systems. You may also receive a score of zero if you have plans for a sound system, but you have not yet implemented it. This would indicate no deployment. Plans and intentions will not earn you points on the Baldrige scale until you have deployed the system. Most companies that do self-assessments tend to score themselves between 10 and 30% for good intentions in the future. A score of zero may indicate that the organization has some "pockets of excellence," but these pockets are tied to key individuals rather than the existence of a systematic approach. In general, the company's approach to quality tends to be the traditional inspection/correction approach.

Scores of 0 on Results

A score of zero in an Area to Address or Examination Item that asks for results would indicate that one or more of the following conditions are present:

- There are no results other than anecdotes—no graphs or data
- Data presented are irrelevant to the criteria/requirements of the item
- Data show that performance on key measures has gotten worse, or has not improved at all.

Scores in the 10–30% Range

This is the range in which many Baldrige applicants fall, and the range in which most U.S. companies probably fall on the Baldrige scale. This is also the range in which there is the most misunderstanding on how to score. The biggest reason for this lack of consistency in scoring and misunderstanding is that the descriptors in the scoring scale are the same for all scores in this range. In other words, there is no distinction to indicate how a 10% score differs from a 20% or 30% score.

When I recently worked on a project where I teamed up with a group of internal examiners at one organization, we found that most of our scoring disagreements centered around what was a 10, 20, 30, or 40%. The scoring guidelines provided little help, so we decided to construct our own. Once this matrix was constructed, the consensus discussions took less than than half the time because we all were in agreement about what a 10% looked like versus a 30%. The scale of the 10–30% range is presented below for your reference. It is not the official Baldrige-approved version, but I think that you will find it useful as a guideline.

SCORE	APPROACH	DEPLOYMENT	RESULTS
10%	Beginnings of a systematic approach but system still has major holes/gaps.	Implementation in one or two minor areas or functions in the organization and possibly one major one.	Very slight improvement, or only one data point showing improvement; data on many major indices are missing or flat.
20%	Sound, well thought-out approach (more than a beginning) that shows some evidence of being prevention-based. Multiple pockets of excellence that may lack an overall system architecture.	Deployment of system(s) to 10–30% of the major functions or facilities in the organization.	A couple of data points showing some undramatic improvement in at least 50% of key measures. Other graphs show no improvement and some key data are still missing from the application. Several negative trends.
30%	Early stages of a systematic approach based upon thorough analysis. No real integration yet; immature systems.	Deployment to at least half of the major functions or facilities in the organization.	A few data points that show the beginnings of positive trends in more than half of key indices. Slow steady progress in many areas.

Scores of 10% on Approach/Deployment

A score of 10% is often referred to as a "guilt score." In other words, the organization is very close to a zero, but is doing a few good things in a couple of small pockets of the organization. Or, it has at least acknowledged what it needs to do to improve, even though it does not really yet have a systematic approach. Deployment is often quite limited, in organizations that score at the 10% level. The pockets where systematic approaches are deployed tend to be extremely small. For example, an organization that received a score of 10% in section 4.2 had a team of 12 employees on a self-directed work team, out of a total of over 800 employees, and another team of 8 people had all been cross trained to do each others jobs. An organization at the 10% level would probably not have any deployment to support functions. A systematic approach is only just beginning at the 10% scoring level. This score is also used when the applicant failed to answer much of what is asked for in the criteria.

Scores of 10% on Results

Results at the 10% level will be minimal. The graphs of major performance indices are likely to show very slight improvements, or perhaps one or two data points that show only the beginnings of a positive trend. At the 10% level we might also see that the data show some measures to be improving, some to be getting worse, and some to be remaining about the same.

Scores of 20% on Approach/Deployment

Organizations that receive 20% scores on their approach/deployment items tend to have systematic approaches in bigger pockets than those at the 10% level. They still seem to lack an overall system architecture or structure to their approaches, but a number of good things are happening in a number of different areas of the company. Many pockets of disconnected systematic approaches are often found in organizations at this level. Another way to receive a score of 20% is to have the beginnings of an overall system, that lacks key elements, or has only been implemented in a few portions of the organization. Organizations at the 20% level may also have fairly good systematic approaches that have only been pilot tested in a few areas, and have yet to be implemented throughout the rest of the organization.

Scores of 20% on Results

Results at the 20% level will show more than a data point or two showing slight improvement. To give a score of 20% for results, the Baldrige Examiners would expect to see at least a couple of data points showing improvement in at least half of the key measures in the organization. At this level, it is clear that positive results are starting to materialize. Trends have not really been established yet, and results are not consistent across all measures, but it is clear that improvements are happening. The level of improvements tends to be undramatic at the 20% level. We might see a couple of data points showing slow steady improvement rather than major jumps in the data. Levels of performance compared to competition tend to be about the same, or slightly worse in a few areas.

Scores of 30% on Approach/Deployment

This is the level at which a great number of companies fall. This should be considered to be a good score, indicating more than a good start with implementing a customer-focused culture. In order to receive a 30% score, your approaches need to be based upon thorough analyses of needs, indicate a fairly strong prevention basis, and be quite complete. At this level, your performance improvement effort is still seen by many employees as a program or add-on structure, rather than a way of life. What this means is that integration has not yet occurred. Systems tend to lack maturity at the 30% level, but they are well designed and clearly indicate transition toward a prevention-based approach.

Deployment at the 30% level will be to at least half of the major functions or facilities in the company. Again, we would probably not see implementation in the staff functions or support departments. A 30% score would indicate that roughly half of the employees are working to implement a customer-focused approach in the company.

Scores of 30% on Results

The difference between results at 20% and 30% is that a 30% company would show the beginnnings of positive trends in *more* than half of the company's major indices of performance. Typically, most graphs will contain at least three data points, showing the beginnings of a trend, and the trends will be mostly positive. The level of results are not that impressive yet, and the company may not be doing better than most competitors, but they are getting better each year. You might still expect to see that some of the graphs show no improvement. You may also see inconsistencies in the data at this level. Even though more than half of the graphs show the start of an improving trend, other graphs show no trends, flat performance, and even that performance on a few indices has gotten worse. The bottom line is that more than half of the key indices show the start of positive trends for this level of scoring. At the 30% level there may be key data that are still missing from the application. Levels of performance tend to be at or slightly above competitors'.

SCORE	APPROACH	DEPLOYMENT	RESULTS
40%	Beyond the early stages of a preventive approach, but no refinement or integration of approach yet. Evidence of innovation in design of systems/approaches.	Implementation at beginning stages in some functions and more advanced in others. Many major functions show fairly complete deployment.	Beginnings of positive trends can be seen in areas deployed, and there are no significant adverse trends. Levels of results are good compared to many key competitors.
50%	Some evidence of a more refined, prevention-based approach. A fact-based improvement process in place for key areas addressed in the item. Integration beginning to occur.	Deployment to all major functions in the company —no gaps in deployment to major areas. Beginnings of deployment to several support functions.	Clear positive trends seen on many graphs of key measures addressed in the item. Some trends can be evaluated against relevant comparisons and benchmarks and compare favorably.
60%	Systematic prevention-based approach that has been evaluated and improved at least once. Some systems may show two or more iterations based on evaluation. Integration shown across several major areas.	More than deployment to a few support functions. Most major support departments show at least the start of deployment. Deployment is more advanced in major functions than at 50% level.	Majority of graphs show slow, steady improvements over several years or sustained high levels of performance. Many graphs show competitor and/or benchmark data and applicant's performance better than at least half of these comparisons.

Scores of 40% on Approach/Deployment

This is the top end of the band that indicates that you are off to a good start with your performance improvement effort. Systems at this level of scoring tend to be more comprehensive and more innovative. Approaches are based upon thorough analysis and sound logic, and are tied into the key business and cultural factors in the organization. Companies at the 20–30% level tend to have systems that do not show creativity and tailoring to their individual organization's needs. They may have copied their systems from others. Organizations with scores at the 40% level tend to have developed their own "home grown" approaches and systems that are characterized by being innovative, truly prevention-based, and tailored to their company. Systems may still lack maturity at the 40% level, with no evidence of evaluation and improvement cycles.

Deployment of approaches will be to many major functions and/or facilities, which means more than half of the plants or service delivery areas of the business. The support department employees have yet to adopt a customer-focused approach, even though they may be familiar with the concepts through eduation and training. The organization has probably been working hard on implementing a customer-focused culture for several years to achieve a score at this level.

A large company may have been working at implementing systematic approaches to being customer-focused for 5 or more years and still receive a score at the 40% level, because they still employ an add-on structure of committees, teams, and initiatives.

Scores of 40% on Results

The differences between results at this level and at the 30% level are:

- Lack of significant adverse trends
- Consistency of results across all key performance indices
- Number of data points indicating trends
- Overall level of results compared with competitors
- Slope of trend lines or rate of improvement

We would not expect to see sustained world-class results to give a 40% score. Graphs in most or all of the areas where TQM has been deployed will show positive trends that are not yet conclusive. Statisticians generally believe that seven data points are needed to establish any kind of trend. We would not expect this yet. Three or four data points (typically years versus weeks or months) that show the start of a good trend is more of what we would see at this level.

Scores of 50% on Approach/Deployment

In the Baldrige scale, a score of 50% is not considered average. A 50% is considered to be quite a high score and is fairly difficult to achieve. If you recall the distribution of the scores we discussed earlier, the majority of Baldrige applicants received a score of less than 50%. It must be remembered that this is still a 100% scale. Even though a score of

50% or higher is very hard to achieve, it is possible. In a set of scoring guidelines prepared for Baldrige Examiners, award director Dr. Curt Reinmann describes the 50% score as follows:

> *The 50% point represents a sound approach for accomplishing the principal purposes addressed in the Item. The basic approach should be the way the company actually operates and should affect most of the people and operations addressed in the Item. The approach should project reasonable confidence that over time, there are very likely to be further learning and more complete deployment.*

In order to receive a 50% score for your approach, two characteristics separate it from a score in the 10–40% range. First of all, your approach will include at least one evaluation and improvement cycle. In other words, there will be evidence that you have assessed how well your approach or systems are working, and made changes or enhancements to the systems, based upon this assessment. If your approach has not been improved or changed over the years, you will not receive a 50% score. The second characteristic of a 50% score for approach is some evidence of integration. Many companies approach implementation of a customer-focused culture as an add-on approach by creating teams, committees, and reports/plans. This is contrasted with the organization that approaches the Baldrige criteria as a different way of running the organization rather than an add-on structure. Integration is not complete yet at the 50% level, but is beginning to occur. As Dr. Reimann says, "The basic approach should be the way the company actually operates."

Deployment at the 50% level is characterized by implementation of a customer-focused culture in most major areas of the business, and at least some of the support functions. Scores below 50% tend to show no deployment to departments such as finance, facilities, maintenance, HRD, material, procurement, and other support departments. What we are likely to see at this level is that several major support functions are in the early stages of implementing a customer-focused approach.

Score of 50% on Results

In addition to having no significant adverse trends, results at the 50% level should clearly show improvement trends in most of the major indices asked about in the Examination Item. Not all graphs will show clear trends, but many will. Another factor that differentiates results at this level is that the company's levels of performance on some graphs compare favorably to key competitors and possibly benchmarks. There is usually a lack of comparative data in results below 50%. Or, the company's performance is below that of key competitors and benchmarks. At 50% there is not only comparative data, but the applicant's results are better than levels exhibited in the comparative data. We're certainly not expecting that the company show world-class results on all measures at the 50% level, only that some of the graphs of key measures have comparative data, and that the applicant's performance is at least slightly better than points of comparison. Again, not all graphs will show strong positive trends. Some graphs may still be flat or show slow steady improvements.

Scores of 60% on Approach/Deployment

Companies that receive an overall score of 60% or 600 points on the Baldrige scale are among the best companies in the country. These companies tend to have been working at implementing customer-focused culture for many years, and show a degree of maturity in their approaches. Companies at this level tend to be finalists in the Baldrige competition, and receive site visits. The major difference between a 50% and 60% score in approach is the degree of:

- Integration
- Evaluation and improvement

Evaluation may be informal and lack rigor, but there is evidence that the company performs some evaluation of approaches, and uses the feedback from these assessments to improve its approaches. At the 60% level, we might expect to see at least one iteration of minor enhancements or changes to a number of major systems in the company. Integration of a customer-focused culture as a way of life is occurring in a number of major areas in the company as well. This tends to occur in the areas or facilities that have been developing the culture the longest, and integration is not yet deployed across the company.

Scores at the 60% Level on Results

Results at the 60% level tend to be quite impressive. The majority of graphs depicting results will show either slow steady improvements over several years, or sustained high levels of performance over a number of years. Graphs at the 60% level also tend to show a lack of variability in the data, indicating that the company has these key measures in control as much as possible. Results at this level also tend to be superior to a number of different points of comparison. Most graphs will include two or three comparison points (e.g., industry average, largest competitor, and benchmark). Performance of the applicant will be better than industry averages, key competitors, and other comparison points on many graphs. Results may even approach or exceed benchmark levels on a few graphs.

Scores in the 70% to 90% Range

The problem with using the matrix in the Baldrige Award Guidelines for scoring is the same as the problems with the 10%–30% for 40%–60% ranges—there is no guidance given for the individual scores at 10% intervals. This isn't much of a problem because very few companies fall into the 70% to 90% range. One of the problems that has occurred with the Baldrige scale over the last five years is that Examiners have gotten increasingly stingy in their grading. Examiners function as if the scale were a 0–70% scale rather than a 0–100% scale. In other words, Examiners almost never give out scores of higher than 70%. Scores for outstanding companies tend to be in the 60%–75% range rather than in the 80–95% range as one might expect with a 100% scale. A great deal of emphasis is placed on this in the training of Baldrige Examiners, and some overcompensate—especially when evaluating small companies. One consensus call that I participated in had many items where there was a 0–100% range across the six Examiners. Those who gave out the zeros saw no evidence of a systematic approach, and those that gave out 100% felt that we should give them the benefit of the doubt because they were a small company. A score in the 70% to 90% range should never be given out without serious scrutiny and evidence of a sound systematic approach. However, the company does not need to have a perfect world-class system with 100% deployment to receive a score in this range. (See chart on following page.)

SCORE	APPROACH	DEPLOYMENT	RESULTS
70%	Systematic approach with thorough evaluation and evidence of several iterations of improvement. Good integration of approach into the day-to-day operation of the company.	Deployment is complete in at least 75% or more of major functions and facilities, as well as more than half of all support functions. Few support areas have yet to implement approach, even though integration levels may vary.	Majority of graphs show dramatic improvements or sustained high levels of performance over several years. Few or no graphs show flat or declining performance. Many to most graphs show that performance is better than competitors' and industry averages. Benchmark level results on some key indices.
80%	Excellent integration of an approach that has been systematically evaluated and improved several times. Indication of a mature system that shows innovation. Difficult for Examiners to think of "area for improvement" comments.	Deployment to more than 75% of major functions and between 60 and 75% of all support functions. All departments show some deployment of customer-focused approach, and integration is complete in most areas/elements.	Good to excellent trends in almost all graphs with demonstrated ability to achieve world-class results in industry over a sustained period of time. Many graphs show that company is at benchmark levels for key indices.
90%	A sound systematic approach that has gone through many iterations showing evaluation and improvement. Integration is near complete. World-class approach that demonstrates many innovations.	Deployment is complete to all major functions/facilities and to at least 75% of the support functions/departments. All areas of the company have implemented prevention-based approaches.	Excellent trends showing either dramatic improvements or ability to sustain benchmark level results over a number of years. Results clearly superior to all competitors on most indices.

Scores of 70% on Approach/Deployment

At this level, we are approaching a world-class organization in its approach, deployment, and results. A company at this level may be a year or two away from winning a Baldrige Award. Approaches and systems tend to be very mature and demonstrate at least two iterations or evaluation and improvement cycles. A 70% company usually has been working on a customer-focused culture for more than three or four years, and is getting to the point where the approach is invisible. In other words, TQM is not an add-on structure or viewed as a program or initiative. It is viewed by employees as a way of life and just good common sense. Quality efforts and measures are blended with financial and operational efforts and measures. The approach to achieving world-class performance has filtered down and resulted in changes to the company's major systems such as:

- Leadership
- Business Planning
- Information
- Human Resource Development
- Compensation
- Quality Assurance
- Customer Relationship Management

An organization will never achieve this level if it looks at culture change initiatives as consisting of training, quality improvement teams, and measurement of customer satisfaction using some surveys.

Deployment in companies at the 70% scoring level is complete in at least 75% or more of the major product manufacturing or service delivery functions and to more than half of all the support functions in the organization. There are still a few areas where a customer-focused culture has yet to be implemented. For example, we may find a customer-focused approach absent in the law department or the finance department, where there is a tendency of resistance to the ideas of process control and measurement of internal customer satisfaction.

Scores of 70% on Results

Results in companies at this level tend to show dramatic improvements in performance or sustain very high levels of performance over many years. Most graphs show performance levels to be superior to industry competitors and may even be approaching benchmark levels in some areas. Few or none of the graphs show flat or declining performance and cause/effect relationships are clearly demonstrated. Results in support departments also show very positive trends or sustained high levels of performance.

Scores of 80% on Approach/Deployment

These are companies that achieve scores high enough to win a Baldrige Award. This does not mean that there is nothing that they could do to get better. Their approach has been evaluated and improved three or more times and shows a great deal of refinement and maturity. Major changes have already been made and they are at the point where minor enhancements are all that are needed each year to continue to improve the approaches. Approaches are probably very innovative and clearly tailored to the organization's culture and business factors. All systems show evidence of a prevention-based or proactive approach to quality and customer satisfaction. Integration is complete in at least 75% of the company.

Approaches have been completely implemented or deployed in more than three-fourths of all functions in the company, and all departments/functions are working to improve quality and customer satisfaction.

Scores of 80% on Results

Results show good to excellent trends in almost all major measures, with demonstrated ability to achieve world-class or benchmark-level performance on a number of important measures. Results at this level of score need to go beyond just being the best in the industry. Trends tend to show at least 5–7 data points that are almost exclusively positive. Results at this level demonstrate that the company can keep improving over the long run. It is relatively easy to show two or three years' worth of data that show improvement. It is very difficult to demonstrate continuous improvement over a five or more year period. This does not mean that all graphs need to show five to seven years' worth of data. However, you do need to provide enough data to show *sustained* improvement over time.

Scores of 90% on Approach/Deployment

While it may be next to impossible to earn an overall score of 900 or more on the overall Baldrige scale, it is possible to receive a 90% or even 100% on an individual Examination Item. Your approach will demonstrate many evaluation and improvement cycles, and integration is nearly complete. A customer-focused culture is almost completely invisible in an organization at this level. Employees don't need a flip chart or meeting to trigger their use of quality improvement tools. Employees at all levels have internalized these tools and approaches to the point that they now think differently.

Concern with internal and external customers has become second nature and no longer requires committees, meetings, and forms to make it happen.

Deployment is complete in all major functions and facilities of the company and in almost all of the support functions. The systems in support functions may still require some additional evaluation and improvement, but they are well along in their efforts to concentrate on quality and customer satisfaction. The TQM approach has been fully integrated in most of the major systems in the company.

Scores of 90% on Results

Results at the 90% level would show world-class levels of performance in many major areas. Performance is clearly better than all competitors on most indices and is as good or better than world-class benchmark levels.

Scores of 100% on Approach/Deployment

It's a little tough to say what an organization at this level would look like, because I've never seen one. Some of the early Baldrige winners such as Motorola and Federal Express may be approaching the 100% level in many areas. An overall score of 1000 points should be considered impossible to achieve. However, it is possible to receive a score of 100% for an individual Examination Item. Your approach would need to be truly innovative, and show many cycles of evaluation and improvement. Systems at this level should require only minor adjustments over time. The Award Guidelines explain that the approach should show:

> *Excellent improvement trends and/or sustained excellent performance levels in most areas. (p. 41)*

The guidelines also explain that your approach should address all of the requirements of the Examination Item at the 100% level. Deployment is complete at the 100% level. All employees, facilities, and functions in the organization have implemented a customer-focused preventive approach to quality. Integration is so complete that employess can barely remember what it was like before the company adopted this new approach to management. The Baldrige criteria are truly second nature and intuitive at this level of scoring, and the company is often benchmarked by others.

Scores of 100% on Results

It's impossible for any company to have all of its measures show perfect results and trends, but that's close to what's expected at the 100% level. The Award Criteria Booklet defines the following characteristics of results at the 100% level:

- *Current performance is excellent in most areas of importance to the applicant's key business requirements*

- *Excellent improvement trends and/or sustained excellent performance levels in most areas*

- *Strong evidence of industry and benchmark leadership demonstrated in many areas (p. 25)*

SCORING AREAS TO ADDRESS

When assigning scores, Baldrige Examiners are taught to score an organization on each of the 24 Examination Items and not the 52 Areas to Address. This often leads to inconsistencies in scoring because each Examiner puts a different value on each of the Areas to Address (or subpoints) within a single Item. For example, Item 1.1 includes Areas to Address a–d. Let's say that the applicant does a great job (70%–80% on a and b), but does a poor job (10%–20%) in responding to c and d. How will this be scored? Some Examiners assume that all Areas to Address are equal; since there are four in this Item, each is worth 25%. This, however, can be a faulty assumption. Generally, the a's and b's tend to be more important than the c's, d's, and other Areas to Address.

To increase the amount of precision in the scoring process, some organizations have internal examiners score on Areas to Address as well as the 24 Items. To aid them in doing this, I developed a straw model of values to assign to each of the 52 Areas to Address, found on the following page. These values are expressed in percentages, and are based on my professional experience regarding the importance of each Area to Address. This is not, therefore, an official part of the Baldrige scoring process—and some examiners might even frown upon the assignment of such percentages to the Areas to Address. If, however, you are evaluating internal improvement applications, you could stand to benefit from using this scoring approach. I recommend that you start with these weights and then assign your own based on the situation in your own organization.

1996 WEIGHTS OF AREAS TO ADDRESS			
1.1	A. 80%	B. 20%	
1.2	A. 65%	B. 35%	
1.3	A. 70%	B. 30%	
2.1	A. 70%	B. 30%	
2.2	A. 75%	B. 25%	
2.3	A. 55%	B. 45%	
3.1	A. 65%	B. 20%	C. 15%
3.2	A. 65%	B. 35%	
4.1	A. 65%	B. 35%	
4.2	A. 60%	B. 40%	
4.3	A. 35%	B. 65%	
4.4	A. 40%	B. 25%	C. 35%
5.1	A. 50%	B. 30%	C. 20%
5.2	A. 60%	B. 40%	
5.3	A. 40%	B. 20%	C. 40%
5.4	A. 60%	B. 40%	
6.1			
6.2			
6.3	Not applicable—there is only one area to address for each item.		
6.4			
7.1	A. 55%	B. 30%	C. 15%
7.2	A. 30%	B. 25%	C. 20% D. 25%
7.3	A. 55%	B. 25%	C. 20%
7.4	A. 45%	B. 55%	

ADDITIONAL SCORING GUIDANCE

No amount of guidance in a publication can take the place of practice and feedback in learning the Baldrige scoring scale. I encourage you to obtain a copy of the 1995 or 1996 case study that was used to train current Baldrige Examiners. Score the case yourself, and then compare your score to the textbook answer to see how your scoring differs from a group of Senior Baldrige Examiners. By going through this exercise, you will gain a good understanding of what a 30% looks like, a 60%, an 80%, etc. A copy of the 1994 and 1995 case studies and textbook answer is available by calling the ASQC at 800-248-1946. The 1996 case studies will be available in May, 1996.

Chapter 6

Interpreting the Criteria
for Leadership (1.0)

OVERVIEW OF THE LEADERSHIP CATEGORY

The 1996 Award Criteria define the Leadership category as follows:

> *The **Leadership** category examines senior executives' personal leadership and involvement in creating and sustaining a customer focus, clear values and expectations, and a leadership system that promotes performance excellence. Also examined is how the values and expectations are integrated into the company's management system, including how the company addresses its public responsibilities and corporate citizenship. (p. 6)*

The 1.0 Leadership category is broken down into the following three Examination Items:

1.1 Senior Executive Leadership (45 points)
1.2 Leadership System and Organization (25 points)
1.3 Public Responsibility and Corporate Citizenship (20 points)

As stated in the excerpt above, this category relates to the activities of the organization's senior executives as well as the management system as a whole. The term "senior executives" refers to the highest ranking official of the organization and the executives that report directly to the CEO or president. This would seem very clear, but applicants have been known to report on only the activities of their most senior executive, the CEO, with no information being provided on the activities of any of the other executives in the organization.

The sections below describe each of the Areas to Address, organized under each of the three Examination Items in the Leadership category. Each section begins with a double-ruled box containing the Examination Item, the point value, and any applicable Notes.* Areas to Address falling under that Item follow in a single-ruled box. In the upper right corner of each Area to Address box is an indication [brackets] of whether the Area pertains to approach, deployment, or results. All definitions and information appearing within these boxes are taken directly from the Baldrige criteria. Following each Area to Address is an explanation defining what the examiners are looking for in assessing your application. Next, I have supplied a list of indicators or evaluation factors that will assist you in interpreting the criteria and in preparing your application.

---

* Item Notes that apply to a specific Area to Address are appropriately listed in the box containing that Area.

1.1 SENIOR EXECUTIVE LEADERSHIP

Describe senior executives' leadership and personal involvement in setting directions and in developing and maintaining an effective, performance-oriented leadership system. (45 points)

Note:

(1)   **"Senior executives" means the applicants' highest-ranking official and executives reporting directly to that official.**

AREA TO ADDRESS   [APPROACH/DEPLOYMENT]

1.1a How senior executives provide effective leadership and direction in building and improving company competitiveness, performance, and capabilities. Describe how senior executives: (1) create and maintain an effective leadership system based upon clear values and high expectations; (2) create future opportunity for the company and its stakeholders, set directions, and integrate performance excellence goals; and (3) review overall company performance, capabilities, and organization.

Notes:

(2)   **Values and expectations [1.1a(1)] should take into account needs and expectations of key stakeholders—customers, employees, stockholders, suppliers and partners, the community, and the public.**

(3)   **Review of overall company performance is addressed in 1.2b. Responses to 1.1a(3) should focus on senior executives' roles in such reviews, and their use of the reviews to set expectations and develop leadership.**

What They're Looking For Here

The actions of senior executives are highly correlated with a company's ability to achieve world-class levels of performance. Robert Galvin of Motorola, Bob Allen of AT&T, David Kearns of Xerox, and other CEOs or former CEOs of Baldrige-winning companies all demonstrate certain key characteristics. These executives:

- Lead by active involvement in running the business—they spend time with customers, employees, suppliers, and other stakeholders, and they listen.

- Consistently exhibit behaviors that are consistent with the companies mission and values.

- Take risks and encourage their employees to make major changes in their quest for world-class performance.

- Review all measures of performance on a regular basis and encourage breakthrough approaches through the use of benchmarking and stretch goals.

What the criteria asks for here is evidence that the senior executives are actively involved in promoting a customer-focused culture throughout the organization. The first part of the criteria [1.1a] asks for evidence that the senior executives create and demonstrate the values that the organization wants to live by. Many executives don't do much more than write the company's values, post them on walls, and make speeches about the importance of following the values. Their own behavior seldom exhibits the values. For example, I've seen a number of corporations that have a stated value such as "Employees are our greatest asset." These companies are the same ones that immediately lay off employees and cut budgets for HR activities like training whenever there is a slight business down-turn. This portion of 1.1.a asks for evidence that executives' behavior is consistent with the values. A matrix chart is an effective way of summarizing the actions of individual executives who demonstrate their commitment to a customer-focused culture. An example of such a chart follows.

MATRIX OF ACTIONS OF SR. EXECUTIVES TO DEMONSTRATE CUSTOMER FOCUS							
Executives	Speeches	Employee Orientation	Conf. Presentations	Staff Mtgs.	Team Mtgs.	Leadership Survey Action Plan	Lead Training on Values
CEO	X	X	X	X		X	X
V.P. H.R.	X	X	X	X		X	X
V.P. Finance	X		X	X	X	X	
V.P. Mkt.	X		X	X	X	X	
V.P. Operations			X	X	X	X	X

Several themes the Baldrige Examiners will look for in the leadership approach are:

- Employee participation

- Focus on continuous improvement

- Preventive approach to quality

- Management by "walking around" or staying close to the business

Executives who do a good job on this Area to Address tend to spend a large percentage of their time walking around various facilities in the company, getting to know managers, supervisors, and employees, and asking them about quality improvement activities. Executives also tend to spend a fair percentage of time personally communicating with customers. This helps to:

- Keep executives in touch with customers and their needs

- Promote the company's quality orientation among customers

- Convince employees that executives are concerned with customer satisfaction

The late Sam Walton of WalMart is probably a role model for item 1.1. In general, Baldrige Award applicants tend to score fairly well on Item 1.1. It's hard to find a company today where the executives are not committed to customer satisfaction and performance excellence. However, many fall because most of the commitment and the activity is coming from the CEO, rather than from all senior executives. This is a common reason why Baldrige applicants receive lower scores on this item. Executives often see the performance excellence effort as something they can delegate to others. The CEO appoints a Vice President of Total Quality whose job it is to manage the implementation of TQM throughout the company. The problem with appointing a position like this is that the rest of the executives feel they are off the hook. They don't need to worry about this quality business because that's the quality VP's job. Appointing a quality Vice President is not necessarily a bad idea. It only is a problem if it allows other executives to avoid involvement in the performance excellence effort.

The three most important dimensions of involvement that are assessed in this item are:

- Types of quality-related activities executives spend time on
- Amount of time executives spend on these activities
- Extent to which all senior executives participate in these activities

I've seen companies that limit their executive involvement to only a couple of activities. For example, executives attend quality steering committee meetings and hand out quarterly quality awards. Other companies I've worked with show evidence that executives engage in a wide variety of quality-related activities, but overall spend very little time participating in these actions. Finally, I've seen companies that do a good job on the first two items, but there are a few executives that do most of the quality-related work, and a few executives who don't do anything. This is how deployment is evaluated in this area to address—by looking at the extent to which the activities are deployed across all the senior executives.

1.1a(2) asks about how the senior executives are involved in creating future opportunities for the company. This is not about establishing some empty slogan like "Vision 2000." This portion of the criteria asks about executive involvement in deciding the future direction of the competition, including factors such as products/services, markets that will be served, growth, etc. One important job of an executive is to make sure that the company survives in the long run. Consequently, it is important to clearly articulate a vision for the future, and clearly communicate that vision to employees. A vision needs to be translated into more specific goals, which is also something that needs to be done by the executives. Explain what your senior executives do to set major goals for the organization's future, and describe how strategies are formulated to help achieve the goals.

For example, one of Northrop Corporation's long-term goals was to establish new aerospace contracts and business to ensure their long-term survival in an industry where demand has weakened. One major strategy they employed to help further this goal was the acquisition of Grumman in 1994. This acquisition was a major cornerstone in the company's overall strategy for ensuring their survival.

The third and final point in this area to address [1.1a(3)] asks about what data get reviewed by executives on a regular basis. What executives review is what gets concentrated on. In order to receive high marks for your response to this area, it is important that executives review all important measures in your company's scorecard on a regular basis. Executives in many companies review financial and operational data on a weekly or at least monthly basis. Customer satisfaction data get reviewed once a year, and employee satisfaction data are reviewed every other year. Executives in these companies never review product/service quality or supplier data, unless a major problem occurs. The macro measures for your organization should be identified in section 2.1a of your application. Executives need to review performance on all of these macro measures on a regular basis, such as once a month.

Indicators for Area 1.1a

- Senior executives have developed a clear and concise set of values for the organization that explains what the company stands for and believes

- The behavior of all senior executives is consistent with the stated values

- Executives are continually looking for opportunities to grow the organization's future business

- Thoroughness with which senior executives communicate and reward behavior that is consistent with the future vision

- Extent to which recent major business decisions are consistent with the company's vision and values

- Leadership styles of all senior executives is consistent with the philosophies of Baldrige (e.g., continuous improvement, empowerment of employees, delighting customers, staying close to the business, etc.)

- Senior executive involvement in establishing major long-term goals for the company to ensure its future survival and success

- Number of hours of training completed each year by senior executives, and the extent to which executives have learned about the philosophies and processes involved in becoming a customer-focused organization

- Executive participation in benchmarking other companies, and in leading groups who want to benchmark their own company

- Existence of an inside service culture in support functions led by senior executives such as the vice president of finance or human resources

- Degree to which employees believe that senior executives model the company values, and promote a customer-focused culture

- Amount of time senior executives spend interacting with employees in the plants, field, or areas of the business where services are delivered to customers

- Extent to which visible executive perks, such as special parking, lunch rooms, bathrooms, etc. have been eliminated to promote a more egalitarian culture.

- Frequency with which senior executives review customer satisfaction, employee satisfaction, and product/service quality data.

- Senior executive involvement in recognizing employees for their accomplishments

- Evidence that senior executives are open and honest in communicating important issues to employees

- Executives engage in a variety of activities to demonstrate their customer orientation and company values

- Evidence that quality values are integrated into the organization's approaches to:
    - Planning
    - Decision making
    - Monitoring performance
    - Collection and analysis of data
    - Organization and job design
    - Workflow design
    - Performance planning and appraisal
    - Employee education and training

- Employees' view, at various levels in the company, of the extent to which managers and executives have integrated the quality values of the organization into their leadership approach

---

AREAS TO ADDRESS   **[APPROACH/DEPLOYMENT]**

1.1b How senior executives evaluate and improve the company's leadership system, including their own leadership skills

Notes:

(4) Evaluation of the company's leadership system (1.1b) might include assessment of executives by peers, direct reports, and/or a board of directors. It might also include use of surveys of company employees.

<u>What They're Looking For Here</u>

This is the first of many such Areas to Address that you will see throughout the various categories. It asks for evidence that the organization systematically evaluates how well the executives do in demonstrating their commitment to quality and customer satisfaction. Begin your explanation with a list of the specific measurement indices that you use to evaluate executives' performance in this area. Your measurement indices should be broad, including data from a variety of sources. Some example measurement indices might be:

- Evaluation of executives by Board of Directors

- Employee survey items that address executive commitment to quality

- Percentage of time executives spend interacting with customers

- Employee focus group data

- Leadership survey executives complete with regard to each other and which executives' subordinates also complete

I've seen several Baldrige applicants mention that they use customer satisfaction data as the measure of the effectiveness of their leadership approach. But customer satisfaction data are impacted by too many other variables to be a good index of the effectiveness of the leadership approach. After listing the various leadership measurement indices, explain how you collect the evaluation data, how you aggregate the data, and use it to make decisions about what the executives need to do in the future to better demonstrate their commitment to quality. Finally you should provide several examples of changes that have resulted from evaluation data, and improvements you have made in your approach to getting executives to demonstrate quality in their leadership approach. The examiners are not only looking for a systematic approach to integrating total quality into their leadership approach.

Indicators For Area 1.1b

- Identification of a variety of measurement indices that can be used to evaluate executives' leadership and involvement

- Appropriateness and objectivity of measurement indices as indicators of executive leadership

- Extent to which measures directly relate to the effectiveness of leadership practices

- Evidence of a systematic approach to evaluation of executive leadership and involvement

- Clear explanation of how evaluation data are aggregated and compared

- System in place for follow-up planning in response to evaluation data

- Evidence of continuous improvements in executives' personal leadership and involvement based upon evaluation data

- Scope and breadth of changes that have been made over the last few years to improve executives' personal involvement and leadership

---

1.2 LEADERSHIP SYSTEM AND ORGANIZATION

Describe how the company's customer focus and performance expectations are integrated into the company's leadership system, management, and organization. (25 points)

AREA TO ADDRESS   **[APPROACH, DEPLOYMENT]**

1.2a How the company's values, expectations, and directions are integrated into its leadership system, management, and organization. Describe: (1) how the organization and its management of operations are designed to achieve companywide customer focus and commitment to high performance. Include roles and responsibilities of managers and supervisors; and (2) how values, expectations, and directions are effectively communicated and reinforced throughout the entire work force.

What They're Looking For Here

This examination item is about **integration.** Many organizations have attempted to implement a quality and customer-focused culture by creating an add-on structure of committees, teams, and initiatives. These organizations usually end up scoring between 200 and 400 on the old Baldrige criteria, because they have not really changed the way their companies operate on a day-to-day basis, and are often stuck with hierarchical organization structures that slow decision making. Changes to the Baldrige criteria for 1995 and 1996 suggest that a TQM program or initiative will no longer get much credit. Many of these TQM programs have died an early death because they are programs. Baldrige winners have made fundamental changes in how work is done, jobs are designed, and how the organization is structured. In other words, they have gone way beyond a quality or TQM program or initiative.

This may have seemed like a new area to address for 1995, but it is actually an old one that has been resurrected from the 1992 Baldrige criteria. What used to be 1.2b in the 1992 criteria asked about how the company has changed its organization structure to promote a focus on quality, customer satisfaction, and efficiency. The new area to address has been made broader to address the company's leadership system and management approach, as well as its organization structure.

The first question you might ask about this area to address is "what is a leadership system?" A leadership system is the company's approach for defining and communicating the company direction, vision, and major objectives. The leadership system should help ensure that every employee is working together toward the achievement of common goals. A leadership system might consist of the following factors or components:

- Senior management positions and major responsibilities

- Methods for developing future direction, products/services, and values

- Roles of senior executives, board of directors, and stakeholders/stockholders

- Methods for cascading measures, goals, and improvement strategies down throughout various functions, levels, and facilities in the company

- Responsibilities of each major layer of management.

The second question asked in this area to address is about the company's management. What you need to discuss is what is the role of management in your organization. If you are trying to implement a culture that focuses on issues like empowerment, trust, efficiency, and delighting employees and customers, you need to explain management's role in facilitating this type of culture. The focus in item 1.1 is the senior executives. The focus in this item is on all levels of management, from first-level supervision on up to senior executives. One way of responding to this portion of the area to address is to create a matrix that shows the major responsibilities of each level of management in your organization. It might also be a good idea to show how the roles and responsibilities of managers have evolved and changed over the years. This will help your score by indicating evaluation and continuous improvement.

The third factor assessed is your organization structure. One of the first hurdles you must get over is to convince the Baldrige Examiners that your structure was designed in a logical manner to encourage achievement of performance goals. Most organization structures were never deliberately designed and have little logic to them. Rather, they were built over time in a reactive fashion, around the strengths and weaknesses of individual managers and leaders. Structures also tend to switch back and forth as often as senior leadership changes. If the company has a decentralized structure for a while, you can bet the new President will try making the organization more centralized, or vice versa.

You need to present your organization structure in chart format, explain the logic behind the structure, and how it will reduce wasted time, promote empowerment of employees, and achievement of long- and short-term performance goals. You might also present your old organization structure and point out differences and improvements you have made. Two common approaches of changing organization structures are "de-layering" and implementation of cross-functional teams based on processes, rather than traditional functional departments. If your structure has been "de-layered" or flattened, explain how and why these changes have been made, and what the impact of the new flatter structure has been. If you have eliminated functional departments, explain how the new structure allows you to perform better. In general, you need to explain how your new organization structure has impacted major performance measures in your organization. This does not mean presenting results or data. What it means is that you need to explain some of the improvements or benefits that have resulted from your new structure.

Changing your organization structure for the sake of change is certainly not called for or necessary. Yours might be a relatively young company that has always had a flat, logical, organizational structure that promotes high performance. To receive a high score, you would still need to show how the structure has been evaluated and fine-tuned over the last few years, however. This portion of the Area to Address (1.2.a.(2)) asks about what the *company* does to communicate and reinforce the company's customer focus and values.

There are really two parts to this Area to Address that should be discussed separately. Begin your response by explaining how you communicate the company's focus on the customer and your values. An important dimension of how the values are communicated is the methods used for communication. Some companies simply post the values on plaques that are posted on walls all over the company. It is important that you use a variety of methods and media to communicate the company's values and customer focus. Employees need reminders of the values to help keep their behavior aligned with those values. Because of this, the frequency of your communication is also important. Values need to be communicated in speeches, newsletters, training programs, meetings, reports, plans, and various other ways in which the company conveys information to its employees. It is also important to vary the media used. One company I worked with programmed every computer terminal so that the company values would appear on the screen when employees signed on in the morning. Since almost every employee worked with a computer terminal, they saw the values every day. Yet, not one of the approximately 50 employees I interviewed could recite those values for me off the top of their heads. The lesson to learn here is that it is important to vary the communication medium. People get used to seeing a plaque on the wall or words on a screen every morning, and don't really see it any more after a while.

The second half of the area, which I think is the more important part, asks about how you reinforce the customer focus and quality values. We first need to make clear what the word *reinforcement* means. Many will interpret this to mean how the company reminds employees of the quality values. Reminding is just more communication; it is not reinforcement. Reinforcement is being used in the Skinnerian sense here, to mean:

> How do you reward employee behavior that is consistent with your customer focus and quality values?

The company I mentioned above that has the values on the sign-on screen on the computer terminals may not communicate their values well, but they do an excellent job of reinforcing employee behavior that is consistent with the values. One way they do this is by putting all customer contact and many support employees on incentive pay. The incentive is based upon customer satisfaction scores. The company also gives out monthly and quarterly awards to employees for behaviors that are consistent with a focus on the customer. Employees may not be able to recite the words in the company's value statements, but they certainly live by the values, which is what's important.

Your response should explain the methods that you use to reward or reinforce employees for behavior that is consistent with your quality values. Describe the various methods used, the criteria for receiving the rewards, and the employees that are eligible for the awards. An ideal system would include methods for rewarding all levels and types of employees for following the values, as opposed to just the customer contact employees. An ideal system would also make sure that the items or actions that are used for rewards are, in fact, rewarding to the recipients. For example, lunch with the boss is often used as a reward for individuals or teams in companies. Most employees I talk to find this to be more of a punishment than a reward. So, provide evidence that you tailor your rewards and reinforcement strategies to the likes and dislikes of the employee group being rewarded.

Indicators For Area 1.2a

- Evidence that leadership system has been designed in a logical manner rather than something that just evolved over time with no plan

- Extent to which leadership approach encourages flexibility, empowerment, and excellence in all measures of performance

- Evidence that all levels of management are measured on the degree to which they satisfy their internal and/or external customers

- Degree to which all portions of the organization work together to achieve common goals, rather than at cross-purposes

- Evidence that organization structure and jobs have been defined based on key success factors for the company.

- Evidence that the organization has considered the philosophies of TQM and the Baldrige principles in the design of their organization structure.

- The current organization structure helps to eliminate bureaucracy and speed decision making.

- Redundant jobs and layers of management have been eliminated to make a flatter organization

- Appropriateness of leadership system and organization structure to the size and type of organization

- Identification of specific measures or indicators to evaluate the effectiveness of the leadership system and organizational structure.

- Use of a systematic process to collect data on evaluation indices

- Evidence to suggest that the organization structure is effective

• Degree to which organization structure and leadership system have been evaluated and continuously improved over the last several years.

AREA TO ADDRESS   **[APPROACH, DEPLOYMENT]**

1.2b How overall company and work unit performance are reviewed. Include a description of: (1) the principal financial and nonfinancial measures used and how these measures relate to key stakeholders' primary needs and expectations; (2) how progress relative to plans is tracked; (3) how progress relative to competitors is tracked; (4) how asset productivity is determined; and (5) how review findings are used to set priorities for improvement actions.

Notes:

(1)   **Reviews described in 1.2b might utilize information from results Items—6.1, 6.2, 6.3, 6.4, and 7.4—and also might draw upon evaluations described in other Items and upon analysis (Item 2.3).**

(2)   **Reviews might include various economic measures as well as financial ones.**

(3)   **Assets [1.2b(4)] refers to human resources, materials, energy, capital, equipment, etc. Aggregate measures such as total factor productivity might also be used.**

What They're Looking For Here

This area to address is quite a bit different than it was last year; it asks about the specific types of performance data that are reviewed, along with how and by whom they are reviewed. What is asked for in 1.2b(1) is a list of the macro metrics or measures on the organization's scorecard. This same information is essentially asked for in more detail in 2.1.a. This area to address also asks you to explain how the performance measures are related to meeting the needs of key stakeholders. An easy way of responding to this item is to prepare a matrix that lists the measures along the left side of the chart, grouped into categories, such as financial, supplier performance, customer satisfaction, etc. Along the top of the matrix, you should list the key stakeholders for your organization. Stakeholders typically include: customers, employees, shareholders, the community, and various regulatory agencies and groups. Using the matrix chart format, indicate which measures relate to which of the stakeholders' needs. In addition to this chart, you might also need to explain the primary needs and expectations of each group of stakeholders, so that the Examiners will see the connection between your measures and their needs. Make sure that the information you present in this section is consistent with the information on performance measures in section 2.1.a.

The remaining criteria in this area to address ask about how performance data are reviewed and used to develop action plans and make the right business decisions. This information sounds very much like what used to be asked for in 2.3. The difference, is that this area to address focuses more on review of data, whereas 2.3 asks about aggregation of data, and the establishment of correlations between key metrics. 1.2.b(2) asks about how you review performance against goals or plans. This information could be presented in narrative or chart format. Either way, make sure to explain who does the reviews, what data are reviewed, and how often reviews are conducted. What is important is that executives regularly review non-financial performance as often and in as much detail as financial performance measures.

The next portion of this area to address 1.2b(3) asks about how performance levels of competitors are reviewed on a regular basis, and compared to your own performance. This obviously relates closely to 2.2, that asks about what information you collect on competitors. Your answer to this portion of the Area to Address should list the specific types of competitor data that are reviewed and compared to your own performance. 1.2b(4) asks about how you evaluate asset productivity. This is typically done through the use of performance indices that are important to your industry. For example, a hotel might look at occupancy or fill rates. Many companies have adopted a financial measure called EVA, or economic value-added as a way of assessing the organization's ability to make productive use of its capital investment. MVA, or market value-added is another similar statistic that is used by GE, Coca Cola, WalMart, and others, to measure their ability to create wealth for shareholders. In any case, you need to explain the measures you use in your own organization to track asset productivity.

The last portion of this Area to Address asks about how the findings from performance reviews are used to set priorities and develop interventions or action plans. Beware of a generic answer to 1.2b(5) that says something like: We employ a systematic process for establishing priorities to decide on improvement actions needed to drive improvement planning. You need to go into a little more detail in explaining exactly how you establish priorities, and provide a few examples to add credibility to your process description.

Indicators For Area 1.2b

- Existence of a well-balanced set of financial and non-financial performance metrics

- Extent to which measures are linked to the needs of customers, shareholders, employees, and other primary stakeholders.

- Frequency of performance review meetings

- Evidence that performance on all key performance metrics is reviewed on a regular basis.

- Consistency of performance reviews across levels and functions in the organization

- Scope of competitor data collected and the frequency with which it is reviewed.

- Consistency between measures and goals listed here and those found in sections 2.1 and 3.2

- Consistency between measures listed here and actual results presented in sections 6.0 and 7.0

- Identification of specific metrics of methods used to calculate asset productivity

- Evidence of a systematic process for prioritizing actions needed to improve performance.

- Examples or evidence that the systematic prioritization process is actually deployed.

- Number of times new employees are exposed to the company's values and customer focus during their first year on the job

- Number of different methods and media that are used to communicate the values

- Extent to which employees at all levels and in all locations are equally exposed to the values

- Evidence that media used to communicate quality values are continually changed to promote increased and continued awareness

- Extent to which employees know what the values are—not whether they can recite them word for word, but whether they understand the essence of the values

- Number of different techniques used to reward employee behavior that is consistent with the values

- Extent to which strategies exist for rewarding all categories and functions of employees for behavior consistent with values

- Evidence that items or activities chosen for rewards actually are rewarding to employees

- Use of innovative approaches to reinforce behavior consistent with values

1.3 PUBLIC RESPONSIBILITY AND CORPORATE CITIZENSHIP

Describe how the company addresses its responsibilities to the public in its improvement practices. Describe also how the company leads and contributes as a corporate citizen in its key communities. (20 points)

Notes:

(1) **Public responsibility issues (1.3a) relate to the company's impacts and possible impacts on society associated with its products, services, facilities, and operations. They include environment, health, safety, and emergency preparedness as they relate to any aspect of risk or adverse effect, whether or not these are covered under law or regulation. Health and safety of employees are not addressed in Item 1.3. Employee health and safety are covered in Item 4.4.**

(2) **Major public responsibility or impact areas should also be addressed in planning (Item 3.1) and in the appropriate process management Items of Category 5.0. Key results, such as environmental improvements, should be reported in Item 6.2.**

(3) **If the company has received sanctions under law, regulation, or contract [1.3a(3)] during the past three years, briefly describe the incident(s) and its current status. If settlements have been negotiated in lieu of potential sanctions, give an explanation. If no sanctions have been received, so indicate.**

(4) **The corporate citizenship issues appropriate for inclusion in 1.3b relate to efforts by the company to strengthen community services, education,**

health care, environment, and practices of trade or business associations. Examples of corporate citizenship appropriate for inclusion in 1.3b are:

- influencing and helping trade and business associations to create school-to-work programs;
- communicating employability requirements to schools;
- influencing national, state, and local policies which promote education improvement;
- partnering with and charitable giving to schools, e.g., sharing computers and computer expertise;
- developing trade and business consortia to improve environmental practices;
- promoting volunteerism among employees;
- partnering with other businesses and health care providers to improve health in the local community; and
- influencing trade and business associations to engage in cooperative activities to improve overall U.S. global competitiveness.

AREA TO ADDRESS   [APPROACH, DEPLOYMENT]
1.3a How the company integrates its public responsibilities into its performance improvement effort. Describe: (1) the risks and regulatory and other legal requirements in setting operational requirements and targets; (2) how the company looks ahead to anticipate public concerns and to assess possible impacts on society of its products, services, and operations; and (3) how the company promotes legal and ethical conduct in all that it does.

What They're Looking For Here

Being a Baldrige Award winning company takes more than having the right financial and customer satisfaction results and having the right systems in place. You also have to be a good corporate citizen. Examination Item 1.3 asks about how you develop plans and implement activities relating to corporate citizenship and public responsibility. What does this mean? It means factors such as environmental protection, charity, support of the arts, support of education, and help of the community. The only thing that is not included in this Area to Address is self-serving actions. For example, the money that a defense contractor donates to key congressmen's campaigns might be considered self-serving.

Begin your response for this area to address by describing how your company sets standards or goals relating to public responsibility and corporate citizenship. Explain the process for setting these goals and/or standards and who is involved in the process. Your discussion should also mention the key legal and regulatory requirements that must be adhered to. Explain how the levels of performance in your own standards or goals relate to required levels. Obviously it will be more impressive if your approach is to do more than just satisfy the requirements—you have no choice in this. The examiners want to see evidence of going beyond meeting basic legal and regulatory requirements in how you set your goals and standards. Also, you should explain how you evaluate risks and possible consequences when setting these standards or requirements.

The best companies are those that anticipate the future public concerns about their products or services and deal with those issues in a preventive fashion. Your response for this area should explain how you look into the future to identify trends that may impact your business, and how you plan for those trends.

An important aspect of judging your response to this area is the thoroughness and objectivity of your sources of information on future trends. Some companies rely on one or two sources of data. Others rely on a great many sources and devote a good deal of effort to predicting future trends that will impact their business. These tend to be the companies that are around for the long haul. Once you explain how and where you obtain data used to predict future trends, explain the process for using these data as inputs to your planning. An example or two will help to add credibility to your response, illustrating that you actually have used this data to change your plans.

Finally, 1.3a(3) asks how your company promotes legal and ethical conduct in all it does. Again, forget the general statements. Give us specifics of how you do this. For example, Northrop has an anonymous hotline number that employees can call to report unethical behavior or practices they have observed. This setup is combined with very thorough training for employees on what constitutes unethical behavior. These would be the types of activities that should be discussed here. Education and awareness are usually the first steps in the process, but there also needs to be measurement and control strategies in place to ensure that legal and ethical practices are followed on a continual basis.

Indicators For Area 1.3a

- Response includes delineation of key measures of corporate citizenship and public responsibility that are relevant and important to the company

- A systematic process is used to define standards and goals relating to matters of corporate citizenship and public responsibility

- Goals or standards specify levels of performance that will lead the company to a world-class level of performance on these factors

- Evidence that risks and possible consequences are thoroughly assessed in the process of coming up with goals and standards in the area of public responsibility

- Evidence provided to demonstrate how key goals and standards for public responsibility and corporate citizenship are translated into operational policies and procedures

- Thorough communication of operational policies and procedures relating this item to all appropriate employees and locations within the company

- Regularly scheduled review meetings are held to discuss progress in meeting goals and standards in the areas of public responsibility and corporate citizenship

- Plans are revised as necessary based upon changes in requirements, the business environment, or other factors

- Number of different sources of data company uses to predict future trends that may impact their products, services, or operations

- Objectivity of sources of data on future trends

- Evidence that company acts to prevent possible problems with their products/ services in the future, rather than to cover them up

- Amount and thoroughness of testing done on products/services sold by the company, and relevance of this testing to current and future public concerns

- Evidence that information on future trends in public concerns are incorporated into the company's planning process

- Existence of a specific process for integrating trends in public concerns into the planning process

- Existence of a systematic approach to educating employees regarding legal and ethical behavior/practices

- Extent to which employees at all levels and in all locations are provided with this education/training on legal/ethical issues

- Existence of a system for monitoring extent to which employee behavior is consistent with legal/ethical guidelines

- Control strategies are in place to ensure that legal/ethical practices are followed

---

AREA TO ADDRESS   **[APPROACH , DEPLOYMENT]**
1.3b How the company leads and contributes as a corporate citizen in its key communities. Include a brief summary of the types of leadership and involvement the company emphasizes.

What They're Looking For Here

This area to address looks at two factors. First, it asks for information on what you are doing as a company to be a leader in demonstrating your corporate citizenship and involvement in the communities in which you operate. Second, it asks how you help other organizations in their quality improvement efforts. Sometimes these efforts overlap. For example, Baxter Healthcare, the world's largest manufacturer of medical supplies, held a workshop for area high school principals to teach them about Total Quality and how it may be applied in educational institutions. Since these principals are from the community surrounding Baxter's corporate offices, it is a community outreach effort. However, since it also involved helping promote Total Quality, it qualifies for the second half of this area to address as well.

A good way of responding to this area to address is to summarize in chart form the activities you engage in that make you a good corporate citizen. A sample of a portion of such a chart is shown in the example below.

ORGANIZATION	DESCRIPTION	NOTEWORTHY ACCOMPLISHMENTS
OPAR	Organization that funds and promotes AIDS research	• CFO is chairman • Company donated $50,000 in '93 • Meetings held at company facilities • Employees donated over 20,000 hours and $30,000 in '93
Portage Works Project	Workshop run by the mentally challenged	• All major mailings done by PWP • PWP one of our certified suppliers • Work from our company pays salaries of nine individuals from PWP
Juvenile Diabetes Foundation	Charitable organization for children with diabetes	• CEO is on the board • Company sponsors fundraising banquet each year, devoting many hours and dollars • Prepare all print advertising free for JDF • Company donates over $50,000 each year to JDF

In presenting information on the activities you engage in that make you a good corporate citizen, it may be helpful to provide some comparative data to help illustrate the importance of your accomplishments. For example, if your company donated $80,000 per quarter in 1994 to the United Fund, through employee contributions, and you have 18,000 employees, that works out to less than $5.00 per employee. The Baldrige Examiners may not know whether this is exceptional, average, or below par. Therefore, you might mention that for companies your size, it is typical for employees to average $3.20 per quarter in donations to the United Fund. This makes your performance look much better than the average company.

This area to address also asks about how you seek to enhance your leadership in corporate citizenship. Again, the worst thing to do is to present a general statement such as: "Our company continues to review and improve our approaches to corporate citizenship and promotion of community involvement, and hope to continually enhance our leadership position in these areas in the coming years." Most examiners would read a statement like this and write a comment such as: "It is not clear how the company plans to seek and exploit opportunities for improving its leadership in the areas of corporate citizenship." You need to get specific and explain how you intend to do this, and what your specific goals for leadership are in these areas.

Indicators For Area 1.3b

- Breadth and scope of activites that indicate that the company is a good corporate citizen and concerned with the public welfare

- Significance of the company's accomplishments in these areas

- Evidence from news media and outside sources that the company is, in fact, a good corporate citizen

- Comparison of the corporate citizenship and public responsibility activities of the applicant company to other companies that are similar in size

- Evidence that the company has increased its efforts to be a good corporate citizen over the last few years

- Number of presentations, tours, and publications that company employees have made that promote implementation of the Baldrige principles

Chapter 7

Interpreting the Criteria for Information and Analysis (2.0)

OVERVIEW OF THE INFORMATION AND ANALYSIS CATEGORY

The 1995 Baldrige Award Criteria define the Information and Analysis category as follows:

*The **Information and Analysis** category examines the management and effectiveness of the use of data and information to support customer-driven performance excellence and marketplace success. (p. 8)*

The 2.0 Information and Analysis category is worth a total of 75 points and is broken down into the following three Examination Items:

- 2.1 Management of Information and Data (20 points)
- 2.2 Competitive Comparisons and Benchmarking (15 points)
- 2.3 Analysis and Uses of Company-Level Data (40 points)

The purpose of this category is to assess the types of data you collect relating to quality and company performance and to examine the process by which you analyze those data in order to make decisions. This chapter describes each of the three Examination Items and the six Areas to Address that fall under this category. Again, each section begins with a double-ruled box containing the Examination Item, the point value, and any applicable Notes.* Areas to Address falling under that Item follow in a single-ruled box. In the upper right corner of each Area to Address box is an indication [brackets] of whether the Area pertains to approach, deployment, or results. All definitions and information appearing within these boxes is taken directly from the Baldrige criteria. Following each Area to Address is an explanation defining what the Examiners are looking for in assessing your application. Next, I have supplied a list of indicators or evaluation factors that will assist you in interpreting the criteria and in preparing your application.

This category forms the foundation of a sound performance system. If you have a poor information and analysis system, this will lead to a low score in the sections that deal with planning (3.0), human resource development and management (4.0), management of process (5.0), results (6.0), and customer satisfaction results (7.0). If you select the wrong indices to measure, this will lead to low scores in a number of different areas that ask for results. Even if your graphs look great, you won't end up with a good score for results if the performance indices on the graphs are inappropriate.

---

* Item Notes that apply to a specific Area to Address are appropriately listed in the box containing that Area.

The 1996 Baldrige application guidelines explain:

> *In simplest terms, Category 2.0 is the "brain center" for the alignment of a company's information system with its strategic directions. (p. 35)*

Even though this category is only worth a possible 75 points out of 1000, it is critical to high scores in other sections. In fact, if you do a poor job on this section of your application it will have an impact on all of the sections that ask for *results*. Thus, section 2.0 actually impacts 75 points on its own, plus 410 points relating to results.

It used to be that this item asked for information on the *quality* data that a company collected. The focus now is on *all* important data that a company gathers and analyzes. Certainly quality and customer satisfaction data are still asked for. However, this category also asks for financial, operational, productivity, and any other type of performance data a company might gather and use in running the business.

2.1 SCOPE AND MANAGEMENT OF QUALITY AND PERFORMANCE DATA AND INFORMATION

Describe the company's selection and management of information and data used for planning, management, and evaluation of overall performance. (20 points)

AREA TO ADDRESS   **[APPROACH, DEPLOYMENT]**

2.1a How information and data needed to support operations and decision making and to drive improvement of overall company performance are selected and managed. Describe: (1) the main types of data and information and how each type supports key business operations and business strategy; (2) how the company's performance measurement system is designed to achieve alignment of operations with company priorities, such as key business drivers; and (3) how key requirements such as reliability, rapid access, and rapid update are derived from user needs and how the requirements are met.

Notes:

(1) **Reliability [2.1a(3)] includes software used in information systems.**

(2) **User needs [2.1a(3)] should consider knowledge accumulation such as knowledge about specific customers or customer segments. User needs should also take into account changing patterns of communications associated with changes in process management, job design, and business strategy.**

What They're Looking For Here

This is one of the most important of the 24 Baldrige items. This is a foundation item because it impacts your score in many of the other items; particularly those that ask for results. The basic questions asked in this item are:

- How do you measure performance in your organization?

- Why were these measures selected?

- How do you relate your performance measures to your priorities or key success factors?

The first portion of Area to Address 2.1.a(1) asks you to list the performance measures on your organization's scorecard, and to explain how each relates to the operation of your organization, or to your overall business strategy. What is important here is that you collect data on a reasonable number of performance measures, and that you have good balance in your metrics. If your CEO or President regularly looks at more than 20 performance measures, you may receive a lower score. Leading organizations such as three-time Baldrige winner AT&T focus on a few key measures: Economic Value-Added, People Value-Added, and Customer Value-Added. Many companies have scorecards that include 10 to 15 measures, which is also reasonable. The problem with recording too many measures is that it clouds your focus and ends up distracting you from the vital few performance metrics. The best indicator of a balanced scorecard approach to measurement is a relatively equal number of measures in each of the categories in your data base. This is an area where many organizations have problems. Seventy to ninety percent of the data they collect and review on a regular basis is financial and operational. They prepare 50 pounds of financial reports each month, and maybe one pound of customer-related or employee satisfaction data. Financial performance is measured a hundred different ways every single day, and employee satisfaction is measured once a year with a single survey. Examples of practices that will lead to a low score are in section 2.1.a.

Along with a reasonable number of performance measures, the concept of balancing the time perspective of your data is also important. Performance measures in many organizations focus almost exclusively on measuring the past. A good balanced scorecard includes measures from three perspectives: past, present, and future. Another aspect of balance that is important is that measures focus on the needs of more than just your shareholders or owners. Measures should focus on how well you satisfy customers, employees, and stakeholders, such as the community in which you operate.

The second part of this Area to Address 2.1.a(2), asks about how your performance measures relate to your priorities or key business drivers. Key business drivers are not generic things like quality, productivity, or being customer-focused. Key business drivers, which are discussed in more detail in section 3.2.a, are those things that you need to concentrate on to differentiate your business from major competitors. Key business drivers or success factors should be specific to your business, and may relate to strengths that need to continue to exploit, or weaknesses that need to be corrected. For example, a company that provides cellular phone service identified competitive pricing, wide variety of rate plans, and transmission sound quality as its three key business drivers. If they are better than their competitors on all three of these measures, they will continue to grow market share at a faster rate than their competitors. For additional information on linking performance measures to key business drivers, consult my new book: *Keeping Score: Using Strategic Metrics to Drive World-Class Performance* (Quality Resources, 1996).

In responding to this Area to Address, an effective format might be to list your performance measures down the left side of a table, grouped by category of data. For example, a common set of categories include:

- Financial measures

- Customer-related measures

- Employee-related measures

- Supplier performance measures

- Innovation/growth measures

- Operational/process measures

Along the top of your table, you could list key business drivers, and an additional column labeled "Business Fundamentals." Business fundamentals are used to indicate the measures that may not relate specifically to your key success factors or business drivers, but are important for running the business. For example, you will probably want to have some measure of profit, and perhaps safety in your scorecard, even though these might not be key business drivers for the organization right now. Using X's in the boxes in your matrix, indicate which of the performance measures relate to which of the key business drivers or to business fundamentals. Assigning a percentage weight to each of the measures based on its importance in your overall business strategy is another good way of showing the linkage between your measures and your strategy.

The third portion of this area to address 2.1.a(3) asks about how you identify the needs of the users or consumers of the performance data you collect. This does not ask how the data are used to make business decisions. This information is asked for in 2.3. What 2.1.a(3) asks for is evidence that you thoroughly analyze the needs of managers and others who will use the performance data to find out:

- How often data should be reported

- The format for presentation of the data

- How often the data needs to be updated

- Types of breakdowns available

- How much data is automatically reported and how much should be available as requested

After explaining how and how often you determine the needs of the users of your performance data, explain how you ensure that these needs are being met. In other words, describe how your overall performance data base was designed around user needs.

The examiners also look at the standardization of data collection and reporting techniques. One manufacturing organization I worked with produced 24 different quality reports every week. The reports were produced independently by various departments (e.g., engineering, quality control, production, industrial engineering, etc.), and were all in different formats. What the examiners want to see is that quality reporting is standardized and that there is no overlap or redundancy in the data. Quality reports should be as brief and easy to interpret as possible. The use of graphs and charts to summarize data rather than printouts of statistics is preferable. The examiners also look at the recipients of each of the quality reports. Reports should be only sent to individuals who need the data to make decisions. Use of specific reports for specific levels and functions is a positive indicator, as compared with using a single report that attempts to meet the information needs of all levels of employees in all different functions.

Another factor that is examined in this area is the degree to which quality reports and on-line data are kept up to date and accurate. Many organizations have excellent reporting systems, but they don't maintain the data base frequently enough, so the data are not current.

Indicators For Area 2.1a

- Organization has developed a specific set of criteria for screening out unnecessary measures from their data base

- Evidence that the data base was built with a plan, rather than being something that just evolved over time

- CEO or President looks at not more than 20 measures every month to evaluate the overall organization's performance

- Degree to which macro measures have been derived from key business drivers or analysis of future success factors for the company

- Extent to which measures have been developed for all business drivers

- Consistency of performance measures with mission, vision, and values

- Consistency of measures across business units and/or locations

- Evidence that the organization has a well-balanced set of metrics, with approximately equal amounts of data in each of the following categories: financial performance, operational/process measures, customer satisfaction, employee satisfaction, product/service quality, supplier performance, and safety/environmental performance

- Inclusion of both hard (customer buying behavior) and soft measures (customer opinions) of customer satisfaction in overall measures

- Use of multiple measures of employee satisfaction

- Selection of 3–6 key financial metrics that are a good mix of short- and long-term indicators of success

- Operational/process measures are related to customer or stakeholder requirements

- Company data base includes measures of cycle time and productivity or efficiency

- Several overall measures of safety and environmental performance are included in the overall data base

- Measures of supplier performance include indices of quality, service, price, and responsiveness/timeliness

- Use of regular and systematic approach for testing and calibrating all automated and manual measurement equipment/devices

- Systematic evaluation, testing, and calibration of nonhardware measurement instruments (e.g., surveys, checklists, etc.)

- Validity of methods used to evaluate accuracy of measurement instruments

- Degree to which performance data available to employees are current and accurate

- Timeliness with which performance data are disseminated to employees

- Ease of employee access to performance data needed to do their jobs

- Standardization of data and report format across all functions/departments in the organization

- Readability and ease of use of performance reports

- Quality reports tailored to specific levels and functions so that employees only receive the data they need

- Use of graphs and charts to summarize quality data in reports

- Responses of employees regarding the usability and accuracy of the quality reports distributed

- Responses of managers and supervisors regarding the usability and accuracy of the performance reports

- Systematic process for ensuring that software used for various purposes is useful, accurate, and up to date

---

AREA TO ADDRESS   **[APPROACH, DEPLOYMENT]**

2.1b How the company evaluates and improves the selection, analysis, and integration of information and data, aligning them with the company's key business drivers and operations. Describe how the evaluation considers: (1) scope of information and data; (2) use and analysis of information and data to support process management and performance improvement; and (3) feedback from users of information and data.

Note:

(3)   **Feedback from users [2.1b(3)] might entail formal or informal surveys, focus groups, and teams. Factors in the evaluation might include completeness, timeliness, access, update, and reliability. The evaluation might also include assessment of the information technologies used.**

What They're Looking For Here

Your response for this Area to Address should explain how you systematically evaluate your data collection systems and instruments. Describe how the evaluation is done, the procedures used, instruments, etc. Don't respond with a statement such as: "We regularly evaluate and improve the scope and accuracy of our measures and data collection." Be specific. Explain exactly how you evaluate the data collection system. Your approach will be assessed based upon its thoroughness, objectivity, validity, and use of accepted evaluation methodologies. You should begin by listing the specific indices you use to measure the effectiveness of your data base. The measurement indices should include internal customer satisfaction, process, and output measures. Follow this list with a flowchart or list of steps involved in the evaluation process.

In this section you might also talk about any actions you have taken to get business units and/or facilities to work together to develop common measures. If you have employed any objectives or incentives to encourage sharing of data it would also be appropriate to mention this here.

The Baldrige Examiners are also looking for evidence that you have taken actions to streamline the information processing cycle and to implement countermeasures to improve quality. Many organizations that have only just begun to work on total quality management in the last few years find that quality improvement teams take a great deal of time collecting and processing data before any corrective countermeasures are introduced. While adequate data and thorough analysis are certainly important, too much time can be spent on these activities. The examiners want to see that you are thorough, as well as efficient and improvement-oriented.

A typical response for this area is to describe that you have taken a number of steps to shorten the data gathering and processing cycle. As in the other areas, you need to be specific. Start out by explaining the situation in the past. Be sure to include some statistics if you have them. Your response to this area should also include an explanation of your efforts to broaden employees' access to data and information. The Baldrige people are looking for evidence that many employees are provided with access to the company's data base.

Question 2.1b(2) asks about how you have integrated your data base with process improvement needs and plans. What's being asked for here is evidence that your data base includes key process measures that you have decided are critical to control, in order to produce consistently high quality products/services. Your response for this portion of 2.1c should directly relate to and be compatible with your response to Item 5.2, which asks about your key processes, how you measure them, and how you control them. Your data base should not be limited to output measures such as defects, customer satisfaction, and financial accomplishments. Key process measures also should be included. What the Examiners would like to see here is that the process indices you have chosen to measure are tied in to your key processes and key process variables that are discussed in Item 5.2.

Indicators For Area 2.1b

- Evidence that measures or metrics have been improved to be more closely linked to business drivers

- Existence of a systematic approach for evaluating quality data collection systems

- Evaluation measurement indices include measures of internal customer satisfaction, process, and output quality

- Evidence that company has increased employees' access to data and information

- Validity and objectivity of evaluation instruments and methodologies

- Number of years during which evaluation has been done

- Evidence of improvements in data collection system based upon evaluation

- Evidence that data gathering, analysis, and reporting process has been streamlined over the last several years

- Amount of data indicating that cycle time of data collection and dissemination has been reduced

- Description of specific strategies and tactics that have been employed to reduce cycle time of collecting, summarizing, and disseminating data

- Evidence of steps taken to closely align the company's performance measures with process improvement efforts

---

2.2 COMPETITIVE COMPARISONS AND BENCHMARKING

Describe the company's processes and uses of comparative information and data to support improvement of overall performance and competitive position. (15 points)

Note:

(1)   **Benchmarking information and data refer to processes and results that represent best practices and performance, inside or outside of the company's industry. Competitive comparisons refer to performance levels relative to direct competitors in the company's markets.**

AREA TO ADDRESS   **[APPROACH, DEPLOYMENT]**

2.2a How competitive comparisons and benchmarking information and data are selected and used to help drive improvement of overall company performance. Describe: (1) how needs and priorities are determined; (2) criteria for seeking appropriate information and data—from within and outside the company's industry and markets; (3) how the information and data are used to improve understanding of processes and process performance; and (4) how the information and data are used to set stretch targets and/or to encourage breakthrough approaches aligned with the company's competitive strategy.

Notes:

   (2)   **Needs and priorities [2.2a(1)] should show clear linkage to the company's key business drivers.**

   (3)   **Use of benchmarking information and data within the company [2.2a(3)] might include the expectation that company units maintain awareness of related best-in-class performance to help drive improvement. This could entail education and training efforts to build capabilities.**

   (4)   **Sources of competitive comparisons and benchmarking information might include: (a) information obtained from other organizations such as customers or suppliers through sharing; (b) information obtained from the open literature; (c) testing and evaluation by the company itself; and (d) testing and evaluation by independent organizations.**

What They're Looking For Here

Benchmarking is a process of studying other organizations that are known to be the best in the country or the world at performing one or a series of functions. The data from benchmarking studies are used both to set goals and to determine what level of performance is possible, as well as to adapt some of the practices of the successful companies to one's own organization. The selected organizations against which one's company benchmarks will not necessarily be competitors, and may not even be in a related industry. Xerox Business Products benchmarked itself against many of the functions performed in a mail order clothing company—L. L. Bean, for example. This section of the application should begin with a description of your criteria for selecting competitive comparisons and benchmarks. Many applicants explain that they use specific criteria for selecting benchmarks, but don't list those criteria. Make sure that your response includes a list of your criteria, or at least the major criteria.

Competitive comparisons are different from benchmarking. Competitive comparisons are simply comparisons of how your company does vis-à-vis your major competitors. Competitive comparisons should be selected based upon the similarities between the two organizations. The competitors you choose should be about the same size, have similar products/services, and operate in similar markets. Companies you select to benchmark yourself against need not be in the same business as your organization. Benchmarks should be selected based upon the level of quality they deliver in a particular area that is similar to an area in your own organization. For example, if your company is a computer manufacturer, you might compare your company to an auto manufacturer, because it may have the best inventory control system. The organizations you choose to benchmark or compare yourself against should be the best in the country or even in the world, in a particular area or function.

One factor on which your response for this item will be evaluated is the number of different functions or indices used to compare yourself to competitors and benchmark organizations. If you compare your company with one other competitor who is also one you benchmark yourself against, you won't receive a very high score for this Area to Address. Many organizations select one or two past Baldrige winners and compare every function in their organization to them. This approach will not necessarily be effective because being a Baldrige winner does not mean that every function in the company is world-class. If, on the other hand, you have identified a dozen or more functions and compare yourself to world-class benchmarks on each function, you might end up with a perfect score in this Area to Address.

What the examiners want to hear about in your response for this Area to Address is how you select those organizations to which you compare your own performance and practices. It is important to do both competitive comparisons and benchmarks. You might select your direct competitors as the companies you use for benchmarking purposes, or you might select companies that are totally outside your industry. A good approach employed by many exemplary organizations is to collect comparison data on all major competitors and to benchmark yourself against a variety of different functions in a variety of different organizations. In this section (2.2), you need to explain the process by which you select comparative organizations or "benchmarking partners."

What is also considered important here is that the functions or processes you select as benchmarking and comparison targets must relate to your own goals and priorities for performance improvement, as outlined in the company's strategic and annual plans. Benchmarking is often done independently of the organization's performance improvement goals and plans. You should explain how the benchmarking and competitive comparison activities you engaged in during the past few years have supported your long-term and annual performance goals and priorities.

Within your response to this Area to Address, you should also explain how you determined which organizations were the best at performing a particular function. Some organizations do a much better job of self-promotion than others. It may be that the best organizations get overlooked in benchmarking studies because no one knows that they are the best. Explain what type and how thorough a job you did in identifying the world-class organizations used for benchmarking purposes. The more thorough your research the better. Use of benchmarking data bases has received mixed reviews, so don't use this as your only source of data.

What the Baldrige people want to see in this section is that you actually use the competitive and benchmark data as stimuli to encourage improvements. Many companies conduct benchmarking studies, review the findings, and go about business as usual. You need to have some sort of process in place for using the benchmarking studies and competitive comparisons as a way to improve processes in your company. Your response for this section should begin with an explanation of what happens to benchmarking studies and competitive analyses. Explain how studies are reviewed, who reviews them, and how action plans are developed to use the data to capitalize on improvement opportunities. As with many of the other Areas to Address that ask about processes, it may be a good idea to use a graphic of a process model that depicts your approach. What the examiners don't want to see is that you simply copy what other companies are doing. Rather, you should take what other companies are doing and adapt these practices to your own organization.

After explaining how studies are reviewed and action plans developed, you should provide a list of process improvements that have been made as a result of benchmarking studies or competitive comparisons. A matrix might be a good way of presenting this information.

COMPETITIVE/ BENCHMARKING STUDY	COMPANY FUNCTION	ACTION PLAN
MBNA Benchmarking Study of Employee-Related Programs	Human Resources	Instituted "Parents Day" Concept in 1992
Boeing Supplier Certification Study (Competitive Comparison)	Procurement	Plan Developed for Implementation of Supplier Certification Process in 1993

Along with getting ideas of how to improve your own processes, another reason for gathering competitive and benchmark data is to determine how good performance can be on a particular dimension of process. This information is used to set targets or objectives for improvement. Goals and objectives should not be set in an arbitrary fashion. They should be based upon sound research that indicates that someone in the world has performed at the level of performance you have stated in your goal. For example, let's say that it takes your Human Resources function an average of 13 weeks to process a change of pay rate request for an employee. Two common ways of setting goals are to look at current performance and try to get 10–20% better for next year (to reduce cycle time to 10 or 11 weeks, for example). Another way of setting improvement goals is to set a "stretch" target, by picking a number out of the air simply because it seems like a good one. For example: "Our 1998 goal will be to process all pay rate changes within 5 weeks." Why 5 weeks? Because it seems like a good number and it is much better than current performance? This is not the way to set stretch targets either. Stretch targets should be based upon research that indicates that someone has achieved this level of performance.

This is where benchmarking comes in. Benchmarking tells us what is possible. In benchmarking the company that seems to have the best compensation system, we may find that they process pay rate changes in two weeks. Our own stretch target can then be based on reality—information that someone has achieved this level.

Stretch targets derived from benchmarking studies can then be used to encourage breakthrough approaches. To get the cycle time from 13 weeks down to 2 weeks will require major changes in the process used to review and approve these changes. Benchmarking should also help in figuring out how to do this. It may be that you can copy some of the ideas and approaches used by the companies in your benchmarking study.

Indicators For Area 2.2a

- Evidence of a systematic process for selecting competitive organizations for comparison purposes

- Scope and breadth of data collected on competitors

- Strong relationship between process/functions selected for competitive comparisons and benchmarking and quality goals and plans for the organization

- Thoroughness of research done to identify organizations that are the best at particular functions or processes

- Use of comparisons to both competitors and benchmarks for setting improvement goals

- Evidence that organizations selected as benchmarking partners are in fact world-class for the particular functions or processes studied

- Number and appropriateness of criteria used for selecting competitors with which to compare your organization

- Number and appropriateness of criteria used for selecting benchmark organizations with which to compare your organization

- Number of different functions or processes in the organization that is compared or benchmarked against others

- Objectivity and clarity of the criteria for selecting competitors and benchmarks for comparison purposes

- Linkage of competitor/benchmark data with key business drivers

- Number of different sources of data on competitors

- Objectivity and reliability of sources of data on competitors

- Number of different sources of data on benchmark organizations

- Objectivity and reliability of data sources on benchmark organizations

- Number of different functions and/or processes for which competitive or benchmark data are gathered

- Systems within the company to coordinate benchmarking activities to ensure consistency and avoid duplication of benchmarking efforts

- Evidence that a systematic process is used to review and follow up on competitive comparisons and benchmarking studies that are done

- Evidence that a consistent process is used to follow up on benchmarking studies and competitive comparisons

- Training is done for key employees to teach them how to interpret and use competitive comparisons and benchmarking studies

- Breadth and scope of follow-up actions or changes implemented as a result of competitive comparisons and benchmarking studies

- Number of processes, systems, and programs currently in place that were initiated from competitive comparisons and benchmarking studies

- Degree to which the organization adapts, modifies, and customizes practices of competitors and benchmarkers versus simply copying what others do

- Evidence that competitive comparisons and benchmarking studies are used to set "stretch" objectives

- Breadth and scope of improvement goals/objectives that have been derived from competitive comparisons or benchmarking studies

- Evidence that benchmarking studies and competitive comparisons serve as a stimulus for "breakthrough" changes in processes

---

AREA TO ADDRESS   **[APPROACH, DEPLOYMENT]**
2.2b How the company evaluates and improves its process for selecting and using competitive comparisons and benchmarking information and data to improve planning, overall company performance, and competitive position.

Note:
(5)   The evaluation (2.2b) might address a variety of factors such as the effectiveness of use of the information, adequacy of information, training in acquisition and use of information, improvement potential in company operations, and estimated rates of improvement by other organizations.

What They're Looking For Here

In this section you should explain how you evaluate the scope and validity of your competitive analyses and benchmarking processes and data. You should describe a specific evaluation process and possibly provide an example or two to demonstrate how you have evaluated and improved your process for gathering and using benchmark data and data on competitors.

As in many of the previous Areas to Address, the examiners are looking for evidence that you plan to expand the scope of your data on competitive and benchmark organizations. A typical response for this section might be written as follows:

> *In the future we plan to expand the scope of the data we collect on competitors and benchmark organizations by gathering more information on a wider variety of companies that are known for their world-class quality products/services.*

While this response may sound promising, it lacks details and specifics. A response such as this would earn a score of no more than 10–20%. Not enough information is provided to give credibility to the statements that the organization is expanding the scope of its data collection efforts. In order to earn a high score for this Area to Address, you might begin with an overall statement such as the one above, but follow it with a list of the specific actions or strategies you will employ over the next year or so to expand the scope of your competitive and benchmark data. This type of information will tell the examiners that you in fact have a plan for expanding the scope of your data collection and that you have identified specific strategies and actions.

Indicators For Area 2.2b

- Evidence that a systematic process is used to evaluate processes for gathering competitive and benchmark data

- Validity of evaluation methodologies and data collected to assess process for doing benchmarking studies and competitive comparisons

- Overall strategy for expanding the scope of data collection on competitors and on benchmarking organizations

- Documented plan for expanding the scope of data collection on competitors and benchmark organizations

- Specific actions that have been identified that will improve either the quantity or quality of information on competitors

- Specific actions identified that will improve either the quantity or quality of information on benchmark organizations

- Use of benchmarking data to help develop strategic performance and business goals

---

2.3 ANALYSIS AND USES OF COMPANY-LEVEL DATA

Describe how data related to quality, customers, and operational performance, together with relevant financial data, are analyzed to support company-level review, action, and planning. (40 points)

Notes:

(1) **Item 2.3 focuses primarily on analysis for company-level purposes, such as reviews (1.2b) and strategic planning (Item 3.1). Data for such analysis come from all parts of the company and include results reported in Items 6.1, 6.2, 6.3, 6.4, and 7.4. Other Items call for analyses of specific sets of data for special purposes. For example, the Items of Category 4.0 require analysis to determine effectiveness of training and other human resource practices. Such special-purpose analyses should be part of the overall information base available for use in Item 2.3.**

(2) **Analysis includes trends, projections, cause-effect correlations, and the search for deeper understanding needed to set priorities to use resources more effectively to serve overall business objectives. Accordingly, analysis draws upon all kinds of data: operational, customer-related, financial, and economic.**

AREA TO ADDRESS   **[APPROACH, DEPLOYMENT]**

2.3a How information and data from all parts of the company are integrated and analyzed to support reviews, business decisions, and planning. Describe how analysis is used to gain understanding of: (1) customers and markets; (2) operational performance and company capabilities; and (3) competitive performance.

Notes:

(3)   **Examples of analysis appropriate for inclusion in 2.3a(1) are:**

- **how the company's product and service quality improvement correlates with key customer indicators such as customer satisfaction, customer retention, and market share;**
- **cost/revenue implications of customer-related problems and problem resolution effectiveness; and**
- **interpretation of market share changes in terms of customer gains and losses and changes in customer satisfaction.**

(4)   **Examples of analysis appropriate for inclusion in 2.3a(2) are:**

- **trends in improvement in key operational performance indicators such as productivity, cycle time, waste reduction, new product introduction, and defect levels;**
- **financial benefits from improved employee safety, absenteeism, and turnover;**
- **benefits and costs associated with education and training;**
- **how the company's ability to identify and meet employee requirements correlates with employee retention, motivation, and productivity;**
- **cost/revenue implications of employee-related problems and problem resolution effectiveness; and**
- **trends in individual measures of productivity such as manpower productivity.**

(5)   **Examples of analysis appropriate for inclusion in 2.3a(3) are:**

- **working capital productivity relative to competitors;**
- **individual or aggregate measures of productivity relative to competitors;**
- **performance trends relative to competitors on key quality attributes; and**
- **cost trends relative to competitors.**

What They're Looking For Here

What this area to address asks about is how you summarize data on various different performance measures so this data can be used for analysis of company performance, and for making business decisions. One way of summarizaing data to make it easier to analyze and spot trends is to develop indices that are a combination of individual measures. For example, AT&T has developed several macro measurement indices that are composed of a number of subordinate measures. They are best known for their aggregate financial index called economic value-added, or EVA. EVA, which is a way of calculating profit by figuring in the cost of capital, is the company's overall index of their financial health. AT&T, the only company to bag three Baldriges so far, has also expanded the concept of measuring value. In some parts of their business they also have measures of employee value added and customer value added. These overall indices are a great way of summarizing overall measures of performance to make analysis much easier.

Another key to getting a good score in this area to address is to have consistent performance measures across different business units or locations. If each unit has different measures of performance, it becomes very difficult to summarize and compare measures across the different units.

EXAMPLE CUSTOMER SATISFACTION INDEX

INDEX	% WEIGHT
Customer Satisfaction Survey	40%
Customer-Focus Group Data	10%
Market Share	25%
Gains/Losses of Customers	25%
CUSTOMER SATISFACTION INDEX	100%

As you can see in the example, each of four different indices is assigned a percentage weight based upon its importance as an indicator of customer satisfaction. Establishment of a single CSI is certainly not a requirement; this is just an example of how an organization might aggregate and compare various customer-related measures.

A similar approach can be applied to any type of data, such as supplier performance or product/service quality.

Most companies collect a great deal of data on the quality of the products and services they sell and other aspects of their performance. What separates the exceptional from the average company in this Area to Address is how one aggregates and uses all of these data. The Baldrige Examiners are looking for an explanation of how you interpret all of the data you collect. When Baldrige Examiners interview supervisors and managers during a site visit, they often find out that employees aren't really sure how to interpret and use all of the data in the reports they receive on company performance. In this section of your application, you need to explain how the various measures of performance are interpreted. If you compile several individual measures into something similar to a CSI, as I have described earlier, explain how this is done.

After explaining how performance results indices are aggregated, describe how these data are used to establish priorities for performance improvement. To add credence to your description, you might include a list of the various actions that were considered for short-term performance improvement, showing how you prioritized these alternatives to decide which ones to take action on.

Make sure to provide specific examples of how analysis of results data was used to improve cycle time, productivity, and reduce scrap or waste. Your response for this Area to Address should also explain how you use performance results data to develop plans and strategies for future improvements. After describing the approach that you use, provide a couple of examples of key goals and strategies for achieving them that were initiated based upon analyses of quality results data.

It is also important that you explain how aggregated statistics on overall company performance are used to help gain understanding of relationships between different measures. For example, you might look at the relationship between pricing and market share, or between improved productivity and earnings. You also need to explain how performance data are used to make important business decisions. For example, how were data used to decide to expand the organization, narrow product mix, close or sell off certain units, invest in new technology, etc. Probably the best way of showing that you make data-based business decisions is to summarize some of the major business decisions made during the last few years, and indicate for each the performance data and analyses that were used to help make the decisions. This information would probably be best presented in a chart or table. Failing to provide examples like this may lead the Examiners to write a negative comment, or at least write a site visit issue about the lack of evidence that data are used to make key business decisions.

Indicators For Area 2.3a

- Evidence that a systematic process is used to aggregate various performance indices in different categories (e.g., financial, supplier, customer satisfaction, etc.)

- Approach to aggregating and comparing various performance indices is logical and understandable by employees who must analyze and act upon these data

- Evidence that a planned and systematic approach is used to analyze performance data

- Deployment of analysis approach across the organization's various departments and functions

- Clear description and evidence to suggest that customer-related data are analyzed and used to establish priorities and develop action plans to improve customer-related problems

- Clear description and evidence to suggest that customer-related data are compared to internal product/service quality data

- Evidence that performance data are analyzed and used to develop goals and strategies for improving customer satisfaction, market share, and retention of customers

- Evidence that data are analyzed and used to make key business decisions

- Breadth and scope of aggregate statistics used to evaluate overall company performance

- Evidence that data are analyzed and used to plan improvements

- Linkage between aggregate or summary performance measures or ratios and key success factors (business drivers)

AREA TO ADDRESS   [APPROACH, DEPLOYMENT]

2.3b How the company relates customer and market data, improvements in product/service quality, and improvements in operational performance to changes in financial and/or market indicators of performance. Describe how this information is used to set priorities for improvement actions.

Note:

(6)   **Examples of analysis appropriate for inclusion in 2.3b are:**

- **relationships between product/service quality and operational performance indicators and overall company financial performance trends as reflected in indicators such as operating costs, revenues, asset utilization, and values added per employee;**

- **allocation of resources among alternative improvement projects based on cost/revenue implications and improvement potential;**

- **net earnings derived from quality/operational/human resource performance improvements;**

- **comparisons among business units showing how quality and operational performance improvement affect financial performance;**

- **contributions of improvement activities to cash flow, working capital use, and shareholder value;**

- **profit impacts of customer retention;**

- **market share versus profits;**

- **trends in aggregate measures such as total factor productivity; and**

- **trends in economic and/or market indicators of value.**

What They're Looking For Here

As I have mentioned several times already, the key to success in the new Baldrige criteria is **balance.** Quality has to be balanced with financial results, process improvements and improvements in productivity need to be balanced with employee satisfaction, and so forth. To receive a high score, 1995 Baldrige applicants will need to show world-class levels of both financial and quality-related results. One way of achieving good results in all areas is to understand the relationships between individual measures on the company's scorecard. For example, how much will a 5-point improvement in customer satisfaction impact profits or repeat business? Some leading companies today have conducted the research to identify and understand these correlations. For example, IBM recently completed research that shows the correlation between their Net Satisfaction Index (NSI), which is an overall measure of customer satisfaction, and future revenue for the corporation. IBM has found that even a 1-point improvement on the overall NSI translates into several million dollars in future revenue. Satisfied customers not only stay with IBM, but they are more likely to spend more on IBM products and services in the future. By understanding the relationships between these measures, IBM can make intelligent business decisions regarding investments and are supposed to increase their NSI score.

AT&T, another Baldrige winner, has conducted similar research to define the relationships between various value-added statistics that they use as overall performance measure for their businesses. You don't need to be an IBM or AT&T to learn about these relationships, however. A small or medium-sized business may not have the time or resources to conduct formal research on these correlations. The research may be informal, based on small samples and observational data. For example, I remember reading a Baldrige application several years ago from a family grocery store that understood very well the relationships between customer satisfaction and harder measures like revenue and repeat business.

The reason that the relationships between different performance measures are so important to understand is that you can then make scientific business decisions. This removes much of the guesswork of running a business. When decisions are made with data, and those data are well understood, there are no, or at least few, surprises. For example, when McDonalds took a risk and became the first fast-food chain to ban smoking, do you think they wondered how it would impact their business? I doubt it. McDonalds does not make a move without research and data to tell them that it is the right move. McDonalds took the risk, while their competitors waited and watched to see what happened. When it turned out to be a smart move that did not hurt business, and further enhanced McDonalds' image as a clean, family-oriented place, their competitors followed suit. If you want to be a leader rather than a follower, it is imperative that you measure the right things, and understand how those measures impact each other. This is the essence of what 2.3 is all about, and why it is so important in Baldrige.

In previous years, the Baldrige criteria did not address financial data collection, analysis, or results. This has been one of the primary criticisms of the criteria as a measure of a successful organization. The critics have stated that if application of the criteria outlined by the Baldrige officials leads to a more successful company, then the Baldrige Examiners should look at financial as well as other types of data. A study conducted by the U.S. General Accounting Office in 1991 suggests that adherence to the Baldrige criteria does lead to financial success. The changes to the point values of financial/operational results are testimony to the fact that Baldrige also believes that customer satisfaction and quality can be achieved along with financial results rather than at their expense.

This area to address asks about how you translate improvements in customer satisfaction or the quality of products or services into financial measures. What the examiners want to see here is an explanation of how you measure the return on investment in your quality efforts. Let's say, for example, that you reduced the percentage of defects in your products from 2% down to .03%. The examiners will want to know how improvements in defect rates translate into financial benefits for the company. You also need to explain the relationship between key operational measures and key financial measures. A good way of presenting this data would be a matrix that lists your key financial measures along the top and the key quality and operational measures along the left side. The matrix should indicate which quality and operational measures have a strong degree of impact upon the key financial measures. An example of such a matrix chart is shown below.

KEY MEASURES	PROFITS	MARKET SHARE	SALES	ROA
Customer Satisfaction Index	M	H	H	M
Product Defects	H	M	M	H
Design Cycle Time	L	M	M	L

A chart such as this should be supplemented with an explanation of how and why key measures of quality and operational indices lead to financial measures. You need to explain, for example, how your customer satisfaction index has a high degree of impact on both market share and sales.

Following the explanation of the review and data-analysis processes, you need to provide some examples of how analysis of financial information has led to decisions or the initiation of changes that resulted in improved levels of operational results or improvements in customer satisfaction. The examples will add credibility to your process description. One of the major factors that the Baldrige Examiners look for once they have determined that you have a sound systematic approach is deployment. A good way of giving them information on deployment is through a series of examples that include various functions and levels of employees in your organization. Space limitations will prevent you from listing as many examples as you might like, but matrices and charts are a good way of presenting a number of examples in a limited amount of space. You might create a four-column chart that looks like the following.

EXAMPLES—FINANCIAL ANALYSIS AND ACTION PLANS			
FINANCIAL DATA	ANALYSIS	DECISION/ACTION	RESULTS
Loss of market share in Midwest region	11 new Wal-Mart stores open in 1994	Increased newspaper and direct mail advertising More competitive pricing Increased staffing Additional service training	1st quarter results show improvements

Indicators For Area 2.3b

- Evidence that the company has conducted research to identify correlations between customer satisfaction measures and financial performance

- Evidence of research being conducted to identify correlations between measures of product/service quality and customer satisfaction

- Evidence of research being conducted to identify correlations between measures of supplier performance, product/service, quality, and other performance measures

- Analysis of relationships between individual performance measures is used to make key business decisions

- Understanding of relationships between different performance measures has been documented for all key areas of the business

- Continued monitoring of trends and correlations is done to identify changes in correlations and possible new ones

- Validity/rigor of research done to demonstrate correlations between measures

- Deployment of correlations across all key performance measures identified in 2.1a

- How well understanding of correlations between measures have been communicated throughout the organizations

- Evidence that major business decisions are based upon anaylses of data and an understanding of how each measure relates to others

- Evidence of continous improvement of data-analysis approaches

Chapter 8

Interpreting the Criteria for
Strategic Planning (3.0)

OVERVIEW OF THE STRATEGIC PLANNING CATEGORY

Category 3.0 addresses the area of strategic business planning. It used to be called "Strategic Quality Planning," but they removed the word "quality" because it suggested that quality planning is somehow separate from overall business planning. The criteria in Category 3.0 now truly focuses on how the organization develops short- and longer-term business plans. Although it is the least important of the seven categories according to point value (55 points), your responses to this section can help or hurt your scores in other sections.

The 1996 Award Criteria Booklet defines this category as follows:

> The **Strategic Planning** Category examines how the company sets strategic directions, and how it determines key plan requirements. Also examined is how the plan requirements are translated into an effective performance management system. (p. 10)

This category is purposely vague about how a company needs to do strategic planning, because approaches may differ widely between a big corporation and a very small business. The small business is unlikely to have a formal strategic planning process and document, whereas the big corporation probably has many plan documents for its different businesses and has a much more structured approach to planning. As with any item that asks about your approach in Baldrige, what's important is that you tailor your approach to what's appropriate for your company or organization. A company with 25 employees that has a long and structured approach to planning with many levels of goals, objectives, and strategies may end up with a low score because their approach is overkill for a business their size.

This Category is divided into Examination Items:

3.1 Strategy Development (35 points)
3.2 Strategy Deployment (20 points)

Following are the descriptions of each of the two Examination Items and the Areas to Address that fall under them. As before, each section here begins with a double-ruled box containing the Examination Item, the point value, and any applicable Notes.* Areas to

---

* Item Notes that apply to a specific Area to Address are appropriately listed in the box containing that Area.

Address falling under that Item follow in a single-ruled box. In the upper right corner of each Area to Address box is an indication [brackets] of whether the Area pertains to approach, deployment, or results. All definitions and information appearing within these boxes are taken directly from the Baldrige criteria. Following each Area to Address is an explanation defining what the Examiners are looking for in assessing your application. Next, I have supplied a list of indicators or evaluation factors that will assist you in interpreting the criteria and in preparing your application.

3.1 STRATEGY DEVELOPMENT

Describe the company's strategic planning process for overall performance and competitive leadership for the short term and the longer term. Describe also how this process leads to the development of a basis (key business drivers) for deploying plan requirements throughout the company. (35 points)

Notes:

(1)   Item 3.1 addresses overall company strategy and business plans, not specific product and service designs.

(2)   Strategy and planning refer to a future-oriented basis for major business decisions, resource allocations, and companywide management. Strategy and planning, then, address both revenue growth thrusts as well as thrusts related to improving company performance. The sub-parts of 3.1a are intended to serve as an outline of key factors involved in developing a view of the future as a context for strategic planning.

AREA TO ADDRESS   **[APPROACH, DEPLOYMENT]**
3.1a How the company develops strategies and business plans to strengthen its customer-related, operational, and financial performance and its competitive position. Describe how strategy development considers: (1) customer requirements and expectations and their expected changes; (2) the competitive environment; (3) risks; financial, market, technological, and societal; (4) company capabilities—human resource, technology, research and development and business processes—to seek new market leadership opportunities and/or to prepare for key new requirements; and (5) supplier and/or partner capabilities.

Notes:

   (3)   **Customer requirements and their expected changes [3.1a(1)] might include pricing factors. That is, competitive success might depend upon achieving cost levels dictated by anticipated market prices rather than setting prices to cover costs.**

   (4)   **The purposes of projecting the competitive environment [3.1a(2)] are to detect and reduce competitive threats, to shorten reaction time, and to identify opportunities. If the company uses modeling, scenario, or other techniques to project the competitive environment, such techniques should be briefly outlined in 3.1a(2).**

What They're Looking For Here

This section is about the types of data that are collected and used to determine future direction and develop specific business plans. This phase in the planning process is often referred to as "situation analysis." This area to address also asks how various sources of data are translated into long- and short-term goals and strategies.

The first and most important question asked in this area to address is: how does your organization do its planning? The best way to answer this through the use of a graphic or process flow diagram that depicts the major phases or steps in the planning process. It is important that you show that you have a systematic approach, but also that your planning process is efficient. Many large corporations have systematic approaches to strategic and annual operating plan development. However, most of these same companies spend far too much time and money developing and rewriting plans, and far too little time using them for managing. Plans go through seven or eight drafts until they are finally approved by senior management and then they are put away in file drawers until it becomes time to begin writing next year's plans. I heard a story about the new CEO of Kodak who was horrified when he first took over the company, and found out that it took about 24 weeks each year to write the company's annual business plans. He set a goal that the plans had to be written and approved in 12 weeks the next year, and 4 weeks the following year. Four weeks is a reasonable amount of time to spend writing an annual business plan.

In your application, you need to get across the idea that your planning process is very thorough but also very efficient. I worked with a small shipping company in Long Beach, California, that won the California version of the Baldrige Award this year. A couple of years ago they did not do strategic planning, even though they were an amazingly successful company. They had figured out a good market niche for themselves and did an outstanding job on all measures of performance, including both profits and customer satisfaction. They simply had never bothered writing a formal strategic plan. Even a small company like this needs to do some planning, which they did. However, you can bet they don't spend six months writing the plan, and they actually use it to manage with.

Once you have defined your overall planning process, you need to go into some detail on the specific types of data that are collected in the situation analysis phase of the planning process, and talk about how these data are used to set goals and develop strategies.

The first point in this area to address [3.1a(1)] asks about how information on current and projected customer requirements is used in the planning process. This is directly linked to sections 7.1a and b, which ask about customer requirements now and in the future. The information you present in section 7.1 should define exactly what the most important requirements are for the different types of customers you serve. 7.1b asks you to project who your customers might be in the future, and what you expect their requirements to be. Do not repeat this customer requirements information in this section. Rather, refer back to 7.1, and explain how customer requirements data are used to develop goals and improvement strategies. After briefly describing this in a couple of sentences, provide a couple of examples of how customer needs or requirements were used to initiate goals or strategies in your current plans. For example, you might talk about the fact that future customers are projected to want more ability to order small lots of product that are more customized to their specifications. This information has helped you to develop goals and strategies regarding small lot-size orders, and more flexibility in tailoring products to customer needs.

The next point in this area to address [3.1a(2)] asks about how data on your competitors today and in the future are used in the planning process. If you recall, section 2.2 asks about data that you collect on your current and future competitors. Explain how information on competitor products/services and strategies is used to initiate goals and plans in your own organization. Again, examples will help lend credibility to your response. It is important that you illustrate a proactive approach rather than being a "me too" company that waits for competitors to come up with something new and then copies them. A recent example is United Airlines' Shuttle, which offers flights from cities in California and other locations. The United Shuttle, which was designed by a cross-functional team, spent a lot of time studying Southwest Airlines, the major competitor on the routes they were to serve. Rather than just copying Southwest's strategy, United tried to improve on their approach to take away some of their market share. United offers fares as low or even lower than Southwest's, but also offers what they hope customers will perceive as better service. For example, United has assigned seats; Southwest does not.

3.1a(3) asks about how risks are identified and considered in the development of goals and plans. The types of risks asked about are financial, market, technological, and societal. As with the other sections, explain how data on risks are gathered and used in the development of strategies, and provide an example or two. Many companies don't do a realistic job of assessing their own capabilities when developing improvement strategies. We've all seen companies that are in one business that decide to diversify by buying another company that is in a totally different business. Business is business right? Many of these companies fail with their new acquisitions because they don't know enough about the type of business they bought. Northrop was smart with their recent acquisition of Grumman, because the two companies are very similar. Both have similar technologies, products, people, and customers. This has helped make the transition go very smoothly, and the merging of the two company cultures very easy in comparison to what some companies have gone through. Analyzing supplier capabilities is also important in developing plans if you are heavily reliant on suppliers for your own performance. Just mentioning that you use supplier data in the planning process won't get you much credit. An example or two of how you gather and use supplier data to develop goal or strategies will help add credibility to your response.

One Baldrige applicant that received a very high score for this area presented a table that listed the various types of information used in the planning process, according to the five categories of data addressed in this area. A sample follows.

DATA USED IN PLANNING PROCESS				
Customer Requirements	Competitor Data	Risks	Company Capabilities	Supplier Data
• Focus group data	• Mascor Data	• Financial	• Telecommunication	• Northern Telecom
• Telephone survey	• Andress, Inc.	• Market	• Order processing	• NCR
• Mail survey	• J. Crew	• Societal	• Buying office	• Various

Indicators For Area 3.1a

- Evidence that the planning process is systematic and appropriate for the organization's size and complexity

- Evidence that the planning process is efficient

- Degree to which quality and customer satisfaction goals, strategies, and issues are addressed in the long-term strategic business plan for the company/organization

- Degree to which quality and customer satisfaction goals, strategies, and issues are addressed in the annual business plan for the company/organization

- Degree to which short- and long-term quality and customer satisfaction goals are consistent with goals in other areas such as growth, profits, and markets/products

- Planning and goal-setting processes are systematic, well organized, and include all functions in the organization

- Evidence that customer requirements are thoroughly identified and that this information is used in developing goals and plans for the organization

- Quality and customer satisfaction goals are based upon current and future quality requirements of customers in key markets, as well as projections of changes in customer requirements

- Quality, customer satisfaction, and other performance improvement goals are set based upon performance of major competitors in target markets

- Planning is done in a hierarchical fashion and at all levels in the organization, starting from the top

- Feedback or "catchball" sessions are used to review and improve goals and plans.

- Availability of data on the capabilities of all important processes and technologies in the organization

- Evidence that process and technology capabilities/limitations are taken into consideration when developing long- and short-term plans and goals

- Extent to which supplier data are used as an input to the planning process

- Degree to which the future competitive environment is addressed in the plan

- Evidence that financial, market, and societal risks are considered in the development of goals and strategies

- Evidence of systemic risk analysis being done as part of the planning process

---

AREA TO ADDRESS   **[APPROACH, DEPLOYMENT]**

3.1b How strategies and plans are translated into actionable key business drivers.

Notes:

(5)   **Key business drivers are the areas of performance most critical to the company's success. (See Glossary, page 4.) The purpose of the key business drivers is to ensure that strategic planning leads to a pragmatic basis for deployment, communications, and assessment of progress. Actual key business drivers should not be described in 3.1b. Such information is requested in Item 3.2, which focuses on deployment.**

What They're Looking For Here

Many organizations do a commendable job creating strategic business plans, but few do a good job translating those plans into actions throughout the year. The plans get written, reviewed, and often end up in a file drawer until the end of the year or until a periodic review meeting occurs. This section of the application should describe the mechanisms and systems you have in place to ensure that plans do not remain in file drawers but are actually implemented. Explain how plans are reviewed by various levels of employees and translated into individual performance plans. All levels of goals and objectives should be based upon and contribute to the overall plans of the organization.

Your response should explain how plans drive regular and ongoing work activities. Explain how major projects as well as recurring work tasks relate to major business and quality goals. Be as specific as possible, citing an example or two to illustrate that plans really do drive day-to-day activities in your company.

There should be regular review meetings that occur among various levels of employees to review plans, discuss progress toward meeting the goals outlined in the plans, and change/update the plans as necessary. Describe when these meetings occur and who attends. Explain how plans have been revised based upon changing business conditions, changing customer requirements, or other factors. Also, explain what you do when performance is not reaching projected goal levels. Be specific. The Examiners are looking for a positive approach rather than a punitive approach. One applicant who received a low score said, "Individuals who are not meeting their goals are talked to and reminded of the consequences to them of not meeting their goals." The mechanism for implementing strategies outlined in organizational plans may consist of projects, priority initiatives, task forces, teams, or other approaches. The specific approach you use is not important. What is important is that you have a clear and workable approach for translating your plans into actions and results. The leadership of the senior executives is critical to the success of implementing the plans.

This section of your application should also describe how requests for capital expenditures are evaluated and the extent to which improvement of quality is part of the criteria used to assess capital funds requests. Evidence should be provided to show that a large portion of the capital projects being undertaken in the organization will at least contribute to, if not directly improve, quality and customer satisfaction.

Indicators For Area 3.1b

- Existence of a well defined and workable process for deployment of long- and short-term plans in the organization to achieve quality and customer-satisfaction leadership

- Scope of deployment includes all functions and levels of employees in the development of individual improvement plans that support overall plans for the company

- Amount and objectivity of data to suggest that the plan implementation/ deployment process is successful in the organization

- Clear criteria for evaluating capital projects in relation to goals in long- and short-term plans

- Manner of assigning and deploying resources is consistent with long- and short-term goals and quality priorities

- Evidence that plans are used to direct and control day-to-day work activity in the organization, with management involvement to ensure implementation and follow-up

- Plans are used to make decisions and control actions and priorities in the organization

- Process for deploying quality requirements to suppliers is systematic and timely

---

AREA TO ADDRESS   **[APPROACH, DEPLOYMENT]**

3.1c How the company evaluates and improves its strategic planning and plan deployment processes.

Notes:

(6)   **How the company evaluates and improves its strategic planning and plan deployment process might take into account the results of reviews (1.2b), input from work units, and projection information (3.2b). The evaluation might also take into account how well strategies and requirements are communicated and understood, and how well key measures throughout the company are aligned.**

What They're Looking For Here

It's rare to find an organization that does any type of evaluation of its planning process, but that is exactly what the Baldrige Examiners are looking for in this Area to Address. If you do any kind of evaluation of your planning process, describe the sources of data you examine to determine how well the process is working. Evidence that you have adjusted your planning process based upon the evaluation data is also desirable. Like all other processes used in the organization, planning should show a cycle of continuous improvements. You need to evaluate not only the planning process itself, but how you deploy the plans to various work units in the organization. A major factor in the success or failure of planning is the extent to which plans guide day-to-day activity. Evaluation of this phenomenon should be part of your assessment. Reviewing performance against plans is *not* what is being asked for here. The criteria ask about how you proactively evaluate and improve your strategic and annual planning processes. Make sure you also list the specific improvements you have made over the last few years.

Indicators For Area 3.1c

- Evidence that a systematic evaluation process is used to assess the organization's approach to planning

- Extent to which deployment of plans throughout the organization is part of evaluation

- Objectivity and thoroughness of the process used to evaluate planning

- Changes made in the planning process as a result of the evaluation data

- Evidence of continuous improvement in the planning process over the last few years

- Scope of changes made to the planning process

- Changes made in the communication and deployment of plans throughout the organization

- Degree to which all levels of employees are involved in the evaluation of the planning process

- Reduction in cycle time in the planning process.

3.2 STRATEGY DEPLOYMENT

Summarize the company's key business drivers and how they are deployed. Show how the company's performance projects into the future relative to competitors and key benchmarks. (20 points)

Note:

(1)   The focus in Item 3.2 is on the translation of the company's strategic plans, resulting from the process described in Item 3.1, to requirements for work units, suppliers, and partners. The main intent of Item 3.2 is alignment of short- and long-term operations with strategic directions. Although the deployment of these plans will affect products and services, design of products and services is not the focus of Item 3.2. Such design is addressed in Item 5.1.

AREA TO ADDRESS [APPROACH, DEPLOYMENT]

3.2a Summary of the specific key business drivers derived from the company's strategic directions and how these drivers are translated into an action plan. Describe: (1) key performance requirements and associated operational performance measures and/or indicators and how they are deployed; (2) how the company aligns work unit and supplier and/or partner plans and targets; (3) how productivity and cycle time improvement and reduction in waste are included in plans and targets; and (4) the principal resources committed to the accomplishment of plans. Note any important distinctions between short-term plans and longer-term plans.

Note:

(2)   **Productivity and cycle time improvement and waste reduction [3.2a(3)] might address factors such as inventories, work-in-process, inspection, downtime, changeover time, set-up time, and other examples of utilization of resources—materials, equipment, energy, capital, and labor.**

What They're Looking For Here

This section of your application is designed to provide you with an opportunity to explain in narrative fashion what your vision is for the company and its products or services over the next few years. You might start out with an explanation of what is likely to happen to your industry over the next three to five years. For example:

> *The employee relocation business is expected to continue the shrinking trend we have observed during the past few years. Large corporations will be transferring fewer employees during the coming years because of escalating relocation costs and an increase in the number of individuals who refuse to accept frequent moves as simply a way of life in a large corporation. This means that there will be less business for all of us in the relocation business.*

You should explain not only what will happen to your industry in the future, but how customer needs are likely to change and how this will impact your products and services.

It appears that the reemergence of videodisc technology will have a major impact on the buying habits of consumers in the video market. Once thought to be a dead technology, discs and disc players will be the medium of choice for many consumers who are ready to replace old videotape units.

Once you have explained what is likely to happen in your industry, and how customer requirements may change the market, you should explain what will be needed for a company in your industry to remain a leader in the future. It may be a matter of producing the best quality product, of being the first to introduce new products, or of having products that are sold at a more competitive price than the competition. If you are planning to introduce new products and/or services in the coming years, describe them, and explain how they will impact the market. Next, you should describe the requirements that your organization will need to meet in order to maintain its leadership position in the marketplace. Explain how you will need to change and what the key elements are likely to be to ensure your future success.

After describing your prediction of what is happening in your industry, and what is likely to happen in the future, you need to list your key business drivers. What are key business drivers? These are factors that you need to focus on that will determine whether or not you are successful in the future. For example, one key business driver for Northrop Grumman over the next few years is to reduce their costs to customers. Customers like the U.S. Air Force have told Northrop Grumman that their quality is exceptional; their products just cost too much. Hence, Northrop Grumman is expending a lot of effort on process improvements that will enable them to lower their cost to customers, while still maintaining profitability. One of IBM's key business drivers is to reduce reliance on hardware sales, and increase income from services. A key business driver for many of the telephone companies today is to offer competitive rates on local telephone service, while maintaining existing quality levels. Many of the baby Bells now, or soon will, have competition for local phone service. Key business factors are performance areas that must be targeted to ensure your current success, given projected changes in your industry and market.

A good way of presenting the information on key business drivers and how these translate into specific plans is to create a chart that shows the relationship between key business drivers, measures of performance (from section 2.1), annual goals, longer-term goals, and improvement strategies. Presenting the information this way shows the relationship between sections 2.0 and 3.0. An example of this type of chart follows.

BUSINESS DRIVERS	MEASURES	1995 GOALS	1998 GOALS	STRATEGIES
Expand sales in Pacific Rim	$ International Sales	$2 million	$6 million	• Marketing campaign • Hire new salespeople • Special incentives
Increase new product development	% of sales of new products	12%	22%	• Increase R&D $ • Increase R&D staff • Reduce development cycle time
Reduce turnover of technical staff	Employee satisfaction index	85	95	• Increase training opportunities
	Turnover	20%	8%	• Recognition programs • Pay for performance • Technical ladder

A chart like this provides specifics on how your measures and plans are all linked to key business requirements.

This area to address also asks how plans are deployed [3.2a(1)]. In other words, how do you take the overall goals for the company and cascade them down to different units, functions, and areas of the organization? Again, a graphic might help show this cascading process. The key is to illustrate that plans at all levels are linked, so that every employee is working toward the common goals of the entire organization.

3.2a(2) asks about how plans and goals are communicated to suppliers, so they can help you achieve your own goals. Often this is an area where disconnects are found. Not only should you explain how goals are linked to the formation of supplier requirements, but you might want to provide a few examples.

It is also important that you explain how process reengineering or process improvement efforts are linked to the overall goals in the business plan. One way that former Baldrige winner AT&T Transmission Systems does this is by identifying what they call: "The 10 Most Wanted." These are the 10 process improvement efforts that are underway in the company at any one time. Each of the 10 most wanted is linked to strategic business goals, and only 10 projects are going at any one time, to help ensure that process improvement efforts are not too disjointed. Companies that tell every employee to go off and improve their processes frequently find that this leads to chaos, and the improvements in one area cause problems in others. Process improvement efforts need to be prioritized and channeled. Linking them to the strategic business plan is the way to do this. A good way of responding to this portion of the criteria is to list your major process/productivity improvement efforts and indicate how each is linked to measures and goals in your business plan.

The last section of this long area to address asks about how you allocate resources to the goals and strategies identified in the strategic and annual business plans. Often the budgeting and planning processes are completely separate. To receive high marks for this portion of 3.2a, you need to demonstrate that budgeting and capital equipment expenditures are closely linked to the strategic and annual business plans. A graphic that shows how and where the budgeting and planning processes are linked might be a good idea if there is room. Supplement this with a couple of examples that show how funds were allocated to past strategies and goals that were part of your plan.

Indicators For Area 3.2a

- Consistency between business drivers identified here and information on analysis of current and future customers' needs (7.1), leadership vision and direction of the company (1.1), and analysis of the competitive environment (3.1 and 2.2)

- Annual goals have been developed for each major performance measure from section 2.1, and performance measures are linked back to key business drivers

- Longer-term goals are developed for each major performance measure from section 2.1, and performance measures are linked back to key business drivers

- Goals are measurable and are not confused with projects or activities—goals must be linked to result measures

- Goals will cause the company to stretch to achieve them, and help propel them to world-class levels of performance

- Goals are based on research of what is possible (i.e., through benchmarking and other means), rather than just being arbitrarily picked out of the air

- Goals and strategies are cascaded down throughout all units and levels of the company

- Breadth of annual and longer-term goals cover all products/services, and all units in the company's organization

- The extent to which the budgeting and planning processes are closely linked

- Specific strategies are developed that articulate how goals will be achieved

- Evidence that the capital expenditure budget is well linked with the annual and longer-term business plans

- Evidence that employees at all levels are aware of the overall company goals, and how their own goals help contribute to the overall company's

- Strategies to achieve goals are defined in enough detail for the Examiner to evaluate them

- Goals and plans are communicated to suppliers and linked to supplier requirements

- Productivity, cycle time, and other process improvement efforts are all linked to the goals and strategies outlined in the strategic plan

- Resources committed to achieve goals appear to be reasonable and well thought out

- Employees generally believe that goals are challenging but achievable

---

AREA TO ADDRESS   **[APPROACH/DEPLOYMENT]**

3.2b Two-to-five year projections of key measures and/or indicators of the company's customer-related and operational performance. Describe how product and/or service quality and operational performance might be expected to compare with key competitors and key benchmarks over this period of time. Briefly explain the comparisons, including any estimates or assumptions made regarding the projected product and/or service quality and operational performance of competitors or changes in key benchmarks.

Notes:

(3) **Area 3.2b addresses projected progress in improving performance and in gaining advantage relative to competitors. This projection may draw upon analyses (Item 2.3) and data reported in results Items (Category 6.0 and Items 7.4 and 7.5). Such projections are intended to support reviews (1.2c), evaluation of planning (3.1c) and other items. Another purpose is to take account of the fact that competitors and benchmarks may also be improving over the time period of the projection.**

(4) **Projections of customer-related and operational performance (3.2b) might be expressed in terms of costs, revenues, measures of productivity, and economic indicators. Projections might also include innovation rates or other factors important to the company's competitive position.**

What They're Looking For Here

This section should read like an annual report to shareholders. Your task is to convince the Examiners that you know exactly where your business will be in the future, relative to your competitors. Avoid the term "world class" in your response. This is an overused, meaningless phrase that I often see in this section. It adds no value. "We're projecting that we will become the world-class supplier of . . ." does not say anything. Examiners are looking for specifics. Some examples of statements that are specific enough are as follows:

- By 1998, we will have at least 300 of the Fortune 500 companies as our clients

- We will become the #1 supplier (in market share) of any company in our industry by the end of this century

I saw a credit card company that has a projection to put American Express out of business by the end of the century. These statements are specific. It is in this section that you are allowed to talk about what you want to do. In every other Baldrige category, you are only given credit for what you have already done. The key is to be realistic and specific. Do not get too specific either. The criteria do not ask for measurable goals. Rather, explain where you think your company will be in the market, and how you will be performing on key measures. Talk about major factors such as the quality of your products and services, customer satisfaction, financial results, and operational measures.

You also need to explain where you think you will be relative to your major competitors. Keep in mind what the note to this area to address says. Your competition is getting better also, and they will be trying to take business away from you. Acknowledge the fact that competitors will not be standing still, and project what will happen to them as well. Will they be bigger, smaller, more profitable, etc.

Along with projections of how your performance will compare to direct competitors, you need to explain how your organization will compare to benchmark companies that may not be in your same industry. Again, avoid empty statement like: "By the end of the century, companies will be benchmarking us, rather than us going to them." If you are projecting benchmark-level performance for your company, on what measures and on what processes or products? If you can get specific about areas where you are expecting to show benchmark-level performance, Examiners will be less likely to find fault with your response. Referring to the results sections of the application (6.0, 7.4, and 7.5) may also be appropriate to show the progress you have already made in achieving your longer-term projections.

Indicators For Area 3.2b

- Breadth and scope of projections cover major business areas and products/services

- Projections are specific and show that a thorough analysis has been done

- Projections are consistent with long-term goals and strategies outlined in response to 3.2a

- Level of specificity of projections

- Comparisons are projected between applicant and major competitors

- Information is presented on how competitors are expected to improve and change over the next two to five years

- Comparisons of projections of how performance levels will compare to benchmark companies that go beyond those in the company's industry

- Validity of sources of information used to make projections regarding company's position relative to competition in the future

- How realistic projections are

Chapter 9

Interpreting the Criteria for Human Resource Development and Management (4.0)

OVERVIEW OF THE HUMAN RESOURCE DEVELOPMENT AND MANAGEMENT CATEGORY

The fourth category of the Baldrige criteria is Human Resource Development and Management. It is worth 14 percent of the evaluation, or 140 possible points. According to the Baldrige Award Criteria, the human resource development and management category is defined as follows:

> The **Human Resource Development and Management** Category examines how the work force is enabled to develop and utilize its full potential, aligned with the company's performance objectives. Also examined are the company's efforts to build and maintain an environment conducive to performance excellence, full participation, and personal and organizational growth.

As it is explained here, the Baldrige Examiners are not really concerned that you use a particular set of approaches or processes, but only that your human resource strategies are appropriate for your organization. Many applicants end with a low score in this category because their approach is not systematic. Results of HR systems and approaches are no longer asked for in Category 4.0. Any pertinent HR data should be presented in section 6.3. As with all of the categories, examiners are concerned here with your approach, its deployment, and the results you can demonstrate. A description follows of all four Examination Items and the Areas to Address that fall under them. Each section begins with a double-ruled box containing the Examination Item, the point value, and any applicable Notes.* Areas to Address falling under that Item follow in a single-ruled box. In the upper right corner of each Area to Address box is an indication [brackets] of whether the Area pertains to approach, deployment, or results. All definitions and information appearing within these boxes is taken directly from the Baldrige criteria. Following each Area to Address is an explanation defining what the examiners are looking for in assessing your application. Next, I have supplied a list of indicators or evaluation factors that will assist you in interpreting the criteria and in preparing your application.

---

* Item Notes that apply to a specific Area to Address are appropriately listed in the box containing that Area.

4.1 HUMAN RESOURCE PLANNING AND EVALUATION

Describe how the company's human resource planning and evaluation are aligned with its strategic and business plans and address the development and well-being of the entire workforce. (20 points)

AREA TO ADDRESS   [APPROACH, DEPLOYMENT]

4.1a How the company translates overall requirements from strategic and business planning (Category 3.0) to specific human resource plans. Summarize key human resource plans in the following areas: (1) changes in work design to improve flexibility, innovation, and rapid response; (2) employee development, education, and training; (3) changes in compensation, recognition, and benefits; and (4) recruitment, including critical skill categories and expected or planned changes in demographics of the workforce. Distinguish between the short term and the longer term, as appropriate.

Note:

(1)   Human resource planning addresses all aspects of designing and managing human systems to meet the needs of both the company and the employees. This item calls for information on human resource plans. This does not imply that such planning is separate from overall business planning. Examples of human resource plan (4.1a) elements that might be part(s) of a comprehensive plan are:

- redesign of work organizations and/or jobs to increase employee responsibility and decision making;
- initiatives to promote labor–management cooperation, such as partnerships with unions;
- creation or modification of compensation and recognition systems based on building shareholder value and/or customer satisfaction;
- creation or redesign of employee surveys to better assess the factors in the work climate that contribute to or inhibit high performance;
- prioritization of employee problems based upon potential impact on productivity;
- development of hiring criteria and/or standards;

- **creation of opportunities for employees to learn and use skills that go beyond current job assignments through redesign of processes or organizations;**
- **education and training initiatives, including those that involve developmental assignments;**
- **formation of partnerships with educational institutions to develop employees or to help ensure the future supply of well-prepared employees;**
- **establishment of partnerships with other companies and/or networks to share training and/or spread job opportunities;**
- **introduction of distance learning or other technology-based learning approaches; and**
- **integration of customer and employee surveys.**

What They're Looking For Here

The 1996 Award Criteria booklet explains that Item 4.1 serves as the point of direct linkage between human resource planning and the company's strategic directions. The reason this Area to Address is so important is that it asks for information on all of your goals and plans that impact the employees in your organization. All aspects of the human resource function are included in this criterion.

The first point you need to make in your response for this Area to Address is how your human resource plans are derived from your business plans. The examiners want to see that your human resource goals are driven by the goals in your overall business plans. In some organizations the HR plan is developed by individuals who have no knowledge of the company's overall business goals. In order to receive a good score for this area, you need to demonstrate that there is a clear and logical relationship between your business plans and your HR plans. For example, if one of your business goals is to increase your market share in the telecommunications industry with more new products, this fact might lead to an HR goal that calls for increasing the levels of knowledge and skills among employees who design, manufacture, and market telecommunications-based products. You might also have a goal for recruiting more telecommunications experts into the company over the next few years. Examples will help the Baldrige Examiners see the relationship between human resources and overall business planning. Simply making a statement that "Our human resource planning is based upon our goals for quality and operational performance outlined in our business plan" is obviously vague and will not elicit favorable comments from the Examiners. In order to make your response more credible, you need to use illustrations and examples that are specific. Generalizing your response does not enable the Examiner to get a true picture of how well you really meet the criterion.

Up to this point, we have been discussing ways to explain how your HR planning process is integrated with your overall business planning process. Now, you need to present information in your response on the specific types of HR goals and plans asked for in the criteria. This Area to Address asks about four different types of HR goals and plans:

- Employee development (including education, training, and empowerment)
- Mobility, flexibility, and work scheduling
- Rewards, recognition, compensation, and benefits
- Recruitment and selection

It is important to understand that HR goals are not projects or activities like: "Implement 360° appraisal process in all business by the end of the 3rd quarter." HR goals should be set for specific HR measures such as employee satisfaction ratings, safety, training hours per employee, etc.

For each of these four areas of human resources, you should list both your long-term and short-term plans or goals. If you use a chart, all of this information can be easily summarized on a page or less. Along with a summary of the goals for these four HR areas, the chart might also include information on which business goals each HR goal is tied into. If you present all of this information, you will have a very strong response to 4.1a.

Indicators For Area 4.1a

- Demonstration that human resource plans and strategies are determined based upon long- and short-term quality and operational performance goals of the organization

- Amount and credibility of evidence presented to suggest that business and HR planning are linked/integrated

- Human resource plans are developed as part of the overall strategic business planning process, rather than as a separate planning activity

- There are no arbitrary HR goals such as "Reduce head count by 10%," or "Every employee will receive 80 hours of training"

- Specific goals and plans exist for educating, training, and empowering employees

- Specific goals and plans exist for improving mobility, flexibility, and workforce organization

- Specific goals and plans exist for improving reward, recognition, compensation, and benefits

- Specific goals and plans exist for improving recruiting and selection

- Goals and objectives are measurable and specific

- Both long- and short-term plans are presented for all of the four major HR areas asked about in the criterion

- Clear relationship between long- and short-term plans for each of the four major HR areas asked about in the criterion

AREA TO ADDRESS [APPROACH, DEPLOYMENT]

4.1b How the company evaluates and improves its human resource planning and practices and the alignment of the plans and practices with the company's strategic and business directions. Include how employee-related data and company performance data (Item 6.2) are analyzed and used: (1) to assess the development and well-being of all categories and types of employees; (2) to assess the linkage of the human resource practices to key business results; and (3) to ensure that reliable and complete human resource information is available for company planning and recruitment.

Notes:

(2) **"Employee-related data" (4.1b) refers to data contained in personnel records as well as data described in Items 4.2, 4.3, 4.4, and 6.3. This might include employee satisfaction data and data on turnover, absenteeism, safety, grievances, involvement, recognition, training, and information from exit interviews.**

(3) **"Categories of employees" [4.1b(1)] refers to the company's classification system used in its human resource practices and/or work assignments. It also includes factors such as union or bargaining unit membership. "Types of employees" takes into account other factors, such as work force diversity or demographic makeup. This includes gender, age, minorities, and the disabled.**

(4) **Human resource information for company planning and recruitment [4.1b(3)] might include an overall profile of strengths and weaknesses that could affect the company's capabilities to fulfill plan requirements.**

What They're Looking For Here

A typical response to this area is to explain: "Employee-related data are collected and evaluated to look for ways to continually improve human resource strategies and plans."

What examiners want to see here, however, is specific information on how you *use* employee-related data. Examples will go a long way in convincing the Baldrige Examiners that you really do utilize your employee data to fine-tune your human resources strategies. You might explain, for example, how employee performance-appraisal scores are used to evaluate the quality of the company's selection systems and the quality of training and supervision. Show how selection systems have been improved and how that improvement has led to improvements in other dimensions such as reduced turnover and improved performance appraisal ratings.

As in many of the Baldrige criteria, the examiners are looking for an approach that is based upon the following sequence of activities:

1. Collection of objective data
2. Analysis of data
3. Feedback to employees who can improve performance on these indices
4. Change or improvement in practices to improve the indices being measured
5. Data-based evaluation and modification (if necessary) of improvement strategies

Your score in this area will depend upon the extent to which you have a systematic approach such as the one above, and can provide evidence that such an approach is really followed.

This area to address asks for information on how HR data are used with performance data to evaluate the effectiveness of human resource systems and initiatives. For example, you might talk about the impact of a new incentive compensation system on employee productivity and satisfaction levels. Or, you could discuss how analysis of data on turnover of technical professionals has led you to develop new recruiting/selection criteria. This section does not ask for any results. It asks for evidence that you collect and use employee-related data to make business decisions. It is very similar to Item 2.3 that asks for evidence that all types of performance data are analyzed and used to make business decisions. This section asks specifically about HR or employee-related data.

The Examiners are looking for information on the effectiveness of your efforts to improve employee satisfaction and other human resource measures. For example, let's say that you redesigned your offices and put in new furniture and fixtures, using ergonomic experts to help you design a pleasing and productive environment for employees. You would describe that effort here, along with how the effort has impacted key measures of employee satisfaction. Does this mean that the Examiners want to see data? No. This is an approach/deployment item only. What they want to know about is your approach to improving employee satisfaction, and how fully deployed this approach has been to all categories and levels of employees.

This area to address also asks about how you have improved your human resource planning process to better align it with business strategies and plans. Mention specific examples of how the HR planning process has been streamlined or otherwise improved over the last few years. Describe how the HR planning process is different or better in 1995 as compared to previous years.

Indicators For Area 4.1b

- Amount of employee-related data collected by the organization

- Extent to which indices currently being measured are good indicators of the success of the organization in the area of human resource management

- Length of time data have been collected for employee-related indices

- Objectivity of employee-related data

- Degree to which employee-related data are reported in a systematic and easy-to-understand fashion

- Evidence that employee-related data are periodically analyzed to identify causes of problems or deviations from standards

- Evidence that human resource plans and strategies are evaluated based upon employee-related data

- Regular reports of employee-related data are created and distributed to appropriate personnel

- Evidence that feedback on employee-related data is used to evaluate and improve human resource strategies, plans, and practices

- Extent to which evaluation includes data from all levels and types of employees

- Analyses are done to show linkages between HR results or measures and overall performance measures

- Evidence that HR data are considered in the development of annual and longer-term business plans

- Evidence that employee satisfaction factors are used to reduce adverse indicators of employee morale

- Changes that have been made to improve the HR planning process to make it simpler and better aligned with business strategies

4.2 HIGH PERFORMANCE WORK SYSTEMS

Describe how the company's work and job design and compensation and recognition approaches enable and encourage all employees to contribute effectively to achieving high performance objectives. (45 points)

AREA TO ADDRESS   **[APPROACH/DEPLOYMENT]**
4.2a How the company's work and job design promote high performance. Describe how work and job design: (1) create opportunities for initiatives and self-directed responsibility; (2) foster flexibility and rapid response to changing requirements; and (3) ensure effective communications across functions or units that need to work together to meet customer and/or operational requirements.

Notes:
  (1)   Work design refers to how employees are organized and/or organize themselves in formal and informal, temporary or longer-term units. This includes work teams, problem-solving teams, functional units, departments, self-managed or managed by supervisors. In some cases, teams might involve individuals in different locations linked via computers or conferencing technology.
  Job design refers to responsibilities and tasks assigned to individuals. These responsibilities and tasks help define education and training requirements.
  (2)   Examples of approaches to create flexibility [4.2a(2)] in work design might include simplification of job classifications, cross training, job rotation, work layout, and work locations. It might also entail use of technology and changed flow of information to support local decision making.

<u>What They're Looking For Here</u>

This was a brand new Examination Item for 1995, and it calls for very different information than was asked for in 4.2 in previous versions of the Baldrige criteria. Actually, this new 4.2 is a combination of what used to be 4.2 (employee involvement) and 4.4 (employee performance and recognition) from the 1994 Baldrige criteria. The scope of this item is much broader and ask for different information. You used to get credit by having employees work in teams to solve problems, and for installing suggestion boxes to encourage employees to submit ideas for improving the company. Not any more. The Baldrige criteria are now asking for evidence that you go way beyond teams and suggestion boxes and make fundamental changes in the way jobs are designed and work is accomplished.

Business Week and other national magazines have presented feature or cover stories recently on the changing nature of jobs and work. In case you haven't noticed, the traditional job, office, and organization structure are disappearing. IBM eliminated several floors of offices in its 590 Madison Avenue building in New York City by eliminating offices for salespeople and others. IBMers are given laptop computers, cellular phones, and told to spend work time at customer locations, or at home. If they need an office, they can rent one for the day in IBM's facilities, plug in a phone and computer, and go to work. When employees complained that they missed the personal touches of their own office, IBM scanned pictures of their husbands, wives, kids, and even dogs into their laptop computers to take with them wherever they go. Desert Hospital in Palm Springs, California, has practically eliminated separate departments such as radiology. Employees work on cross-functional teams to provide a variety of different services to patients. Examples like these can be found all over America in all different industries. These are exactly the types of things that will earn you a good score in the new 4.2.

The first part of your answer to this area to address should explain how you have designed jobs and work flow. This explanation should refer back to and build upon the explanation of your organization structure that appeared in section 1.2. Begin by explaining your approach to job and work design. Expand upon this explanation with examples of how jobs and work have changed over the years. This information will help Examiners assess the degree of deployment. Keep in mind that if you have an innovative approach to design of jobs for your salespeople, but salespeople only make up 7 percent of your workforce, you may still end up with a fairly low score because of a lack of deployment.

It is important that you explain how job designs make it easier for employees to contribute to improving the organization. Empowerment is not specifically asked for in the criteria this year, but it is still hidden in there. It is referred to as "self-directed responsibility." Self-directed work teams that are given authority to monitor their own performance are not a requirement, but are an approach that would likely earn you some positive comments from the Examiners. If you still form teams to work on problems or projects, this is not necessarily a negative. Problem solving teams and cross- functional teams do serve a purpose. Baldrige is asking that you go beyond simply adding some teams to traditional jobs and work methods. Although the Baldrige criteria for 1996 are much less prescriptive than they used to be, they still promote concepts like:

- Teamwork
- Empowerment
- Flexibility
- Employee involvement

You will not find the word "team" in the criteria for this item, but you will see it all through Note (1) that accompanies 4.2. Since many will read the notes as part of the requirements rather than suggestions on how you might respond to the Item, teams are still likely to be talked about in Baldrige applications.

4.2a(1) asks about how your approach to jobs and work design encourages employees to contribute ideas for improving the company, and how you have empowered employees or given them more authority than they had in the past. 4.2a(2) asks about how jobs, organization structure, and work methods promote efficiency, flexibility, and short cycle times. To get this across, you may need to talk about how different current job and work designs are different and better than old approaches. Although this section does not ask for any results, you could talk about improvements in efficiency or cycle time that have resulted from your new job/work designs. The third part of 4.2a(3) asks about how your approach to work and jobs facilitates better communication across functions or locations that need to work together. With traditional departments and jobs, employees are often more concerned with their own department's needs than the needs of their customers. Departments that should work together and talk to each other often don't. Hopefully, your approach to jobs, departments, and the assignment of tasks eliminates these barriers and makes it easy and necessary for employees to talk and work together. Organizing work around key processes is one way some companies I've seen help encourage this communication and teamwork.

In order to get a high score for this area to address, you also need to show how your approaches to job and work design have been evaluated and improved over the last few years. Explain the factors that are used to measure effectiveness, describe your evaluation methodology, and tell the Examiners what you have changed or improved over the last few years based on this analysis. If the measures that you use to evaluate job designs and organization structure are not tied back to overall performance measures, this will end up hurting your score. Having a lot of empowerment or teamwork is not how to get a good score. You need to show the link between approaches like self-directed teams and flexible job designs and business results like profits, productivity, and customer satisfaction.

Indicators For Area 4.2a

- Significance of changes to work and job design compared to traditional approaches

- Use of self-directed work teams to complete day-to-day work in the company

- Evidence that jobs are more flexible than they used to be

- Extent to which the organization structure and job designs allow employees many different opportunities to suggest and implement ideas for improving the company's practices and performance

- Innovation in creativity in job/work design

- Evidence that employees in various positions have more authority than they did in the past—empowerment

- Employee opinions on the effectiveness of new approaches to job and work design

- Deployment of new approaches to job and work design across all functions, levels, and locations in the company

- Evidence that new approaches to job and work design promote more open communication and more cooperation between department units, and locations that need to work together

- Evidence that all employees are evaluated on how well they satisfy their internal and/or external customers

- Job performance measures are consistent with overall performance measures defined in section 2.1 of the application

- Evidence of the effectiveness of new approaches to job and work design

- Employee opinions on empowerment or levels of authority that exist today versus the past

- Evidence that company management listens to employees and adopts their suggestions, or allows employees to implement their own ideas/suggestions

- Evidence that motivation for redesign of jobs and work flow goes beyond saving money and getting more work out of employees

- Identification of specific measurement indices for evaluating the effectiveness of new approaches to job and work design

- Evidence of continuous improvement in job and work design approaches

---

AREA TO ADDRESS   **[APPROACH/DEPLOYMENT]**

4.2b How the company's compensation and recognition approaches for individuals and groups, including managers, reinforce the effectiveness of the work and job design.

Notes:

(3)   **Compensation and recognition (4.2b) refer to all aspects of pay and reward, including promotion and bonuses. The company might use a variety of reward and recognition approaches—monetary and non-monetary, formal and informal, and individual and group. Compensation and recognition approaches could include profit sharing and compensation based on skill building, use of new skills, and demonstrations of self-learning. The approaches could take into account the linkage to customer retention or other performance objectives.**

Employee evaluations and reward and recognition approaches might include peer evaluations, including peers in teams and networks.

What They're Looking For Here

A high performance work system includes mechanisms for rewarding the desired behavior and results from employees. One of the big disconnects in many companies is their compensation systems don't reward anything except sticking around for another year, or they exclusively reward short-term financial results.

Many organizations claim to be committed to quality and customer satisfaction, but they compensate employees based upon seniority, level, or job function. Few of the companies that have performance-based pay plans base the pay that employees receive upon quality. Performance-based pay is most often based upon sales, profits, and other financial measures. Some past Baldrige applicants have explained that they've implemented a gainsharing plan as a way of promoting improved quality. However, gainsharing in many cases is nothing more than profit sharing.

Based upon my own experience consulting with large companies, the ideal situation is that a large percentage of all employees' compensation is based upon their individual and group performance against quality goals and standards. Many organizations have bonus programs for executives and upper management, but not for other levels of employees. Three criteria are important in assessing the compensation systems in a company. First, a portion of employees' compensation should be based upon the degree to which individual and group performance goals have been met. The second criterion is that all levels and categories of employees should participate in quality-based compensation programs. Third and last, a large enough percentage of income should be based upon quality results to make a difference in motivating employees. Allowing employees who earn an average of $30,000 to earn an annual bonus of up to $500 for exceeding their quality goals is not going to do much to motivate them.

Your task in this section is to convince the Examiners that your compensation plan drives performance excellence from teams and individual employees. Many former Baldrige winners have very traditional compensation systems. The new criteria ask for evidence of a compensation program that rewards performance that is critical to organization performance. For example, the key business drivers and performance measures and goals that you discussed in sections 2.0 and 3.0 might be the foundation of your compensation or bonus plan. In some leading edge companies, all employees earn a bonus, and that bonus is based upon achieving a balance between all of their measures on their own score cards. For example, in Federal Express, employee bonuses are based on how well you satisfy internal and/or external customers (Service), how well you satisfy your employees or teammates/peers (People), and how well you achieve or control financial results (Profit). All employees from the CEO to the package sorter are on this bonus plan, and it keeps everyone focused on their three priorities.

Another aspect of your high performance work system that is evaluated here is how you recognize employees in nonfinancial ways. Everyone likes money, but motivating employees and influencing their behavior through compensation alone is very limiting. Nonfinancial recognition is probably more important and more powerful if it is done right. Some of the important factors that will be assessed regarding your approach to recognition are:

- How much of it do you do?

- How well have you analyzed the needs and preferences of employees in designing recognition programs?

- How much creativity has been put into recognition programs to make them interesting and fun for employees?

- To what extent are the behaviors and accomplishments that are recognized consistent with organizational values, goals, and key performance measures?

Most companies and organizations pay very little attention to employee recognition, other than a few unimaginative mostly useless programs like "Employee of the Month." No imagination is put into the effort, very few employees receive any kind of recognition, and the items and privileges that are given out for recognition are often perceived by employees as insulting or at best small "thank yous." Certificates, hats, t-shirts, and coffee cups may not be too rewarding if you and your team just saved the company $15,000. Future Baldrige winners will need to put a great deal of emphasis on the approaches they use to motivate and recognize individuals and teams of employees. AT&T Universal Card Systems, a 1992 Baldrige winner, puts a great deal of emphasis on employee recognition, and has many different programs going at once. It seems like every other day they are celebrating some accomplishment. They make a big deal out of employee recognition, and spend time and money thinking of things they can do to keep employees motivated. Not everything works. What is rewarding to one person may not be to others. AT&T UCS keeps trying different approaches though, and they make recognition a priority.

The most important factor in a successful recognition program is to have senior management that believes in the importance of recognition and positive reinforcement, and is willing to make this a priority that does not get delegated down to an HR clerk who updates the employee of the month bulletin board once a month. Your approach to recognition should also be consistent with your organization structure and job design. If you have organized your organization around teams, for example, you wouldn't want all of your recognition to be based on individual performance.

Noncontingent recognition, such as periodic parties or celebrations that everyone attends regardless of their performance, may help build morale, but it is not relevant here. Talk about things you do to boost overall morale in section 4.4, not here.

Indicators For Area 4.2b

- Percentage of employees who have pay at risk, and percentage of overall compensation that is at risk—percentage is large enough to properly motivate desired performance

- At-risk compensation is tied to overall performance measures over which employees have strong influence or control

- Compensation system is consistent with organization structure, job, and work design

- Compensation system is considered fair by employees

- Compensation system rewards exceptional levels of performance from individuals and groups of employees

- Evidence of creativity and use of leading edge approaches to compensation

- Percentage of employees who receive recognition of some sort each year

- Involvement of employees in the design of recognition programs

- Recognition is based upon performance on key measures from 2.1, rather than separate factors

- Creativity in approaches to recognition

- Good mix of team and individual recognition efforts

- Items and/or privileges used for recognition of employees promote peer reinforcement

- Evidence of constant evaluation and improvement of approaches to compensation and recognition

4.3 EMPLOYEE EDUCATION, TRAINING, AND DEVELOPMENT

Describe how the company's education and training address company plans, including building company capabilities and contributing to employee motivation, progression, and development. (50 points)

Note:

(1) Education and training address the knowledge and skills employees need to meet their overall work objectives. Education and training might include leadership skills, communications, teamwork, problem solving, interpreting and using data, meeting customer requirements, process analysis, process simplification, waste reduction, cycle time reduction, error-proofing, priority setting based upon cost and benefit data, and other training that affects employee effectiveness, efficiency, and safety. This might include job enrichment and job rotation to enhance employees' career opportunities and employability. It might also include basic skills such as reading, writing, language, and arithmetic.

(2) Training for customer-contact (frontline) employees should address: (a) key knowledge and skills, including knowledge of products and services; (b) listening to customers; (c) soliciting comments from customers; (d) how to anticipate and handle problems or failures ("recovery"); (e) skills in customer retention; and (f) how to manage expectations.

AREA TO ADDRESS   **[APPROACH/DEPLOYMENT]**
4.3a How the company's education and training serve as a key vehicle in building company and employee capabilities. Describe how education and training address: (1) key performance objectives, including those related to enhancing high performance work units; and (2) progression and development of all employees.

What They're Looking For Here

Employee knowledge and skills are becoming an increasingly important determinants of a company's success. Even formerly low-tech jobs and industries have become high-tech. Today's auto mechanic needs to understand computer hardware, software, on-board diagnostics, as well as all the old mechanical and electrical skills. Successful companies have found that their employees need to continuously upgrade their knowledge and skills to remain competitive. This section of the Baldrige criteria is all about what you do to maintain and continually develop employee knowledge and skills. Because training is so important, and also so expensive, it is crucial that the company link its education and training to the key business drivers and overall goals of the company. One way of doing this is by developing a strategic training plan. A strategic training plan is a method for identifying needed competencies and skills based upon the long-term goals of the business. This approach begins with the business goals and works backward until specific training needs have been identified. Knowledge and skills identified in this manner are those that will help the company to meet its long-term goals.

4.3a asks for evidence that training is linked to the overall goals of the business. It is not necessary that you develop a strategic training plan. It is important that you have a mechanism for ensuring that education and training are one of the stones in your foundation for improving organizational performance. Refer back to previous sections of the application where you discuss your key business drivers, and longer-term goals and strategies. Next, explain how training needs are identified and linked to these goals and plans. A clear way of presenting this is a chart that lists long-term business goals along the left side, major training initiatives or curriculums along the top, creating a matrix. Using this format, you can show which types of education and training are liked to which business goals, or key business drivers.

The criteria in this area to address also ask about how your education and training help lead to the development of employees. 4.3a(2) asks for evidence that you do not just concentrate on knowledge and skills needed to perform today's jobs. One of the big changes to this item in the 1995 Baldrige criteria was an increased emphasis on employee development. One way of responding to this item is to discuss your approach to succession planning or individual career development of all employees. Indicate how education and training needs for future jobs are identified, and how these requirements are met. To show deployment on this area to address, make sure you provide a number of different examples that show that your development approaches are not just limited to a few select groups of employees.

Indicators For Area 4.3a

- Development of a strategic training plan or similar approach for linking training and education to business goals

- Evidence that all training and education can be directly linked to one or more key business drivers or long-term business goals

- An ongoing process exists for ensuring that training and education are closely tied to business goals and success factors

- Linkage between training/education activities and HR goals outlined in Item 4.1

- Consistency of education and training with new work and job design approaches discussed in Item 4.2

- Evidence of a systematic approach to identifying future training needs of employees to promote their development and growth

- Existence of a career development plan for each employee, with an identification of education and training needs for potential future assignments

- Depth and breadth of developmental plans and related training/education needs

---

AREA TO ADDRESS   [APPROACH/DEPLOYMENT]

4.3b How education and training are designed, delivered, reinforced, and evaluated. Include: (1) how employees and line managers contribute to or are involved in determining specific education and training needs and designing education and training; (2) how education and training are delivered; (3) how knowledge and skills are reinforced through on-the-job application; and (4) how education and training are evaluated and improved.

Notes:

(3)   **Determining specific education and training needs [4.3b(1)] might include use of company assessment or employee self-assessment to determine and/or compare skill levels for progression within the company or elsewhere. Needs determination should take into account job analysis—the types and levels of skills required—and the timeliness of training.**

(4)   **Education and training delivery [4.3b(2)] might occur inside or outside the company and involve on-the-job, classroom, computer-based, or other types of delivery. This includes the use of developmental assignments within or outside the company to enhance employees' career opportunities and employability.**

(5)   **How education and training are evaluated [4.3b(4)] could address: effectiveness of delivery of education and training; impact on work unit performance; and cost effectiveness of education and training alternatives.**

What They're Looking For Here

Many organizations approach training and education by buying a series of packaged programs from vendors who tell them what their employees need. What the Baldrige Examiners are looking for in this area is that you conduct a systematic needs assessment to determine the specific knowledge, skills, and competencies needed by different categories of employees in your organization. A systematic needs analysis does not mean conducting a survey to ask employees which courses they would like to take. A training/education needs analysis is a process that involves an initial analysis of the functions and jobs, and then a determination of the knowledge and skills needed to do the jobs and functions correctly. Group or individual interviews are conducted to identify the specific tasks employees must perform in their jobs, as well as how quality tools and concepts can be integrated into those job tasks. The key to this process is that the knowledge and skills are derived from analyzing job tasks. From this, relationships are identified between particular job tasks and specific skills and knowledge.

It is also important that training needs are derived from an analysis of the company's business goals. Identification of key competencies that are needed to meet business goals is the first step. Current employee skills and competencies then need to be assessed. The gap between existing and needed competencies form the foundation for a needs analysis.

Some organizations adopt the one-size-fits-all approach to quality training/education. While it is true that all employees at all levels need education on the basic concepts of quality, such as prevention versus detection, not all employees need to learn about specific tools and techniques such as facilitating team meetings or the Taguchi method of conducting experiments. Giving all of the same quality courses to all employees only produces the result that:

- Training is not tailored to individual needs
- Time and money are wasted on training that is irrelevant
- There will be no discussion of job/function-specific applications of the quality tools and techniques
- Skills and knowledge learned in the classroom will not translate into changed behavior on the job

Needs analysis for education and training should also be based upon individual performance appraisals and developmental plans created for each type of employee. Succession plans also can provide key data to be used for training needs analysis. Area to Address 4.3b(1) asks about how employees' input is sought for the needs analysis process. This does not mean, as I mentioned earlier, that you should do a survey to find out which courses employees want to take. Instead, employees are involved in needs analysis through the techniques called job and task analyses, which were discussed earlier. It is impossible to conduct a thorough training needs analysis without involving employees.

When describing the methods used for the delivery of education and training, it is important to explain why certain methods and media are used for particular audiences and topics. The Examiners expect that the methods and media used are matched to both the audience and the content of the education. For example, use of reading assignments for a population with poor reading skills would not be advised.

When discussing on-the-job reinforcement of training, a typical response is to explain that "employees at all levels are encouraged to use the skills they learn in performance training throughout various aspects of their jobs." What the Examiners are looking for here is that you have planned and implemented a systematic process for ensuring that skills learned in training are reinforced in the work environment. Most organizations have no such plan, and end up with a low score. I consult with many large organizations who spend millions of dollars on quality and related training and nothing on following up the training with coaching and reinforcement to make sure that the trainees apply the skills on the job. Consequently, the training fails to change job behavior or produce any improvements in performance. What usually follows is that the training itself is blamed, and the organization buys a different program, hires a different consultant, or develops a new program of their own. They usually find that the second or third training program works no better than the first one. All that a good training or education program can do is provide people with knowledge and skills. It cannot ensure that those knowledge and skills are applied and used on the job.

A lack of systematic and planned follow-up is the number one reason why training of any sort fails in organizations. As much—or more—time and money need to be spent on what happens after the classes as is spent preparing and conducting the classes.

Another effective approach is to teach employees job-specific applications for the tools and techniques they learn. This will help in bridging the gap between the classroom and the job environment. A more formalized reinforcement program would result in an even higher score in this area. One award applicant describes a program whereby supervisors and managers hand out coupons and "thank you" notes to employees when they see them going beyond quality standards or making use of the quality improvement techniques learned in training courses. Coupons are posted on sheets, and completed sheets are used to earn symbolic recognition or a small monetary/privilege award. The existence of a program such as this, along with data on its effectiveness, would help to earn a high score in this area.

This Area to Address also asks about how you evaluate the effectiveness of your education and training. This education and training should be evaluated on four dimensions:

- Reaction

- Learning

- Behavior Change

- Results

Reaction data are the most common, and are collected via questionnaires or surveys filled out by participants at the end of a class. The typical questionnaire asks the participants to rate the course, the instructor, the content, and the relevancy of the material on a five-point scale, along with a few open-ended questions.

The second education/training evaluation dimension is *learning*. This is another index that provides data on the effectiveness of the training delivery. This set of data should not simply report what the trainees/participants thought of the courses, but rather should indicate whether or not employees have mastered the material covered. Testing is the only appropriate means of measuring learning in an education/training program. Many large organizations do no testing in any of their quality courses, and hence have no data to demonstrate that participants learned any of the material. Testing does not have to consist of a paper-and-pencil, multiple-choice test. In any course in which skills are taught, performance tests are much better than written tests. A performance test might be a case study, a simulation, a role play, a demonstration, or any other situation where the trainee must demonstrate that he/she has mastered the skills taught in the course. Tests should be developed based upon the objectives of the courses, and should simulate how the trainees will use the skills in the job environment.

The third dimension of training/education evaluation is *behavior change*. This dimension considers whether trainees' behavior on the job has changed as a result of the training/education they received. Many large and small organizations do not have data on behavior change. This type of data, however, is even more important than data on what was learned. If skills learned in training are not used on the job, performance will not improve, and the money and time spent on the training will have been wasted. The degree to which employees apply and use the knowledge and skills they have learned in training is usually a direct result of the strategies employed in doing follow-up coaching and reinforcement. Data on behavior change are often collected via follow-up surveys of the trainees, their bosses, and their peers. An even more objective way of gathering such data is a measurement or audit of the actual products of people's behaviors and/or behavior changes. For example, an auditor might count the number of correctly prepared control charts posted in offices and work areas, or the number of quality improvement project reports that have been completed according to the criteria outlined in the training. A combination of process (behavior) and output (accomplishments/products) measures will earn high marks from the Baldrige Examiners in this area.

The final type of evaluation data that should be collected on training/education programs and courses is data on quality *results*. Employees might like the course, master the tests, and apply the skills on the job, but results may not improve. The major reason an organization invests in training and education is to produce better results from its employees' performance. If courses on quality improvement tools and techniques don't result in improved quality, something is wrong. The examiners want to see that you identify and measure key dimensions of performance that will be impacted by each course in your education/training curriculum. You should compare performance results data both before and after the training to see whether the training has made any difference. Of course, various other activities occurring in the organization will also impact performance, so it is important that you use a sound, applied research/ experimental design in your evaluation effort to rule out alternative explanations for the improvements seen in quality results. Present your response for this area using key graphs of major quality indices that have been impacted by the training.

In summary, the examiners are looking for four types or dimensions of evaluation data here. They are also looking to see that you can demonstrate clear cause–effect relationships between the education/training and improvements in both employee behavior and quality results.

Indicators For Area 4.3b

- Evidence that a systematic needs analysis has been done to identify specific training needs of various functions and levels of employees

- Scope of needs analysis includes all functions and levels of employees, including executives

- Degree to which needs analysis is based upon the study of job tasks to identify the key knowledge and skills needed by various groups of employees

- Use of appropriate data gathering techniques, such as group or individual interviews, rather than surveys

- Use of appropriate needs analysis processes, such as job or task analysis

- Needs analysis identifies where and how quality and performance improvement tools and techniques will be utilized in specific job tasks

- Needs analysis is updated and changed as jobs, functions, and training needs change

- Degree to which training need analyses are integrated with performance appraisal and individual employee development plans

- Training needs analysis linked to career development and succession planning as appropriate

- Extent to which employees are involved in the needs analysis process

- Use of a variety of methods (if appropriate) for delivery of quality education/training. For example, self-study, group instruction, video, case studies, etc.

- Education/training methods and media match characteristics of various target audiences within the organization

- Education/training methods and media match knowledge and skills to be taught

- Supervisors and managers have been trained to provide on-the-job reinforcement of employees' use of quality improvement tools and concepts

- Employee opinion about the degree to which supervisors/managers reinforce/encourage their use of quality tools and techniques

- Executives and upper management reinforce managers' use of quality tools and techniques

- Existence of a systematic plan to ensure that training/education courses on quality are followed up with appropriate coaching and reinforcement

- Training is scheduled in a "just-in-time" fashion so that skills and knowledge have immediate application on the job

- Degree to which employees receive follow-up coaching on the use of quality and performance improvement tools and techniques

- Employees are given adequate time to practice and master quality improvement tools/techniques on the job after formal training is completed

- Evidence that the company has a systematic approach to evaluating its education and training

- Deployment of evaluation methods across all types of education and training

- Collection of data on trainee reactions or satisfaction levels with courses

- Learning or mastery of material is tested in courses designed to teach specific knowledge and skills

- Where appropriate, employee use of skills learned in training on the job is measured

- Training process measures such as the quality of instruction or delivery are measured as part of the education/training evaluation approach

- The company measures the impact of certain courses on performance results such as customer satisfaction, financial results, productivity, or product/service quality

- Evidence of continuous improvement in training and education as a result of evaluation data

---

4.4 EMPLOYEE WELL-BEING AND SATISFACTION

Describe how the company maintains a work environment and a work climate conducive to the well-being and development of employees. (25 points)

AREA TO ADDRESS   **[APPROACH/DEPLOYMENT]**

4.4a How the company maintains a safe and healthful work environment. Include: (1) how employee well-being factors such as health, safety, and ergonomics are included in improvement activities; and (2) principal improvement requirements, measures and/or indicators, and targets for each factor relevant and important to the work environment of the company's employees. Note any significant differences based upon differences in work environments among employees or employee groups.

What They're Looking For Here

Companies that are known for their efforts to delight employees are rare today. Many have words in their vision and value statements about the importance of employees to their success, but few really operate that way. Downsizing, right-sizing, or simply laying off employees has become the favored approach to get a short-term boost in lagging profits for American companies. One former Baldrige winner waited until a week after they received the award to announce that they were laying off ten percent of the workforce. Sometimes cutting staff is unavoidable, even in a very well-run organization. Most of the time it is avoidable, though, through careful planning, prudent hiring, and other methods. This Examination Item is about what you do to make your organization a safe and enjoyable place to work.

Something that Examiners will look for in your response to this Area to Address is that you approach safety and employee health with the same systematic prevention-based approach as you employ for ensuring the production and delivery of high quality products and services. Most organizations and virtually all manufacturing companies have some type of safety program. Having a decent safety program may not earn you many points, but you will certainly lose some if you don't have one. What Examiners will need to see to give you a good score is a preventive approach to safety. Most safety programs are not preventive. Companies approach safety in much the same manner that fire departments approach fire prevention. Fire departments spend about 10 percent of their time on prevention-oriented activities, and the rest of the time fighting fires. One key indicator of a detection approach to safety is in how the organization measures safety. Most companies measure safety in lost time accidents or incident rates. This is like measuring quality by counting the number of defects found in products after they are made. Once an accident has occurred, it's too late to do anything about it. We can learn from the accident and correct the situation that allowed it to occur, but this is a detection approach to safety.

One organization I worked with measures employee behavior and inspects the work environment on a regular basis as their major safety measures. Safety boils down to employee behavior. If you can get employees to always follow safety rules and practices, you will not have safety problems. This company that I worked with monitors employee behavior for safe practices on almost a daily basis. They still measure defects such as incidents, near misses, and lost time related to accidents, and their safety record is near benchmark level for their industry.

Having a proactive to preventing safety problems would tend to earn you a very good score from Examiners. If your approach is characterized by safety audits conducted a few times a year, some safety training, and a few posters placed throughout the facility, you will probably end up with a very low score. Meeting OSHA or other regulatory requirements will also not earn you many points. You have no choice but to do this. Baldrige is looking for organizations that go way beyond minimum requirements.

4.4a(1) asks about how health, safety, and ergonomics (human factors engineering) are improved. The approach you use to achieve good performance in these areas is the same as the approach you employ to achieve good results in other areas, such as quality or customer satisfaction. You need to identify good measures of health, safety, and ergonomics, benchmark other organizations to identify world-class levels of performance, set stretch goals based on benchmarks, assign resources, and improve processes to achieve excellent levels of performance on these measures.

4.4a(2) asks for specific information on your measures and goals or targets. This information is probably best presented in a chart that lists measures along the left side, followed by annual targets and longer-term targets or goals. As I mentioned earlier, what is important is that all of your measures are not defect-detection oriented. You need to have a good mix of prevention-based measures and detection-based measures. A good prevention-based measure is not the number of safety training programs conducted or poster put up on the wall, either. The frequency with which you collect data on safety, health, and ergonomic factors is also important. To have a prevention-based approach, you need to collect data more often than once every few months.

Measures of employee health need to be preventive as well. Tracking employee health problems or sickness and absenteeism/sick leave by themselves are detection-oriented measures. You need to be careful with preventive measures to ensure that you drive the right behavior. One organization that had an on-site gym/health club used to measure the percentage of employees who used the gym, and the average amount of time spent in the gym per employee. Many used the gym as a social activity, however. They'd go to the gym, do 10 minutes on the Stairmaster, do a couple of sit-ups, and spend 45 minutes talking with co-workers, or sitting at the juice bar reading the newspaper. After realizing that hours spent in the gym was not a good measure, the company started measuring cardiovascular fitness, body fat percentage, blood pressure, and other health-related factors that were really important in maintaining employee health.

The last part of 4.4a asks you to note any significant differences in approaches based on different facilities or work groups. Often the company corporate headquarters will have a health club, medical clinic, stop smoking, weight loss, and any number of other programs to promote employee health. However, only 20 percent of the company's employees might work at headquarters. The rest are in plants or offices in remote locations that have none of these facilities or services. In assessing deployment on this Area to Address, Examiners are interested in what you are doing for all of your employees in all of your facilities. This last sentence in the criteria also asks about different approaches you might have for different employee groups—read diversity. If you have locations in different locations including international facilities, you may need to use different approaches to employee health safety and ergonomics. Examiners will look for evidence that you do not adopt a one-size-fits-all approach, but that you tailor your approaches to the culture and demographics of the employees in different locations if appropriate.

<u>Indicators For Area 4.4a</u>

- Absence of citations from health/safety regulatory agencies, or lawsuits relating to health/safety issues

- Identification of a good set of measures for employee safety that is a good mix of prevention and detection types of metrics

- Benchmarking and other comparative information are used to set stretch goals for safety performance

- Specific goals and targets have been set for all measures of employee safety

- How employees feel about the degree to which the company promotes health and safety

- Evidence of process changes and improvements that will promote better employee safety performance

- Evidence of a preventive approach to employee health, safety, and ergonomics

- Evidence that the company goes way beyond regulatory requirements in this area and strives to be a role model for others

- Frequency with which data are collected on health and safety issues

- Levels of resources devoted to health and safety efforts compared to companies of similar size in the same industry

- Scope and breadth of improvements made in ergonomics

- Programs the company has in place to promote the health of their employees (e.g., weight loss, stop smoking, health club, smoke-free environment, etc.)

- Existence of a systematic process for analyzing the causes of accidents when they do occur

- Evidence that employee health and safety initiatives are tailored to different cultures, locations, and employee groups if appropriate

---

AREA TO ADDRESS   **[APPROACH, DEPLOYMENT]**

4.4b What services, facilities, activities, and opportunities the company makes available to employees to support their overall well-being and satisfaction and/or to enhance their work experience and development potential.

Notes:

(1) **Examples of services, facilities, activities, and opportunities (4.4b) are: personal and career counseling; career development and employability services; recreational or cultural activities; non-work-related education; day care; special leave for family responsibilities and/or for community service; safety off the job; flexible work hours; outplacement; and retiree benefits, including extended health care. These services also might include career enhancement activities such as skill assessment, helping employees develop learning objectives and plans, and employability assessment.**

(2) **Examples of specific factors which might affect satisfaction, well-being, and motivation are: effective employee problem or grievance resolution; safety; employee views of leadership and management; employee development and career opportunities; employee preparation for changes in technology or work organization; work environment; workload; cooperation and teamwork; recognition; benefits; communications; job security; compensation; equality of opportunity; and capability to provide required services to customers. An effective determination is one that provides the company with actionable information for use in improvement activities.**

What They're Looking For Here

Almost all companies do something in this area. What the examiners are looking for is the breadth and depth of the special services you provide to employees, and the degree to which these services have been tailored to the special needs of the organization's employees. For example, in an organization populated largely by women, child care might be an appropriate and appreciated special service. In a situation in which an organization's surrounding community education system is poor, remedial reading or other similar programs may be needed. If you have done a thorough analysis of your employees and have identified their special needs, and have tailored your employee assistance programs to those needs, you will do well in this area.

Most organizations approach this area either by offering what other companies offer in the way of employee services, or waiting until a problem occurs and then developing a program to deal with the problem (e.g., drugs or alcohol). If, however, you take a proactive/preventive approach to employee assistance, this will be noticed more by the examiners. If you can demonstrate that you offer more than your competitors do in the area of employee services, this too will be of interest to examiners. Your response might consist of a table that lists all employee assistance programs on the left side of the page, and the name of your organization and a few of its competitors along the top. A matrix like the one that follows then could be created to illustrate which employee assistance programs you offer, as compared to your competition.

EMPLOYEE ASSISTANCE PROGRAMS			
	Your Organization	Competitor A	Competitor B
Child Care	X	X	
Home Financing Assistance	X		X
Health Club Membership	X		
Weight Control Program	X		
Stop Smoking Program	X		
Drug/Alcohol Program	X		
Discount Symphony Tickets	X		
Annual Family Picnic	X	X	X
Counseling	X	X	
Outplacement Assistance	X	X	

Indicators For Area 4.4b

- Whether or not a needs analysis has been completed to determine the employee assistance programs that may be needed in the organization

- Number of different employee assistance programs offered

- Breadth/variety of employee assistance and special services offered

- How the organization's employee assistance programs compare to major competitors'

- Employee opinion on the assistance programs offered

- Evidence that services and programs are offered to all employees in all locations

---

AREA TO ADDRESS   **[APPROACH, DEPLOYMENT]**

4.4c How the company determines employee satisfaction, well-being, and motivation. Include a brief description of methods, frequency, the specific factors used in this determination, and how the information is used to improve satisfaction, well-being, and motivation. Note any important differences in methods or factors used for different categories or types of employees, as appropriate.

Notes:

(3)   **Measures and/or indicators of satisfaction, well-being, and motivation (4.4c) might include safety, absenteeism, turnover, turnover rate for customer-contact employees, grievances, strikes, worker compensation, as well as results of surveys.**

(4)   **How satisfaction, well-being, and motivation information is used (4.4c) might involve developing priorities for addressing employee problems based on impact on productivity.**

(5)   **Trends in key measures and/or indicators of well-being and satisfaction should be reported in Item 6.3.**

What They're Looking For Here

What they are looking for in this Area to Address is that you use a thorough and objective approach to measuring employee satisfaction, and that you do so with reasonable frequency. An annual 10-item morale survey that has been completed by only a portion of employees will not earn you many points in this area. An annual morale survey is a good start, but the Baldrige Examiners will be looking at how thorough and how frequent your survey is, and at the percentage of employees who actually complete it.

Surveys are only one means of measuring employee satisfaction. Other types of data are much better indicators of the level of employee satisfaction in an organization. You should include statistics on:

- Average hours worked per week
- Turnover
- Reasons why employees leave the company (obtained via exit interviews or follow-up surveys)
- Absenteeism
- Incidence of stress-related illnesses or disorders
- Requests for lateral transfers in and out of locations or functions

The extent to which your data on employee satisfaction are based upon multiple measures will have a large impact on the score you receive in this area. What your organization does with the data on employee satisfaction is also examined in this area. Many organizations conduct morale surveys that end up being reviewed and thrown away, with the issues never being dealt with. The Baldrige people are looking for evidence that you have a process for reviewing these data and for developing action plans to improve the issues uncovered in the survey. Examples of situations where you uncovered problems relating to employee satisfaction and have corrected them will help make your response more credible.

Indicators For Area 4.4c

- Use of thorough employee morale/satisfaction surveys on a regular basis

- Objectivity of survey methodology and instruments

- Frequency with which employee satisfaction is measured

- Good mix of hard (e.g., turnover) and soft (e.g., morale survey) measures of employee satisfaction

- Percentage of employees at all levels and in all functions who complete surveys (return rate and sample)

- Use of multiple measures/indices over and above surveys to measure employee satisfaction

- Objectivity of employee satisfaction data

- Evidence that a systematic process is used to review employee satisfaction data and develop corrective action plans for dealing with problems or situations with which employees are dissatisfied

- Evidence that approach to measuring employee satisfaction is evaluated and continuously improved

- Extent to which safety issues are addressed as part of employee satisfaction measures

Chapter 10

Interpreting the Criteria for Process Management (5.0)

OVERVIEW OF THE PROCESS MANAGEMENT CATEGORY

Category 5.0 covers Process Management. This category is worth 14 percent of the award evaluation, or a possible 140 points. The category addresses how you assure and improve the quality of the products and services you offer to customers through process management strategies. Emphasis should be placed on the word *how*. This category deals with *processes*, not results. Results are assessed in Category 6.0, Business Results. The Award Criteria define Category 5.0 as follows:

Process Management (Category 5.0) is the focal point within the Criteria for all key work processes. Built into the Category are the central requirements for efficient and effective process management—effective design, a prevention orientation, evaluation and continuous improvement, linkage to suppliers, and overall high performance.

An increasingly important concept in all aspects of process management and organizational design is flexibility. In simplest terms, flexibility refers to the ability to adapt quickly and effectively to changing requirements. Depending on the nature of the business' strategy and markets, flexibility might mean rapid changeover from one product to another, rapid response to changing demand, or the ability to produce a wide range of products. Flexibility might demand special strategies such as modular designs, sharing of components, and specialized training. (p. 39)

In this chapter we'll discuss the four Examination Items and the ten different Areas to Address that fall within this category. As in previous chapters, each section begins with a double-ruled box containing the Examination Item, the point value, and any applicable Notes*. Areas to Address falling under that Item follow in a single-ruled box. In the upper right corner of each Area to Address box is an indication [brackets] of whether the Area pertains to approach, deployment, or results. All definitions and information appearing within these boxes is taken directly from the Baldrige criteria. Following each Area to Address is an explanation defining what the examiners are looking for in assessing your application. Next, I have supplied a list of indicators or evaluation factors that will assist you in interpreting the criteria in preparing your application.

---

* Item Notes that apply to a specific Area to Address are appropriately listed in the box containing that Area.

5.1 DESIGN AND INTRODUCTION OF PRODUCTS AND SERVICES

Describe how new and/or modified products and services are designed and introduced and how key production/delivery processes are designed to meet both key product and service quality requirements, company operational performance requirements, and market requirements. **(40 points)**

Notes:

(1) **Design and introduction might address:**
- **modifications and variants of existing products and services, including product and service customization;**
- **new products and services emerging from research and development or other product/service concept development;**
- **new/modified facilities to meet operational performance and/or product and service quality requirements; and**
- **significant redesigns of processes to improve customer focus, productivity, or both.**

   Design approaches could differ appreciably depending upon the nature of the products/services—entirely new, variants, major or minor process changes, etc. If many design projects are carried out in parallel, responses to Item 5.1 should reflect how coordination of resources among projects is carried out.

(2) **Applicants' responses should reflect the key requirements for their products and services. Factors that might need to be considered in design include: health; safety; long-term performance; environmental impact; "green" manufacturing; measurement capability; process capability; manufacturability; maintainability; supplier capability; and documentation.**

(3) **Service and manufacturing businesses should interpret product and service design requirements to include all product- and service-related requirements at all stages of production, delivery, and use.**

AREA TO ADDRESS   **[APPROACH, DEPLOYMENT]**
5.1a How products, services, and production/delivery processes are designed.
Describe: (1) how customer requirements are translated into product and
service design requirements; (2) how product and service design requirements
are translated into efficient and effective production/delivery processes,
including an appropriate measurement plan; and (3) how all requirements
associated with products, services, and production/delivery processes are
addressed early in design by all appropriate company units, suppliers, and
partners to ensure integration, coordination, and capability.

Notes:

 (4)   **A measurement plan [5.1a(2)] should spell out what is to be measured,**
        how and when measurements are to be made, and performance levels
        or standards to ensure that the results of measurements provide
        information to guide, monitor, control, or improve the process. This
        may include service standards used in customer-contact processes. The
        term, "measurement plan," may also include decisions about key
        information to collect from customers and/or employees from service
        encounters, transactions, etc. The actual measurement plan should not
        be described in Item 5.1. Such information is requested in Item 5.2.

 (5)   **"All appropriate company units" [5.1a(3)] means those units and/or**
        individuals who will take part in production/delivery and whose
        performance materially affects overall process outcome. This might
        include groups such as R&D, marketing, design, and product/process
        engineering.

What They're Looking For Here

The Examiners want to see that you employ a systematic approach to gathering
information about customers' requirements and desires, and have a process for translating
this information into product or service characteristics and standards. A well-accepted
technique for doing this is Quality Function Deployment (QFD). The approach is best
explained by Hauser and Clausing (of Harvard and MIT) in the May/June, 1989, issue of
the *Harvard Business Review* (see "The House of Quality," pages 63–73). The process
begins by gathering information on the specific requirements customers have regarding
the components of the products you produce. The example given in the article is about

car doors. Customers make a list of 15 to 20 different characteristics they consider important in car doors. These characteristics are then prioritized by the customers. The prioritized list of customer requirements is given to design engineers, who design the new product or portion of a product (e.g., car door) based upon the list of requirements.

A similar process for defining customer requirements in the design of services is described by me in the May, 1990, issue of the *Journal For Quality and Participation*. The process is similar, except that the customer requirements lead to service characteristics and standards instead of engineering characteristics and product design specifications. It is not necessary that you use either of these approaches, but you should use something similar. Your approach should demonstrate that you collect a great deal of data on customer requirements for various aspects of the products and/or services you offer and that you use that information extensively to guide the design of new or enhanced products/services.

Some applicants respond to this section by explaining that they have a systematic process for defining customers' requirements and using this information to design new products and services, but they don't explain the process. One applicant who received a very high score on this area provided a graphic representation of the phases and steps in its process and described each step in detail. Examples were provided to illustrate the process. Make sure, however, not to use an example as your actual response. Examples should be used only to clarify and illustrate processes.

A frequent problem in large organizations is that individuals and functions that should provide input to product/service designs don't have a chance to do so until it is too late. Each individual or function that will be involved in producing, delivering, or servicing the product/service needs to be able to provide input early in the design process. Don't respond simply by saying that this involvement occurs. Explain how you ensure that everyone's input is gathered and considered. Systems, procedures, and the meeting(s) you have in place to encourage this should be described.

Once you have obtained everyone's input, you also need to ensure that they are involved at key points in the design and introduction cycle. Requiring consensus meetings or sign-offs may be a way of ensuring this. It may be appropriate to present a diagram that shows the major phases in the product/service design cycle, and which functions have responsibility for which phases. For example, engineering may have heavy involvement in the first few phases and lesser degrees of involvement as you're getting ready to introduce the product/service.

If you list the critical process characteristics or measures to be controlled and the methods for controlling each process for your major products and/or services, you will demonstrate to the examiners that you have good control plans.

Indicators For Area 5.1a

- Thoroughness with which data on customer requirements are gathered

- Designs are coordinated and integrated to include all phases of production and delivery

- Use of multiple methodologies and sources of data on customer requirements

- Evidence that the company is close to the customer

- Extent to which customer requirements are identified for parts of products/services as well as the products/services as a whole

- Use of sound statistical methods to collect and analyze market research data

- Prioritization of customer requirements is done using large samples of customers

- Evidence that customer requirements have been translated into engineering specifications and characteristics during the design phase of the new product development cycle

- Evidence that customer requirements have been translated into service characteristics and standards during the design phase of the new service development cycle

- Evidence that all appropriate personnel and functions are involved in early stages of the design process—when their input has the most value

- Objectivity and validity of process for using customer requirements as inputs for the product/service design process

- Use of systematic methodology such as Quality Function Deployment to translate customer requirements into product/service characteristics

- Quantity of evidence to suggest that existing products and/or services have been designed based upon customer requirements

---

AREA TO ADDRESS   **[APPROACH, DEPLOYMENT]**
5.1b How product, service, and production/delivery process designs are reviewed and/or tested in detail to ensure trouble-free and rapid introduction.

What They're Looking For Here

This section of your application should describe the overall process you use to design and test new products and services. You should include a graphic that shows the phases and steps in your product/service development cycle. Most applicants that are manufacturing companies do a pretty good job on this section of their applications. Most organizations have a process defined for developing new products and services. Simply having a systematic product/service development process won't earn you many points by itself. What the examiners are looking for in this Area to Address is the extent to which quality is built into the development process. Moreover, they are looking for evidence of a preventive approach to quality, rather than a production spot-check and correction cycle.

One important criterion for the design phase of a new product or service is that all the important functions that will be involved with the product/service participate in the design process. A major problem in many large companies is the number of changes made to designs, drawings, and specifications due to input from manufacturing, field service, marketing, legal, etc. Every department responsible for some detail of the product or service will offer its input. The problem is that the input is usually too late, causing numerous revisions to the product/service designs. A preventive approach involves getting representatives from each of these functions involved early in the design phase of the product/service and obtaining their input at key points, before all the drawings are done and the specifications finalized.

Another aspect of your development process examined in this area is the number and thoroughness of tests you perform on the product/service. Explain the types of tests you conduct, when they are conducted, and what the test is used to determine. Remember that the Baldrige Examiners may not understand your business or technology well, so make sure you avoid industry jargon and technical terms if at all possible.

In reviewing your process for designing new products or services, the Baldrige Examiners will be looking for evidence that key factors such as product and service performance, and process and supplier capabilities, are taken into consideration. Capabilities need to be considered in reviewing the feasibility of product and service designs. Involving suppliers in the design review process is critical when outside parts, materials, and/or services are required in order to meet key product/service requirements.

Indicators For Area 5.1b

- Novel ways of improving product design and introduction

- Systematic process for designing new products and/or services

- Suppliers are involved in reviewing product/service designs

- Evidence of a participative approach to the design phase of a new product/service, involving all of the functions/departments that will work with the product/service

- Reviews take into account product/service performance data

- Use of a preventive approach to assuring quality in the design of new products/services

- Reviews involve an assessment of process capabilities when appropriate

- Thorough testing of new products and/or services before they are introduced

- Use of techniques such as Alpha Tests, Beta Tests, and controlled market introductions, if appropriate

- Objectivity and reliability of methods used for testing new products/services

- Number and frequency of changes that occur in product/service designs (changes should be minimized)

- Thoroughness of design reviews

- Continued deployment of the voice of the customer through QFD or similar process

---

AREA TO ADDRESS   **[APPROACH, DEPLOYMENT]**
5.1c How designs and design processes are evaluated and improved to achieve better product and service quality, time to market, and production/delivery process effectiveness.

What They're Looking For Here

This Area to Address is more relevant to products than to services. Design of new products often gets bogged down and products end up taking much longer to be released than originally planned. In this area, the Examiners are looking for a description of the process or approach you use to evaluate the design process and reduce the amount of time it takes to design, test, and introduce new products and/or services. This is not what is sought in Areas 5.1a and 5.1b. In those areas the examiners want to make sure that your new product/service design process is systematic and thorough. Systematic and thorough is sometimes equated with time-consuming and inefficient, however. Your response to this area should stress the timeliness and efficiency of your process. In addition, you should explain some of the steps you have taken in recent years to minimize product/service design time. Results included here would be helpful in supporting your claims. Cite statistics on the average time required from design to the introduction of new products/services this year in comparison with past years, and you will have a stronger case. Although this section does not ask for data, information on reductions in cycle time will help give you a better score from Examiners.

You should also provide evidence that you systematically evaluate your design process. Describe the evaluation procedures, methodologies, and instruments. If you can explain how the process has been improved over the last few years, this will be considered a positive sign.

Indicators For Area 5.1c

- Evidence of a systematic plan for evaluating the product/service design process that includes customer feedback on product/service quality

- Evidence of a systematic plan for reducing product/service design time

- Specific actions that have been taken to reduce product/service design time

- Validity and thoroughness of evaluation process

- Data to demonstrate that plans/steps that have been implemented actually have reduced the time it takes to design new products/services

- Number and significance of improvements that have been made in the product/service design process over the last few years

5.2 PROCESS MANAGEMENT: PRODUCT AND SERVICE PRODUCTION AND DELIVERY PROCESSES

Describe how the company's key product and service production/delivery processes are managed to ensure that design requirements are met and that both quality and operational performance are continuously improved.
(40 points)

Note:

(1)   Key production/delivery processes are those most directly involved in fulfilling the principal requirements of customers—those that define the products and services.

AREA TO ADDRESS   [APPROACH, DEPLOYMENT]

5.2a How the company maintains the performance of key production/delivery processes to ensure that such processes meet design requirements addressed in Item 5.1. Describe: (1) the key processes and their principal requirements; and (2) the measurement plan and how measurements and/or observations are used to maintain process performance.

Notes:

(2)   Measurement plan [5.2a(2)] is defined in Item 5.1, Note (4). Companies with specialized measurement requirements should describe how they ensure measurement effectiveness. For specialized physical, chemical, and engineering measurements, describe briefly how measurements are made traceable to national standards.

(3)   The focus of 5.2a is on <u>maintenance</u> of process performance using measurements and/or observations to decide whether or not corrective action is needed. The nature of the corrective action depends on the process characteristics and the type of variation observed. Responses should reflect the type of process and the type of variation observed. A description should be given of how basic (root) causes of variation are determined and how corrections are made at the earliest point(s) in processes. Such correction should then minimize the likelihood of recurrence of this type of variation anywhere in the company.

Once you have identified your key products and services, and identified the three to six major processes associated with the production and delivery of each one, you need to prepare a second matrix that indicates how you measure and control your processes. This matrix chart might look like the one below.

KEY PROCESSES	REQUIREMENTS	MEASURES	STANDARDS	CONTROL STRATEGIES

The key processes are taken from the first chart in this section, where you indicated which processes are associated with which products and services. Chances are there will be a number of generic processes that cut across all products and/or services, like delivery or distribution. Make sure that processes have verbs in them, and that you don't go too deeply into subprocesses. Requirements are important dimensions of the process that directly relate to important customer requirements. For example, at Alcoa plants that manufacture aluminum that is used for beverage cans, one of the customers' key requirements is the thickness of the aluminum. In a hotel, if we were looking at delivery of room service as a process, one of the key customer requirements is how long it takes to get the meal delivered. Requirements sometimes translate directly into measures; sometimes they do not. In the room service example, a good measure obviously would be cycle time from the time the customer calls in the order until it is delivered to her room. In the Alcoa example, some of the measures are not so obvious. One of Alcoa's key manufacturing processes is rolling. They start off with a big hunk of aluminum called an ingot that is about two feet thick and ten feet long. This ingot is rolled until it becomes longer and thinner. One of Alcoa's key process measures is the temperature of the aluminum as it is being rolled. Do customers care about the temperature of the finished product? No. If it is cold outside when it is delivered, the aluminum is cold. Customers do care about thickness and strength though, which are two product dimensions that are influenced by the temperature of the aluminum as it is being rolled.

After identifying several key measures for process that are tied back to requirements, you need to identify the targets, standards, or control limits for each measure. Measures are meaningless without standards or goals. You might have a band consisting of an upper and lower control limit, or simply one standard. In the hotel example, the standard for the delivery of room service might be 45 minutes or less. If the meal is delivered in 30 minutes that is not a problem, so we don't need an upper and lower standard or control limit. Standards or targets for process measures should tie back to customer requirements that are identified in section 7.1 of your application. As you will come to learn, almost everything ties back to 7.1 eventually. This is why I advise applicants to write 7.1 first to help ensure that everything else is consistent with it.

The final column in your matrix chart is used to identify the control strategies that are used to keep the process performance within the standards or levels that have been set. In the Alcoa example, the control strategy is easy. Everything is automated. If you go into an Alcoa plant, there are almost no people. The place almost runs by remote control. In most service businesses, and many manufacturing businesses such as aerospace, most processes have human behavior as a major component. If this is the case, the Baldrige Examiners want to know what control strategies you have in place to ensure that employee behavior stays within acceptable limits or standards. Procedures are not a control technique because they are usually not looked at. McDonalds is a company that is a master at controlling processes dependent upon human behavior. They have automated where they can, but some things just can't be automated yet. McDonalds' control strategies consist of thorough training, clear and precise procedures and work rules, constant monitoring, feedback, and consequences. Employees are rewarded for desired behavior and following process rules, and punished for failure to conform to standards.

Your response to this item should explain the various methods you employ to ensure that your product and/or services meet the standards outlined in the design specifications. These approaches might include in-process inspection of components, products, or services as they are delivered, as well as an inspection of the final products or accomplishments. An accomplishment produced by a service might be a repaired car, a served meal, or a completed set of architectural drawings. The examiners will also assess the degree to which your approach is prevention-based. In other words, do you have systems in place for preventing the occurrence of defects, or are your systems focused on the detection and correction of defects?

Some processes, particularly those related to service delivery, are better handled by humans than controlled through automation. In this case, you need to describe your methods for controlling the behaviors of the employees delivering the service. Training them does not qualify as a control process. A control process involves specifying desired performance, tracking performance against standards, providing feedback to employees involved in the process, and setting up positive and negative consequences to encourage meeting or exceeding standards.

Many applicants believe that they must use a specific cause-analysis process such as Ishikawa/fishbone diagramming in order to receive a high score for this Area to Address. This is not true. Remember, the Baldrige criteria are designed to be nonprescriptive. The Examiners want to see that you employ a systematic method for analyzing the causes of process upsets. I once worked on a project for Toyota's plant in Georgetown, Kentucky, where we were teaching the American employees to solve problems Japanese-style.

When I asked the Japanese managers how their style was different from ours, they said that most of the time Americans do not do any analysis. They go from problem to solution. If one solution doesn't work, they try a different one.

If you use this type of problem-solving technique, you will earn a low score in this section. The Baldrige Examiners want to see that you *thoroughly* and *completely* analyze the root causes of process upsets and other types of quality problems before implementing a solution or countermeasure. The approach you use should be based upon a major model, but it can be customized to fit your own needs. For example, some organizations use the comparative approach to cause analysis as taught by the consulting firm of Kepner-Tregoe. Others use the Ishikawa diagram as the base for their approach. These and other proven models are all appropriate.

Within this Area to Address you also need to explain how process deviations are corrected and the corrections verified. Once single or multiple causes have been identified, there are usually several different alternatives for countermeasures. Your response to this area should explain how you decide on the most appropriate countermeasure, how you implement it, and how you verify that the change produced the desired result. As in most other areas, the examiners are looking for evidence of a systematic process.

This area should address your follow-up after the implementation of countermeasures designed to improve quality. Many organizations do not do follow up. For example, a large bank conducted an experiment that showed that if clerks in the operations area were put on incentive pay, their productivity and quality would improve. Upon implementation of the pay system, they found that the incentive pay worked well only for about three months. After that time, productivity stayed up but quality began to deteriorate. If the bank had not conducted a thorough follow-up evaluation, it might have left the incentive system intact for quite some time before realizing that it was no longer producing the desired results.

One important criterion regarding your follow-up approach is the scope of your follow-up activities. Do you conduct follow-up of *all* changes implemented to improve quality, or only the major ones that impact the whole organization? Do you conduct follow-up assessments in the support organizations as well as in the line organization? Another important criterion is the objectivity of the approach and instruments you use to conduct follow-up evaluations. Conducting a survey of employees' bosses six months after the employees have been through quality training is a poor way of evaluating the impact of training, for example. It's analogous to "the emperor's new clothes." People expect to see a change after the training, so that's how they respond to the survey. Surveys should never be used when it is possible to obtain "hard" data on quality measures.

The duration of your follow-up is also considered important. Some side effects don't appear immediately. If your evaluation occurs only a couple of months following implementation of a countermeasure, you won't know what happens after six months or a year. The effectiveness of countermeasures may deteriorate significantly after the first few months.

Indicators For Area 5.2a

- Clear identification of all important processes relating to the production and delivery of products and/or services

- Use of statistical process control where appropriate

- Relationships identified between individual products/services and processes

- Approach to process control is preventive in nature

- Process owners and/or accountabilities identified, if appropriate

- Degree to which process control is automated where appropriate and possible

- Frequency of measurement of key process variables

- Thoroughness of control mechanisms used to ensure that processes stay within specified tolerances or guidelines

- Control mechanisms for ensuring that processes based upon employee behavior are systematic and thorough

- Adequate sample sizes used to collect data on end-of-process measures

- Adequacy of in-process measures

- Use of valid statistical procedures for analyzing process data

- Number of different process measures for which data are collected

- Use of established and acceptable model for cause analysis

- Use of different processes for analyzing common-cause and special-cause problems

- Thoroughness and rigor of cause-analysis process

- Examples or evidence to suggest that the analysis process is successful for discerning the root causes of process upsets and other quality-related problems

- Clear linkages between customer requirements, process measures, and standards

---

AREA TO ADDRESS   **[APPROACH, DEPLOYMENT]**

5.2b How processes are evaluated and improved to improve products and services and to achieve better performance, including cycle time. Describe how each of the following is used or considered: (1) process analysis and research; (2) benchmarking; (3) use of alternative technology; and (4) information from customers of the processes—within and outside the company.

Notes:

  (4) **The focus of 5.2b is on improvement of processes—making them perform better than the original design. Better performance might include one or more of the following: operational, customer-related, and financial performance. After processes have been improved, process maintenance (5.2a) needs to adjust to the changes. Process improvement methods might utilize financial data to evaluate alternatives and set priorities.**

  (5) **"Process analysis and research" [5.2b(1)] refers to a wide range of possible approaches to improving processes. Examples include process mapping, optimization experiments, basic and applied research, error proofing, and reviewing critical encounters between employees and customers from the point of view of customers and employees.**

  (6) **Information from customers [5.2b(4)] might include information developed as described in Items 7.2, 7.3, and 2.3.**

  (7) **Results of improvements in products and services and in product and service delivery processes should be reported in Items 6.1 and 6.2, as appropriate.**

<u>What They're Looking For Here</u>

This section should include an explanation of how you analyze and improve or reengineer the key processes in your organization. The foundation of any process improvement effort is to begin by documenting current processes. This is often more difficult than it would seem. Getting a group of employees to all agree on how a process

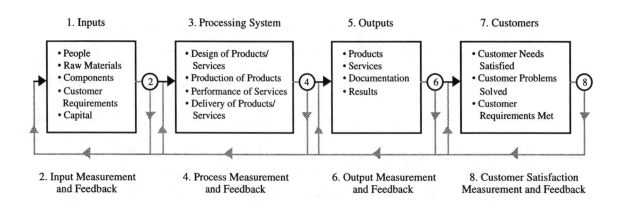

Figure 10.1: Macro Process Model of an Organization

is performed is sometimes a time-consuming activity. The most common approach to this effort is to create process models or systems diagrams that depict inputs, outputs, and key process steps. An example of a macro process model is shown in Figure 10.1.

Modeling all processes in an organization is a great way to identify opportunities for improvement. Many processes have never been documented. The act of documenting a process forces employees to question whether all of the steps are really necessary and to see ways in which the processes may be streamlined. Many large and small companies are currently working on modeling all of their processes, which number in the thousands, and are finding that it is a great deal of work. The activity, however, has already produced numerous improvements.

Evaluation of new or updated technology is another way to identify opportunities for improvement. Acquiring new technology may give you the ability to significantly reduce customer processing time in a service business, for example. The clerks at Hertz Rental Car now use hand-held terminals to record your mileage and gas and print out a receipt on the spot. This technology allowed Hertz to greatly reduce the amount of time the customer spends returning a rental car.

Opportunities for continuous improvement are also identified by reviewing competitive and benchmark data. A competitor or company you have benchmarked yourself against may exhibit performance superior to yours on a particular measure. Their level of performance should then become the goal for your company to achieve or surpass.

Your approach to continuous improvement should be well rounded. In other words, do not base all your opportunities for continuous improvement around what the competition is doing. You will never rise to the top using such an approach because you will be too busy playing catch-up. Include data from a variety of sources in your approach, and make your approach proactive as well as reactive. Employees from all levels and functions within the organization should be involved in the continuous improvement process.

Your response for this Area to Address should also explain how you evaluate various process improvement alternatives to decide on the best approach. The Baldrige Examiners are looking for evidence of a systematic approach to deciding on the best way to improve processes. A typical response to this area is to explain that "We use a participative group process to brainstorm possible process improvements and decide upon the most appropriate approach." This may sound good, but the Examiners want more information.

As with many of the Areas to Address relating to quality assurance processes, a good way to respond here is to include a flow chart or similar graphic that depicts the steps in your decision-making process. Describe who uses the process and how and when it is used. If every employee has been trained in the process, state this in your response. Your approach should have certain characteristics. First, it should be participative; the process should allow for input from several employees who have knowledge of any problems. Second, it should involve brainstorming or a similar approach for generating alternative actions. Finally, it should include a process for evaluating alternative actions or countermeasures against specific criteria and constraints found in the work environment. For example, a particular action may be very effective, but if there is not enough time to implement it, or if it costs too much money, it is not a good choice.

This Area to Address asks for information on a variety of stimuli, which may be used to initiate process improvement. The first segment (1) asks about how simply analyzing a process and conducting research can serve as a stimulus for improving it. Sometimes all it takes is to draw a flow chart of a process to realize how inefficient it is, and to spot key steps that can be eliminated. Benchmarking, which is asked about in 5.2b(2), often stimulates process improvement since one sees how another company performs the same or a similar process. It may be that you never considered it possible to perform a process the way the benchmarked company does. Process improvements are also sometimes generated based upon research.

Examining alternative technology (3) may allow you to make improvements in a process. The hand-held computers that I described earlier in the Hertz example are a great illustration of how a new technology was used to greatly improve and simplify the process of returning a car and obtaining a receipt.

Sometimes internal and external customers (4) provide inputs that lead to process improvements. Customers can sometimes see a lack of logic in processes, or opportunities for improvement that those performing the processes can't discern. I recently was a passenger on a foreign airline and was amazed at the approach it used to count the number of passengers on the plane. There were no assigned seats, so everyone rushed into the plane at once, fighting for the best seats. Even when everyone had found a seat, we realized that there was still almost an hour before takeoff time. It was a big plane, holding at least a couple of hundred people. In looking around, the plane appeared almost completely full—there were only about six to eight empty seats in the entire plane. While we waited, a flight attendant walked slowly down the aisle with a hand counter, counting the passengers on the left side of the airplane. Once she got to the back, she walked back toward the front, clicking off the number of passengers on the right side of the plane. The entire process took about ten minutes because she was being very careful. The man next to me was extremely annoyed at the apparent lack of sense to this procedure. He said, "They know how many seats are in this plane. Why don't they just count the number of empty seats—wouldn't that be a lot easier?" While we were all laughing about this silly procedure, another flight attendant started down the aisle, with a hand counter. The man next to me stopped the attendant and said, "What are you doing? Someone already counted the passengers. Why don't you just count the number of empty seats? The plane is almost full." You can just guess the answer: "Our procedure is that we need to do a count of all passengers twice to ensure accuracy. We would not be following the procedure if we did it any other way." With this, he proceeded to walk through the entire plane again, repeating the counting procedure that was performed by the other flight attendant ten minutes before. You may think this is a funny story that would never happen in another airline, or certainly not in your company. But every company I've ever seen has some processes like this one—processes that may have made sense at one time but are laughable under changed circumstances. Listen to your internal and external customers when they ask: "Why do you have to do it this way?"

Using challenge goals based on benchmarks is a good way of stimulating process improvement. Once a process has been mapped and data are collected on current levels of performance for key process variables, a stretch goal is set to force people to do the process differently. I once heard the chief financial officer of Motorola talk about how they do this in his function. A process that had always caused them a great deal of grief and overtime was completing the month-end close of the books. Everyone in the department ended up working late at the end of every month, and the antacids flowed freely because of the high stress. After mapping and measuring this process, the CFO set a stretch goal for the process improvement team. They had to figure out how to do the month-end close in half the usual time (labor hours) and without any overtime. They were told that they could change anything they wanted, as long as they didn't violate any regulations or generally accepted accounting practices. Big surprise—they did what they all thought was impossible at first. They did a major overhaul of the process, cutting out many unnecessary steps. Closing the books at the end of the month is no longer a nightmare for those who work in the finance department of Motorola. This is the type of example the Examiners want to see in your use of stretch or challenge goals to stimulate process improvements.

Indicators For Area 5.2b

- Use of process modeling as a means for identifying opportunities for improvement in processes and resulting products/services

- Objectivity and methodological rigor of process modeling approach

- Scope of process modeling to include all functions in the organization

- Use of field data, when appropriate, as a way of identifying opportunities for continuous improvement

- Systematic analysis of new and changing technology as a means for identifying quality improvement opportunities

- Number of different stimuli used as impetus for continuous improvement efforts

- Use of competitor or benchmark data as stimuli for identifying opportunities for quality improvement

- Scope of continuous improvement efforts includes all departments/functions and all levels of employees

- Existence of a systematic process for making decisions regarding countermeasures designed to correct quality-related problems or process upsets

- Approach to deciding on process improvement strategy is participative and adaptable for use with groups, as well as with individuals

- Approach to process improvement is based upon one or more established models for systematic decision making

- Use of brainstorming or similar technique to generate a variety of alternative actions to consider for improving processes

- Evidence that process analysis is used as a stimulus for process improvement

- Breadth and scope of process improvements initiated via process analysis

- Evidence that benchmarking is used as a stimulus for process improvement

- Breadth and scope of process improvements initiated from benchmarking studies

- Evidence that process research and discovery of alternative technologies have led to process improvements

- Breadth and scope of process improvements that have been initiated based upon research, testing, or the use/discovery of alternative technologies

- Evidence that inputs from internal and external customers has led to changes and improvements in processes

- Breadth and scope of changes and improvements to processes that have been initiated based upon internal or external customer inputs

- Evidence that stretch goals or challenge goals have been used to initiate process improvements

- Breadth and scope of process improvements that have been initiated based upon the setting of challenge goals

---

5.3 PROCESS MANAGEMENT: BUSINESS AND SUPPORT SERVICE PROCESSES

Describe how the company's key business and support service processes are designed and managed so that current requirements are met and that operational performance is continuously improved. (30 points)

Notes:

(1) **Support services are those that support the company's product and/or service delivery but which are not usually designed in detail with the products and services themselves because their requirements do not usually depend a great deal upon product and service characteristics. Support service design requirements usually depend significantly upon internal requirements. Support services might include finance and accounting, software services, sales, marketing, public relations, information services, supplies, personnel, legal services, plant and facilities management, research and development, and secretarial and other administrative services.**

(2)   The purpose of Item 5.3 is to permit applicants to highlight separately the design (5.3a), maintenance (5.3b), and improvement (5.3c) activities for processes that support the product and service design, production, and delivery processes addressed in Items 5.1 and 5.2. The support service processes included in Item 5.3 depend on the applicant's type of business and other factors. Thus, this selection should be made by the applicant. Together, Items 5.1, 5.2, 5.3, and 5.4 should cover all key operations, processes, and activities of all work units.

(3)   Measurement plan [5.3a(2)] is described in Item 5.1, Note (4). Process maintenance (5.3b) is described in Item 5.2, Note (3). Process improvement (5.3c) is described in Item 5.2, Note (4).

AREA TO ADDRESS   [APPROACH, DEPLOYMENT]

5.3a   How key support service processes are designed. Include: (1) how key requirements are determined or set; (2) how these requirements are translated into efficient and effective processes, including operational requirements and an appropriate measurement plan; and (3) how all requirements are addressed early in design by all appropriate company units to ensure integration, coordination, and capability.

What They're Looking For Here

This area to address is similar to Examination Item 5.1, which asks how you design new products and services. This Area to Address asks how you design products and services that are produced by the support functions in your organization. For example, product literature, accounting reports, and training programs are all products that are produced by support departments in companies. Support functions also frequently introduce new services, or change/improve existing services. The procurement function, for example, might introduce a new simplified process for issuing a purchase order.

What the Baldrige Examiners are looking for in this section is that support functions do a thorough job of identifying the requirements of their internal customers. These customer requirements are then used as the driver to revise existing services/products, or design new ones. Your response for this area to address can be very revealing because usually only the companies that are far along on their performance excellence journey design support services based on internal customer requirements.

The first part of this area to address [5.3a(1)] asks how support functions identify the most important requirements for the products and services they provide. Your response should explain that this process begins by having each support function identify all of their internal and/or external customers. Once customers have been identified, explain how requirements are determined for each major product and service area for the support function. It is not expected that your approach will be as formal or systematic as the one you will describe in section 7.1a, but you need at least to define an informal process for determining customer requirements in support areas. Internal customers often want things from support departments that are unreasonable or not possible given resource constraints. For example, an HR function might find out that most managers and supervisors in the company want to get rid of the performance appraisal system—they think it adds no value to the company and takes up valuable time. Does this mean that HR should eliminate the performance appraisal system? Or, to take another example, internal customers might tell the legal department that they want a 48-hour turnaround on documents sent to them for review. Should the legal department automatically figure out a way to meet the 48-hour customer requirement? The answer is *not necessarily* in both cases. You need to explain how you take customer requirements and translate these into reasonable and achievable requirements.

The second part of this area to address [5.3a(2)] asks how you take the requirements you defined in 5.3a(1) and turn them into actual services or products. Your response might include a flow chart or similar graphic that outlines the major steps in this design process. To lend credibility to this process description, you might provide a couple of examples of how this was done in several support areas. The example should explain how customer requirements were determined and how these requirements were met by the design of the new product/service. This area to address also asks how you develop measures to evaluate the extent to which customer requirements are being met.

The third and final portion of this area to address asks about how you get appropriate personnel involved early in the design process where it is easy and inexpensive for them to have input. Waiting until a new system is pilot tested to get user feedback, for example, makes it unlikely that it will be changed other than in minor ways. This approach is often called concurrent engineering or integrated product development. Whatever you call it, it is important that users or customer of services and products of support areas are actively involved in all phases of the design process.

Indicators For Area 5.3a

- A systematic process has been defined that support departments use for identifying their customers, and the requirements of those customers

- Evidence that the process for defining customer requirements is used by *all* support functions in the organization rather than only a few

- Information is presented that explains how conflicting customer requirements are resolved

- A systematic process has been defined for taking customer requirements and using them to design new/enhanced products and services in support functions

- Evidence that the process is actually used by all support functions to design new products and/or services

- Evidence that support functions have an approach for measuring the degree to which customer requirements are being met for the products they produce and the services they provide for internal and/or external customers

- Evidence that measurement plans exit that specify data collection methods, frequencies, and reporting methods

- Standards have been set for each measure based on customer requirements

- Measures of product/service quality in support functions are fed back to appropriate personnel who are empowered to make any necessary changes to improve performance.

- Evidence that customers of support services are involved at all phases in processes used to design new products and services in support areas.

AREA TO ADDRESS   **[APPROACH, DEPLOYMENT]**
5.3b How the company maintains the performance of key support service processes to ensure that such processes meet design requirements. Describe: (1) the key processes, and their principal requirements; and (2) the measurement plan and how measurements are used to maintain process performance.

What They're Looking For Here

Your response for this Area to Address should be a condensed version of your response to Examination Item 5.2. The examiners want to see that you employ the same process for assuring quality in your support departments as you use in the line function of the organization. This is an area in which many organizations receive a very low score. Applying a customer-focused approach in support departments is more difficult and the results obtained are harder to quantify. However, more than half of the personnel and operating costs go to support functions in many of the large companies. This means that a performance improvement effort cannot simply concentrate on the line organization. Similar improvements must also be made in the staff functions.

The first thing that the examiners will look for in your response is your approach. You need to have defined performance indices and standards for each support function based upon internal customer requirements. Not many organizations have done this, so yours will get greater credit if it has. You also need to have process and output measures in place, and a way of feeding back these data to the employees who control the performance measures. While it is probably not necessary that you have actual control plans written, it *is* necessary that you have procedures in place for controlling the key quality variables. In short, your approach to quality assurance of support functions will be judged against the same criteria as those appearing in 5.2a–b.

The second aspect that will be evaluated in your response is your deployment. Make sure that your response explains how and in which support departments/functions you have implemented systems and procedures for assuring quality. In order to receive a high score for this section, you should have fully implemented a quality assurance process in all support/staff functions. Don't state simply that you have "fully implemented a customer-focused approach in all of our support departments." Discuss each department and explain which aspects of TQM, or a customer-focused approach have been implemented. Again, a table or matrix chart listing the support departments vertically along the left side and the features of your quality system horizontally along the top of the chart offers an excellent way to present this information. An example is shown in Figure 10.2.

Obviously, your approach to root cause analysis in support areas should mirror your response to 5.2a. Cause analysis is often done well in the factory, or in the service delivery functions, but forgotten about in the support functions such as finance, HR, facilities, and procurement. Whatever cause-analysis model you use in your primary functions or line organization should also be used in staff or support organizations. Many applicants will be tempted to save valuable space in this section by simply making a brief statement indicating that you use the same approach for cause analysis as you described in 5.2a. While this may be true, you need to convince the examiners that you actually use this model to analyze the causes of problems in support functions.

QUALITY SYSTEM FEATURES					
Support Departments	Definition of Requirements	Process Measurement	Output Measurement	Control Procedures	Problem Solving
Accounting	X				X
Human Resources	X		X	X	X
Engineering		X	X		
Quality	X		X		X
Maintenance	X	X	X	X	X
Sales	X	X	X		
Marketing			X		X
Information Services		X	X	X	X

Figure 10.2: Example of Matrix Chart Showing Deployment of Quality Systems in Support Departments

Indicators For Area 5.3b

- Procedures and mechanisms are in place to control key variables associated with quality

- In-process as well as output measures are used to assess quality in support departments

- A systematic cause-analysis process is used to diagnose the causes of quality problems and process deviations that occur in support departments

- Various alternatives are generated and evaluated prior to the implementation of countermeasures or changes designed to solve problems or improve performance

- Quality assurance procedures and systems have been implemented in all support departments

- Support departments and employees within these departments are evaluated according to how well they satisfy internal customer requirements

- Evidence that employees in support functions have been trained to use cause-analysis process

- Examples or evidence that suggests that cause-analysis process is effective for discerning the root causes of support department problems

---

AREA TO ADDRESS   **[APPROACH, DEPLOYMENT]**

5.3c How processes are evaluated and improved to achieve better operational performance, including cycle time. Describe how each of the following is used or considered: (1) process analysis and research; (2) benchmarking; (3) use of alternative technology; and (4) information from customers of the processes— within and outside the company.

Notes:

   (4)   **"Process analysis and research" [5.3c(1)] refers to a wide range of possible approaches for improving processes. See Item 5.2, Note (5).**

   (5)   **Information from customers [5.3c(4)] might include information developed as described in Items 7.2, 7.3, and 2.3. However, most of the information for improvement [5.3c(4)] is likely to come from "internal customers"—those within the company who use the support services.**

   (6)   **Results of improvements in support services should be reported in Item 6.2.**

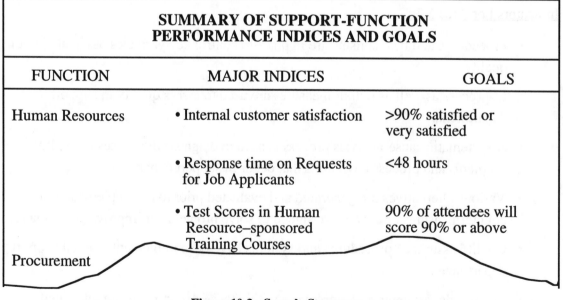

SUMMARY OF SUPPORT-FUNCTION
PERFORMANCE INDICES AND GOALS

FUNCTION	MAJOR INDICES	GOALS
Human Resources	• Internal customer satisfaction	>90% satisfied or very satisfied
	• Response time on Requests for Job Applicants	<48 hours
	• Test Scores in Human Resource–sponsored Training Courses	90% of attendees will score 90% or above
Procurement		

Figure 10.3: Sample Summary

Chart of Support-Function Performance Indices and Goals

What They Are Looking For Here

You should begin your response to this Area to Address by listing the major performance improvement goals that have been developed for each of the major support functions in the organization. You might make a chart like the one shown in Figure 10.3 that depicts support functions, goals, and performance indices.

Following your description of measurement indices and goals for each of the major support functions in your organization, you need to explain how processes are examined and improved. Your response should include an examination of performance data, new technologies, and benchmarking as stimuli that lead to process improvement activities. An example or two will help illustrate how this has occurred in your support areas. Your response should also explain how data on internal customer requirements are used to initiate process improvements in support functions. Many organizations' support functions are currently at work to improve their processes, but few are using customer requirements as the stimulus for these improvement actions. Provide some examples to illustrate how internal customer needs and requirements have driven you to make changes or enhancements in support processes, explaining how performance has improved since the changes were made. Finally, explain how and how often progress on quality improvement projects is reviewed in support departments.

Indicators For Area 5.3c

- Identification of quality indices for all support functions

- Validity of indices

- Existence of goals or standards for each of the quality indices in support functions

- Use of a systematic and participative process to define performance indices and set improvement goals

- Approach for ensuring that continuous improvement occurs in all support departments

- Deployment of continuous improvement activities throughout all locations and all support functions

- Defined systematic process for evaluating and improving performance

- Breadth and scope of efforts during last 12 months to improve performance within support departments

- Systematic and planned approach for reviewing progress of performance improvement efforts in support departments

- Frequency of progress reviews

- Use of process modeling/documentation as a means for identifying opportunities for quality improvement in support functions

- Use of a proactive and reactive approach to identify opportunities for continuous improvement

- Systematic analysis of new and changing technology as a means of identifying opportunities for improvement in support functions

- Evidence that analysis of support processes is used to initiate process improvements

- Breadth and scope of process improvements in support functions initiated via process analysis

- Evidence that benchmarking is used as a stimulus for process improvement in support functions

- Breadth and scope of support process improvements made that were initiated by benchmarking studies

- Evidence that process research, testing, and exploration of alternative technologies have led to improvements in support processes

- Breadth and scope of support process improvements that have been initiated based on input of support function customers—inside and outside of the organization

- Evidence that challenge or "stretch" goals are used to initiate process improvements in support functions

- History and success stories that demonstrate continuous improvement efforts have paid off in various support functions in the organization

- Use of competitor and benchmark data as stimuli for identifying opportunities for quality improvement

- Plans to define internal customer requirements for support functions

- Plans to improve scope or accuracy of data collection and feedback systems in support functions

5.4 MANAGEMENT OF SUPPLIER PERFORMANCE

Describe how the company assures that materials, components, and services furnished by other businesses meet the company's performance requirements. Describe also the company's actions and plans to improve supplier relationships and performance. (30 points)

Note:

(1)   The term "supplier" refers to other-company providers of goods and services. The use of these goods and services may occur at any stage in the production, design, delivery, and use of the company's products and services. Thus, suppliers include businesses such as distributors, dealers, warranty repair services, transportation, contractors, and franchises as well as those that provide materials and components.

If the applicant is a unit of a larger company, and other units of that company supply goods/services, this should be included as part of Item 5.4.

The term "supplier" also refers to service suppliers such as health care, training, and education.

AREA TO ADDRESS   **[APPROACH, DEPLOYMENT]**

5.4a Summary of the company's requirements and how they are communicated to suppliers. Include: (1) a brief summary of the principal requirements for key suppliers, the measures and/or indicators associated with these requirements, and the expected performance levels; (2) how the company determines whether or not its requirements are met by suppliers; and (3) how performance information is fed back to suppliers.

Notes:

(2) **Key suppliers [5.4a(1)] are those that provide the most important products and/or services, taking into account the criticality and volume of products and/or services involved.**

(3) **"Requirements" refers to the principal factors involved in the purchases: quality, delivery, and price.**

(4) **How requirements are communicated and how performance information is fed back might entail ongoing working relationships or partnerships with key suppliers. Such relationships and/or partnerships should be briefly described in responses.**

(5) **Processes for determining whether or not requirements are met [5.4a(2)] might include audits, process reviews, receiving inspection, certification, testing, and rating systems.**

<u>What They're Looking For Here</u>

Begin this section with an explanation of your approach to determining performance requirements for goods and services you receive from key suppliers. Many large organizations use hundreds or even thousands of suppliers. If this is true of your company, you may want to identify who your most critical 10 to 50 suppliers are, and discuss your efforts with them rather than trying to include all of them. Once you've identified your key or critical suppliers, list the critical quality requirements for perhaps the top 10 or so. One way of doing this might be by means of a table or chart. Next, list the critical measures or indicators you use to monitor and evaluate supplier performance. All of this information could be neatly summarized in a chart like the one shown in Figure 10.4.

Make sure that your response also includes a clear explanation of how you communicate quality indicators and requirements to suppliers. You should also have mechanisms in place to provide regular feedback to key suppliers on how they do in meeting

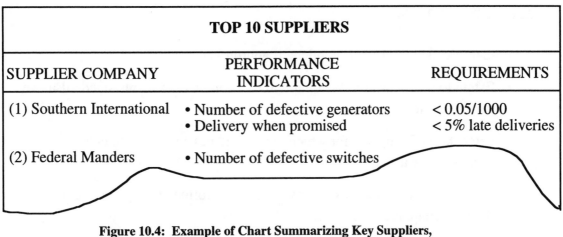

**Figure 10.4: Example of Chart Summarizing Key Suppliers,
Performance Indicators, and Performance Requirements**

performance requirements. This means that you need to have a thorough approach in place for measuring supplier quality.

It is important that you have a well-defined and successful approach for ensuring that your suppliers meet your performance standards. All organizations have suppliers, but in some they play a more important role than in others. For instance, a manufacturing company may buy all of the components for the products it produces from outside suppliers. Hence, supplier performance is critical to the quality of the final products. A service business such as a bank may have relatively few suppliers who perform non-critical services or sell supplies to the bank. The effort your organization puts into ensuring quality from its suppliers should be directly proportional to the degree to which you rely on suppliers for your success.

Begin your response for this area with a general description of the approach you use to assure performance excellence. Explain how you determine your requirements for the goods and services provided by suppliers, and how you communicate these to suppliers. Next, explain how you monitor supplier performance and feed back the data to them so that they may correct existing problems and/or prevent future ones. If you use an audit or periodic assessment, describe how it is conducted, how often it is done, etc.

As in many of the other areas, using a chart or table is a good way to summarize the information. Rather than listing each supply company, you might group them according to the type of products or services you buy from them. Using a matrix, indicate which quality assurance strategies you employ with each group of suppliers. It doesn't matter whether you use certification, testing, audits, or another approach. What matters is that your approach is effective for your organization and suppliers, and is multifaceted. In other words, it should include more than just one strategy/approach.

Indicators For Area 5.4a

- Identification of critical suppliers, if appropriate

- Extent to which measurable quality indices and requirements/standards have been identified for suppliers

- Percentage of suppliers for which quality indices and requirements/standards have been identified

- Degree to which suppliers are involved in the formulation of indices and standards/requirements

- Existence of an effective system for communicating standards/requirements to suppliers

- Feedback system for keeping key suppliers informed on a regular basis of their performance on key quality indicators

- Amount of effort devoted to assurance of supplier performance is appropriately geared to the degree to which organization relies on suppliers

- Use of a multifaceted approach to assure supplier performance

- Organization's requirements have been defined and clearly communicated to suppliers

- Systems exist for measuring supplier performance on a regular basis and for feeding back the data to suppliers to help them improve their performance

- Objectivity and reliability of measures of supplier performance

- Procedures are in place for periodically auditing or assessing supplier processes, products, and services

---

AREA TO ADDRESS   **[APPROACH, DEPLOYMENT]**

5.4b How the company evaluates and improves its management of supplier relationships and performance. Describe current actions and plans: (1) to improve suppliers' abilities to meet requirements; (2) to improve the company's own procurement processes, including feedback sought from suppliers and from other units within the company ("internal customers") and how such feedback is used; and (3) to minimize costs associated with inspection, test, audit, or other approaches used to verify supplier performance.

Notes:

    (6)   **"Actions and plans" (5.4b) might include one or more of the following: joint planning, rapid information and data exchanges, use of benchmarking and comparative information, customer-supplier teams, partnerships, training, long-term agreements, incentives, and recognition. Actions and plans might also include changes in supplier selection, leading to a reduction in the number of suppliers.**

    (7)   **Efforts to minimize costs might be backed by analyses comparing suppliers based on overall cost, taking into account quality and delivery. Analyses might also address transaction costs associated with alternative approaches to supply management.**

<u>What They're Looking For Here</u>

In this area to address you need to report what you, as the buyer of the goods and services, are doing to improve your own performance in the procurement area. Suppliers always tend to get the blame when things go wrong. Often, it is the buyer who is at fault for failing to communicate requirements to suppliers, or for failing to keep them abreast of changes that will impact their products or services.

In describing how you evaluate your procurement function, the ideal situation would be to get feedback from two sources:

- Internal customers who use procurement to get them the goods and services they need to do their jobs

- External suppliers who must interact with procurement to do business with your company

Procurement functions in many companies seem to forget that their role is to help others in the company obtain the materials and services they need from outside suppliers in a cost-efficient and timely fashion. Procurement people often see themselves as more of a policing function to prevent managers in the company from selecting suppliers that are their friends, or from selecting those suppliers that take them out to lunch and provide them with tickets to sporting events every year. Part of procurement's role is to serve this policing function and to be aware of unethical practices. However, their primary role is to serve the needs of the managers in the organization that need to buy goods and services from outside suppliers. Procurement people also tend to be obsessed with making sure that all the correct forms are filled out and all the appropriate procedures are followed. If you got your parts late because the P.O. didn't go out on time, it was probably your fault because you didn't fill out a few of the lines on the Request for Purchase Order Form.

Ideally, procurement should seek regular feedback from employees who use their services. In the ideal situation, a number of different methods would be used to seek feedback from internal customers of procurement. Telephone surveys, face-to-face meetings, service pacts or contracts, mail surveys, and other methods might be used to stay in touch with procurement's internal customers' needs. Summarize what you do to obtain feedback from internal customers of procurement in your company. A table or chart like the one shown below might be an efficient way of summarizing this information.

SUMMARY OF CUSTOMER SATISFACTION MEASURES—PROCUREMENT

CUSTOMER GROUP	METHODOLOGY	FREQUENCY	SAMPLE
Senior Executives	Face-to-Face Meetings	Biannually	All
Function Directors	Telephone Survey	Quarterly	50%
2nd & 3rd Level Mgrs.	Mail Survey	Quarterly	20%
2nd & 3rd Level Mgrs.	Focus Group	Biannually	8 Mgrs.

If you choose to use a chart or table like this to summarize how you collect feedback from procurement's internal customers, you need to supplement this with some explanation. Briefly explain why you decided to use the approaches you use, and describe how the satisfaction measures seem to work.

After explaining how you gather internal customer satisfaction data on procurement, you need to explain how you get feedback from suppliers. What is being asked here is not how you rate them, but how they rate you. What kind of a company are you to deal with compared to other companies they sell to? Questions like this can be very revealing. Companies I've worked with often seem to blame the supplier when things go wrong. Being a supplier to big corporations myself, it sometimes seems like the only reason they hire a consultant is to have someone to blame when things go wrong.

Your response for this Area to Address should explain how you get feedback from your suppliers on how they rate you. Again, you might want to use a chart or table to summarize the various methods you use to obtain feedback. Of course, this will only be appropriate if you use multiple methods. Make sure you explain how many of your total suppliers are contacted, how you decide who gets contacted, and what types of questions get asked. You obviously don't have enough room to include your surveys, but you can describe how many questions are asked and what types of scales are used. In addition to surveys and devices to seek supplier opinions, you may also collect "hard" data on indicators such as the number of suppliers that have refused to deal with your company because of bad experiences, or the average seniority of suppliers. If you've been dealing with the same suppliers for 20 years, both of you must be pretty happy with each other.

The Examiners are also looking for evidence that you have established solid, cooperative relationships with your suppliers. This can be done in a number of different ways. For example, some organizations develop long-term relationships with suppliers who are able to consistently demonstrate that they meet or exceed requirements. Others work together to set goals and develop plans and strategies for reaching the goals.

Your response for this Area to Address should describe all the major efforts you have underway or have planned that will improve your relationship with your suppliers. List those activities and approaches you have employed over the past several years. Discuss joint activities such as training programs and meetings in which employees from your company and from suppliers' organizations have both participated. Describe any incentives or awards you offer to suppliers based upon their performance. Some organizations give out awards each year to suppliers who demonstrate exemplary performance.

Another important factor to address in your response to this section is the methods you have employed to improve supplier selection.

Indicators For Area 5.4b

- Number of different sources of data on levels of internal customers' satisfaction with procurement

- Extent to which all users of procurement services are queried as to their satisfaction levels

- Frequency with which internal customer satisfaction is measured regarding procurement

- Reliability and validity of instruments and methods used to gather data on levels of internal customer satisfaction with the procurement function

- Number of different sources of data used to assess suppliers' levels of satisfaction in dealing with your company

- Extent to which all suppliers' feedback is sought

- Use of valid and reliable methods to gather data on supplier satisfaction ratings

- Frequency with which supplier feedback is obtained

- Use of hard data such as loss of key suppliers to supplement opinion data gathered from surveys or interviews

- Evidence that a cooperative relationship exists between applicant's organization and its suppliers

- Joint performance improvement activities are performed by applicant's and suppliers' employees (e.g., training, planning meetings, etc.)

- Selection criteria for suppliers indicates that quality is just as important as price and other factors

- Evidence to suggest that suppliers are selected based upon quality and performance, and not just price

- Existence of incentives to encourage suppliers to improve their performance

- Awards or recognition programs to reward suppliers for exemplary performance

- Use of long-term partnerships or contracts with suppliers who consistently demonstrate that they can meet or exceed organization's requirements

- Evidence that inspections of supplier goods have been eliminated or reduced, based on demonstrated good performance

Chapter 11

_____

Interpreting the Criteria for Business Results (6.0)

OVERVIEW OF THE BUSINESS RESULTS CATEGORY

This sixth category, Business Results, is one where organizations are really put to the test. The previous five categories concentrate on processes and activities. A good writer may even make your approach and processes seem like they meet all the criteria in the first five categories, but this section (6.0) and the next one (7.0 Customer Focus and Satisfaction) tell the true tale of the success (or lack thereof) of your performance improvement efforts. In this section, you must provide evidence that all of the processes and programs you employ have really worked to improve quality and overall performance in your organization.

The Baldrige Award Criteria define this category as follows:

> The **Business Results** Category examines the company's performance and improvement in key business areas—product and service quality, productivity and operational effectiveness, supply quality, and financial performance indicators linked to these areas. Also examined are performance levels relative to competitors. (p. 19)

It is important that you understand the difference between what is being asked for in this section and what is asked for in the section that covers Customer Focus and Satisfaction (7.0). Figure 11.1 depicts a systems diagram of an organization. All organizations have inputs, processes, and outputs. Outputs don't have to be products. In a service business, an output is usually an accomplishment such as a transported passenger, a repaired car, a delivered package, or a meal served. Outputs are received by customers, who then provide information (inputs) on their level of satisfaction with the product or service.

As you can see from Figure 11.1, measurement occurs at four different points:

- Measurement of inputs
- In-process measurement
- Measurement of outputs
- Measurement of customer satisfaction

The business results asked for in this section of your application pertain to only the *first three* types of measures. Data on customer satisfaction should be discussed in your response to Category 7.0.

Again we begin with a description of the first Examination Item and Area to Address falling under category 6.0, Business Results. Subsequent Examination Items are

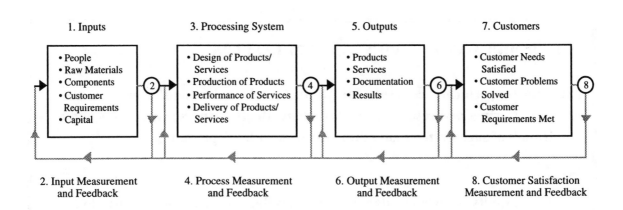

Figure 11.1: Macro Process Model of an Organization

contained in a double-ruled box together with the point value and any applicable Notes[*]. Areas to Address falling under that Item follow in a single-ruled box. In the upper right corner of each Area to Address box is an indication [brackets] of whether the Area pertains to approach, deployment, or results. All definitions and information appearing within these boxes is taken directly from the Baldrige criteria. Following each Area to Address is an explanation defining what the examiners are looking for in assessing your application. Next, I have supplied a list of indicators or evaluation factors that will assist you in interpreting the criteria and in preparing your application.

---

[*] Item Notes that apply to a specific Area to Address are appropriately listed in the box containing that Area.

6.1 PRODUCT AND SERVICE QUALITY RESULTS

Summarize performance results for products and services and/or product and service offerings and results of improvement efforts, using key measures and/or indicators of such performance and improvement. (75 points)

Notes:

(1) **Results reported in Item 6.1 should reflect performance relative to key non-price product and service requirements—those described in the Business Overview and addressed in Items 7.1, 3.1, and 5.1. The measures and/or indicators should address factors that affect customer preference—performance, timeliness, availability, and variety. Examples include defect levels, repeat services, delivery response times, and complaint levels.**

(2) **Data appropriate for inclusion might be based upon one or more of the following:**

- **internal (company) measurements;**
- **field performance;**
- **data collected by the company or on behalf of the company through follow-ups (7.2c) or surveys of customers on product and service performance; and**
- **data collected or generated by organizations, including customers.**

Although data appropriate for inclusion are primarily based upon internal measurements and field performance, data collected by the company or other organizations through follow-ups might be included for attributes that cannot be accurately assessed through direct measurement (e.g., ease of use) or when variability in customer expectations makes the customer's perception the most meaningful indicator (e.g., courtesy).

(3) **Comparative data might include industry best, best competitor, industry average, and appropriate benchmarks. Such data might be derived from independent surveys, studies, laboratory testing, or other sources.**

AREA TO ADDRESS   **[RESULTS]**

6.1a Current levels and trends in key measures and/or indicators of quality of products and services and/or product and service offerings. Graphs and tables should include appropriate comparative data.

What They're Looking For Here

In this extremely important area, the examiners are looking for a summary of your major product/service quality results over the past several years. In general, the more data you have, the better. If you have ten years' worth of historical quality data, this is good. If you don't have such data, present the data you do have. You should, however, have at least three years' worth of data. An important consideration in evaluating your response to this area is the completeness of your data. In a sample application used to train Baldrige Examiners, a bank claims to collect data for 160 different indices of quality. Yet in this section, it presents data for only three or four indices. This might lead the Examiners to think that it selected only those indices that put its performance in a good light, while deliberately ignoring the other 150+ measures that may have indicated declining quality.

While there is not space to include 160 graphs in this section, it is important to provide a summary of data for all major quality indices. A good way of doing this would be to include graphs of data for four to six major measures of quality, and then summarize the remaining statistics in a table such as the one that follows.

SUMMARY OF QUALITY DATA ABC ACCOUNTING, INC., 1990-1994					
Index	1990	1991	1992	1993	1994
% Repeat Business	18%	23%	28%	36%	44%
# of Report Drafts	3.8	3.3	2.5	2.3	1.6
% of Rewrite Time	28%	29%	22%	18%	14%
Number of Points/Audit	127	116	88	72	57
Number of Errors per Page	3.4	3.0	2.5	0.96	0.62

Obviously, you would present more data for more indices than the five included in this example. By using such a table, though, you can include a great deal of information in a limited amount of space. You might even add a "Percent Improvement" column at the far right that lists the improvement percentage over the time period measured (e.g., 26% improvement in repeat business between 1990 and 1994). Using this format, you could present data for 20–30 different indices on a single page of your application.

Graphs and graphics can be used to illustrate information, but be careful how they are drawn. In attempts to save space, some applicants have included four or five different data lines in a single line graph. This makes the graph confusing and very difficult to read. Never include more than two lines of data on a single graph. Another good rule to follow is to always include a goal or standard line on a graph, like the one shown in Figure 11.2 below. Without a goal or standard on the graph, it is very difficult to evaluate performance.

Although there are many different types of graphs that can be used to present data, it is best to use either line or bar graphs. Place a time scale on the horizontal axis and some measure of quality performance on the vertical axis. Be sure to adjust the performance scale of your graph to depict the maximum amount of improvement. For example, if performance has improved from 82% to 94% over the last four years, the scale should be between 80% and 100% to best show the improvement.

Another common problem to avoid in this section is not adequately explaining your graphs and figures. Explain in the text what the graph depicts and the significance of the results shown. For example: "Figure 6.4 depicts the total number of rejects per thousand in product line A over the last five years. As you can see, rejects have fallen from a high of 73 per thousand to a low of 21 per thousand in 1994." Be careful not to go overboard, as some applicants have done, and describe every piece of data in the graph, point by point, year by year. This is redundant and wastes valuable space in the application. (Further details on preparing graphics appear in Chapter 3).

If you are presenting data for 25 or more different indices of performance in your organization, there are bound to be some adverse trends or anomalies that may make the organization look bad in certain areas. Indeed, if the data reveal *no* adverse trends, their credibility might be questioned. It is not expected that all trends will be consistently positive. It is expected, however, that *most* of your performance data will show positive trends. When a drop in performance has occurred, you are expected to provide an explanation. It is best if only drops caused by factors outside your control, such as the economy, the environment, regulations, etc., have occurred.

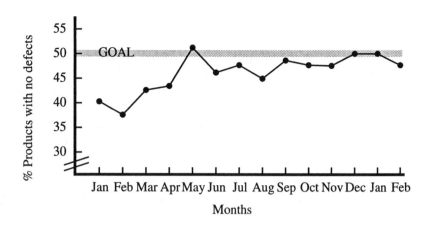

Figure 11.2: Graph with Goal Depicted

You will be judged in this section on whether you address all adverse trends and anomalies in the data presented for section 6.1a. Furthermore, you will be evaluated on the credibility of your explanations. It is easy to rationalize poor performance as being due to factors lying outside your control. However, the Baldrige Examiners will be looking for strong evidence that your explanations are valid and are not just rationalizations.

The number and credibility of data sources you have for comparing your performance results to competitors are important in your response to this Area to Address. The biggest and perhaps most common mistake applicants make in this section is the failure to be specific enough. A typical response for this area is as follows:

> *We use a variety of different sources of data to compare ourselves to our competitors. Market research reports by independent marketing companies, industry reports from professional associations, and our own intelligence gathered by our employees are among the many sources of competitive data.*

A response such as this will earn you very few points in this area because it lacks details and, therefore, credibility. The more specific your response is, the more convincing it is. One applicant who received a very high score for this area began with a statement or two similar to the example above, but followed it with a detailed table in which the various sources of competitive data were listed. An example of such a chart is as follows.

SOURCES AND TYPES OF COMPETITOR DATA Arons Oil Company			
Information Provided	Frequency	Source	Methodology
Quality Data – # Defects 4 major customers	Monthly	Exxon	Laboratory Samples
Market Share Data	Annually	Nat. Petrochemical Association	Survey

A chart such as this shows the examiners the types of data you collect, the objectivity of the data (based upon who collects it), and the number of different sources of information you have on competitors. You might also include a column in your chart that explains how the data are used. For example, the market share data from the National Petroleum Association might be used for goal setting in your planning sessions.

A good way to excel in this Area to Address is to demonstrate that you provide higher quality products and/or services than any of your competitors—locally, nationally, and internationally. In your response, you should provide data on a number of different measurement dimensions to indicate that you are better than all competitors. What many applicants do is provide their own comparisons to results of a few competitors. They pick only those competitors that show a poorer performance than their own companies. Other applicants explain that they are in a very poorly defined market and that it is therefore impossible to gather competitive data for comparison purposes. Being a small company or being in a new field are certainly valid reasons why competitive data are more difficult to gather, but these reasons do not serve as an excuse for having none. Company size and access to competitive data are both taken into consideration in evaluating your application. The complete absence of competitive data, however, makes it virtually impossible to assess your own quality results to determine just how good or impressive they may be.

Remember that this section should address how your quality results compare with those of your competitors. You should *not* provide statistical comparisons on market share, size, number of employees, profits, growth, etc. In order to earn a high score for this area, you will need to provide numerous comparisons of your organization's *quality performance* against a number of your biggest competitors. By comparing yourself to world-class leaders in your field, you give your response additional credibility. Although your organization does not have to be the best in all areas, you should rank highest in most of the performance measures.

You should present additional data here on how actual results compare with your goals on all important quality indices. Explain whether you are ahead of your goals, behind them, or on target. A table or chart is a good way of summarizing this information, even if some of it was presented in section 6.1. A sample format you could use for your summary table follows.

COMPARISON OF QUALITY RESULTS TO GOALS				
Index	Current Performance	Goal	Difference	Comments
% Comebacks	14%	10%	4% below goal	Showing steady progress
% Correct Diagnoses	92%	90%	2% above goal	
% Jobs Done on Time	94%	98%	4% below goal	10% better than last year

The applicant who prepared the chart in this example has not done especially well in relation to the three quality goals listed, but the format for presentation of the information is good. The examiners will look not only at the extent to which you have met or exceeded each of your quality goals, but also at the level of difficulty of your goals in relation to past performance. For example, if last year you met your deadlines for delivery of customer orders 78% of the time, and this year you met these deadlines 95% of the time, you would get credit for the amount of improvement shown, even if you didn't make your goal of 98% on-time orders.

This section of your application is assessed on the completeness of your data and the degree to which you meet or exceed your goals on each index. If you have 56 quality measures and present data for only 15 of them, you won't receive a very high score. This is not to say that you must present data for all 56 indices. You may choose to present data for only the most critical of the measures. Similarly, if you present data for all 56 indices but have met your goals on only 12 of them, you won't receive a very high score. Finally, make sure that you adequately explain any conditions or situations where you fell significantly short of your goals. Saying that the goal wasn't realistic in the first place is a frequent disclaimer that must be avoided in offering your explanation. Make sure that you explain all adverse trends or failures to meet goals, and that your explanations are both clear and credible.

Indicators For Area 6.1a

- Number of different quality indices for which data are presented

- Data are presented for all important quality indices, not just a few

- Number of years' worth of historical data presented to show trends

- Degree to which all indices show continuous and steady improvement

- Clarity of graphs included in this section

- Amount of variability in performance.

- Clarity of explanations of quality results

- Measures include inputs, processes, and outputs (the scope should not be limited to outputs alone)

- Number of adverse trends or anomalies noted in quality data

- Credibility and clarity of explanations for anomalies or adverse trends

- Evidence that when adverse trends are the fault of the organization, the situations causing the problems have been thoroughly investigated and corrected (this should be indicated by level of performance following the adverse trend)

- Use of outside sources of data on competitors

- Use of reliable and appropriate sources to gather data on competitors

- Use of ethical and fair methods of gathering data on competitors

- Number of different sources of competitor data

- Number of different aspects of the business that are compared to competitors

- Amount of competitor data relating specifically to quality as against financial or market standing

- How applicant's quality results compare with major competitors

- How much better the applicant's quality results are than those of major competitors

- How applicant's quality results compare to world-class leaders in the field

- Number of different quality indices on which comparisons are made with competitors

- Length of time applicant's quality results have been superior to competitors'

- Percentage of total quality indices (for which data are presented) that relates to leadership goals, objectives, or standards

- Percentage of indices for which performance meets or exceeds goals

- Degree to which performance exceeds goals

- Level of difficulty of goals compared with past performance—how challenging are goals?

- Importance of indices for which performance meets or exceeds goals relative to importance of indices for which performance goals have not been met

---

6.2 COMPANY OPERATIONAL AND FINANCIAL RESULTS

Summarize results of the company's operational and financial performance and performance improvement efforts using key measures and/or indicators of such performance and improvement. (110 points)

Notes:
(1)   Key measures and/or indicators of company operational and financial performance include the following areas:

- **productivity and other indicators of effective use of manpower, materials, energy, capital, and assets. (Aggregate measures such as total factor productivity, ROI, margin rates, operating profit rates, and working capital productivity are encouraged. Aggregate economic and/or market value measures are also appropriate.);**

- **company-specific indicators such as innovation rates, innovation effectiveness, cost reductions through innovation, and time to market;**

- **environmental improvements reflected in emissions levels, waste stream reductions, by-product use and recycling, etc. (See Item 1.3);**

- **cycle time, lead times, set-up times, and other responsiveness indicators; and**

- **process assessment results such as customer assessment or third-party assessment (such as ISO 9000).**

> **(2)   Comparative data might include industry best, best competitor, industry average, and appropriate benchmarks.**

AREA TO ADDRESS   [RESULTS]
6.2a Current levels and trends in key measures and/or indicators of company operational and financial performance. Graphs and tables should include appropriate comparative data.

<u>What They're Looking For Here</u>

The results you present in this section of your application should correspond to the indices that you stated you measure in section 2.1, and the measures on which you set goals as described in section 3.2. What is considered important about your response to this Item is the scope and breadth of the data you present. You should present data for a variety of operational and financial measures. The key here is to select and present data for those measures that reflect *overall company performance*. An error that Baldrige applicants could make in this section (judging from errors made in similar sections in the past) is to present graphs showing only those indices that signal an improving trend. When Examiners see this they tend to wonder what performance looks like on the other indices for which there are no graphs. When the criteria refer to "operational results," they are not asking about quality data. Operational measures typically fall into three categories:

- Productivity
- Timeliness
- Quantity

Keep in mind that Examination Item 6.2 is a catchall category where you would report a wide variety of results. Results that used to be asked for in Categories 1.0 and 4.0 are now to be reported in 6.2. Along with financial and operational results, some of the major types of data that might be presented in this section are:

- Ethics measures
- Environmental performance
- Public health/safety results
- Corporate responsibility results

Read over the example indices listed in the criteria for types of indices that should be taken into account. A study that was done by the U.S. General Accounting Office in 1991 on the impact of using the Baldrige criteria to improve organizational performance lists eight operating indices used to evaluate past Baldrige finalists:

- Reliability
- Order processing time
- Product lead time
- Costs of quality
- Timeliness of delivery
- Errors or defects
- Inventory turnover
- Cost savings

The only one of these indices that doesn't fit into a response for Item 6.2 is "Errors or defects." Data on product/service errors or defects are reported in 6.1. The other seven indices are all appropriate, however. I am not suggesting that you need to present data on these indices, only that these should be considered in determining what is appropriate for your company.

Another type of data that should be presented in this section is data on measures that are unique to your industry or your organization. These should be indices by which the company measures itself. Unique measures of customer satisfaction are reported on in section 7.0, not here.

The criteria in this Examination Item also ask for financial data. Financial measures may include some of the following:

- Sales
- Operating expenses
- Return on sales
- Profits
- Return on assets
- Sales per employee

Overall trends in your financial performance over the last five years or so will be examined to determine the degree of improvement and the extent to which improvements have been maintained. Something the examiners will specifically look for is return on investment (ROI) data from your efforts to implement and other performance excellence techniques. Many large companies have literally spent millions of dollars on activities relating to implementation of total quality. You should present data in this section that demonstrate the financial benefits that have resulted from your investment in change initiatives. Part of these data might be all of the financial benefits that can be attributed to the hundreds of individual team projects that have been completed over the last few years. Other financial benefits may have resulted from any macro-level changes implemented. However you present ROI data, the examiners will be interested in the overall level of ROI, as well as the level of confidence in any claim you make about a change initiative like re-engineering or TQM being the key variable responsible for the improvements. It could be that many other variables impacted financial results. For this reason, it is important that you show before-and-after data to help demonstrate that TQ has had a major positive impact on financial measures in your company.

In order to determine how significant or insignificant your results are, you need to present data on competitors and industry averages. What is important about your response to this Area to Address is the extent to which several different comparative statistics are presented for each of the indices presented in 6.2a. A good way of presenting these data is to prepare a chart that lists the various performance indices along the left, and performance of your company and several others in the remainder of the chart. A portion of an example of such a chart is shown below.

Comparison of Operational Results					
Measures	Our Company	Competitor A	Competitor B	Industry Best	Benchmark
Order Processing Time	8 days	14 days	11 days	6 days	3 days
Sales per Employee	$140,000 per employee	$113,000 per employee	$110,000 per employee	$150,000 per employee	N/A
% On-Time Delivery	96%	95%	88%	98%	N/A
Profit (% of total income)	18%	12%	8.4%	20%	N/A

Another way of presenting these data is to present graphs showing trends over the last three to five years in your performance as compared with competitors and others. The problem with using a matrix like the one shown above is that only one year's worth of data is presented. The examiners are interested in how your overall levels of results compare with competitors', but they are also interested in how your *trends* compare with others. If other companies have improved at about the same rate as you have, your positive trends will not be nearly as impressive. The sources of your data on competitors and other companies will also be questioned, so make sure that you explain where these data come from.

Obviously, what is important for this Area to Address is that your levels of performance are better than your major competitors', and, in the best-case scenario, than industry leaders' and other benchmarks you use for improvement planning.

Indicators For Area 6.2a

- Scope and breadth of indices for which operational and financial data are presented

- Correspondence between measures identified in 2.1 and data presented in 6.2

- Extent to which positive trends are demonstrated in productivity, waste, cycle time, and other key operational measures

- Presentation of enough data to establish trends (typically three to five years)

- Amount of improvement occurring over the last three to five years for key indices

- Extent to which indices are appropriate measures of overall company performance

- Presentation of data on key financial performance measures

- Levels and trends in measures of environmental performance

- Levels and trends in measures of employee satisfaction

- Presentation of financial data shows consistently improving trends over the last three to five years

- Levels of financial performance have significantly improved over the last three to five years

- Consistency of trends across all different financial indices for which data are presented

- Percentage of indices for which competitor and industry-leader results data are presented

- Competitors are the companies against which the applicant most often competes

- Credibility of sources for competitor data and benchmark data

- Extent to which data are presented for major competitors, industry leaders, and benchmarks

- Extent to which current levels of performance by the applicant are better than all major competitors, industry leaders, and benchmarks

- Extent to which positive trends exhibited by applicant are significantly better than trends in competitor data

- Length of time (number of years) during which applicant's performance on financial and operational measures is superior to the competition

6.3 HUMAN RESOURCE RESULTS

Summarize human resource results, including employee development and indicators of employee well-being and satisfaction. (35 points)

Notes:

(1)   Measures and/or indicators should include safety, absenteeism, turnover, and satisfaction. Comparative data might include industry best, best competitors, industry average, and appropriate benchmarks. Local or regional data on absenteeism and turnover are also appropriate. Financial measures such as worker compensation cost or turnover cost reductions are appropriate for inclusion.

(2)   Measures and/or indicators of development should cover not only extent (for example, percent of employees trained or hours of training per year) but also effectiveness. Financial information such as benefit cost ratios for training is appropriate for inclusion.

(3)   Examples of satisfaction factors are given in Item 4.4, Note (2).

(4)   The results reported in Item 6.3 derive from activities described in the Items of Category 4.0. Results should address all categories and types of employees.

AREAS TO ADDRESS   **[RESULTS]**

6.3a Current levels and trends in key measures and/or indicators of employee development, well-being, satisfaction, self-directed responsibility, and effectiveness. Graphs and tables should include appropriate comparative data.

What They're Looking For Here

This section asks for quantitative data that illustrates the effectiveness of all the human resource (HR) development processes you discussed in sections 4.2, 4.3, and 4.4. As with any of the other sections that ask for results, levels of performance are the most important dimension of performance, and levels can only be assessed against relevant competitor and comparative statistics. All graphs or data should include comparative data of some sort, so that your own level of performance can be appropriately judged. Performance data relating to item 4.2, High Performance Work Systems, might include measures such as:

- Percentage of workforce who have been trained to perform more than one job

- Reductions in levels of management over the years

- Spending authority levels of various categories of employees (empowerment)

- Employee opinion data on empowerment

- Percentage of the workforce whose jobs have been re-designed

- Percentage of employees who are on incentive compensation

- Percentage of employees who receive recognition

- Number of suggestions received per employee and acceptance rate.

This item also asks for data relating to 4.3, which asks about employee training and development. Measures of training activity or volume might be presented here, such as average hours of training per employee per year, or percentage of payroll dollars spent on training over the years. Even more important are measures of the effectiveness of training. Effectiveness measures might include employee reaction data gathered via end-of-course surveys, pretest and posttest scores, behavior change measures for particular courses, and data on how training has impacted bottom-line results, such as sales or product/service quality. As with the other types of data, levels and trends are what Examiners will assess, so make sure that graphs include data presented over multiple years, and that comparative data are included on all graphs. Data on benchmark companies from outside of your industry is also appropriate to include on any graph; particularly if your own performance is at or above benchmark levels.

This section should also include safety data that is both process and output based. For example, you might report safety audit scores, near misses, or data on other preventive measures, along with the typical output measures like worker compensation costs, number of lost-time accidents, days of work lost due to safety incidents, etc. Data on employee well-being factors should be included in this section. Employee climate or morale survey data over a multiple year period are important to present, along with relevant comparative or benchmark data. Many companies use the Mayflower group to track employee satisfaction, because they have a broad data base with which they can compare their own performance to other companies. Other measures of employee satisfaction and well-being should also be presented here. Measures like turnover, requests for transfers, complaints, grievances, stress-related illness, average hours worked per week/overtime, and absenteeism are generic measures that should at least be considered. Keep in mind, that without comparative statistics, your own level of performance will be difficult to judge. For example, one company reported that they had maintained less than 5% turnover for over five years, which sounds great, until you realize that they are in a town where they are just about the only employer.

Your performance will be evaluated on this item based on how your results demonstrate consistently improving trends over multiple years, and/or levels of performance that are consistently above industry averages, major competitors, and even benchmark levels in some cases.

Indicators For Area 6.3a

- Number of different HR measures for which results are presented

- Levels of performance compared to industry averages, major competitors, and benchmark organizations

- Objectivity/reliability of data

- Credibility of sources of competitor and benchmark data

- Evidence of continuous improvement in most or all key measures of HR performance

- Relation of HR performance measures for which results are presented to the company's key business drivers

- Results indicate that the company invests major resources (time, money, equipment) to ensure that employees are properly trained and motivated

- Results indicate a balance between focus on the needs of employees as well as shareholders and customers

- All measures indicate that the company would be considered a good place to work

- Safety performance is significantly better than industry averages, and has consistently improved over the last few years

- Results show that performance system changes like job re-design, teams, suggestion systems, compensation, recognition, and other approaches actually lead to improvements in financial and operational performance, or have positive impact on important measures on the company's performance metrics

- Measures of HR process focus more on effectiveness than activity measures like hours of training or percentage of employee on teams.

6.4 SUPPLIER PERFORMANCE RESULTS

Summarize results of supplier performance and performance improvement efforts using key measures and/or indicators of such performance and improvement. (30 points)

Notes:

   (1)   **The results reported in Item 6.4 derive from activities described in Item 5.4. Results should be broken out by key supplies and/or key suppliers, as appropriate. Results should include performance of supply chains and/or results of outsourcing, if these are important to the applicant. Data should be presented using the measures and/or indicators described in 5.4a(1).**

   (2)   **Results reported should be relative to all principal requirements: quality, delivery, and price. If the company's supplier management efforts include factors such as building supplier partnerships or reducing the number of suppliers, data related to these efforts should be included in responses.**

   (3)   **Comparative data might be of several types: industry best, best competitor(s), industry average, and appropriate benchmarks.**

AREA TO ADDRESS   **[RESULTS]**
6.4a Current levels and trends in key measures and/or indicators of supplier performance. Graphs and tables should include appropriate comparative data.

<u>What They're Looking For Here</u>

Once again the word "trends" appears in the criteria statement. This should tell you that they want graphs and statistics, not just words. Often, applicants formulate a written response to this area by simply explaining how suppliers' performance has improved due to the applicant's efforts. Without supportive data, however, they end up with a very low score in this area—regardless of how well written the description may be.

The examiners want to see evidence that key measures of supplier performance have improved over the last few years. If you have over 500 suppliers, obviously you don't have room to present data on every one of them. What you might do is select the two or three that you conduct the most business with, and present graphs on their performance trends. You could then summarize results for other suppliers in a table or chart similar to the one which follows.

SUPPLIER QUALITY DATA					
Company	Measure	1988	1989	1990	1991
Canon	Photocopiers Uptime	82%	78%	88%	94%
Cleansweeps Janitorial	Cleanliness Ratings	3.4/5	3.7/5	4.3/5	4.6/5
ABC Office Supplies	% On-time Deliveries	82%	88%	90%	90%

Your response for this area will be evaluated both on the amount of supplier data you present and the degree to which supplier performance shows a trend of continuous improvement. Where there have been drops in supplier results, you will be expected to provide explanations.

You also need to explain how your suppliers' performance compares to that of your competitors' suppliers, and/or to benchmark organizations. Begin your response for this section by explaining the bases for your comparisons. You should address such questions as:

- How are competitors selected for comparison?
- How are suppliers for which comparative data are presented selected?
- How are benchmark organizations selected for examining supplier performance?

After explaining how you select supplier data from competitors and benchmark organizations, you should present the comparative data. As in the other sections, it is a good idea to present supplier data using graphs. Your response will be judged according to the amount of data you present and the level of quality your suppliers achieve in relation to competitors' suppliers.

Indicators For Area 6.4a

- Percentage of suppliers for which performance data are presented

- Trend showing continual improvement in supplier performance over the last several years

- Overall levels of supplier performance are high

- Percentage of suppliers showing trend toward improved quality

- Evidence to suggest that actions by applicant to help suppliers improve their performance have resulted in improved performance

- Objectivity and reliability of data presented on suppliers

- Percentage of suppliers for which comparative data are presented

- Importance of suppliers for which comparative data are presented

- Presentation of benchmark data on suppliers

- Degree of difference between quality performance of applicant's suppliers and that of competitors' suppliers

- Number or percentage of suppliers for which the applicant's supplier performance is superior to competitors' suppliers

- Trend of performance improvement in applicant's suppliers as compared to competitor's suppliers

Chapter 12

Interpreting the Criteria
for Customer Focus
and Satisfaction (7.0)

OVERVIEW OF THE CUSTOMER FOCUS AND SATISFACTION CATEGORY

The seventh and final category in the Baldrige Award Criteria is Customer Focus and Satisfaction. This category is worth 250 points. The reason this is one of the most important categories is because customers are the final judge of performance. You might do all the things that quality gurus such as Deming and Juran tell you to achieve impressive improvements, but if your customers still think that your products are average or inferior compared to the competition, it is extremely unlikely that you'll become a Baldrige Award winner. Although advertising and other factors can influence customers to buy your product or service the first time, quality is what keeps them coming back. You might buy a certain brand of car because it has great styling and a good price, for example. But you will never buy another one of these cars if the quality is poor and the car is in the shop all of the time. A balance between quality and price is what keeps people buying your products and services.

According to the 1996 Award Criteria, Category 7.0, Customer Focus and Satisfaction, is defined as follows:

> ***Customer Focus and Satisfaction*** *(Category 7.0) is the focal point within the Criteria for understanding in detail the voices of customers and of the marketplace. The Category emphasizes relationship management as a key requirement and calls for a variety of listening and learning strategies as well. However, much of the information needed for understanding the voices of customers and of the marketplace must come from measuring results and tracking trends. Such results and trends provide hard information not only on customers' views but also on their marketplace behaviors. The results and trends offer a means to determine whether or not priorities for improvement activities are appropriately directed.*

Figure 12.1 is repeated from the previous chapter on Business Results. Customer satisfaction is measured after the external customers have purchased the products or services produced by the organization. As you can see in the figure, this occurs at point 8, and this information is then fed back to the organization to aid them in producing better performing products and services.

The satisfaction level of internal customers is not addressed in Category 7.0. This category relates only to external customer satisfaction. Company results with internal customers are evaluated in section 6.2.

This chapter describes each of the eight Examination Items in this category of the Award Criteria. As in previous chapters, each section begins with a double-ruled box containing

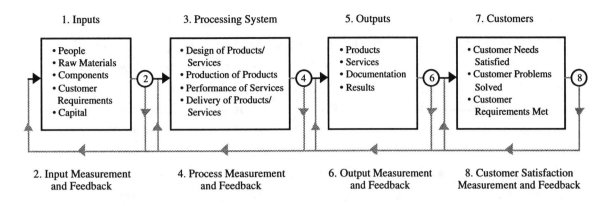

Figure 12.1: Macro Process Model of an Organization

the Examination Item, the point value, and any applicable Notes.* Areas to Address falling under that Item follow in a single-ruled box. In the upper right corner of each Area to Address box is an indication [brackets] of whether the Area pertains to approach, deployment, or results. All definitions and information appearing within these boxes are taken directly from the Baldrige criteria. Following each Area to Address is an explanation defining what the examiners are looking for in assessing your application. Next, I have supplied a list of indicators or evaluation factors that will assist you in interpreting the criteria and in preparing your application.

7.1 CUSTOMER AND MARKET KNOWLEDGE

Describe how the company determines near-term and longer-term requirements, expectations, and preferences of customers and markets, and develops listening and learning strategies to understand and anticipate needs. (30 points)

---

* Item Notes that apply to a specific Area to Address are appropriately listed in the box containing that Area.

AREA TO ADDRESS [APPROACH, DEPLOYMENT]

7.1a How the company determines *current and near-term requirements* **and expectations of customers. Include: (1) how customer groups and/or market segments are determined and/or selected, including how customers of competitors and other potential customers are considered; (2) how information is collected, including what information is sought, frequency and methods of collection, and how objectivity and validity are ensured; (3) how specific product and service features and the relative importance of these features to customer groups or segments are determined; and (4) how other key information and data such as complaints, gains and losses of customers, and product/service performance are used to support the determination.**

Notes:

(1)   **The distinction between near-term and future depends upon many marketplace factors. The applicant's response should reflect these factors for its market(s). Methods used in 7.1a(2) and 7.1b might be the same or similar.**

(2)   **The company's products and services might be sold to end users via other businesses such as retail stores or dealers. Thus, "customer groups" should take into account the requirements and expectations of both the end users and these other businesses.**

(3)   **Some companies might use similar methods to determine customer requirements/expectations and customer satisfaction (Item 7.3). In such cases, cross-references should be included.**

(4)   **Customer groups and market segments [7.1a(1)] might take into account opportunities to select or** *create* **groups and segments based upon customer- and market-related information. This might include individual customization.**

(5)   **How information is collected [7.1a(2)] might include periodic methods such as surveys or focus groups and/or ongoing processes such as dialogs with customers.**

(6)   **Product and service features [7.1a(3)] refer to all important characteristics and to the performance of products and services that customers experience or perceive throughout their overall purchase and ownership. The focus should be primarily on features that bear upon customer preference and repurchase loyalty—for example, those features that differentiate products and services from competing offerings. This might include price and value.**

What They're Looking For Here

What the Baldrige Examiners are looking for in this section is how well you know your current and potential customers. To maintain positive relationships with all of your customers, you need to be in constant touch with their ever-changing wants, desires, and expectations. The first thing you should explain is that you have divided customers into different market segments, which you examine separately, rather than considering all customer needs as identical. While it is true that all of your customers have some common requirements and expectations about the products and services you sell, those in different markets have their own unique requirements as well. You are also expected to explain how and why you segment your customers the way you do. For example, if more than half of your business comes from the automotive industry and the rest from many other different types of industries, it might make sense to segment your customers into two groups:

- Automotive
- Nonautomotive

A manufacturer of printing equipment uses the following segments to categorize its customers:

- Manufacturing companies
- Service companies
- Government
- Educational institutions
- Printers

The Baldrige Examiners are not searching for a specific segmentation strategy. They want to see that you have accurately identified your market segments and that you have sound reasoning for the categories chosen.

Your response for this area should also include an explanation of what the common requirements for all your customers are and what the requirements for customers in the different market segments you serve are. A common way to respond to this area is to make the following statement: "We have identified all of the requirements and expectations unique to each of the different market segments we serve." But as you have learned by now, using broad statements such as this will not earn many points. Listing the requirements and expectations of your different groups of customers will earn points in this area. A matrix with customer requirements and expectations listed along the left side, and market segments listed horizontally along the top is a great way to show common and unique customer requirements. A sample of a portion of such a chart follows.

CUSTOMER REQUIREMENTS BY MARKET SEGMENT			
CUSTOMER REQUIREMENTS	LARGE-COMPUTER MANUFACTURERS	SMALL-COMPUTER MANUFACTURERS	OTHERS
Timely Delivery	X	X	X
Assembly of Components	X		X
Special Packaging	X		
Quality Inspection of 25%		X	

You also need to explain how you gather data on customer requirements. Your response will be evaluated according to the objectivity and reliability of your research methodologies and instruments. The examiners will also be looking at factors such as sample size, frequency of data collection, and use of a variety of different methods to gather data on customer requirements. Your own market research should be supplemented with data collected by outside firms to increase the objectivity of your data.

A great many customers may not be included in your efforts to gather data on customer requirements, and you may not hear from them when they have a service or product complaint. In fact, for every eight customers who are unhappy with a product or service, only one complains. Rather than complain, most unhappy customers simply take their business elsewhere. Two valuable sources of data on customers requirements are complaint data and an analysis of lost customers to determine why they leave. The examiners are looking for evidence that you gather data from customers who decide to buy their product/service elsewhere and that you use both this and customer complaint data to identify customer requirements that may not be apparent from the other market research you do.

Another good source of data is new customers. Surveying new customers to find out why they selected your product or service can provide valuable information. In your response, explain how data on lost and new customers is gathered and directed back through the appropriate channels to serve as input to the product/service design process.

This area to address not only asks how you determine customer requirements, it also asks what you do with them. Question 7.1a(3) asks about the process you use to define product/service features, based upon the customer requirements. In 5.1a, I mentioned the approach called Quality Function Deployment for translating customer requirements into product/service design features. This is one very good approach that would earn you points in this section, but it is certainly not a requirement. What the Examiners want to see is that you employ some systematic approach to using the customer requirements as inputs to the product/service design process. Your response should include a flowchart or process description that outlines how you use the customer requirements to determine product/service features. To give your response credibility, you should follow your process description with several examples that illustrate how customer requirements have been used to design product or service features. Explain what the research revealed about high-priority customer needs, and how you met those needs with a new feature or new product/service. Two or three examples should be enough.

Your response for this Area to Address should also explain how you use complaints and performance data as a way of identifying possible customer requirements. For example, a car company may look at the number of warranty repairs that customers have done on their cars during the first year as a set of performance data relevant to customer requirements for reliability.

Indicators For Area 7.1a

- Thoroughness of process for identifying market segments and potential customers

- Data on requirements collected from your own and competitors' customers

- Degree to which customer requirements have been identified for each market segment your company serves

- Identification of the common and unique requirements and expectations for each market segment

- Objectivity of data collection methods used to identify customer requirements and expectations

- Frequency of data collection on each market segment

- Sample sizes are large enough to be adequate representation of customer populations

- How the company provides information to customers to help ensure that their expectations are realistic

- Use of multiple methodologies (e.g., telephone interviews, mail surveys, focus groups, etc.) to gather data on customer requirements

- Use of comparative data for such areas as product/service performance, complaints, and gains/losses of customers to help determine customer requirements

- Use of outside sources of data to supplement the applicant's own data on customer requirements

- How the role of and logistical support for customer-contact personnel are determined

- Use of a systematic process for gathering customer requirement data

- Evidence that customer complaint data are summarized and used as input for design or enhancement of products/services

- Use of a systematic process to design product/service features based upon customer requirements

- Evidence that the process for defining products/services based on customer requirements is actually used

- Lost customers are tracked and follow-ups are done to determine their reasons for buying products/services elsewhere and why they were dissatisfied with your products/services

- Thoroughness of a system for following up with lost customers

- Data gathered from new customers to determine why they selected the product/services offered by your company

- Use of performance data on products/services to identify customer requirements

- Evidence that data from new or lost customers are used to design, enhance, or change products and/or services

- Extent to which requirements have been identified for all dealers or distributors if appropriate

---

AREA TO ADDRESS   **[APPROACH, DEPLOYMENT]**

7.1b How the company addresses future requirements and expectations of customers and potential customers. Include an outline of key listening and learning strategies used.

Note:

(7)   Examples of listening and learning strategy elements (7.1b) are:
- relationship strategies, including close integration with customers;
- rapid innovation and field trials to better link R&D to the market;
- close monitoring of technological, competitive, societal, environmental, economic, and demographic factors that may bear upon customer requirements, expectations, preferences, or alternatives;
- focus groups with demanding or leading-edge customers;
- training of frontline employees in customer listening;
- use of critical incidents to understand key service attributes from the point of view of customers and frontline employees;
- interviewing lost customers;
- won/lost analysis relative to competitors;
- posttransaction follow-up (see 7.2c); and
- analysis of major factors affecting key customers.

What They're Looking For Here

The purpose of this item is to suggest that companies need to focus on determining what customers are likely to want and expect in the future. This may seem a difficult task, but being able to predict future customer demands is what separates the leading companies from the followers. Many large manufacturing companies are designing products now that won't be on the market for several years. These companies need to be aware of how tastes and expectations of customers are likely to change in the future so that their new products will meet or exceed those expectations.

You should explain the time horizon for determination of future customer requirements. The time horizon should be based upon the trends and frequency of changes in your industry, and a reasonable time frame within which you can predict trends. The amount of time you need to develop and test new products also should be considered in determining the time frame for your predictions. Some pharmaceutical companies are working on drugs that may not be on the market for more than five years. Clothing designers, on the other hand, come up with their product designs about a year or so before they hit the stores. In a fashion-oriented business, it is much more difficult to predict trends and customer tastes more than a couple of years in advance. Your response should explain the logic behind your selection of a particular time frame for predicting future customer expectations.

Your response should explain how needs of current and potential new customers are likely to change. You should also explain how you are in touch with the current and future expectations of competitors' customers. Explain how you predict your existing and potential customers' buying behavior. If you do market research, explain how you ensure that predictions made by this research have turned out to be valid.

The final segment of your response for this Area to Address should list various trends that are relevant to your business, and how each of these trends will impact upon requirements and expectations of your current and potential customers. I suggest preparing a matrix that lists the factors in the first column, the trends for each of the factors in the second column, the impact on your customers' requirements in the third column, and your strategy for capitalizing on each trend in the final column. An example that depicts the relationship between trends and current customer requirements for a real estate firm follows.

Factors	Trends	Customer Requirements	Strategies
Demographics	Move Away From Large Cities	• Better Home Value • Less Traffic • Better Schools • Less Materialistic Values	• Open More Offices in Medium-Sized Cities • Train Agents in Benefits of Small City Living

You also need to explain how you use the information you gather on future customer requirements to design new products and services, or to enhance existing products/services. A very clear way of presenting this information might be to build upon the matrix you presented in 7.1a. List the trends again, and prepare a matrix that shows the trends against your products and services, as well as market segments. Your matrix might also show how new features of your products/services will be designed to meet or exceed future customer requirements. The following example chart depicts a portion of a matrix for a fast-food chain that is concerned with the increasing societal trend of eating more healthy foods.

FACTOR	TRENDS	MARKETS/PRODUCTS
Societal	• Less Fat in Diets • Less Cholesterol in Diets	Children—D Adults—A, B, C
Products A=Salads C=Carrots/Celery Sticks	B=Chicken Sandwich D=Healthy Meal	

Explain how data on future trends and customer expectations are used by engineers and/or product/service design teams. Your response should also explain how you evaluate the importance of various future customer requirements so that you concentrate your efforts on designing product/service features that address the most important requirements. Describe the process for incorporating future trends into the design process. You might describe this process using a process model or flowchart. It will also be helpful for you to provide a couple of examples of how you have capitalized on past trends in the way you design new products/services. Your response should also explain how you will capitalize on future trends in order to gain market share and attract a larger customer base.

Indicators For Area 7.1b

- Explanation of a time horizon for determination of how future customer requirements match applicant's business, products/services, and technology

- Time frame for determination of future requirements is far enough in the future to allow the organization to capitalize on trends by designing and introducing products and services to meet future customer expectations

- Extent to which projections are made about requirements of existing customers in the future and requirements of potential customers who currently do not buy the organization's products or services

- Identification of important trends in technology, competition, society, economy, demographics, and other factors that may impact the business

- Extent to which the company has identified how each of these trends will impact its business

- Identification of specific strategies the company will use to capitalize on future trends in all areas listed above

- Evidence that future customer requirements are used in the product/service design process

- Use of a systematic process to evaluate the importance of various future customer requirements

- Demonstration that only the most important future customer requirements are translated into new product/service features

- Clarity and completeness of explanation of how future trends are translated into customer requirements leading to design of new or enhanced products/services

- Extent to which response addresses existing customers and potential future customers

---

AREA TO ADDRESS   **[APPROACH, DEPLOYMENT]**

7.1c How the company evaluates and improves its processes for determining customer requirements, expectations, and preferences.

Note:

(8)   **Examples of evaluation and factors appropriate for 7.1c are:**
- **the adequacy and timeliness of the customer-related information;**
- **improvement of survey design;**
- **the best approaches for getting reliable and timely information—surveys, focus groups, customer-contact personnel, etc.;**
- **increasing and decreasing importance of product/service features among customer groups or segments; and**
- **the most effective listening/learning strategies.**

The evaluation might also be supported by company-level analysis addressed in Item 2.3.

<u>What They're Looking For Here</u>

If you've come this far in this book, this Area to Address should look very familiar to you. The last in a sequence of Areas to Address typically calls for evidence that you systematically evaluate and improve a process. This is exactly what is being asked for here. The Baldrige Examiners are looking for evidence that you employ a systematic process to evaluate your market research and other investigations to determine future customer expectations. Begin your response with a list of the various types of research you do to determine customer requirements in the future. Along with a list of the various types of research, you might also mention who does the research, indicating whether you use outside firms or do it all using your own internal resources. For each type of research that is done, list the type of evaluation factors or measures used for assessment. Next, describe the methodology used to gather the evaluation data. Explain how the evaluation data are compiled and how conclusions are drawn.

Following your description of the methods used to evaluate your research approaches, you should explain how you use these evaluation data to improve your research methodology or expand the time horizon for your research. One area you should work on improving is the accuracy of your predictions and the length of your time horizons. The best companies in the future will be those that accurately predict long-range trends. You might end your response with an example or two of how you have used evaluation data to improve your research methodology, leading to improvements in the accuracy of your predictions or in the time horizons of your research.

Indicators For Area 7.1c

- Evidence that a systematic process is used to evaluate the approaches used to determine future customer requirements

- Extent to which evaluations are done on all methodologies employed to conduct research on future customer requirements

- Degree to which evaluation methods are appropriate for the research methods used

- Validity of measurement indices used for evaluation

- Validity of evaluation approaches used

- Clear description of a system to compile evaluation results and follow up on them

- Evidence that evaluation results are acted upon and result in improvements in research approaches

- Evidence to indicate that improvements have been made in the last few years in the accuracy and/or time frames of predictions about future customer requirements

7.2 CUSTOMER RELATIONSHIP MANAGEMENT

Describe how the company provides effective management of its responses and follow-ups with customers to preserve and build relationships, to increase knowledge about specific customers and about general customer expectations, to improve company performance, and to generate ideas for new products and services. (30 points)

Note:

(1) Customer relationship management refers to a process, not to a company unit. However, some companies might have units which address all or most of the requirements included in this Item. Also, some of these requirements may be included among the responsibilities of frontline employees in processes described in Items 5.2 and 5.3.

AREA TO ADDRESS   [APPROACH, DEPLOYMENT]

7.2a How the company provides information and easy access to enable customers to seek assistance, to comment, and to complain. Describe how contact management performance is measured. Include key service standards and how these standards are set, deployed, and tracked.

Notes:

(2) How the company maintains easy access for customers (7.2a) might involve close integration, electronic networks, etc.

(3) Performance measures and service standards (7.2a) apply not only to employees providing the responses to customers but also to other units within the company that make effective responses possible. Deployment needs to take into account all key points in a response chain. Examples of measures and standards are: telephonic, percentage of resolutions achieved by frontline employees, number of transfers, and resolution response time.

What They're Looking For Here

This is one area in which many quality-oriented companies have difficulty. Probably the best way of ensuring easy access for customers to comment on an organization's products or services is to have a company representative visit each customer frequently. In some organizations this may not be feasible, so other methods must be used. The key here is to make it easy for the customer. Most organizations place the burden upon the customer to exert the effort and take the initiative to comment on service or product quality. If, however, you take the initiative to determine customer comments rather than waiting for them to complain, you will excel in this section.

Another aspect of your response for this area is that of how easy it is for the customer to take the initiative to comment or complain about your products or services. Many organizations have customer service 800-numbers or hotlines. While this is a great idea, many of the companies I've dealt with don't adequately staff their customer service phone lines, so that the lines are either busy for hours or you're put on hold forever while waiting for the "next available customer service representative." If you have an 800-number or hotline for customer comments and questions, your response here should include data that indicate the prompt and efficient handling of incoming calls by your staff.

Comment cards are another common technique for allowing customers to voice their opinions. These are frequently used by hotels, restaurants, car dealers, and others. If you make use of these cards or a similar instrument, explain how customers receive or obtain the cards, how much time it takes to fill them out, and what the customers need to do to turn them in. If you simply leave the cards lying out in your place of business for the customer to choose to fill out—in their hotel room, on the seat of a new car, on the restaurant table—only people who are very upset about poor service will take the time to fill them out. If the customer needs to put a stamp on the card and mail it, even fewer of them will bother to fill out and send in the comment card. The same is true of product comment cards that are included with the owners manual of many consumer products. Only people who fill out the cards are part of the sample, so the sample is not representative of all customers.

To receive a high score for your response to this area, you must first have a well-designed and simple system for customers to comment on your products or services, and, second, a set of data from customer surveys and interviews that suggest how truly easy it is to comment, complain, or get a question answered. If 98 percent of your customers say that your customer service department answers the phones in three rings or less and is able to answer questions or resolve problems adequately almost every time, the Baldrige Examiners will take notice.

In your response, define the major customer requirements or needs for each major point of interaction with customer-contact employees. Finally, explain how you track or measure whether or not you meet the requirements. The question says: "Describe contact management performance measures." This means, what do you measure to determine your performance levels in meeting the customer requirements? Once again, this is a situation where a chart might be a good way of presenting all of the information called for. An example is shown below for an accounting firm that presents all three types of information asked for in this Area to Address.

Major Interaction Points	Key Cust. Requirements	Indicators/Measures
Audit planning meeting	• All key players in attendance	Attendance log
	• Major milestones defined	Project plan
	• Labor budget established	Project plan
	• Efficiency of meeting	Customer Satisfaction Survey

As I mentioned in other sections of this book, measures are meaningless without standards or goals. A customer service standard should always have two parts. The first part is the behavior or action the employee should perform, and the second is the standard or criterion that specifies how well the action must be done. Some examples are as follows:

"Approach customers *within three minutes* of the time they enter the department."

"End the transaction by *thanking the customer for using AT&T*."

"Greet members *using their names* when they walk into the club."

The italicized parts of the statements are the criteria or standards that specify how a task should be done or how well it should be done.

Standards should always be stated in a manner that allows conformance to be reliably and objectively measured. Many applicants list standards that include words and phrases such as, "in a friendly manner," "showing empathy for the customer's situation," "promptly," or "in an efficient manner." While these may all be good adjectives to describe service, they are neither precise nor objectively measurable. My definition of "promptness" may be quite different from yours. Standards need to be very specific and quantified whenever possible.

After listing your customer service standards, the second half of your response to this area should concentrate on how the standards are based upon customer requirements. Many organizations base their standards upon either past performance or industry standards. For example, a medical insurance company uses a standard of 30 days for the time that it should take to process a customer's claim. The 30 days is based upon industry standards. If, on the other hand, the company asked *customers* how long it should take (which it hasn't), customers would probably say one week or so. Your score in this area will be partially based upon how well you demonstrate that your major customer service standards are derived from customer requirements and expectations.

In almost all companies, it is impossible for customer-contact employees to meet customer service standards by themselves. In a restaurant, the waiter must rely upon the host/hostess, food buyer, restaurant manager, cooks, chef and others to help meet customer service standards. In a manufacturing plant, the sales representatives must rely upon production, quality assurance, procurement, accounting, production control, and other departments to help meet customer service standards. In any organization, the people who have the face-to-face contact with the customers must count on the cooperation of many others to help them deliver services and products that meet all of the customers' expectations and needs.

For this to happen, it is essential that all the employees who help the customer-contact people to achieve their goals are knowledgeable of the customer service standards and are held accountable for completing the tasks necessary to enable the customer-contact people to meet those standards. One applicant who received a high score in this area presented a list of customer service standards along the left side of a chart, and a list of the various functions in the organization horizontally along the top of the chart. Codes were used to indicate the degree of influence each support department had in helping to achieve the customer service standard. A portion of such a chart is shown as follows.

ACCOUNTABILITIES—CUSTOMER SERVICE STANDARDS					
STANDARDS	ACCOUNTING	PROCUREMENT	ENGINEERING	PRODUCTION	HRD
Deliver all orders by customer deadline	4	3	4	1	3
Provide appropriate prints and documentation with orders	4	4	1	3	3
Answer technical questions within 24 hours	4	4	1	2	3

Key: 1 = Primary Responsibility   3 = Support Responsibility
                2 = Secondary Responsibility   4 = No Responsibility

This chart is only one way of depicting the level of responsibility each function has in assisting customer-contact employees in meeting customer service standards. Your response needs to explain how support departments and others are made aware of the customer service standards and how they are held accountable for helping to achieve them.

Simply setting customer service standards and communicating them to all employees will not ensure that the standards are met. The expression "you get what you measure" is very true. If you do not track and measure the degree to which standards are met, you can almost guarantee that they will not be met on a consistent basis. Performance improvement is a matter of selecting measurement indices, setting standards, measuring performance against those standards, and sending performance feedback to employees who have influence or control over the indices.

Performance of customer-contact employees compared to established standards needs to be measured and the data fed back to employees in a timely and consistent manner. A great many service and manufacturing companies receive low scores for this area because they do not measure performance against the customer service standards, other than by surveying customers. Surveying customers is a very imprecise way to measure performance against standards. It is important to gather customer opinion about how well you meet satisfaction standards, but you should also have your own internal measurement that gets done.

As customers, the expectations and standards we have for the products and services we buy are constantly changing. Because of the poor on-time performance of airlines in recent years, many of us have lowered our expectations. Other standards have been raised. We expect our cars to be more trouble-free, to need less maintenance, and to run more efficiently than in the past.

Your response for this Area to Address should also briefly explain a process for periodically evaluating the validity of your customer service standards. This should be done through ongoing research into customer requirements and expectations. The requirements and expectations should then be translated into new or revised customer service standards. After describing your approach to evaluating customer service standards, present information on how the standards have evolved or changed over the last several years. A trend indicating that the changes have resulted in more stringent standards will earn you points in this section of your application.

Indicators For Area 7.2a

- Amount of effort and trouble customers must go through to comment or complain, or seek assistance

- Use of frequent personal contact with customers where appropriate

- Staffing levels and expertise of personnel manning 800 lines designed to help customers

- How many times customers receive a busy signal when trying to call your 800 lines

- Evidence of a proactive approach to get customers to comment and complain

- Definition of key customer-contact points with customers, and most important requirements for each transaction.

- Identification of specific performance measures for each major interaction with customers

- Extent to which measures have been identified for each customer interaction point

- Evidence that measures are clearly related to customer requirements

- Definition of standards for each measure associated with customer service levels

- Standards exist for all measures

- Standards are set based upon requirements and desires of customers and upon what competitors and benchmark organizations do

- Evidence that data are collected on each major service measure

- Data on extent to which standards are met is fed back to appropriate employees and used to improve performance

---

AREA TO ADDRESS   **[APPROACH, DEPLOYMENT]**

7.2b How the company ensures that formal and informal complaints and feedback received by all company units are resolved promptly and effectively. Briefly describe the complaint management process and how it ensures effective recovery of customer confidence, meeting customer requirements for resolution effectiveness, and elimination of the causes of complaints.

Notes:

(4)   **Responses to 7.2b and 7.2c might include company processes for addressing customer complaints or comments based upon expressed or implied guarantees and warranties.**

(5)   **The complaint management process (7.2b) might include analysis and priority setting for improvement projects based upon potential cost impact of complaints, taking into account customer retention related to resolution effectiveness. Some of the analysis requirements of Item 7.2 relate to Item 2.3.**

What They're Looking For Here

Most companies have systems for filing and summarizing complaint letters and phone complaints made to customer service departments. However, the majority of customers who have comments on the services and products they buy don't bother writing a letter or calling a customer service department. Many organizations we buy from don't even have customer service departments. The Baldrige Examiners are looking for methods and procedures you have in place to capture the formal and informal customer comments or complaints. Most of the informal data get lost in many organizations, creating an unrealistic picture of actual levels of customer satisfaction. For example, the comments you make to the copier machine repair person or the field support representative from the computer company may never be recorded anywhere. Comments made to salespeople, or even customer-contact employees, are often heard and then forgotten.

In order to receive a high score for this area, you need to demonstrate that you have a comprehensive, yet simple, system for documenting all written and/or verbal comments made by customers about the quality of your products and services. You also need to have a system for summarizing and reporting all formal and informal complaints/comments received from customers.

Your response should include a combination of process description and results. A flow chart, algorithm, or a list of steps should be included that depicts the process for responding to and correcting customer complaints. You should also explain the escalation process that occurs when a customer feels that his/her complaint has not been resolved satisfactorily. Your process will be assessed for its logic, thoroughness, and the degree to which it fits your type of business and the size of your company.

The second part of your response for this area should include data covering a variety of different indices that show you are timely in resolving customer complaints, and that complaints are resolved completely and with a minimum of inconvenience to the customer. Data on the number of complaints received is not really relevant to this Area to Address. The number of complaints received is a measure of the quality of services and/or products offered by the organization. This section should focus on how well you handle and resolve the complaints that do come in. Preventing complaints in the first place is addressed elsewhere.

One of the most common mistakes that applicants make in responding to these "process" items is to write a brief and very general description of how they deal with a particular issue or input. A typical response is as follows.

> *Each complaint received is analyzed by customer service representatives to determine its root cause. The cause of the complaint must be recorded on the Complaint Log form. Once a month, a summary report is prepared that lists the causes of complaints and provides statistics on the number of complaints tied to specific causes. Reports are sent to the department managers who have responsibility for correcting the causes of the complaints.*

The problem with a response such as this is that it is too vague and the process described does not explain:

- The steps a customer service representative follows to analyze the cause(s) of a problem

- The knowledge customer service representatives have to analyze the cause(s) of customer complaints

- How the organization follows up on corrective actions that need to be taken to correct problem situations

- Evidence that the company has a system for recording all customer comments and complaints

- Evidence that data on customer comments and complaints from all areas of the organization are aggregated and analyzed to identify trends that may help identify opportunities for improvement

Sending a report to managers once a month is not an effective system for resolving problems.

7.2d(2) asks about how you summarize complaints and comments from throughout the company and use these data to better manage relationships with customers. Many companies do not do this. Complaints or comments are received by individual units or facilities, logged, and resolved. Many comments or minor complaints are never even logged, because they are resolved before they get worse. The only overall data on complaints that the company has are complaint letters or phone calls that made it to some corporate officer. These are few and far between in most companies. Baldrige is suggesting that companies have a tracking system to enable all complaint and comment data to be summarized. The key is to learn as much about customers and their needs as possible. Failure to aggregate these data and look at them across the entire company may handicap the company in making good decisions about how to improve relationships with customers.

Your response for this Area to Address should also explain how you use your analyses of the causes of customer complaints to improve processes, products, and services in the organization. Describe the process, and perhaps give an example or two of how you have used customer-complaint analyses to modify processes or a product/service.

Indicators For Area 7.2b

- Comprehensiveness of system for tracking customer comments and complaints

- Objectivity of the approach for gathering and documenting data on customer comments and/or complaints

- All employees who have telephone or personal contact with customers have a simple but thorough way of documenting any incidental comments or complaints heard about the company's products or services

- Data on customer comments/complaints from a variety of sources are aggregated for overall evaluation and comparison

- Data on customer comments/complaints are fed back to appropriate personnel in a timely fashion

- Customers believe that the comments/complaints they make to any of the organization's employees will get documented and reported

- Existence of a formal and logical process for resolving customer complaints

- Clearly defined escalation procedures for situations in which customers do not feel their complaint has been resolved by lower-level personnel

- Trend showing reductions in the amount of time needed to resolve customer complaints over the past few years

- Current performance on the amount of time needed to resolve complaints is exemplary

- Data showing customer satisfaction with the handling of complaints

- Objectivity and reliability of data on levels of customer satisfaction with the handling of complaints

- Data on the thoroughness with which complaints are handled

- Organized and systematic process for analyzing the causes of customer complaints

- Description of process clearly depicts inputs, process steps, and outputs

- Level of clarity and amount of detail in description of process are appropriate

- Those analyzing the causes of customer complaints have the knowledge and skills to do so

- Information on the causes of customer complaints is fed back to employees who can correct the problems

- Evidence that complaint data are used to initiate improvement projects that prevent the future complaints and potential loss of customers

- Evidence that analyses of causes of customer complaints are used to make changes in processes, products, and/or services

---

AREA TO ADDRESS   **[APPROACH, DEPLOYMENT]**

7.2c How the company follows up with customers on products, services, and recent transactions to determine satisfaction, to resolve problems, to seek feedback for improvement, to build relationships, and to develop ideas for new products and services.

What They're Looking For Here

The frequency, thoroughness, and objectivity of the data you gather on how satisfied current customers are with your products and services are important in this Area to Address. A typical response for this Area is to explain, "We survey our customers once a year to determine their level of satisfaction with our products/services." Conducting a survey once a year represents a very weak follow-up approach. The Examiners look for frequent contact with customers (e.g., quarterly or monthly) to determine how satisfied they are with your products and services. They also want to see that you use a variety of different follow-up methods, such as phone calls, mail surveys, etc. Although the approach should be comprehensive, it is also very important that it minimizes the amount of time the customer must spend giving you feedback. Too much follow-up can be an aggravation to the customer and end up doing more to turn him/her off than anything else. Explain how your approach to follow-up is sensitive to these issues and back it up with any data that indicate customers' opinion of your follow-up system. It is also important that you do informal follow-up with customers—not to collect customer satisfaction data, but simply to build a more positive relationship.

Indicators for Area 7.2c

* Percentage of customers surveyed during follow-up to determine their levels of satisfaction with your products and/or services

* Frequent informal contact is done to build strong relationships with customers

* Use of a variety of different data collection methods as follow-up on customer transactions

* Follow-up approach demonstrates concern for minimizing customer time and hassle

* Proactive follow-up is done for all types of customers and all of the organization's products and services

---

AREA TO ADDRESS   **[APPROACH, DEPLOYMENT]**

7.2d How the company evaluates and improves its customer relationship management. Include: (1) how service standards, including those related to access and complaint management, are improved based upon customer information; and (2) how knowledge about customers is accumulated.

Notes:

   (6)   **Improvement of customer relationship management (7.2d) might require training. Training for customer-contact (frontline) employees should address: (a) key knowledge and skills, including knowledge of products and services; (b) listening to customers; (c) soliciting comments from customers; (d) how to anticipate and handle problems or failures ("recovery"); (e) skills in customer retention; and (f) how to manage expectations. Such training should be described in Item 4.3.**

   (7)   **Information on trends and levels in measures and/or indicators of complaint response time, effective resolution, and percent of complaints resolved on first contact should be reported in Item 6.1.**

<u>What They're Looking For Here</u>

The first thing the Examiners are asking for here is evidence that you systematically evaluate and improve your approaches to managing relationships with customers. Explain the types of data that are collected to evaluate customer relationship management, as well as the evaluation methodology that is employed. If you have a formal approach for doing this, you might even want to present a graphic that depicts the evaluation process. As with other Baldrige approach/deployment criteria, your response should demonstrate the following pattern of events:

- Definition of evaluation measures and factors
- Collection of data on evaluation measures
- Analysis of data
- Implementation of changes and corrective actions to improve relationships with customers

As you get into more of the specifics in this area to address, you will see that subpoint 7.2d(1) asks about how service standards have been improved or made more challenging as a result of the evaluation. The service standards that you have in place today should have been listed in 7.2a. In this section you want to show how these standards have evolved and hopefully been made tougher over the last three or more years. In order to demonstrate this, you will need to explain how service standards in previous years were different. A good way of showing this continuous improvement is in a chart that takes the major measures on which you collect data, and list the standards for these measures over the last five years or so. Hopefully, this chart will show that standards have become more challenging each year, as customer expectations have increased.

The third and final point in this area to address, 7.2d(3), asks about the systems you use to document and accumulate knowledge about your customers. Credit card companies monitor our spending patterns and develop classification systems based on how we spend our money. Specific marketing techniques can then be tailored to our individual tastes and buying patterns. Grocery store scanners keep track of what we buy and issue customized coupons with the receipt for products we tend to buy each week, or would be very likely to buy. These are examples of systems for learning about what individual customers like and want, and using this information to more effectively sell to them.

IBM's General & Public Sector Trading Area, a winner of IBM's internal Baldrige Award, is a sales and service organization in New York City, with about 500 employees. The group has designed a tool for documenting intelligence on individual customers called "Organizational Memory." Organizational Memory is a data base that is used to document all sorts of information about each customer. Comments, complaints, changes in needs, previous sales, won and lost proposals, changes in customer personnel, etc., are all given a place in the data base. The system is extremely easy to use by the busy IBM staff members. Data are entered on their laptop computers that all customer-contact people have with them at all times. If a customer-contact employee gets moved to another trading area or is assigned different customers, the data base is passed on to the new person who will handle the account. This is exactly the type of system that would earn a very high score in this area to address. Knowledge about customers and their ever-changing needs and buying patterns needs to be documented and easily accessed when making important marketing and business decisions.

Indicators For Area 7.2d

- Use of a planned and systematic approach to evaluate and improve approaches to customer relationship management

- Identification of specific measures for assessing customer relationship management

- Objectivity of data collection methods used to evaluate customer relationship management

- Strategies to improve customer relationship management were derived from an analysis of data

- Evidence that approaches to customer relationship management have improved as a result of the evaluation data

- Extent to which service standards have changed and been made more challenging over the last several years

- Scope of changes to service standards extends to all areas of customer contact and all products, services, and major customer transactions

- Existence of methods for documenting information on customers and their needs, and for continually building and updating this data base

- Evidence that tools used to document knowledge of customers are actually used appropriately by company employees

---

7.3 CUSTOMER SATISFACTION DETERMINATION

Describe how the company determines customer satisfaction, customer repurchase intentions, and customer satisfaction relative to competitors; describe how these determination processes are evaluated and improved. (30 points)

AREA TO ADDRESS   **[APPROACH, DEPLOYMENT]**

7.3a How the company determines customer satisfaction. Include: (1) a brief description of processes and measurement scales used; frequency of determination; and how objectivity and validity are ensured. Indicate significant differences, if any, in processes and measurement scales for different customer groups or segments; and (2) how customer satisfaction measurements capture key information that reflects customers' likely future market behavior.

Notes:

(1)   **Customer satisfaction measurement might include both a numerical rating scale and descriptors for each unit in the scale. An effective (actionable) customer satisfaction measurement system provides reliable information about customer ratings of specific product and service features and the relationship between these ratings and the customer's likely future market behavior—repurchase and/or positive referral. Product and service features might include overall value and price.**

(2)   **The company's products and services might be sold to end users via other businesses such as retail stores or dealers. Thus, "customer groups" or segments should take into account these other businesses and the end users.**

(3)   **Customer dissatisfaction indicators include complaints, claims, refunds, recalls, returns, repeat services, litigation, replacements, downgrades, repairs, warranty work, warranty costs, misshipments, and incomplete orders.**

What They're Looking For Here

There are many ways to measure customer satisfaction. Most companies rely upon only two methods:

- Comment/feedback cards
- Annual mail survey sent to all or a sample of customers

While these two approaches are certainly valid, if this is all you do, it is not likely that you are obtaining a clear view of the degree to which customers are satisfied with your products/services. The problem with comment cards and surveys is that most customers can't be bothered to take the time to fill them out. Or if they do fill them out, they do so quickly and carelessly, rating everything average or above average. As consumers of numerous goods and services, we are inundated with requests for our opinions and feedback. Most of us respond to a few of these requests and ignore the rest, unless we are extremely unhappy with the level of service or product quality. And when we are very unhappy, we usually don't bother with filling out a comment card or waiting for the annual survey—we write a letter or make a phone call right away.

The most objective way to measure customer satisfaction is by examining customers' behavior, not their opinions. The fact that Mr. Green traded in his 1990 Ford Taurus for a 1994 model from the same dealership says more about Mr. Green's level of satisfaction than any survey could. In fact, if you surveyed Mr. Green, you might find that there are a number of things he didn't like about his Taurus. The bottom line, though, is that he bought another one. The amount of repeat business an organization receives is one of the best indicators of customer satisfaction. (Unless you're the only game in town. If you live in Butte, Montana, for example, there may be only one car dealer who sells or services exclusively Mercedes.)

Market share can be an indicator of customer satisfaction, but it is not a good one. Market share is influenced by too many extraneous factors such as competition, advertising, and pricing. In this Area to Address, the Examiners are looking for an approach to measuring customer satisfaction that takes into account a variety of different sources of data. Opinion data should be gathered using several approaches and large representative samples of all the organization's customers. Other measures, such as repeat business, need to be used to supplement opinion data. The specific measures you utilize will depend upon the nature of your products/services. A single measure can be misleading, so the use of multiple indices and data gathering methodologies adds a great deal of objectivity and reliability to your approach.

If you are a large corporation with many products and/or services, chances are that you serve a variety of customers with differing needs and levels of satisfaction with your products/services. For example, a large service company might have hotels, restaurants, and amusement parks, each catering to different types of customers. A company that makes only personal computers may have many different types of customers for their single product. Customers may be segmented based upon how they will use their personal computers.

In this Area to Address, the Baldrige Examiners are also looking for evidence that you segment your customers in a logical manner and that your customer satisfaction efforts address the various segments. In some cases, it won't make sense to segment them at all. However, even if you are a small business you probably should be categorizing your customers somehow. If 60 percent of your business is conducted with AT&T, for example, and the rest is with miscellaneous small companies, you might segment your customers into two groups: (1) AT&T and (2) all others.

Indicators For Area 7.3a

- Number of different sources of data on customer satisfaction

- Use of objective measures such as repeat business along with opinion data

- Frequency with which customer satisfaction is measured

- Adequate sample sizes used when measuring customer satisfaction

- Extent to which customers in all segments/markets are included in customer satisfaction data

- Validation done with customer satisfaction instruments prior to their use

- Reliability of instruments used to measure customer satisfaction

- Use of multiple approaches to gather customer opinion data, such as surveys, focus groups, etc.

- Logical approach for segmenting customers and customer satisfaction data

- Use of measurement indices and instruments that are unique to each customer group's expectations and needs regarding your products/services

- Separate sets of data collected on levels of customer satisfaction for each major market group or segment

- Use of data collection instruments and methods that minimize the time customers must spend providing you with feedback

---

AREA TO ADDRESS   **[APPROACH, DEPLOYMENT]**

7.3b How customer satisfaction relative to that for competitors is determined. Describe: (1) company-based comparative studies; and (2) comparative studies or evaluations made by independent organizations and/or customers. For (1) and (2), describe how objectivity and validity of studies or evaluations are ensured.

Note:

(4)   **Comparative studies (7.3b) might include indicators of customer dissatisfaction as well as satisfaction.**

What They're Looking For Here

This Area to Address refers to how you determine how your levels of customer satisfaction compare with those of your competitors. We are not looking for data here; the criteria ask *how* you determine comparative levels of customer satisfaction. Including a question or two on your customer surveys to ask your customers what they think of your competition is a common way of doing this. This is certainly not the most objective way, however. You are surveying your own customers and they may never have bought the competition's products/services, even though they may have an opinion about them. A more complete approach is to use an outside research firm to measure customer satisfaction among your own and your competitors' customers. J. D. Power, the market research firm used by the automotive industry, uses the same instruments to measure customer satisfaction among customers of all car companies. This way, the data are objective and can be easily compared. Your approach need not be as comprehensive as that used by the automotive industry, but you need to demonstrate that you gather reliable data on the levels of customer satisfaction your competitors achieve relative to your own levels.

Indicators For Area 7.4b

- Use of a variety of sources of data on competitors' levels of customer satisfaction

- Objectivity of data gathered on how your customer satisfaction levels compare with competitors

- Amount of data collected on comparison of customer satisfaction levels to those of competitors

- Reliability of data gathering methods used to assess competitors' levels of customer satisfaction

---

AREA TO ADDRESS   **[APPROACH, DEPLOYMENT]**

7.3c How the company evaluates and improves its processes and measurement scales for determining customer satisfaction and satisfaction relative to competitors. Include how other indicators (such as gains and losses of customers) and dissatisfaction indicators (such as complaints) are used in this improvement process. Describe also how the evaluation determines the effectiveness of companywide use of customer satisfaction information and data.

Notes:

(5)   Evaluation (7.3c) might take into account:
- **how well the measurement scale relates to actual customer behavior;**
- **the effectiveness of pre-survey research used in survey design;**
- **how well customer responses link to key business processes and thus provide actionable information for improvement; and**
- **how well customer responses have been translated into cost/revenue implications and thus provide actionable information for improvement priorities.**

(6)   Use of data from satisfaction measurement is called for in 5.2b(4) and 5.3c(4). Such data also provide key input to analysis (Item 2.3).

What They're Looking For Here

Since customer satisfaction is the most important index of performance in any organization, it is important that effort be put toward constantly evaluating and improving the methods and instruments used to assess customer satisfaction levels. A common response for this area is written as follows: "We evaluate the usefulness of each item on our customer satisfaction questionnaires annually, and revise the instruments based upon both customer feedback and the usefulness of the data each item generates." A response like this is too vague.

You should begin your response here by listing the indices you use to measure and evaluate the organization's approach to determining customer satisfaction. Explain why these indices have been selected as the best measures of the effectiveness of your customer satisfaction measurement system. Next, list the steps or phases involved in your evaluation process, along with the outputs of each phase. Describe how evaluation data are summarized and reported, and explain who receives the reports. Finally, explain the process you use to review the evaluation results and develop an action plan for improving your approach to measuring customer satisfaction. A description of some of the changes you've made over the years to the customer satisfaction measurement system will help demonstrate that you do, in fact, take action based upon the evaluation data. The Baldrige Examiners are looking for a trend of continuous improvements.

Indicators For Area 7.3c

- Explanation of a well-defined and systematic approach to evaluate a customer satisfaction measurement system

- Objectivity and reliability of methodology and instruments used to evaluate customer satisfaction measurement system

- Evaluation data are summarized and sent to appropriate managers and other employees

- Action plans based upon evaluation data are created to identify improvements needed in customer satisfaction measurement system

- Evidence that actions plans are actually implemented and that changes have been made in measurement instruments and/or methodologies based upon evaluation data

- Trends showing continual improvements/enhancements in the approach to measuring customer satisfaction over the last several years

- Evidence that improvements have been made in measurement of customer dissatisfaction indicators

7.4 CUSTOMER SATISFACTION RESULTS

Summarize the company's customer satisfaction and dissatisfaction results using key measures and/or indicators of these results. Compare results with competitors' results. (160 points)

Notes:

(1)   **Results reported in this Item derive from methods described in Items 7.2 and 7.3.**

AREA TO ADDRESS   **[RESULTS]**
7.4a Current levels and trends in key measures and/or indicators of customer satisfaction and dissatisfaction. Results should be segmented by customer groups and product and service types, as appropriate.

<u>What They're Looking For Here</u>

As with any result item, level and trends are the two most important dimensions of your performance. This is the area for which data should be reported that demonstrates how levels of customer satisfaction have improved over the last several years due to performance improvement efforts. This section should include graphs of customer satisfaction data for the different groups of customers you serve. Refer back to the guidelines included in Chapter 3 of this book for a discussion of how to prepare graphs and tables. Don't make the mistake some applicants have made and respond with a single graph of customer satisfaction data. Present several different graphs of customer satisfaction data from at least the past three years. Three data points do not establish much of a trend, so the more historical data you can present, the better.

In evaluating this section, the Baldrige Examiners will be looking for several things. The first is the amount of data you present on customer satisfaction. While you are constrained by the maximum of 70 pages for your entire application, some applicants devote only a couple of pages to this important Area to Address. Include as much data as you can, and don't be afraid to use several pages for this area. It is possible to fit as many as eight separate graphs on one page. Tables or charts also allow you to fit a great deal of data in a small space. (Make sure that your graphs and charts are readable, however.)

Two other related factors examined are the level of customer satisfaction you have achieved and the current level of performance in relation to past levels. If 80 percent of your customers are satisfied or very satisfied with your quality, a large number (20 percent) still remain unsatisfied. If only 50 percent were satisfied three years ago, you will receive some credit for a big improvement, but your overall levels of satisfaction are still low. Improvement is much more difficult when you are already doing well. It may take more effort and thus be more significant if you have raised customer satisfaction levels from 94 to 98 percent in three years. A trend showing steady improvement over the last three to five years is considered very positive.

The final factor examined in this Area to Address is the number of different indices and types of data you present on customer satisfaction. Different measures of customer satisfaction (or the same indices among different segments or groups of customers) should be presented. For example, you might present data on overall levels of satisfaction among new customers, existing customers, large company customers, small company customers, government customers, private sector customers, etc. Choose the breakdowns that make the most sense for your products/services and markets.

Obviously, not all of the indices mentioned regarding dissatisfaction will be relevant to your organization. You should respond to this section by presenting data you have for any indicators that are a good gauge of customers' dissatisfaction with your products and/or services. Present the data graphically and include at least three years of statistics. The number of different indices for which data are presented and the degree to which the data show a steadily decreasing trend are the factors that will be evaluated in your response to this section.

It is likely that not all of the results and trends will be entirely positive. Performance on one or more indicators of customer dissatisfaction may not show a consistent downward trend. It is important that you thoroughly explain each of these anomalies or adverse trends. A thorough explanation does not mean that blame should be placed elsewhere for the occurrence of the anomaly. It simply means that you can describe exactly why these phenomena occurred and explain the steps taken to prevent future lapses in performance.

Indicators for Area 7.4a

- Presentation of a wide variety of customer satisfaction data

- Number of different indices of customer satisfaction for which data are presented

- Presentation of customer satisfaction data by customer or market group

- Trend showing continual improvements over the last several years in all measures of customer satisfaction

- Amount of historical data presented on levels of customer satisfaction

- Overall levels of customer satisfaction (percent of customers satisfied with service, etc.)

- Clarity of graphs and explanations of customer satisfaction data

- Number and types of different breakdowns of customer satisfaction data

- Number of different indices for which data are presented

- Data are presented for all important adverse indices or measures of dissatisfaction in industry

- All adverse indicators show a steady downward trend over the past three or more years

- Minimum number of anomalies or positive trends in dissatisfaction indicators

- Clear and complete explanations provided for all anomalies in data or positive trends in dissatisfaction indicators

- Overall levels of performance on indicators of dissatisfaction

---

AREA TO ADDRESS   **[RESULTS]**

7.4b Current levels and trends in key measures and/or indicators of customer satisfaction relative to competitors. Results should be segmented by customer groups and product and service types, as appropriate.

Notes:

(2)   **Measures and/or indicators of satisfaction relative to competitors (7.4b) should include gains and losses of customers and customer accounts to competitors as well as gains and losses in market share.**

(3)   **Measures and/or indicators of satisfaction relative to competitors might include objective information and/or data from independent organizations, including customers. Examples include survey results, competitive awards, recognition, and ratings. Such information and data should reflect comparative satisfaction (and dissatisfaction), not comparative performance of products and services (called for in Item 6.1).**

(4)   **Customer retention data might be used in both 7.4a and 7.4b. For example, in 7.4a, customer retention might be included as a satisfaction indicator, while in 7.4b, customer retention relative to competitors might be part of a switching analysis to determine competitive position and the factors responsible for it.**

What They're Looking For Here

In this section of your application, you should present data demonstrating that your customers are more satisfied with your products and/or services than any of your competitors' customers are with their products/services. Your performance relative to that of your competitors is the most important factor evaluated in your response to this area. This is an Area to Address on which many applicants lose points because they have little comparison data, or their results are not significant when compared to competitors' levels of customer satisfaction. You can earn a high score on Item 7.4 for your customer satisfaction results and still earn a very low score for this Item if your levels of customer satisfaction are not better than most of your competitors'.

It is important in your response for this area that you compare your performance on several dimensions of customer satisfaction to several key competitors. The organizations you compare yourself to are also important. Comparing yourself to a world-class leader instead of local competitors obviously will earn you more points.

You also need to present data on gains and losses of customers or accounts in this section. It is surprising how many companies don't track this.

If appropriate, you should also present data on market share relative to competitors. As in the previous Area, the Examiners want to see that your market share has increased as a result of your quality and customer satisfaction improvement results. Data should be presented for all of your major products and/or services in all the major markets you serve. If you present information on only a couple of your products/services or a couple of markets, the examiners will probably suspect that the missing data are negative.

Your results should demonstrate continual increases in your market share and show a cause-effect relationship between improvements in your quality and increases in market share. Market share is determined by many factors that have nothing to do with quality. For example, your market share could have increased because you cut your prices. Or, it could have increased because the size of the market increased and the number of competitors decreased. Advertising, marketing, pricing, product availability, and many other factors influence market share. It is not enough to show that your market share has increased steadily over the last few years. You need to demonstrate that your market share has increased primarily because you offer higher-quality goods/services than your competitors.

Indicators For Area 7.4b

- Number of different competitors to which comparisons are made

- Number of different indices of customer satisfaction on which comparisons are made to the competition

- Status/level of competitors (e.g., world-class leader in field) to which comparisons are made

- Percentage of customer satisfaction indices on which applicant is superior to the competition

- Applicant's superiority to competition in measures of customer satisfaction

- Objectivity of data on how the applicant compares to competition

- Extent to which competitors in all major markets and with all major products/services are used for comparison

- A systematic and objective method is used to collect data on gains/losses of customers

- Data trends show continual increase in number of new customers over the past three or more years

- Data trends show continual decreases in number of lost customers over the past three or more years

- Extent to which cause/effect relationships are shown between gains/losses of customers and quality improvement efforts of the organization

- Gains in customers are not due to competitors going out of business or no longer being in the same markets

- Trends show gains in shares in key markets over the last several years

- Cause-effect relationships demonstrated between increases in market share and improvements in quality or customer satisfaction

- Data are presented for all key products/services and for all major markets

- Number of markets in which gains in shares have been demonstrated

- Significance/size of increases in market share

- Competitors show losses in market shares as applicant's shares have increased

- Evidence that increases in market share are not due to loss of competition or other strategies unrelated to quality and customer satisfaction improvement

Chapter 13

How to Audit Your
Organization Against the
Baldrige Award Criteria

The purpose of this chapter is to outline a process for designing a performance audit based specifically upon the Baldrige Award Criteria. Chapter 14 explains various ways of using the Baldrige criteria as a strategic planning tool. This chapter provides a detailed explanation of one of the most thorough of such approaches, the performance audit. The audit can be conducted internally by trained performance auditors. They need to assess current performance against the criteria and make recommendations for improvements.

THE AUDIT CYCLE

Regardless of whether you are doing a performance audit, an accounting audit, a safety audit, or some other kind of audit, you generally follow a four-phase process as outlined in Figure 13.1.

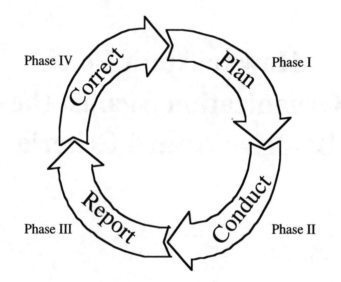

Figure 13.1: Performance Audit Planning Cycle

As you can see, the four phases in the performance audit cycle are Plan, Conduct, Report, and Correct. The majority of the work the audit team has to perform is in the Plan and Conduct phases. Each of these four phases is described in further detail. The first three phases in an audit against the Baldrige criteria could take three to four months to complete. The remainder of the year (eight or nine months) or longer could be spent making corrections based upon the audit findings.

PHASE I: PLANNING THE QUALITY AUDIT

Purpose

The purpose of this phase is to create a detailed plan for completing the audit. This requires a great deal of work for most organizations because you will be starting from scratch. You may already have audited the performance of your products and services periodically or conducted specific audits for safety or regulatory compliance, but you may not have conducted an audit as comprehensive as one based upon the Baldrige criteria. Essentially, you will be looking at all functions and levels of the organization, and examining a great deal of data in order to draw conclusions about the approach, deployment, and results the company is achieving in the area of quality.

Process

The process below outlines the major tasks in planning the Baldrige audit. The specific process you follow may vary slightly.

```
1. Form Audit Teams
2. Write Audit Project Plan
3. Create Audit Instruments
4. Create Data Collection Plan
5. Schedule Interviews and Data Collection Activities
```

Step 1: Form Audit Teams

The size of your audit team will depend upon the size of your organization. If your company has a few hundred employees and sales of under $10 million, an audit team of three or four individuals will probably suffice. If your organization employs thousands of people and has sales of several billion dollars, you might have an audit team of 50 or more. If you are a medium- to large-size company, your audit team should be led by an audit manager. The audit manager is directly responsible for the audit. Beneath the audit manager are several senior auditors. The job of the senior auditors is to supervise and coach the auditors in their collection of data. It makes sense to assign one senior auditor to each of the seven categories in the Baldrige criteria. Each senior auditor then has a team of auditors responsible for auditing the organization's practices and results relating

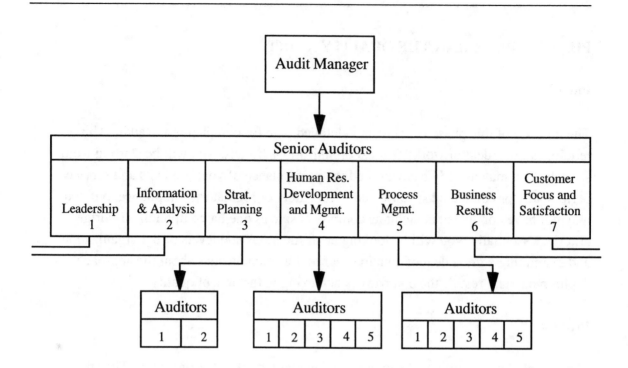

**Figure 13.2: Suggested Audit Team Organization Structure
for Medium or Large Company**

to a single category. Figure 13.2 presents a suggested organizational structure for an audit team in a medium or large company.

As you can see, there are a total of seven senior auditors, each having responsibility for one of the seven Award Criteria categories. Each senior auditor has a team of auditors reporting to him/her. The number of auditors on the senior auditor's team is shown as being equivalent to the number of Items in the Baldrige criteria for that Category. For example, Category 3.0, Strategic Planning, is divided into two Items, so there are two auditors on this team. Process Management, Category 5.0, is divided into four Items, so there are four auditors on this team.

If you are auditing a small organization, the audit team might look like the one depicted in Figure 13.3.

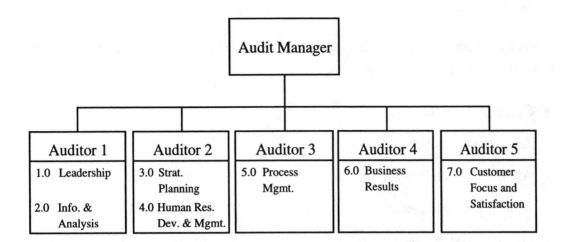

**Figure 13.3: Suggested Audit Team Organization Structure
for Small Organization**

Once you have designed your audit team structure and reporting relationships, you need to select individuals to fill the positions. The audit manager should be someone who has successfully managed large projects in the company, has good rapport and credibility with top management, and has a grasp of the concepts and principles relating to the Baldrige criteria. Senior auditors should be selected based upon their supervisory skills, their attention to detail, and their knowledge of the particular Baldrige Category to which they will be assigned. You will not, however, want to assign senior auditors to be in charge of auditing an area in which they currently work. For example, don't take the human resource manager and assign him/her the senior auditor position for Category 4.0, Human Resource Development and Management. Even though this person obviously knows a great deal about human resources, he/she is probably too close to it to objectively audit human resource practices and results. Select someone who knows a good deal about human resources or who once worked as a manager in this function, but now works in another function. You want a balance of objectivity and knowledge of the function being audited.

The auditors should be chosen based upon their attention to detail, knowledge of quality concepts, and knowledge of the particular Baldrige Category to which they will be assigned. It is not important that those chosen to be auditors or senior auditors be participants from past audits. An audit against the Baldrige criteria will be significantly different from an accounting, safety, or other type of audit conducted in the company.

Step 2: Write Audit Project Plan

Once your audit team has been assembled, the next task is to create a detailed project plan for the audit. The project plan defines the:

- Scope of the audit

- Areas to be examined

- Audit team members and their responsibilities

- Schedule for completion of audit tasks

- Outputs to be produced

- Specific steps or tasks to be completed during each phase of the audit

- Time estimates for each task

- Labor and materials budget for the audit

The project plan should be outlined in a group meeting of the audit manager and the senior auditors. The audit manager facilitates the group in defining both the outputs of each phase of the audit process and the steps involved in producing each of the outputs. Figure 13.4 shows some of the typical outputs that might be listed for the audit phases.

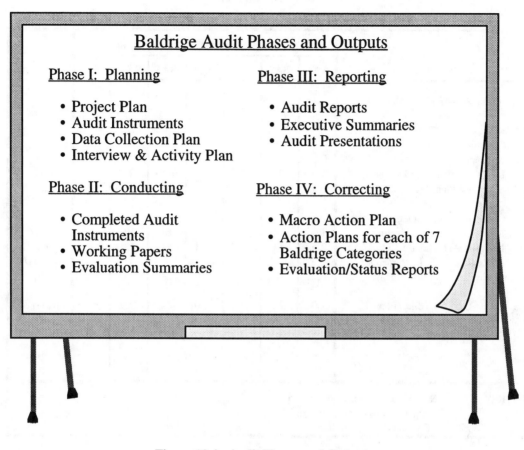

Figure 13.4: Audit Phases and Outputs

Once the outputs for all four phases have been listed, the group must specify the tasks involved in completing the first phase. After the tasks are listed, estimate time requirements for each individual who will be responsible for assisting or completing each task. Figure 13.5 shows a portion of a project plan chart for the first phase of an audit project. Notice that the time estimates are indicated in days or portions of days for each member of the audit team. (The steering committee is a group of top executives who will want to be involved in overseeing the audit.) The final column is used to schedule the various tasks listed. The scheduling is done after listing the tasks and estimating time.

Audit Project Plan

Steps/Tasks	Responsibilities & Time Requirements							Schedule
	SA1	SA2	SA3	SA4	SA5	SAM	SC	
PHASE I: AUDIT PLANNING								
1. Review Project Plan with Steering Committee								
a. Prepare for Meeting	0.5	-	-	-	-	0.5	-	11/1
b. Conduct/Attend Meeting	0.5	0.5	0.5	0.5	0.5	0.5	0.5	11/3
c. Revise Plan Based on SC Input	0.5	-	-	-	-	0.25	-	11/4
2. Create Audit Instruments								
a. Planning/Design Meeting	1.0	1.0	1.0	1.0	1.0	1.0	-	11/8
b. Write Audit Instruments	2.5	3.0	3.0	3.0	3.0	1.5	-	11/9-11/12
c. Review Audit Instruments	-	-	-	-	-	3.0	-	11/15-11/18
d. Revise Audit Instruments	0.75	1.0	1.0	1.0	1.0	-	-	11/19
3. Create Data Collection Plan	2.0	2.0	2.0	2.0	2.0	2.0	-	11/21-11/22
4. Schedule Interviews and Activities	2.5	2.5	2.5	2.5	2.5	3.0	-	11/23-11/26

KEY   SA1-SA5 = Senior Auditors 1-5
                SAM = Senior Audit Manager
                SC = Steering Committee

Figure 13.5: Audit Project Plan

Once the meeting participants have created work plan charts like the one in Figure 13.5 for all the phases of the project, the project plan itself should be outlined. The format of the written plan is flexible and should be based upon the format used for other types of project plans in your organization. It should address the process to be followed in completing the audit and describe outputs that will be produced. An outline of a typical audit project plan appears below.

OUTLINE:

Typical Audit Project Plan

    I.   Introduction and purpose
    II.   Background
    III.   Project scope, goals, and objectives
    IV.   Audit team
    V.   Phase I process and outputs
    VI.   Phase II process and outputs
    VII.   Phase III process and outputs
    VIII.   Phase IV process and outputs

Step 3: Create Audit Instruments

The Baldrige Award Criteria consist of a hierarchy of 7 Categories, 24 Examination Items, and 54 Areas to Address. Your first task in creating audit instruments is to take each of the 54 Areas to Address and break them down into 3 to 8 indicators. Chapters 6 through 12 of this book contain breakdowns of each of the 54 Areas to Address together with suggested indicators. Some examples follow for 2.1a.

2.0 INFORMATION AND ANALYSIS (Category)

2.1 Management of Information and Data (Item)

2.1a How information and data needed to drive improvement of overall company performance are selected and managed. Describe: (1) the main types of data and information and how each type is related to the key business drivers; and (2) how key requirements such as reliability, rapid access, and rapid update are derived from user needs.

INDICATORS

I.   **Existence of specific criteria for selecting measurement indices for products and services produced for external customers.**

II. **Existence of specific criteria for selecting measurement indices for products and services produced for internal customers.**

III. **Degree to which measurement indices are selected based upon their impact on customer satisfaction.**

IV. **Elimination from performance reports of any indices (and corresponding data) that don't meet selection criteria.**

V.   **Degree to which internal and external customers are involved in identifying criteria for selection of quality measurement indices.**

Once indicators have been identified for each of the Areas to Address in the Baldrige criteria, the next task is to create the first-level audit instruments, which include interview questionnaires and checklists. The complete hierarchy of audit instruments and reports is depicted in Figure 13.6.

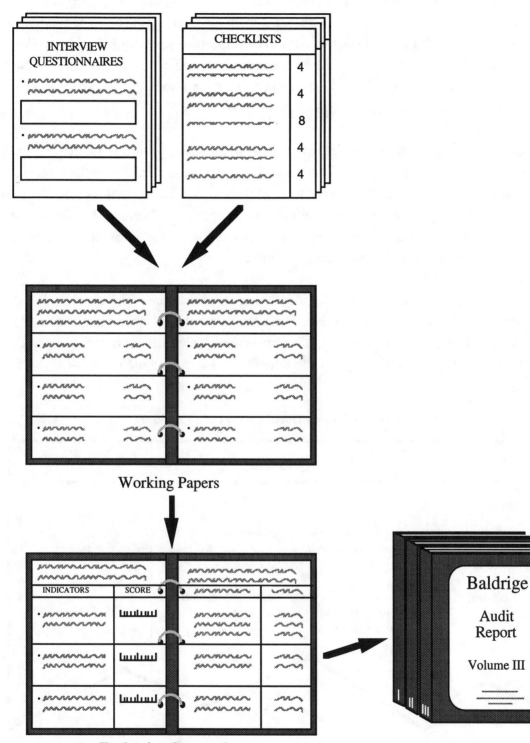

Figure 13.6: Hierarchy of Audit Instruments

To summarize the figure, the Baldrige audit reports, the final outputs, are written based upon the evaluation summaries, which are written from the working papers. The working papers summarize the findings of completed interview questionnaires and checklists. The interview questionnaires and checklists are created from the indicators. Further details on the use of the questionnaires and checklists, and on the preparation of these other reports, are covered later in this chapter.

Once you have identified the indicators, you can begin designing your questionnaire. For each indicator, create one or more questions an auditor could ask during an interview. Your questions should be direct and to the point and should enable the auditor to solicit helpful feedback from the interviewee in relation to the specific indicator. Also, be sure to list the titles of those who should be asked each question. Figure 13.7 presents a sample worksheet for identifying audit interview questions.

A similar worksheet can be developed for identifying checklist items. The checklist is used by the auditor during a review of data, procedures, systems, or observation of practices rather than during an interview. Checklists are detailed lists of criteria reflecting what you should find in a well-designed and integrated total quality management system.

Creating Audit Interview Questionnaires and Checklists

Indicator	Questions	Audience
2.1a III Degree to which measurement indices are selected based upon their impact upon customer satisfaction	• To what degree are the performance measurement indices you have selected for this Area based upon customer satisfaction? • How would improvements in these indices positively impact levels of customer satisfaction?	Directors Function Managers Supervisors Directors Function Managers

Figure 13.7: Worksheet for Identifying Audit Interview Questions

Once you have written interview questions or checklist items for each indicator and identified who you will direct each question to, you can formulate specific questionnaires for interviews. You don't want to go back to the same individual six or seven times with various questions about the Baldrige criteria. You should interview each person once, asking all of your questions in that interview. For this reason, it is important to coordinate your interview plans with other members of the audit team. We will discuss this more later.

Step 4: Create Data Collection Plan

At this point, you have written all of your interview questionnaires and checklists. Now you need to figure out who is going to be responsible for completing each questionnaire checklist. Figure 13.8 shows an example of a data collection plan for Category 1.0 (Leadership). The specific audit instruments are listed vertically along the left side of the sheet, and the auditor's initials are listed horizontally along the top of the sheet.

DATA COLLECTION PLAN

Category: 1.0 Leadership

Interview Questions and Checklists	Auditors			
	AL	BM	JS	SD
1. Senior Executive Interview Questionnaire	X			
2. Director Questionnaire regarding Senior Executives	X			
3. Employee Telephone Survey regarding Senior Executive involvement in TQM			X	
4. Public Responsibility Questionnaire for Managers and Executives		X		
5. Quality Values Checklist				X
6. Quality Values/Employee Behavior Survey				X
			X	

Figure 13.8: Example of a Data Collection Plan

Step 5: Schedule Interviews and Data Collection Activities

The final step in the planning phase of the Baldrige audit process is to schedule all of the interviews and data collection activities. Allocate interview time according to the number of questionnaires that need to be answered by the interviewee. For example, you might need to ask the top executives over a hundred questions, so you should schedule several hours for these interviews. The schedule for other data collection activities is somewhat more problematic, because it is difficult to estimate the amount of time it will take for a tour, a review of a system, etc.

In a large organization with senior auditors and many auditors, each senior auditor should have a master schedule showing the daily interviews and data collection activities of each auditor. Every auditor should prepare his/her own data collection and interview schedule and submit this to the senior auditor. Schedules should be based upon the major deadlines that have been outlined in the audit project plan.

PHASE II: CONDUCTING THE AUDIT

Purpose

The purpose of this phase is to gather and summarize the data needed to assess the organization against the Baldrige criteria. Even in a small organization, this phase will require a great deal of time. There will be many people to interview, a large amount of data to review, and many systems and procedures to observe.

Process

The specific steps that you follow may be more involved than those listed below, but in a general sense, the following three activities should be completed during this phase:

1. Gather and Document Audit Data
2. Prepare Audit Working Papers
3. Write Evaluation Summaries

Each of these steps is described below.

Step 1: Gather and Document Audit Data

Gathering data involves conducting individual and group interviews, observing systems and procedures, and reviewing data. Various data collection methods used in Baldrige audits are listed as follows.

AUDITING DATA COLLECTION TECHNIQUES

- Individual and Group Interviews
  - Executives   - Managers
  - Supervisors   - Employees
  - Customers   - Suppliers

- Review of Data
  - Product Quality Data   - Service Quality Data
  - Safety Data   - Employee Data
  - Benchmark Data   - Competitive Data
  - Customer Satisfaction   - Internal Customer Satisfaction

- Review of Resources
  - Programs   - Procedure Manuals
  - Documentation/Drawings   - Audit Reports
  - Surveys   - Plans

- Demonstrations/Work-Throughs
  - Tours   - Observation of Employees as They Perform Operations
  - Examiner/Auditor Works
    Through Processes

Your goal when conducting the interviews and observations is to find examples of actions and practices that do not meet the Baldrige criteria. The people you will be interviewing and observing will be trying to tell and show you how well they meet or exceed all of the criteria. It's very easy to be persuaded to see only the positive aspects and overlook the negatives. You will be doing your organization a great disservice if you overlook problems or concerns. Problems that are not identified will not get corrected prior to applying for the award, and your organization will lose points with the Baldrige Examiners.

The two major data collection methods used are interviews and observations. When conducting interviews, make sure that you ask the same questions to several different levels of employees. For example, don't just ask executives if they are committed to quality; ask some of the employees how committed to quality the executives are.

Even though your interview questionnaires may contain specific questions, it is better not to run through the questions one at a time. Make the interview a little less structured and ask some open-ended questions to encourage interviewees to talk. Some examples are listed below:

- "Give me some examples of decisions your boss has made that show his commitment to quality."

- "Tell me about the process you use to create the strategic quality plan."

- "How do you determine what training people require on quality topics?"

- "How well do we do in handling customer complaints as compared to our biggest competitors?"

Along with interviews, auditors spend a great deal of time reviewing data and observing practices and procedures. Again, keep in mind that as an auditor you are looking for problems. The people who prepare the data will try to make them look as positive as possible. If there are missing data, this probably means that the auditors are trying to hide something. For example, if data on some dimension are presented from the past five years, but data from only the past two years are presented for other dimensions, the missing data are most likely negative.

When you are conducting tours or observations, people will tend to be on their best behavior. Everyone will know why you are there and will behave accordingly. It will be difficult for you to find anything negative if all of your observations are announced. It is good idea to do some unannounced inspections and observations so you will have a better chance of seeing things the way they really are.

Step 2: Prepare Audit Working Papers

At this point in the audit, you will have generated reams of interview notes, references, graphs, and completed checklists. Your next task is to begin summarizing this information so that it can be reviewed and evaluated. This is done by creating audit working papers. Figure 13.9 presents a sample of what your audit working papers might look like.

1.0 Leadership 1.1 Senior Executive Leadership a. Senior Executives' leadership, personal involvement and visibility in performance excellence goals		1.0 Leadership 1.1 Senior Executive Leadership a. Senior Executives' leadership, personal involvement, and visibility in performance excellence goals	
INDICATOR — Amount and percentage of time each executive spends on performance excellence goals		INDICATOR — Amount and percentage of time each executive spends on performance excellence goals	
ACTIVITIES	**NOTES/EVIDENCE**	**CORRECTIVE ACTIONS**	**FOLLOW-UP NEEDED**
• Interview President	Says he spends more than 50% of his time on performance-related activities. Has no record of time spent or activities completed. Need data to validate this claim.	Have secretary track President's performance-related activities for a couple of months to get some data on how much time he spends. Design data collection form and procedure for secretary.	Check with secretary in 2-3 months
• Interview V.P. Finance	Says that due to the nature of her job, she does not spend much time on activities relating to performance excellence goals. She estimates that she spends 2-4 hours a week.	Develop action plan that identifies specific tasks that V.P. Finance should perform that support performance excellence goals. Develop tracking system to obtain data on time spent on performance improvement activities.	Monitor degree to which tasks are being completed and amount of time being spent

Figure 13.9: Sample Audit Working Papers

As you can see, the page spread covers a single indicator. Data gathering activities such as interviews and observations are listed in the far left column. Notes and evidence relating to the degree to which the indicator is met are written in the next column. Notice that in this example, what the president says about the amount of time he spends on quality-related activities is recorded, but the notes specify that there are no data to back up his claims. On the left side of the facing page you list any corrective actions you think would help improve the organization's or individual's performance on this indicator. In the case of this president, it says that he needs to start tracking the activities and time he spends on the quality improvement effort. For the vice president of finance, it suggests that an action plan be developed that outlines specific activities she should be performing to support the quality improvement effort. The final column on the right side of the facing page is used to list any follow-up needed to collect further data or obtain the answers to questions.

This format for the working papers is simply a suggestion. You should design your own working papers in a way that works best for your organization. The only real guidelines to follow are that the working papers should address each indicator individually and that they should be a summary, and therefore less detailed than your interview/observation notes.

Once the auditors have completed the first draft of the working papers, it should be submitted to the senior auditors for review. The senior auditors review the working papers for clarity and thoroughness and write what accounting auditors call "points." Points are notes or suggestions of issues that the auditor did not address or notes regarding additional information that the auditor needs to gather.

After discussing the "points" with the senior auditor, the auditor goes back to gather additional data and to rewrite portions of the working papers. This cycle may be repeated several times until the senior auditor is satisfied that all important issues have been addressed properly. These "review and revise" cycles are often painful for the auditors, but they are necessary to ensure that the audit is thorough and objective.

Step 3: Write Evaluation Summaries

The third and final step in this phase of conducting the audit is to prepare evaluation summaries that will be used to write audit reports. Up to this point in the audit process, individual auditors have mainly been working on their own, collecting and documenting data. Now is the time when the audit teams get together to discuss and summarize their findings. In a large organization, you should hold separate meetings—one for each audit team assigned to the seven categories of Baldrige criteria. In a small organization with a single audit team of six to eight people, a series of meetings with the team will be necessary. The purposes of these meetings are to obtain input from all auditors and to reach a consensus regarding the ratings to give the organization against the various Examination Items, Areas to Address, and indicators in the Baldrige Award Criteria. Even though the Baldrige Examiners assign a score only to each of the 24 Examination Items, and then to each of the seven categories, it is recommended that you score all aspects as depicted in Figure 13.10.

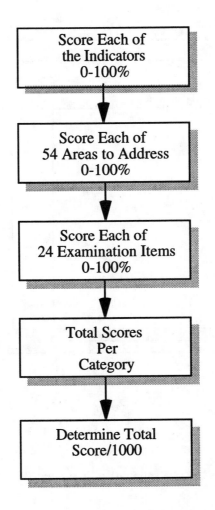

Figure 13.10: Audit Scoring Process

For the sake of the example, let's assume that you work for a large organization that has seven individual audit teams, each consisting of a senior auditor and three to eight auditors. Each of the seven groups will attend a two- to three-day meeting where final scores will be decided and examination summaries written.

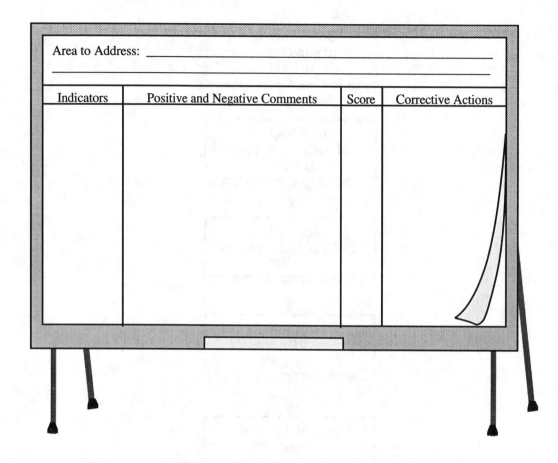

Figure 13.11: Examination Summary Flip Chart

Prior to the meeting you should prepare a series of flip charts, like the one in Figure 13.11, to use in writing the examination summaries.

It is best to use double-wide easels and flip-chart paper for these meetings. If this is not available, two standard flip-chart easels can be placed side by side so that all four columns of information can fit on one sheet. At the top of the sheet, list one of the Areas to Address that falls under the audit team's participation category. Begin the meeting by explaining that you are going to lead the group in discussing and scoring each indicator, one at a time. Write the first indicator for the first Area to Address at the top of the first column of the flip chart. Ask the team members to refer to their working papers and to volunteer some of the significant positive and negative comments they have regarding the organization's performance on this indicator. Ask for input from all of the auditors that examined this indicator and try to get a balance of positive and negative comments. If performance on an indicator is particularly bad, try to find at least one positive comment to write. Figure 13.12 depicts a portion of a flip chart with information on the indicator and comments filled in.

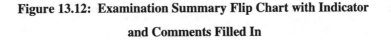

Area to Address:	1.1a. Senior Executive Leadership		

Indicators	Positive and Negative Comments	Score	Corrective Actions
• Amount and percentage of time each exec. spends on performance-related activities	+ President spends up to 50% of his time on performance-related activities + All executives spend at least a few hours a week on performance-related activities		

Figure 13.12: Examination Summary Flip Chart with Indicator
and Comments Filled In

As you are gathering comments from the auditors in the meeting, remember that the goal is to prepare a summary. Therefore, fifteen or twenty comments on a single indicator is probably too many. A better number might be three or four positive and three or four negative comments. Select the ones that are most important and for which you have the most supporting evidence.

Once the comments have been documented, the group must decide on a score for this indicator. A percentage scoring system should be used, similar to the Baldrige evaluation, with 100% indicating perfect performance. The group should reach a consensus on the score based upon the positive and negative comments that have been listed and discussed. Therefore, even auditors who did not examine a particular indicator can offer their input to the scoring decisions. After deciding on a percentage score for the indicator, the group needs to identify corrective actions that should be taken to improve the organization's score on this indicator. Figure 13.13 shows a portion of an evaluation summary flip chart with this information filled in.

Area to Address:	1.1a. Senior Executive Leadership		
Indicators	**Positive and Negative Comments**	**Score**	**Corrective Actions**
• Amount and percentage of time each exec. spends on performance-related activities	+ President spends up to 50% of his time on performance-related activities + All executives spend at least a few hours a week on performance-related activities − No data on the activities or hours executives devote to performance-related activities − Several Vice Presidents spend very little time on performance-related activities	30%	• Begin tracking time and activities of execs. • Assign specific performance-related activities to execs • Monitor completion of performance-related activities by execs. • Set goals for amount of time

Figure 13.13: Examination Summary Flip Chart with all Four Columns Filled In

The corrective actions should come from the auditors' working papers and should be a summary of all of the corrective actions they may have listed. Corrective actions should specify what can be done to improve performance on an indicator, but they should not specify how a particular improvement will be done or by whom it should be done. That will be determined later when action plans are created.

When the group finishes this exercise for the first indicator, post the flip charts on the meeting room wall, and proceed with the next indicator. You can see why this meeting will require several days. The group could spend a few hours creating the charts on each indicator, and there may be over 50 different indicators to discuss in some of the larger categories, such as Customer Focus and Satisfaction. If you want to shorten the length of the meeting, divide the audit team into subgroups that focus upon specific Examination Items. For example, Category 3.0 (Strategic Planning) is divided into two Examination Items. If the audit team that looked at Category 3.0 comprises four members, split the team into two subgroups, each responsible for creating the examination summaries for one of the two Examination Items. This will shorten the overall meeting time, but the quality of the documentation will not be as good because fewer auditors can offer their input in creating the summaries. This second phase of the audit process is complete when all meetings have been conducted and all of the evaluation summaries have been written.

PHASE III: REPORTING AUDIT FINDINGS

Purpose

The purpose of this phase is to prepare audit reports for various audiences, present the contents of the reports, and to revise the reports as necessary.

Process

The audit report is written by a team of senior auditors using the examination summaries created in the previous phase. Although the format of the report is flexible, a suggested outline is as follows.

AUDIT REPORT OUTLINE

    I.   Background on the Baldrige Award and Total Quality Management

   II.   Audit Methodology

  III.   Overview of Baldrige Criteria

        A. Categories, Items, and Areas to Address

        B. Scoring System

  IV.   Category 1.0 Leadership

        A. Findings

        B. Recommendations

   V.   Category 2.0 Information and Analysis

        A. Findings

        B. Recommendations

  VI.   Category 3.0 Strategic Planning

        A. Findings

        B. Recommendations

 VII.   Category 4.0 Human Resource Development and Management

        A. Findings

        B. Recommendations

VIII.   Category 5.0 Process Management

        A. Findings

        B. Recommendations

  IX.   Category 6.0 Business Results

        A. Findings

        B. Recommendations

   X.   Category 7.0 Customer Focus and Satisfaction

        A. Findings

        B. Recommendations

The first section of the report should provide some background information on both the Baldrige Award and total quality management. You should explain how and why the award was developed, talk about organizations that have won in the past, and explain how the criteria for the award serve as a national set of standards by which all organizations can evaluate their efforts to improve quality. This section should also contain the reasons your organization became involved in its assessment and improvement plan and some of the major actions that have occurred relating to the effort.

Finally, you should explain the organization's intentions with regard to the Baldrige Award. If you intend to apply for the award in 1996, say, state this. For many organizations the results of the audit will determine when they apply for the Baldrige Award.

Section II of the audit report is designed to provide information on how the audit was conducted. Some of the specific questions and issues that should be addressed in this section are:

- How was the audit team organized and who was on it?

- Who was interviewed and what types of questions were asked?

- What types of data and printed materials were reviewed?

- What instruments were developed to gather audit data?

- How were observations and reviews of systems accomplished?

- How were data summarized?

- How were scores and corrective actions determined?

This section of the report should be thorough, but not more than 20 pages in length. To maximize space, details such as the specific instruments used can go into appendices.

Section III of the audit report should provide an overview of the Baldrige criteria.

It should include explanations of the seven different categories, along with the Examination Items and Areas to Address that comprise each category. Explain that each Area to Address is broken down into indicators, which are what auditors look for in their evaluation of the organization. This section of the report should be no more than 15 pages in length. Do not go into great detail explaining each Area to Address and indicator. Detailed information is more useful in the individual sections of the report covering the seven categories of criteria.

The seven remaining sections of the audit report address the findings and recommendations relevant to a particular category of the award criteria. These sections should use similar formats and include the same headings of information. Begin each section with a description of the category and a definition of the Examination Items covered, followed by a one- or two-page summary of the findings in this category. The reader ought to be able to get a general feeling of the organization's performance in this category by reviewing this summary. Follow the summary with a discussion of the

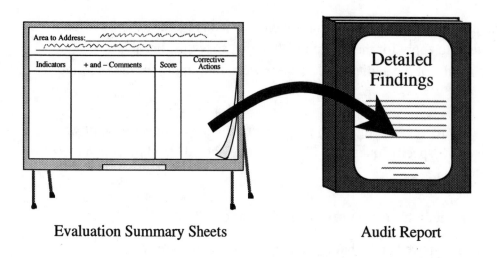

Evaluation Summary Sheets   Audit Report

**Figure 13.14: How to Write Detailed Findings Sections
in the Audit Report**

detailed findings and your recommendations for actions that need to be taken to improve performance (see Figure 13.14).

For example, begin with the first Area to Address under the first Examination Item. Define the Examination Item and Area to Address, using the text from the Baldrige Award Criteria. Next, list and explain the first indicator and provide your evaluation of the organization's performance on this indicator. This information should be presented in narrative style based upon the comments written in the evaluation summaries.

Follow your discussion of the organization's performance against the first indicator with your recommendations for actions that need to be taken to improve performance. This section can best be presented as a list of recommendations followed by an explanation of each recommendation.

Each of the seven sections presenting the detailed findings and recommendations will be between 30 and 60 pages in length, depending on the number of indicators you address and the amount of information there is to present. This is the body of the report, however, and should include a great deal of detail.

Once a draft of the entire audit report has been written, the audit manager, and perhaps an upper-level manager who has not been involved in the audit, should review it. The report is to be reviewed for completeness and clarity. Have the report edited to make it read as if it were written by one person and to make sure the headings and style of each section are consistent. After the necessary revisions are made, make an executive summary of the report. This document should be 6–10 pages in length, cover the same information covered in the larger report, and address the content from the perspective of top management in the organization. I suggest that the audit manager be the one to write the executive summary. This document should also be edited by an editor and reviewed by several people who have been involved in the audit.

After the abbreviated and full-length versions of the audit report have been completed, the next task is to prepare a list of presentations that need to be made. You will probably need three types of presentations:

- Presentation to the audit team
- Presentation to upper management
- Presentation to middle management and key technical professionals

It is important to remember that the audit team needs a review of the entire audit findings and recommendations. Up to this point, they have been exposed only to the particular area they were assigned to audit. This presentation to the audit team will last several hours, as each senior auditor presents his or her audit category to the team. The presentation to the audit team should be done first because it serves as a dry run for the remaining presentations.

The next presentation is to upper management. This can be the same presentation you gave to the audit team or an abbreviated version of it. The length of the presentation and the amount of detail covered depend upon the willingness of management to devote a half day or more of their time to this. Under no circumstances should the presentation to upper management be more than one day in length. Do not attempt to present all of the information contained in the audit report—simply present the highlights.

The final series of presentations to be done are those to function directors, managers, and key technical professionals. Tailor these presentations to the issues that can be dealt with by the individuals in these functions. All groups should get a brief overview of the findings and recommendations that pertain to the entire organization, followed by presentations on the findings and recommendations that are unique to that function.

PHASE IV: CORRECTING AUDIT FINDINGS

Purpose

The purpose of this final phase in the audit cycle is to correct any and all problems and deficits identified during the audit. This is the most critical phase in the audit process; unfortunately, it is also the phase most often done poorly. Accepting the audit findings is difficult enough—none of us likes to hear about our shortcomings. Dealing with the concerns that were identified is time consuming and often quite difficult. Some of the changes required will take several years to properly implement, and are usually resisted.

Process

The major steps in this fourth phase of the audit cycle are outlined and described below.

> 1. Form Steering Committee
> 2. Create Macro Action Plan
> 3. Create Individual Action Plans for Baldrige Categories
> 4. Implement and Evaluate Recommendations

Step 1: Form Steering Committee

After all presentations on the audit findings and recommendations have been completed, the next step is to form a steering committee that will oversee the plans and projects put into action to correct the concerns and problems identified in the audit. The steering committee will provide the resources, impetus, and direction to individuals working on the audit-driven changes, without working on the changes themselves. The steering committee should be made up of 6 to 10 individuals who are members of top management in the organization. Ideally, the steering committee should consist of the president or CEO, along with his/her direct reports. The higher up in the organization the members of the steering committee are, the more likely the audit-driven changes will actually be completed. (If a steering committee was already in place during Phases I through III, you can work with this same committee provided that the members have the necessary authority to bring about change.)

The steering committee members will not need to spend a great deal of time managing the Correction Phase of the audit cycle, but their involvement is critical. Many of the changes needed to correct the concerns identified in the audit will require top management authority to implement. Major changes are often needed in procedures, policies, and practices.

The responsibilities of the steering committee are outlined as follows.

STEERING COMMITTEE RESPONSIBILITIES

- Develop Macro Action Plan for Implementing Audit-Driven Changes
- Assign Responsibilities to Key Managers
- Attend Periodic Status Meetings
- Review Status Reports
- Commit Necessary Resources and Remove Obstacles
- Make Major Policy and Procedure Decisions as Needed

One of the biggest mistakes made when forming a steering committee is to assign individuals to the committee who are at too low a level in the organization. A steering committee made up of function and department managers will not have the clout and decision-making authority to do what it takes to implement the audit-driven changes. Often the top executives don't see why they need to be involved. Implementing total quality management, however, must be done *from the top down.* Every company that has won the Baldrige Award will testify to this. Top management support means more than allocating the necessary resources. Executives must be visibly involved in the quality effort and devote a good portion of their own time to it.

Step 2: Create Macro Action Plan

The steering committee must first meet to create the macro, or long-term, action plan. The overall goals relating to quality are to be included in this plan. Two types of goals that should be set are:

- Performance results goals
- Performance process goals

Samples of macro results and process goals are shown below.

PERFORMANCE RESULTS GOALS

- Achieve customer satisfaction scores of 94 percent satisfaction by the end of 1996.
- Achieve goal of no more than 20 defects per million products by the end of 1995.
- Achieve internal customer satisfaction scores averaging 95 percent by the end of the second quarter of 1995.
- Earn 12 percent before-tax profit on income of $2.5 billion.

PERFORMANCE PROCESS GOALS

- Apply for the Baldrige Award in 1996 and achieve a score of at least 700/1000.
- Implement a comprehensive system for measuring competitors' customer satisfaction levels by the end of 1995.
- Achieve an internal Baldrige Audit score of 700/1000 by the end of 1994.
- Redesign strategic planning process to reduce cycle time from 19 weeks to 6 weeks.

After macro goals have been established for the performance improvement effort, the steering committee must review and prioritize the recommendations contained in the audit report. Begin with the Leadership category and list the major recommendations or changes on a flip chart. Number each one, as shown in Figure 13.15. Once the recommendations are listed, ask the members of the steering committee to individually prioritize the recommendations from most to least important. Write the steering committee members' initials on the chart as shown, and leave two final columns for the sum of the priorities and the numerical order of the group's priorities.

CATEGORY: 1.0 – LEADERSHIP							
RECOMMENDATIONS	Individual Priorities					Total	Final Priorities
	MG	JS	AT	RM	SV		
1. Executive training in quality leadership	1	6	2	5	1	15	1
2. Time Tracking System	7	8	7	2	8	32	6
3. Establishing accountabilities for performance results for all executives	6	1	3	1	4	15	1
4. Develop a clear set of values	3	3	5	4	2	17	2
5. Create Action Plan for improving executives' involvement in employee recognition	2	5	1	6	5	19	3
6. Establish goals for improving executives' involvement in public responsibilities	8	7	8	3	7	33	7
7. Develop system for evaluating extent to which values are demonstrated in employee behavior	4	4	6	7	3	24	4
8. Develop participative process for managing quality and performance	5	2	4	8	6	25	5

Figure 13.15: Prioritizing Recommendations with the Steering Committee

As you can see in Figure 13.15, the individual's ratings are added across the columns, with the sum appearing in the "total" column for each row. The recommendation with the lowest overall score is assigned the highest priority. In the example above, two of the recommendations are tied for top priority: "Executive training in quality leadership," and "Establishing accountabilities for performance results for all executives." This method of prioritizing works well because it is quick, and everyone has an equal say in establishing the overall priorities. The same process is continued for each of the six remaining Baldrige categories. Once all of the recommendations are prioritized, the steering committee should assign one individual to each of the seven categories to be responsible for carrying out the recommendations. These individuals should be high enough in the organization to make the necessary changes and implement the projects initiated by the recommendations. Each of these managers will form his/her own committee to work on creating more detailed plans for developing and implementing the high-priority recommendations.

Before concluding the steering committee meeting, establish a schedule for development of the seven quality improvement teams and the creation of detailed plans by each team. Also establish dates for periodic review meetings, where team leaders will present their progress to the steering committee. It is a good idea to schedule these meetings once each quarter. Monthly meetings are a possibility if the organization is in a hurry to get the changes implemented.

Step 3: Create Individual Action Plans For Baldrige Categories

Each of the seven quality improvement teams has the responsibility to design and implement the recommendations under one of the Baldrige criteria categories. Those recommendations that cut across categories will be assigned to one of the seven teams. The first task of the teams is to hold a meeting to develop detailed project plans for the recommendations for which they are responsible. Each recommendation may require a separate plan, or several recommendations may be combined into a single project. For example, it might make sense to combine recommendations 3 and 5 from Figure 13.15 into one project. The project plans created at this stage are similar to the project plan that was created for the audit itself. You begin by listing the tasks involved in completing the project, then estimating the time required for project personnel, and finally, assigning deadlines to each of the project tasks.

Figure 13.16 depicts a project plan for creating a set of values for the organization.

| | Responsibilities & Time Requirements | | | | | |
Steps/Tasks	PM	AM	ST	PC	WP	Schedule
TEAM: LEADERSHIP						
1. Form Project Committee	0.25	0.5	-	-	-	
2. Review Resources	0.5	0.5	0.5	-	-	
3. Conduct/Attend Meeting to Draft Values						
a. Prepare for meeting	0.25	0.5	0.5	-	-	
b. Conduct/attend meeting	1.0	1.0	1.0	1.0	-	
c. Document meeting outputs	-	1.0	-	-	1.0	
4. Values Feedback Survey						
a. Prepare survey	0.25	0.5	0.5	-	1.0	
b. Administer survey	0.25	1.0	0.25	-	2.0	
c. Document survey results	0.5	1.0	0.5	0	2.0	
5. Project Committee Review Meeting						
a. Prepare for meeting	0.25	0.25	-	-	0.5	
b. Conduct/attend meeting to review feedback and decide on values	0.5	0.5	0.5	0.5	-	
c. Document meeting outputs	-	0.5	-	-	0.5	

KEY   PM = Project Manager   PC = Project Committee
          AM = Al Masters   WP = Word Processing
          ST = Sam Turner

Figure 13.16: Project Plan for Creating Quality Values

This is a simple project compared to some of the other recommendations. Notice that there is a project manager and two other team members working on this project. There is also a project committee made up of executives responsible for determining the values of the organization. Once the executives have drafted a set of values, they are tested with a cross section of employees to determine people's reactions. Based upon the employees' reactions, the values will be revised as necessary and communicated to all employees.

Step 4: Implement and Evaluate Recommendations

There are no specific steps to follow in implementing the recommendations because the approach depends upon the complexity and nature of the recommendation. For example, the values simply need to be communicated to employees to be implemented. Other recommendations, such as a system for evaluating the degree to which employee behavior is consistent with the values, will require much more work.

Because there will be seven different teams working on developing recommendations to improve quality, it is important that all seven teams work together to come up with an implementation plan. The seven team leaders need to meet to review the status of their projects and discuss implementation plans. It is important that the performance improvement effort be an integrated one rather than be seven different groups working independently of one another. In this meeting the leaders must lay out all of the high-priority recommendations to be implemented for the year, and identify an implementation sequence that makes the most sense. Make sure to note whether the implementation of one recommendation is a prerequisite for another. Many of the recommendations in the Leadership category are prerequisites to those in other categories. Basic quality values need to be established before other activities can be initiated.

It is extremely important to evaluate the impact of each recommendation to determine whether the change or new approach actually improves processes or results. Go back to the indicators in the audit report that pertain to a given recommendation. You should be measuring performance on these indicators both before and after introducing the recommendations that pertain to these indicators. Measuring the performance of the indicators before and after implementation of the recommendations will allow you to determine whether they have had the desired effect on the indicators. Plot these before-and-after data on graphs to determine the relative impact the change has had on performance. This type of data is useful not only for demonstrating a return on investment in your performance improvement efforts, but also for diagnostic purposes when a recommendation fails to produce the desired results. Figure 13.17 presents an example of a measure of number of hours per month executives spend with customers or employees before and after they set goals and started having to report this figure to the president.

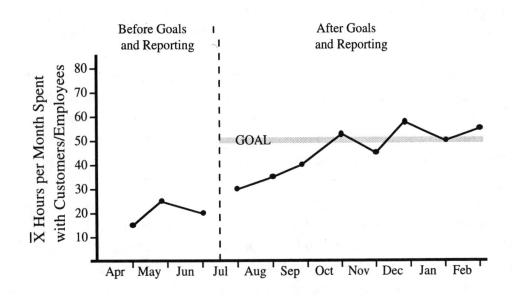

**Figure 13.17: Evaluation of Goals and Reporting on Average Number
of Hours per Month Executives Spend with Customers and Employees**

The results in Figure 13.17 show that executives averaged about 20 hours a month with customers and employees before the goals and reporting started, and that they reached the target of 50 hours a month within four months after the goal and reporting began. This graph clearly shows that the strategy employed was successful. It would be difficult to calculate the return on investment for this particular project, but the cause-effect relationship between the changes introduced and the average number of hours spent with customers and employees is clear.

CONCLUSIONS

In this chapter, I have presented an approach to auditing your organization against the Baldrige criteria. Previous chapters have provided you with lists of indicators that can be used to assess your performance on each of the 54 Areas to Address in the Baldrige criteria. In this chapter, I have explained how to use these indicators to develop audit instruments to audit your own organization against the Baldrige criteria. But, you might ask, why bother? Why not pay the $4,000 and apply for the Baldrige Award so you can have an audit done by actual Baldrige Examiners?

First of all, you will spend a great deal of time and money preparing the application for the award. Unless you are fairly certain of at least being a finalist, this is a great deal of money to spend. If you do actually apply for the award and receive low scores from the Examiners reviewing your application, you will not receive a site visit. A score in the high 600s or better is necessary to warrant a site visit, where a team of Baldrige Examiners spends several days in your company auditing your practices and results.

An internal audit such as the one described in this chapter is more for diagnostic than evaluative purposes. Its goal is to identify areas of weakness and recommend specific actions that can be taken to remedy the areas of weakness. As such, it is much more thorough than a site visit conducted by Baldrige Examiners. The report you receive from the Baldrige Examiners will not include recommendations but only findings regarding the strengths and weaknesses of your quality practices and results.

Once you have conducted several of the internal audits of the sort described in this chapter and have received scores of 600 or more from your internal auditors, you are ready to actually apply for the Malcolm Baldrige Award. I work with a number of companies who think they are a year or two away from applying and possibly winning the Baldrige Award. Going through an audit such as the one described here can be an eye-opening experience for management. Most often they realize they are five or more years away from being ready to apply for the award, and have a great deal of work to do to change their organization to better meet the award criteria.

An audit is valuable only if the organization is willing to make the changes identified and implement the recommendations made by the auditors. I've worked with many organizations that will spend the time and money for a thorough quality audit, but will not commit the resources needed to implement the recommendations that come out of the audit. It is critical to get top management to commit to doing something about the audit findings before embarking upon such a comprehensive evaluation of the organization in the first place. Once management commits to following through on the findings, you may well be on your way to achieving Baldrige Award winning quality.

Chapter 14

Using a Baldrige Assessment as a Strategic Planning Tool

ASSESSMENT ALTERNATIVES

The previous chapter presented details on how to audit your organization against the Baldrige criteria. This approach is very thorough, but many organizations don't have the resources to use it to the best effect. Most of the companies I've worked with in conducting Baldrige assessments over the past few years don't use the full-scale audit approach. Rather, a number of other basic methods are used. These are listed below in order of least to most objective and thorough, and of least to most expensive.

1.   Survey based on the Baldrige criteria

2.   Armchair assessment

3.   Mock Baldrige application

4.   Formal Baldrige application

5.   Audit against the Baldrige criteria

1. Baldrige Survey—The simplest and least expensive method of establishing some baseline data on where you stand in your implementation of the Baldrige standards is to send out a survey to all or a sample of employees, having them rate the organization on how well it has implemented each of the items making up the Baldrige criteria. A large variety of surveys exist that may be used for this purpose. One that has been written by the author was published for the last few years in the *Journal for Quality and Participation.*

Using such a survey, or similar ones available through TQM consulting firms, is the least expensive way of evaluating your own status. However, it is also the least reliable, regardless of which survey instrument you are using. The problem with any survey is that it is subjective. People responding to the survey don't usually have the "big picture" of what is happening in the company, and they often mark their responses to the survey items based upon limited and most recent experiences. I've administered Baldrige surveys to 100 or so people in a single organization and gotten scores that ranged from 250 to 800 out of a possible 1000 points. Does this mean that the survey instrument is poor? Perhaps, but I believe that all TQM surveys are at best a very rough and rudimentary indicator. Considering the low cost of the survey, however, this tool does provide you with a basic idea of where you stand, without spending much money or time.

2. Armchair Assessment—The second approach is a good deal more thorough and more useful than a survey, without much added expense. I have used this approach with a number of large organizations and have talked to a number of others that use a variation on it. Here's how it works. A team of senior executives from the business unit or organization being assessed attend a two-day workshop to learn the Baldrige criteria and gain an understanding of how an assessment is done. Next, the executive team attends a one-day meeting where they begin to assess their own organization. During the meeting, a facilitator begins by reviewing the first Baldrige Examination Item, explaining what it means. Next, the participants brainstorm a list of the organization's strengths and areas for improvement relating to that Item. The pluses and minuses are listed by the facilitator on a flip chart. After listing a page or so of strengths and areas for improvements, the facilitator asks the group to suggest a percentage score in multiples of 10. The group discusses and reaches consensus on a percentage score, the facilitator writes it on the flip chart, and together they move on to the next Item. This process continues until all 24 Items have been completed. A time limit of 15 minutes is observed for discussing each Item, so the meeting is very fast-moving. After listing comments and scoring each of the 24 Baldrige Items, percentage scores are multiplied by the official point value of each Item to compute the final score. The 24 flip chart pages are typed and become the complete assessment report. Total time commitment for the approach is three days.

While this approach is quick and relatively inexpensive, it does have some problems. First, the objectivity of the senior executives is not always what it should be. The executives sometimes find it easier to list the good things than to spend time thinking of areas for improvement. They also tend to give more credit for partial deployment of systems or approaches than a Baldrige Examiner would. Executives also tend to score a little higher than a Baldrige Examiner might. The personality of the CEO or the most senior executive in the meeting also can make this approach problematic. I've observed a few assessment meetings where the participants simply deferred to what the senior executives said and what he/she said the score was.

Even with its problems, this approach is much better than using any kind of survey. The assessment is more thorough; you end up with a page of strengths, areas for improvement, and a score on each of the 24 items; and executives buy in to the results of the assessment more readily because they did it. This approach will only work, however, if the senior executives are willing to devote three days for training and assessment. Executives in many organizations don't feel they need to be involved in such training or assessment and prefer to delegate this task to others. The Armchair Assessment will only work if you can get the senior executives to commit to it.

3. Mock Baldrige Application—This is by far the most commonly used approach for assessment against the Baldrige criteria. This approach is currently being used by, among others, AT&T, IBM, Baxter Healthcare, Northrop, McDonnell Douglas, Roadway Express, Whirlpool, Cargill, Westinghouse, Johnson & Johnson, Appleton Papers, and Boise Cascade. The approach involves having business units, facilities, or even departments in a company prepare their own application using the same format as the Baldrige application. Generally, all 24 Items are required to be addressed and the applications are often about the same size (70 pages) as an official application. Applications are reviewed and individually scored by a team of examiners from other departments or units, who then get together to reach consensus on the final scores. Examiners are usually company employees who have been trained in a 2–4-day workshop. Some companies use outsiders to supplement their team of internal examiners, adding Baldrige consultants, customers, and suppliers, for example.

In some companies, such as Baxter and IBM, the examiners score the written applications and do site visits on the best (usually the top 15%–20%). Most organizations also have their own quality awards that they give out to the best performers. The major difference between the Armchair Assessment and the Mock Baldrige Application is that one always uses examiners from one business unit or department to evaluate another business unit or department. Some organizations have gotten senior executives involved as part of their team of examiners. Cargill, a major agricultural firm with 70,000 employees, has a team of about 50 examiners that includes about 15 senior executives. Most senior executives in the Northrop Corporation also have spent at least one year serving as an examiner for their award. A side benefit of getting executives to be examiners is that they almost always come away from the experience as staunch believers in the value of the Baldrige criteria as a tool for running a better organization.

The advantage of this approach over the previous two, then, is the objectivity and thoroughness of the assessment and feedback. The approach can give you the same level of analysis and feedback that a company would get by applying for the Baldrige Award. The approach also does a great deal to help move the organization toward being an excellent company. Examiners become internal experts on the Baldrige criteria, and can help others to work toward satisfying the criteria. Another advantage is that you can get near immediate feedback on your application and probe the examiners for details if the feedback is unclear. Examiners can provide recommendations about what the organization should do to improve the areas for improvement that were uncovered in the assessment.

The only real disadvantage of this approach is that it is much more expensive than the other two. You will recall from Chapter 3 that it takes a great deal of time to write an application. In this case, time will also need to be spent in training examiners, having them review and score the applications, and possibly go on site visits. Examiners in many companies that use this approach can be expected to spend the following amount of time on the activities listed:

- Attend examiner training   3 days
- Score written applications   2 days × 3 applications = 6 days
- Reach consensus on scores   .5 day × 3 applications = 1.5 days
- Prepare and conduct site visit   5 days
- Prepare and present feedback report   2 days _____
                                              17.5 days

When you consider that some large companies such as AT&T have over 100 examiners, this can add up to a major investment. If you supplement your team of internal examiners with consultants or other outsiders, the cost can become even greater.

4. Formal Baldrige Application—A fourth and less commonly used approach for assessment is to formally apply for the Baldrige Award to see where you stand. This strategy was used by a number of organizations that later went on to win the award. (They applied and failed to win at least once before finally winning the award.) Miliken, Federal Express, Cadillac, and others all used the initial feedback they received to then go on to win. The $4,000 it costs to apply for the award for a large organization is minimal compared to the value of the feedback received. For $4,000 ($1,200 for small companies) you get a team of six to eight official examiners who will individually score your application, reach consensus on your scores, and present you with a feedback report that gives you a page of strengths, areas for improvement, and scores for each of the 24 Baldrige Items. If you are lucky enough to receive a site visit, a team of examiners will spend up to a week in your organization doing a further assessment. If you were to pay an outside consulting firm to conduct such an assessment, you would probably pay $30,000–$50,000 or more. Applying for the Baldrige Award to receive feedback is perhaps one of the government's biggest bargains.

If formally applying for the award offers such advantages, why don't more companies do it? Besides the initial cost (relatively small though it may be), the disadvantages are as follows. First, there is the long delay between the time you send in the application (April 3rd) and the time you receive feedback (November or December). This means that you can't use the feedback for planning purposes until the following year. A second disadvantage is that the approach forces you to apply as an entire company, or at least its major business units; units or facilities that have fewer than 500 employees are not allowed to apply for the Baldrige Award. A third disadvantage is that you do not receive your final score—only ranges are provided. This makes it difficult to gauge the level of improvement each year. Another problem is that you are not allowed to talk to anyone about your feedback. I know of one Baldrige applicant that received a feedback report which was extremely vague. One page had three positive comments, an area for improvement, and a score of 20 percent. When the organization called the Baldrige office and asked to speak to the examiners or someone who could explain their feedback and scores, they were informed that no one was allowed to talk to them about these matters. One final reason why applying for the award as an assessment method may not be a good idea is that a low score might have a negative impact on employee morale. Imagine how the results would play if you received a score of 175 out of 1000 (when you may have been expecting around 600). Such results will be used as ammunition by those employees who believe total quality management is just another passing fad. Baldrige also does not provide you with an overall score, or scores for each of the 24 items.

5. Audit Against the Baldrige Criteria—The most thorough and most expensive way of evaluating your implementation of total quality management is to prepare and conduct an audit of the organization's practices and results based upon the Baldrige criteria (see Chapter 12). This involves developing a detailed audit plan, creating audit instruments, and spending many hours interviewing various levels of employees, reviewing quality data, and observing processes and practices. The advantage of this approach over the other four is its objectivity and the level of detailed feedback provided. The scope of the audit can vary considerably, and can be tailored to the organization's resource constraints. Some large organizations devote thousands of hours to such audits, and assign 10 to 20 employees to work full time for several months on the audit. Another organization I know of assigned a task force of seven people, and each spent a total of about 10 person-days on the audit.

The audit is very similar to the approach taken by the Baldrige Examiners when they do a site visit. However, you don't need to prepare a mock or real Baldrige application to conduct a Baldrige audit. The audit instruments are developed using the Baldrige criteria and the assessments are done based upon interviews, observations, and reviews of data rather than by reading a 75-page summary of the organization's approach to quality. (Again, see Chapter 13 of this book for details on how to conduct an audit against the Baldrige criteria.)

USING THE BALDRIGE ASSESSMENT TO DRIVE IMPROVEMENT

Getting assessed against the Baldrige criteria is the organizational equivalent of getting a three-day physical. The problem, however, is that many organizations have not figured out how to take the information from a Baldrige-style assessment and use it for improvement planning. An organization I'm familiar with has been doing Baldrige assessments of each of its business units for the last three years; each year teams of examiners spend a great deal of time on site visits to evaluate the organization's approaches, deployment, and results. Findings of the assessment are presented to senior management, and the examiners are thanked for doing such an honest and thorough evaluation. In 1991, when this was first done, each of the business units received a score of around 300 points out of a possible 1000. In 1992, the same type of assessment was done on the same business units, and, once again, the organizations all received scores of around

300 points. Some areas were slightly better; some had gotten worse. In 1993, a team of examiners did the third Baldrige assessment, and the scores once again ended up being around 300.

The problem is that this company, like many others, has not figured out how to put *teeth* into the assessment and assure that areas for improvement end up getting addressed in the overall business plan of the organization. This is what I will attempt to provide guidance on here.

Trying to Fix Everything at the Same Time

One commonly used approach in trying to make improvements is to take each area identified in the Baldrige assessment as lacking and developing an action plan for addressing the problem. Committees and task forces are formed and hundreds of people are involved in trying to improve the organization's performance in, often, more than 100 different areas. A year is spent and thousands of dollars in labor are expended working on the various improvement projects. The assessment is done again the following year, and, to everyone's surprise, the overall score does not improve much. The reason for the failure is that such an approach is too diluted, too uncoordinated, too lacking tie-in to the company's strategic business plan. Teams end up stepping on each others' toes, perhaps improving performance in one area only to make it worse in another.

A Smarter Approach—Selecting a Few Major Areas to Work on Improving

A better improvement planning approach is to prioritize the areas for improvement before proceeding to develop action plans. With this approach, you take the 120 or so areas for improvement from the Baldrige assessment and select the most important 10–20 to work on over the next year. Senior executives may assign a score to each area for improvement, using the following variables and scale:

- IMPACT—to what extent will fixing this weakness impact our performance on key measures of quality, customer satisfaction, or financial performance? (1 = no impact; 10 = great impact on a number of performance measures.)

- URGENCY—to what extent do we have to address this weakness immediately? (1 = can be postponed for several years; 10 = this needs to be fixed *now*.)

- TREND—is performance in this area currently getting worse, stable, or better? (1 = performance is improving rapidly; 10 = performance is getting worse all the time.)

By adding the scores for each area for improvement as given by each member of the senior executive team, you should be able to list the 100 or so areas in order of their priority. You then take the top ten and develop action plans for improving performance in these areas. A project manager is assigned to each action plan, and specific tasks and deadlines are developed for each improvement project.

Breaking Into The Next Level

Organizations performing Baldrige assessments often reach a plateau at between 300 and 400 points on the Baldrige scale. It is fairly easy for an organization that does some training, implements some process improvement teams, and starts measuring customer satisfaction to earn a score in this range. Getting a score of 500–600, on the other hand, generally requires some major changes in an organization's leadership, culture, and overall systems. Changing these features in an organization requires risk—and taking risks is something most organizations don't do well, especially if they are not in trouble. Companies that are unwilling or unable to make the changes needed to break out of the 300–400-point range are unlikely to stick with a total quality effort and the results of training and process improvement teams will tend to be short-lived. In companies that score above 500, total quality is not a program or initiative; it is, or is becoming, the way the organization is run.

Linking a Baldrige Assessment With Your Strategic Business Plan

A strategic business plan should focus on *results* before defining strategies and activities. Because two thirds of the Baldrige criteria deal with an organization's approaches or activities rather than with results, it is sometimes difficult to use a Baldrige assessment as a strategic planning tool. However, the assessment can provide important input to your business plan—as long as you avoid using it simply to outline projects or activities rather than concrete goals. For example, I've seen a number of organizations that set goals such as the following:

- Implement a comprehensive system for tracking customer satisfaction levels using a telephone survey by the end of the third quarter, 19_ _.

- All employees will have an individualized training plan by the end of the year.

- Implement QFD in all design functions in the company by the end of 19 _ _.

In this case, all of these goals were written in direct response to areas for improvement identified in a Baldrige assessment. None of them, however, is really a *goal*—they are projects or activities. A goal should include a meaningful *measure* of performance such as ROI, profit, customer satisfaction, market share, or employee satisfaction, and should specify the desired level of performance on the measure. A strategy defines how the goal will be achieved. The results sections of a Baldrige assessment (6.0, 7.4, and 7.5) provide information on current performance and past trends for all key measures in an organization. Data from these sections of an assessment can be used to set annual goals for the following year, and longer-term goals for three to five years. Benchmarking studies, noted in section 2.2 of the Baldrige assessment, can also supply input for setting stretch goals. Once such goals have been set for all key results measures, the remaining sections of the Baldrige assessment can be used to help articulate strategies for accomplishing the goals. For example, you might set a goal to improve employee satisfaction by 40 percent over current levels during the following two years. To achieve this goal, look at the areas for improvement that were identified in section 4.5 of the assessment report. This should tell you where some holes exist in your approach to making your organization a good place to work. It won't tell you how to fix the problems, but it will tell you where to begin. Similarly, let's say that you develop a long-term goal of reducing the number of customers you lose because of poor service by 75 percent over the next three years. Look at areas for improvement that were identified in sections 7.1 and 7.2 of the Baldrige assessment.

In short, a Baldrige assessment can be linked usefully to the business planning process of an organization as long as the data are used to develop concrete business goals and the weaknesses in the company's approach are identified and used as input for the development of improvement strategies.

Developing a Plan to Improve Your Baldrige Assessment Score

An approach used by a number of organizations to improve their score is to develop a separate plan focused on this. Organizations such as Northrop and McDonnell Douglas even set goals for business unit executives to improve their Baldrige assessment score by a certain percentage from one year to the next. The latter kind of goal setting is, in my view, a good idea. The score on a Baldrige assessment is an excellent indication of the overall health of a business unit or organization. It includes an evaluation of all important business results as well as the approaches used to achieve the results. What I would not recommend, however, is developing a separate plan for improving the score. Meeting the Baldrige criteria does not require a separate set of activities distinct from those involved in running the organization. The Baldrige criteria outline a comprehensive approach for running an organization. Goals to improve performance in the areas of customer satisfaction, quality, and other "results" areas need to go into the company's overall business plan—not produced as a separate document.

The Key to Success

Doing assessments against the Baldrige criteria can be an expensive and time consuming activity. Most organization's today have had their staffs cut back, so that there is no longer time for "busy" work such as conducting an audit that doesn't seem to result in any immediate benefits to the organization. Unless your organization is serious about making the changes necessary to satisfy the Baldrige criteria, I wouldn't waste time on doing an assessment. Even if you are serious about using the assessment to improve, you still need a system for making this happen. This system is in using the Baldrige assessment along with other data to develop your strategic business plan. The key to making it all happen is to get senior executives involved in the assessment and the review of findings. Common threads running through all of the organizations that have won the Baldrige Award are a strong commitment among and the active involvement of senior executives. Only then can the organization travel on its journey toward reaching the ideals set by the Baldrige criteria.

FURTHER READING

Bemoski, Karen. "A Pat on the Back is Worth a Thousand Words." *Quality Progress,* March, 1994, pp. 51–54.

Brennen, Niall. *Lessons Taught by Baldrige Winners.* New York: The Conference Board, 1994.

Brown, Mark Graham. *Keeping Score: Using the Right Metrics to Drive World-Class Performance.* New York: Quality Resources, 1996.

———— *The Pocket Guide to the Baldrige Award Criteria.* rev. ed. New York: Quality Resources, 1995.

———— "Measuring Your Company Against the 1995 Baldrige Criteria." *Journal for Quality and Participation*, December, 1994.

———— "The Baldrige Award: How Do You Win?" *Automation,* October, 1991, pp. 34–37.

Brown, Mark Graham, Darcy Hitchcock, and Marsha Willard. *Why TQM Fails and What to Do About It*. Burr Ridge, IL: Irwin Professional Publishing, 1994.

DeCarlo, Nell J., and Kent J. Sterett. "History of the Malcolm Baldrige National Quality Award." *Quality Progress*, March, 1990, pp. 41–50.

Enrico, Dottie. "Winners of Top Awards Blow Their Horns." *USA Today*, October 19, 1994, p. B-1.

Fisher, Donald. *The Simplified Baldrige Award Organization Assessment*. New York: Lincoln-Bradley, 1993.

Garvin, David A. "How the Baldrige Award Really Works." *Harvard Business Review*, November/December, 1991, pp. 80–95.

Hart, Christopher W.L., and Christopher E. Bogan. *The Baldrige: What It Is, How It's Won, How to Use It to Improve Quality in Your Company*. New York: McGraw-Hill, 1992.

Hauser, John R., and Don Clausing. "The House of Quality." *Harvard Business Review*, May/June, 1989, pp. 63–73.

Helton, B. Ray. "Investing in Quality Pays Off." *QPMA's Discover*, September/October, 1993, pp. 4–11.

Henry, Craig A. "Does the United States Need Quality Awards?" *Quality Progress*, December, 1990, pp. 26–27.

Junkins, Jerry R. "Insights of a Baldrige Award Winner." *Quality Progress,* March, 1994, pp. 57–58.

Main, Jeremy. "How to Win the Baldrige Award." *Fortune*, April 23, 1990, pp. 101–116.

———— "Is the Baldrige Overblown?" *Fortune*, July 1, 1991, pp. 62–65.

Moore, Martha T. "Is TQM Dead?" *USA Today,* October 17, 1995, p. B-1.

Rohan, Thomas M. "Do You Really Want a Baldrige?" *Industry Week*, April, 1991.

Schaffer, Robert H., and Harvey A. Thomson. "Successful Change Programs Begin with Results." *Harvard Business Review*, January/February, 1992, pp. 80–89.

Stratton, Brad. "Goodbye ISO 9000: Welcome Back Baldrige Award." *Quality Progress*, August, 1994, p. 5.

U.S. General Accounting Office. "Management Practices—U.S. Companies Improve Performance Through Quality Efforts." U.S. General Accounting Office Publication GAO/NSIAD–91–190, May, 1991.

Wiseman, Paul, and Micheline Maynard. "Bags Deming, Baldrige Same Day." *USA Today,* October 19, 1994, p. B-1.

Wolff, Michael. "Pushing to Improve Quality." *Research and Technology Management*, May/June, 1990, pp. 19–22.

Malcolm Baldrige
National
Quality
Award

1996
Award Criteria

"Because of the astounding success of its winners in taking care of their business, the Baldrige Award has become a symbol of excellence and an inspiration for the rebirth of American competitiveness."

William J. Clinton

"Since 1987, the Baldrige Award has been a powerful agent of change within America's economy."

Ronald H. Brown
Secretary of Commerce

The Award, composed of two solid crystal prismatic forms, stands 14 inches tall. The crystal is held in a base of black, anodized aluminum with the Award winner's name engraved on the base. A solid bronze, 22-karat, gold-plated, die-struck medallion is captured in the front section of the crystal. The medal bears the inscriptions: "Malcolm Baldrige National Quality Award" and "The Quest for Excellence" on one side and the Presidential Seal on the other.

Awards traditionally are presented by the President of the United States at a special ceremony in Washington, D.C.

Awards are made annually to recognize U.S. companies for business excellence and quality achievement. Awards may be given in each of three eligibility categories:

- Manufacturing companies
- Service companies
- Small businesses

Award recipients may publicize and advertise receipt of the Award. The recipients are expected to share information about their successful performance strategies with other U.S. organizations.

Crystal by Steuben
Medal by The Protocol Group

CONTENTS

THE MALCOLM BALDRIGE NATIONAL QUALITY AWARD: A PUBLIC-PRIVATE PARTNERSHIP

Building active partnerships in the private sector, and between the private sector and all levels of government, is fundamental to the success of the Award in improving national competitiveness.

Support by the private sector for the Award Program in the form of funds, volunteer efforts, and participation in information transfer continues to grow.

To ensure the continued growth and success of these partnerships, each of the following organizations plays an important role:

The Foundation for the Malcolm Baldrige National Quality Award

The Foundation for the Malcolm Baldrige National Quality Award was created to foster the success of the Program. The Foundation's main objective is to raise funds to permanently endow the Award Program.

Prominent leaders from U.S. companies serve as Foundation Trustees to ensure that the Foundation's objectives are accomplished. Donor organizations vary in size and type, and are representative of many kinds of businesses and business groups.

National Institute of Standards and Technology (NIST)

Responsibility for the Award is assigned to the Department of Commerce. NIST, an agency of the Department's Technology Administration, manages the Award Program.

NIST's goals are to aid U.S. industry through research and services; to contribute to public health, safety, and the environment; and to support the U.S. scientific and engineering research communities. NIST conducts basic and applied research in the physical sciences and engineering and develops measurement techniques, test methods, and standards. Much of NIST's work relates directly to technology development and technology utilization.

American Society for Quality Control (ASQC)

ASQC assists in administering the Award Program under contract to NIST.

ASQC is dedicated to facilitating continuous improvement and increased customer satisfaction by identifying, communicating, and promoting the use of quality principles, concepts, and technologies. ASQC strives to be recognized throughout the world as the leading authority on, and champion for, quality. ASQC recognizes that continuous quality improvement will help the favorable repositioning of American goods and services in the international marketplace.

Board of Overseers

The Board of Overseers is the advisory organization on the Award to the Department of Commerce. The Board is appointed by the Secretary of Commerce and consists of distinguished leaders from all sectors of the U.S. economy.

The Board of Overseers evaluates all aspects of the Award Program, including the adequacy of the Criteria and processes for making Awards. An important part of the Board's responsibility is to assess how well the Award is serving the national interest. Accordingly, the Board makes recommendations to the Secretary of Commerce and to the Director of NIST regarding changes and improvements in the Award Program.

Board of Examiners

The Board of Examiners evaluates Award applications, prepares feedback reports, and makes Award recommendations to the Director of NIST. The Board consists of business and quality experts primarily from the private sector. Members are selected by NIST through a competitive application process. For 1996, the Board consists of about 270 members. Of these, nine (who are appointed by the Secretary of Commerce) serve as Judges, and approximately 50 serve as Senior Examiners. The remainder serve as Examiners. All members of the Board take part in an Examiner preparation course.

In addition to their application review responsibilities, Board members contribute significantly to information transfer activities. Many of these activities involve the hundreds of professional, trade, community, and state organizations to which Board members belong.

Award Recipients' Responsibilities and Contributions

Award recipients are required to share information on their successful performance and quality strategies with other U.S. organizations. However, recipients are not required to share proprietary information, even if such information was part of their Award application. The principal mechanism for sharing information is the annual Quest for Excellence Conference, highlighted on page 48.

Award recipients in the first eight years of the Award have been very generous in their commitment to improving U.S. competitiveness, and manufacturing and service quality. They have shared information with hundreds of thousands of companies, educational institutions, government agencies, health care organizations, and others. This sharing far exceeds expectations and Program requirements. Award winners' efforts have encouraged many other organizations in all sectors of the U.S. economy to undertake their own performance improvement efforts.

INTRODUCTION

The Malcolm Baldrige National Quality Award is an annual Award to recognize U.S. companies for business excellence.

The Award promotes:

- understanding of the requirements for performance excellence and competitiveness improvement; and
- sharing of information on successful performance strategies and the benefits derived from using these strategies.

Award Participation

The Award has three eligibility categories:

- Manufacturing companies
- Service companies
- Small businesses

Companies participating in the Award process are required to submit application packages that include responses to the Award Criteria.

Awards may be given in each category each year. Award recipients may publicize and advertise their Awards. Recipients are expected to share information about their successful performance strategies with other U.S. organizations.

Award Criteria

The Award is based upon performance excellence criteria created through a public-private partnership. In responding to these criteria, each applicant is expected to provide information and data on the company's improvement processes and results. Information and data submitted must be adequate to demonstrate that the applicant's approaches are effective and could be replicated or adapted by other organizations.

The Award Criteria are designed not only to serve as a reliable basis for making Awards but also to permit a diagnosis of each applicant's overall performance management system.

Application Requirements

Applicants need to submit an application package that consists of three parts:

- An Eligibility Determination Form showing that eligibility has been approved

- A completed Application Form
- An application report consisting of a Business Overview and responses to the Award Criteria.

Detailed information and the necessary forms are contained in the *1996 Business Application Forms and Instructions* booklet. Ordering instructions for this booklet are given on page 47. Deadlines for eligibility determination and Award application are given in the box at the bottom of this page.

Application Review

Applications are reviewed and evaluated by members of the Board of Examiners in a four-stage process:

Stage 1 – independent review and evaluation by at least five members of the Board

Stage 2 – consensus review and evaluation for applications that score well in Stage 1

Stage 3 – site visits to applicants that score well in Stage 2

Stage 4 – Judges' review and recommendations

Board members are assigned to applications taking into account the nature of the applicants' businesses and the expertise of the Examiners. Assignments are made in accord with strict rules regarding conflict of interest.

Applications are reviewed by volunteers without funding from the United States government. Review expenses are paid primarily through application fees; partial support for the reviews is provided by the Foundation for the Malcolm Baldrige National Quality Award.

Feedback to Applicants

Each applicant receives a feedback report at the conclusion of the review process. The feedback is based upon the applicant's responses to the Award Criteria.

Purpose of This Booklet

This booklet contains the Award Criteria, a description of the Criteria, Scoring Guidelines, and other information. In addition to serving as the basis for submitting an Award application, the Criteria are used by organizations of all kinds for self-assessment, planning, training, and other purposes.

If you plan to apply for the Award in 1996, you will also need the booklet entitled
1996 Business Application Forms and Instructions. **Ordering instructions are given on page 47.**

Eligibility Determination Forms due — March 1, 1996

Award Applications due — April 1, 1996

MESSAGE TO EXECUTIVES

This Message to Executives provides basic information on the Baldrige Award and on the factors that might affect your decision to apply. The Message outlines: the Award's purpose; the focus of the Criteria; the benefits you might expect from participation; and what will be expected if your company receives the Award. If you decide not to apply, you are encouraged to undertake a company self-assessment to determine for yourself how your company measures up on the Baldrige Award scoring scale. In the most competitive business sectors, world-class organizations are able to achieve and maintain a score above 70%. However, a score of about 25% would be far more typical of most U.S. companies. We encourage you to challenge *your* business to take the test!

The Award and the Award Assessment

- The Award recognizes companies for business performance excellence and competitiveness improvement. Award recipients need to demonstrate results and results improvement in a wide range of indicators: customer-related, operational, and financial. Results reported need to address all stakeholders — customers, employees, owners, suppliers, and the public.

- The Award assessment is tailored to your company through a focus on factors important to your business, strategy, and competitive success. These factors are spelled out by you in your Business Overview and in the Strategic Planning Category.

- Your company's participation as an applicant, as well as information you submit about your company, are considered confidential. Assignment of Examiners to your application is made in accord with strict rules regarding conflict of interest.

- You will receive a detailed feedback report.

The Award Criteria

- The Criteria's seven Categories and 24 Items focus on requirements that all businesses — especially those facing tough competitive challenges — need to thoroughly understand. The Criteria address all aspects of competitive performance in an integrated and balanced way. This includes improvement of: customer- and market-related performance, productivity in the use of all assets, speed and flexibility, product and service quality, cost reduction, and overall financial performance.

- The Criteria address key business processes and results, and are designed for diagnosis and feedback. All Criteria directly relate to improving business performance; nothing is included merely for purposes of an Award.

- The Criteria do not call for specific practices or organizational structures, because there are many possible approaches. The best choices depend upon many factors, including your business' type, size, strategy, and stage of development.

Benefits of Participation

Over the years, Award applicants have reported numerous benefits. Commonly cited benefits are:

- Responding to the Criteria forces a realistic self-assessment from an external point of view. This self-assessment, when combined with the comprehensive feedback report received from the Award's Board of Examiners, targets key gaps and priorities for improvement. The overall assessment also recognizes and reinforces company strengths.

- The pace of performance improvement is accelerated.

- The knowledge gained from assessment and feedback teaches new and better ways to evaluate suppliers, customers, partners, and even competitors.

- Use of the Award Criteria in assessment leads to the integration and alignment of numerous activities, previously loosely connected. The assessment provides an effective means to measure progress and to focus everyone in the company on the same goals.

- Use of the Award Criteria helps companies understand, select, and integrate appropriate management tools such as reengineering, ISO 9000, quality management, activity-based costing, just-in-time production, lean manufacturing, flexible manufacturing, benchmarking, and high performance work.

- The Award Criteria and Scoring System provide a clear perspective on the distinction between typical performance and world-class performance.

- Participation frequently leads to companies attending information sharing meetings and joining sharing networks, where it is often possible to obtain free or inexpensive advice and help from other business leaders. One networking opportunity is the annual Quest for Excellence Conference (see page 48 of this booklet).

Expectations of Award Winners

- Award winners are expected to share non-proprietary information with other U.S. organizations. The principal mechanisms for sharing information are conferences and written application summaries. Some Award winners hold periodic visitor days. The only conference participation required by the Baldrige Award Program is the Quest for Excellence Conference, held in Washington, D.C., each February. This Conference features the most recent Award winners named in October of each year. Award winners are invited to participate in other conferences, particularly the Baldrige Regional Conferences sponsored jointly by NIST and The Conference Board.

- Award winners may publicize and advertise based upon their Awards. They are asked to adhere to voluntary advertising guidelines established to ensure that the meaning of the Award is appropriately represented.

1996 Categories/Items	Point Values

1.0 Leadership — 90

1.1 Senior Executive Leadership	45
1.2 Leadership System and Organization	25
1.3 Public Responsibility and Corporate Citizenship	20

2.0 Information and Analysis — 75

2.1 Management of Information and Data	20
2.2 Competitive Comparisons and Benchmarking	15
2.3 Analysis and Use of Company-Level Data	40

3.0 Strategic Planning — 55

3.1 Strategy Development	35
3.2 Strategy Deployment	20

4.0 Human Resource Development and Management — 140

4.1 Human Resource Planning and Evaluation	20
4.2 High Performance Work Systems	45
4.3 Employee Education, Training, and Development	50
4.4 Employee Well-Being and Satisfaction	25

5.0 Process Management — 140

5.1 Design and Introduction of Products and Services	40
5.2 Process Management: Product and Service Production and Delivery	40
5.3 Process Management: Support Services	30
5.4 Management of Supplier Performance	30

6.0 Business Results — 250

6.1 Product and Service Quality Results	75
6.2 Company Operational and Financial Results	110
6.3 Human Resource Results	35
6.4 Supplier Performance Results	30

7.0 Customer Focus and Satisfaction — 250

7.1 Customer and Market Knowledge	30
7.2 Customer Relationship Management	30
7.3 Customer Satisfaction Determination	30
7.4 Customer Satisfaction Results	160

TOTAL POINTS — **1000**

GLOSSARY OF KEY TERMS

This Glossary of Key Terms defines and briefly describes concepts that are important to performance management and used throughout the Award Criteria booklet.

Alignment

Alignment refers to unification of goals throughout the company and consistency of processes, actions, information, and decisions among company units in support of these goals.

Effective alignment requires common understanding of purposes and goals and use of complementary measures and information to enable planning, tracking, analysis, and improvement at three levels: the company level; the key process level; and the work unit level.

Cycle Time

Cycle time refers to responsiveness and completion time measures — the time required to fulfill commitments or to complete tasks. Cycle time and related terms are used in the Criteria booklet to refer to all aspects of time performance.

Time measurements play a major role in the Criteria because of the great importance of time performance to improving competitiveness. Other time-related terms in common use are: set-up time, lead time, change-over time, delivery time, and time to market.

High Performance Work

High performance work refers to work approaches *systematically* directed toward achieving ever higher levels of overall performance, including quality and productivity.

Approaches to high performance work vary in form, function, and incentive systems. Effective approaches generally include: cooperation between management and the work force, including work force bargaining units; cooperation among work units, often involving teams; self-directed responsibility (sometimes called empowerment); individual and organizational skill building and learning; flexibility in job design and work assignments; an organizational structure with minimum layering ("flattened"), where decision making is decentralized and decisions are made closest to the "front line"; and regular use of performance measures, including comparisons. Some high performance work systems use monetary and non-monetary incentives based upon factors such as company performance, team and/or individual contributions, and skill building. Also, some high performance work approaches attempt to align the design of organizations, work, jobs, and incentives.

Key Business Drivers

Key business drivers is a term used in the Award Criteria in connection with strategic planning and related goal setting. Key business drivers refer to principal company-level requirements, derived from short- and long-term strategic planning. Key business driver development represents the critical stage in planning when general strategies and goals are made sufficiently specific so that effective companywide understanding and ongoing action are possible. In simplest terms, key business drivers are those things the company must do well for its strategy to succeed.

An effective planning approach results in a clear basis (key business drivers) for consistent focus, communications, and deployment at three levels: the company level; the key process level; and the work unit level. Deployment of key business drivers requires analysis of overall resource needs and creation of aligned measures for all work units. Deployment might require specialized training for some employees or recruitment of personnel.

An example of a key business driver for a supplier in a highly competitive industry might be to develop and maintain a price leadership position. Deployment should entail design of efficient processes, analysis of resource and asset use, and creation of related measures of resource and asset productivity for all work units, aligned for the company as a whole. It might also involve adoption of a cost-accounting system that provides meaningful activity-level cost information to support day-to-day work. Unit and/or team training should include priority setting based upon costs and benefits. Company-level analysis and review should emphasize overall productivity growth. Ongoing competitive analysis and planning should remain sensitive to technological and other changes that might greatly reduce operating costs for the company or its competitors.

Leadership System

Leadership system refers to how leadership is exercised throughout the company — the way that key decisions are made, communicated, and carried out at all levels. It is based upon shared values, expectations, and purposes; communicated and reinforced via interactions among leaders and managers; reflected in the decisions the leaders make; and evident in the actions of the company. It includes the formal and informal bases and mechanisms for leadership development used to select leaders and managers, to develop their leadership skills, and to provide guidance and examples regarding behaviors and practices.

An effective leadership system creates clear values respecting the requirements of all stakeholders of the company and sets high expectations for performance and performance improvement. It builds loyalties and team-work based upon the values and the pursuit of shared purposes. It encourages and supports initiative and risk taking, subordinates organization to purpose and function, and minimizes reliance on chains of command that require long decision paths. An effective leadership system includes mechanisms for the leaders' self-examination and improvement.

Measures and Indicators

Measures and indicators refer to numerical information that quantify (measure) input, output, and performance dimensions of processes, products, and services. Measures and indicators might be simple (derived from one measurement) or composite.

The Award Criteria do not make a distinction between measures and indicators. However, some users of these terms prefer the term indicator: (1) when the measurement relates entirely to performance and not to inputs; (2) when the measurement relates to performance but is not a direct or exclusive measure of such performance. For example, the number of complaints is an indicator of dissatisfaction, but not a direct or exclusive measure of it; and (3) when a performance or measure is a predictor ("leading indicator") of some more significant performance, e.g., gain in customer satisfaction might be a leading indicator of market share gain.

Performance

Performance refers to numerical results information obtained from processes, products, and services that permits evaluation and comparison relative to goals, standards, past results, and to others. Most commonly, the results address quality, efficiency, and time and might be expressed in nonfinancial and financial terms.

Four types of performance are addressed in this Criteria booklet: (1) operational; (2) product and service quality; (3) customer-related; and (4) financial.

Operational performance refers to performance relative to effectiveness and efficiency measures and indicators. Examples include cycle time, productivity, and waste reduction. Operational performance might be measured at the work unit level, the key process level, and the company level.

Product and service quality performance refers to performance relative to measures and indicators of product and service requirements, derived from customer preference information. Examples include reliability, on-time delivery, defect levels, and service response time. Product and service quality performance generally relates to the company as a whole.

Customer-related performance refers to performance relative to measures and indicators of customers' perceptions, reactions, and behaviors. Examples include customer retention, complaints, customer survey results, and market share. Customer-related performance generally relates to the company as a whole.

Financial performance refers to performance using measures of cost and revenue, including asset utilization and asset growth. Financial measures are generally tracked throughout the company and are also aggregated to give company-level, composite measures of performance. Examples include returns on investments, returns on assets, working capital productivity, and total factor productivity.

Process

Process refers to linked activities with the purpose of producing a product or service for a customer (user) within or outside the company. Generally, processes involve combinations of people, machines, tools, techniques, and materials in a systematic series of steps or actions.

In some situations, process performance might require adherence to a specific sequence of steps, with documentation (sometimes formal) of procedures and requirements, including well-defined measurement and control steps.

In many service situations, particularly when customers are directly involved in one or more steps of the service, process is used in a more general way — to spell out what must be done, possibly including a preferred or expected sequence. If a sequence is critical, the service needs to include information for customers to help them understand and adhere to the sequence. Service processes involving customers require guidance to the servers on handling contingencies related to differing circumstances and to customers' actions or behaviors.

In cases such as strategic planning, research, and analysis, process does not necessarily imply formal sequences of steps. Rather, process implies general understandings regarding competent performance such as timing, options to be included, evaluation, and reporting. Sequences might arise as part of these understandings.

Productivity

Productivity refers to measures of efficiency of the use of resources. Although the term is often applied to single factors such as manpower (labor productivity), machines, materials, energy, and capital, the productivity concept applies as well to the total resources consumed in producing outputs. Overall productivity — usually called total factor productivity — is determined by combining the productivities of the different resources used for an output. The combination usually requires taking a weighted average of the different single factor productivity measures, where the weights typically reflect costs of the resources. The use of an aggregate measure such as total factor productivity allows a determination of whether or not the net effect of overall changes in a process — possibly involving resource tradeoffs — is beneficial.

Effective approaches to performance management require understanding and measuring single factor and total factor productivity, particularly in complex cases when there are a variety of costs and potential benefits.

1.0 Leadership (90 pts.)

The *Leadership* Category examines senior executives' personal leadership and involvement in creating and sustaining a customer focus, clear values and expectations, and a leadership system that promotes performance excellence. Also examined is how the values and expectations are integrated into the company's management system, including how the company addresses its public responsibilities and corporate citizenship.

1.1 Senior Executive Leadership (45 pts.)

Describe senior executives' leadership and personal involvement in setting directions and in developing and maintaining an effective, performance-oriented leadership system.

(See page 24 for a description of these symbols.)

AREAS TO ADDRESS

a. how senior executives provide effective leadership and direction in building and improving company competitiveness, performance, and capabilities. Describe how senior executives: (1) create and maintain an effective leadership system based upon clear values and high expectations; (2) create future opportunity for the company and its stakeholders, set directions, and integrate performance excellence goals; and (3) review overall company performance, capabilities, and organization.

b. how senior executives evaluate and improve the company's leadership system, including their own leadership skills

Notes:

(1) "Senior executives" means the applicant's highest-ranking official and executives reporting directly to that official.

(2) Values and expectations [1.1a(1)] should take into account needs and expectations of key stakeholders – customers, employees, stockholders, suppliers and partners, the community, and the public.

(3) Review of overall company performance is addressed in 1.2b. Responses to 1.1a(3) should focus on senior executives' roles in such reviews, and their use of the reviews to set expectations and develop leadership.

(4) Evaluation of the company's leadership system (1.1b) might include assessment of executives by peers, direct reports, and/or a board of directors. It might also include use of surveys of company employees.

1.2 Leadership System and Organization (25 pts.)

Describe how the company's customer focus and performance expectations are integrated into the company's leadership system, management, and organization.

AREAS TO ADDRESS

a. how the company's values, expectations, and directions are integrated into its leadership system, management, and organization. Describe: (1) how the organization and its management of operations are designed to achieve companywide customer focus and commitment to high performance. Include roles and responsibilities of managers and supervisors; and (2) how values, expectations, and directions are effectively communicated and reinforced throughout the entire work force.

b. how overall company and work unit performance are reviewed. Include a description of: (1) the principal financial and nonfinancial measures used and how these measures relate to key stakeholders' primary needs and expectations; (2) how progress relative to plans is tracked; (3) how progress relative to competitors is tracked; (4) how asset productivity is determined; and (5) how review findings are used to set priorities for improvement actions.

Notes:

(1) Reviews described in 1.2b might utilize information from results Items — 6.1, 6.2, 6.3, 6.4, and 7.4 — and also might draw upon evaluations described in other Items and upon analysis (Item 2.3).

(2) Reviews might include various economic measures as well as financial ones.

(3) Assets [1.2b(4)] refers to human resources, materials, energy, capital, equipment, etc. Aggregate measures such as total factor productivity might also be used.

1.3 Public Responsibility and Corporate Citizenship *(20 pts.)*

Describe how the company addresses its responsibilities to the public in its performance management practices. Describe also how the company leads and contributes as a corporate citizen in its key communities.

AREAS TO ADDRESS

a. how the company integrates its public responsibilities into its performance improvement efforts. Describe: (1) the risks and regulatory and other legal requirements addressed in planning and in setting operational requirements, measures, and targets; (2) how the company looks ahead to anticipate public concerns and to assess possible impacts on society of its products, services, facilities, and operations; and (3) how the company promotes legal and ethical conduct in all that it does.

b. how the company leads and contributes as a corporate citizen in its key communities. Include a brief summary of the types of leadership and involvement the company emphasizes.

Notes:

(1) Public responsibility issues (1.3a) relate to the company's impacts and possible impacts on society associated with its products, services, facilities, and operations. They include environment, health, safety, and emergency preparedness as they relate to any aspect of risk or adverse effect, whether or not these are covered under law or regulation. Health and safety of employees are not addressed in Item 1.3. Employee health and safety are covered in Item 4.4.

(2) Major public responsibility or impact areas should also be addressed in planning (Item 3.1) and in the appropriate process management Items of Category 5.0. Key results, such as environmental improvements, should be reported in Item 6.2.

(3) If the company has received sanctions under law, regulation, or contract [1.3a(3)] during the past three years, briefly describe the incident(s) and its current status. If settlements have been negotiated in lieu of potential sanctions, give an explanation. If no sanctions have been received, so indicate.

(4) The corporate citizenship issues appropriate for inclusion in 1.3b relate to efforts by the company to strengthen community services, education, health care, environment, and practices of trade or business associations. Examples of corporate citizenship appropriate for inclusion in 1.3b are:
* *influencing and helping trade and business associations to create school-to-work programs;*
* *communicating employability requirements to schools;*
* *influencing national, state, and local policies which promote education improvement;*
* *partnering with and charitable giving to schools, e.g., sharing computers and computer expertise;*
* *developing trade and business consortia to improve environmental practices;*
* *promoting volunteerism among employees;*
* *partnering with other businesses and health care providers to improve health in the local community; and*
* *influencing trade and business associations to engage in cooperative activities to improve overall U.S. global competitiveness.*

2.0 Information and Analysis (75 pts.)

The *Information and Analysis* Category examines the management and effectiveness of the use of data and information to support customer-driven performance excellence and marketplace success.

2.1 Management of Information and Data
(20 pts.)

Describe the company's selection and management of information and data used for strategic planning, management, and evaluation of overall performance.

AREAS TO ADDRESS

a. how information and data needed to support operations and decision making and to drive improvement of overall company performance are selected and managed. Describe: (1) the main types of data and information and how each type supports key business operations and business strategy; (2) how the company's performance measurement system is designed to achieve alignment of operations with company priorities, such as key business drivers; and (3) how key requirements such as reliability, rapid access, and rapid update are derived from user needs and how the requirements are met.

b. how the company evaluates and improves the selection, analysis, and integration of information and data, aligning them with the company's key business drivers and operations. Describe how the evaluation considers: (1) scope of information and data; (2) use and analysis of information and data to support process management and performance improvement; and (3) feedback from users of information and data.

Notes:

(1) Reliability [2.1a(3)] includes software used in information systems.

(2) User needs [2.1a(3)] should consider knowledge accumulation such as knowledge about specific customers or customer segments. User needs should also take into account changing patterns of communications associated

with changes in process management, job design, and business strategy.

(3) Feedback from users [2.1b(3)] might entail formal or informal surveys, focus groups, and teams. Factors in the evaluation might include completeness, timeliness, access, update, and reliability. The evaluation might also include assessment of the information technologies used.

2.2 Competitive Comparisons and Benchmarking *(15 pts.)*

Describe the company's processes and uses of comparative information and data to support improvement of overall performance and competitive position.

AREAS TO ADDRESS

a. how competitive comparisons and benchmarking information and data are selected and used to help drive improvement of overall company performance. Describe: (1) how needs and priorities are determined; (2) criteria for seeking appropriate information and data — from within and outside the company's industry and markets; (3) how the information and data are used to improve understanding of processes and process performance; and (4) how the information and data are used to set stretch targets and/or to encourage breakthrough approaches aligned with the company's competitive strategy.

b. how the company evaluates and improves its process for selecting and using competitive comparisons and benchmarking information and data to improve planning, overall company performance, and competitive position

Notes:

(1) Benchmarking information and data refer to processes and results that represent best practices and performance, inside or outside of the company's industry. Competitive comparisons refer to performance levels relative to direct competitors in the company's markets.

(2) Needs and priorities [2.2a(1)] should show clear linkage to the company's key business drivers.

(3) Use of benchmarking information and data within the company [2.2a(3)] might include the expectation that company units maintain awareness of related best-in-class performance to help drive improvement. This could entail education and training efforts to build capabilities.

(4) Sources of competitive comparisons and benchmarking information might include: (a) information obtained from other organizations such as customers or suppliers through sharing; (b) information obtained from the open literature; (c) testing and evaluation by the company itself; and (d) testing and evaluation by independent organizations.

(5) The evaluation (2.2b) might address a variety of factors such as the effectiveness of use of the information, adequacy of information, training in acquisition and use of information, improvement potential in company operations, and estimated rates of improvement by other organizations.

2.3 Analysis and Use of Company-Level Data

(40 pts.)

Describe how data related to quality, customers, and operational performance, together with relevant financial data, are analyzed to support company-level review, action, and planning.

(A – D)

AREAS TO ADDRESS

a. how information and data from all parts of the company are integrated and analyzed to support reviews, business decisions, and planning. Describe how analysis is used to gain understanding of: (1) customers and markets; (2) operational performance and company capabilities; and (3) competitive performance.

b. how the company relates customer and market data, improvements in product/ service quality, and improvements in operational performance to changes in financial and/or market indicators of performance. Describe how this information is used to set priorities for improvement actions.

Notes:

(1) Item 2.3 focuses primarily on analysis for company-level purposes, such as reviews (1.2b) and strategic planning (Item 3.1). Data for such analysis come from all parts of the company and include results reported in Items 6.1, 6.2, 6.3, 6.4, and 7.4. Other Items call for analyses of specific sets of data for special purposes. For example, the Items of Category 4.0 require analysis to determine the effectiveness of training and other human resource practices. Such special-purpose analyses should be part of the overall information base available for use in Item 2.3.

(2) Analysis includes trends, projections, cause-effect correlations, and the search for deeper understanding needed to set priorities to use resources more effectively to serve overall business objectives. Accordingly, analysis draws upon all kinds of data: operational, customer-related, financial, and economic.

(3) Examples of analysis appropriate for inclusion in 2.3a(1) are:
* *how the company's product and service quality improvement correlates with key customer indicators such as customer satisfaction, customer retention, and market share;*
* *cost/revenue implications of customer-related problems and problem resolution effectiveness; and*
* *interpretation of market share changes in terms of customer gains and losses and changes in customer satisfaction.*

(4) Examples of analysis appropriate for inclusion in 2.3a(2) are:
* *trends in improvement in key operational performance indicators such as productivity, cycle time, waste reduction, new product introduction, and defect levels;*
* *financial benefits from improved employee safety, absenteeism, and turnover;*
* *benefits and costs associated with education and training;*
* *how the company's ability to identify and meet employee requirements correlates with employee retention, motivation, and productivity;*
* *cost/revenue implications of employee-related problems and problem resolution effectiveness; and*
* *trends in individual measures of productivity such as manpower productivity.*

(5) Examples of analysis appropriate for inclusion in 2.3a(3) are:
* *working capital productivity relative to competitors;*
* *individual or aggregate measures of productivity relative to competitors;*
* *performance trends relative to competitors on key quality attributes; and*
* *cost trends relative to competitors.*

(6) Examples of analysis appropriate for inclusion in 2.3b are:
* *relationships between product/service quality and operational performance indicators and overall company financial performance trends as reflected in indicators such as operating costs, revenues, asset utilization, and value added per employee;*
* *allocation of resources among alternative improvement projects based on cost/revenue implications and improvement potential;*
* *net earnings derived from quality/operational/human resource performance improvements;*
* *comparisons among business units showing how quality and operational performance improvement affect financial performance;*
* *contributions of improvement activities to cash flow, working capital use, and shareholder value;*
* *profit impacts of customer retention;*
* *market share versus profits;*
* *trends in aggregate measures such as total factor productivity; and*
* *trends in economic and/or market indicators of value.*

3.0 Strategic Planning (55 pts.)

The *Strategic Planning* Category examines how the company sets strategic directions, and how it determines key plan requirements. Also examined is how the plan requirements are translated into an effective performance management system.

3.1 Strategy Development
(35 pts.)

Describe the company's strategic planning process for overall performance and competitive leadership for the short term and the longer term. Describe also how this process leads to the development of a basis (key business drivers) for deploying plan requirements throughout the company.

(A – D)

AREAS TO ADDRESS

a. how the company develops strategies and business plans to strengthen its customer-related, operational, and financial performance and its competitive position. Describe how strategy development considers: (1) customer requirements and expectations and their expected changes; (2) the competitive environment; (3) risks: financial, market, technological, and societal; (4) company capabilities—human resource, technology, research and development, and business processes—to seek new market leadership opportunities and/or to prepare for key new requirements; and (5) supplier and/or partner capabilities.

b. how strategies and plans are translated into actionable key business drivers

c. how the company evaluates and improves its strategic planning and plan deployment processes

Notes:

(1) Item 3.1 addresses overall company strategy and business plans, not specific product and service designs.

(2) Strategy and planning refer to a future-oriented basis for major business decisions, resource allocations, and companywide management. Strategy and planning, then, address both revenue growth thrusts as well as thrusts related to improving company performance. The sub-parts of 3.1a are intended to serve as an outline of key factors involved in developing a view of the future as a context for strategic planning.

(3) Customer requirements and their expected changes [3.1a(1)] might include pricing factors. That is, competitive success might depend upon achieving cost levels dictated by anticipated market prices rather than setting prices to cover costs.

(4) The purposes of projecting the competitive environment [3.1a(2)] are to detect and reduce competitive threats, to shorten reaction time, and to identify opportunities. If the company uses modeling, scenario, or other techniques to project the competitive environment, such techniques should be briefly outlined in 3.1a(2).

(5) Key business drivers are the areas of performance most critical to the company's success. (See Glossary, page 4.) The purpose of the key business drivers is to ensure that strategic planning leads to a pragmatic basis for deployment, communications, and assessment of progress. Actual key business drivers should not be described in 3.1b. Such information is requested in Item 3.2, which focuses on deployment.

(6) How the company evaluates and improves its strategic planning and plan deployment process might take into account the results of reviews (1.2b), input from work units, and projection information (3.2b). The evaluation might also take into account how well strategies and requirements are communicated and understood, and how well key measures throughout the company are aligned.

3.2 Strategy Deployment
(20 pts.)

Summarize the company's key business drivers and how they are deployed. Show how the company's performance projects into the future relative to competitors and key benchmarks.

AREAS TO ADDRESS

a. summary of the specific key business drivers derived from the company's strategic directions and how these drivers are translated into actions. Describe: (1) key performance requirements and associated operational performance measures and/or indicators and how they are deployed; (2) how the company aligns work unit and supplier and/or partner plans and targets; (3) how productivity and cycle time improvement and reduction in waste are included in plans and targets; and (4) the principal resources committed to the accomplishment of plans. Note any important distinctions between short-term plans and longer-term plans.

b. two-to-five year projection of key measures and/or indicators of the company's customer-related and operational performance. Describe how product and/or service quality and operational performance might be expected to compare with key competitors and key benchmarks over this time period. Briefly explain the comparisons, including any estimates or assumptions made regarding the projected product and/or service quality and operational performance of competitors or changes in key benchmarks.

Notes:

(1) The focus in Item 3.2 is on the translation of the company's strategic plans, resulting from the process described in Item 3.1, to requirements for work units, suppliers, and partners. The main intent of Item 3.2 is effective alignment of short- and long-term operations with strategic directions. Although the deployment of these plans will affect products and services, design of products and services is not the focus of Item 3.2. Such design is addressed in Item 5.1.

(2) Productivity and cycle time improvement and waste reduction [3.2a(3)] might address factors such as inventories, operational complexity, work-in-process, inspection, downtime, changeover time, set-up time, and other examples of utilization of resources — materials, equipment, energy, capital, and labor.

(3) Area 3.2b addresses projected progress in improving performance and in gaining advantage relative to competitors. This projection may draw upon analysis (Item 2.3) and data reported in results Items (Category 6.0 and Item 7.4). Such projections are intended to support reviews (1.2b), evaluation of planning (3.1c), and other Items. Another purpose is to take account of the fact that competitors and benchmarks may also be improving over the time period of the projection.

(4) Projections of customer-related and operational performance (3.2b) might be expressed in terms of costs, revenues, measures of productivity, and economic indicators. Projections might also include innovation rates or other factors important to the company's competitive position.

4.0 Human Resource Development and Management (*140 pts.*)

The *Human Resource Development and Management* Category examines how the work force is enabled to develop and utilize its full potential, aligned with the company's performance objectives. Also examined are the company's efforts to build and maintain an environment conducive to performance excellence, full participation, and personal and organizational growth.

4.1 Human Resource Planning and Evaluation (*20 pts.*)

Describe how the company's human resource planning and evaluation are aligned with its strategic and business plans and address the development and well-being of the entire work force.

AREAS TO ADDRESS

a. how the company translates overall requirements from strategic and business planning (Category 3.0) to specific human resource plans. Summarize key human resource plans in the following areas: (1) changes in work design to improve flexibility, innovation, and rapid response; (2) employee development, education, and training; (3) changes in compensation, recognition, and benefits; and (4) recruitment, including critical skill categories and expected or planned changes in demographics of the work force. Distinguish between the short term and the longer term, as appropriate.

b. how the company evaluates and improves its human resource planning and practices and the alignment of the plans and practices with the company's strategic and business directions. Include how employee-related data and company performance data (Item 6.2) are analyzed and used: (1) to assess the development and well-being of all categories and types of employees; (2) to assess the linkage of the human resource practices to key business results; and (3) to ensure that reliable and complete human resource information is available for company planning and recruitment.

Notes:

(1) Human resource planning addresses all aspects of designing and managing human resource systems to meet the needs of both the company and the employees. Examples of human resource plan (4.1a) elements that might be part(s) of a comprehensive plan are:
- *redesign of work organizations and/or jobs to increase employee responsibility and decision making;*
- *initiatives to promote labor-management cooperation, such as partnerships with unions;*
- *creation or modification of compensation and recognition systems based on building shareholder value and/or customer satisfaction;*
- *creation or redesign of employee surveys to better assess the factors in the work climate that contribute to or inhibit high performance;*
- *prioritization of employee problems based upon potential impact on productivity;*
- *development of hiring criteria and/or standards;*
- *creation of opportunities for employees to learn and use skills that go beyond current job assignments through redesign of processes or organizations;*
- *education and training initiatives, including those that involve developmental assignments;*
- *formation of partnerships with educational institutions to develop employees or to help ensure the future supply of well-prepared employees;*
- *establishment of partnerships with other companies and/or networks to share training and/or spread job opportunities;*
- *introduction of distance learning or other technology-based learning approaches; and*
- *integration of customer and employee surveys.*

(2) "Employee-related data" (4.1b) refers to data contained in personnel records as well as data described in Items 4.2, 4.3, 4.4, and 6.3. This might include employee satisfaction data and data on turnover, absenteeism, safety, grievances, involvement, recognition, training, and information from exit interviews.

(3) "Categories of employees" [4.1b(1)] refers to the company's classification system used in its human resource practices and/or work assignments. It also includes factors such as union or bargaining unit membership. "Types of employees" takes into account other factors, such as work force diversity or demographic makeup. This includes gender, age, minorities, and the disabled.

(4) Human resource information for company planning and recruitment [4.1b(3)] might include an overall profile of strengths and weaknesses that could affect the company's capabilities to fulfill plan requirements.

4.2 High Performance Work Systems *(45 pts.)*

Describe how the company's work and job design and compensation and recognition approaches enable and encourage all employees to contribute effectively to achieving high performance objectives.

AREAS TO ADDRESS

a. how the company's work and job design promote high performance. Describe how work and job design: (1) create opportunities for initiative and self-directed responsibility; (2) foster flexibility and rapid response to changing requirements; and (3) ensure effective communications across functions or units that need to work together to meet customer and/or operational requirements.

b. how the company's compensation and recognition approaches for individuals and groups, including managers, reinforce the effectiveness of the work and job design

Notes:

(1) Work design refers to how employees are organized and/or organize themselves in formal and informal, temporary or longer-term units. This includes work teams, problem-solving teams, functional units, departments, self-managed or managed by supervisors. In some cases, teams might involve individuals in different locations linked via computers or conferencing technology.

Job design refers to responsibilities and tasks assigned to individuals. These responsibilities and tasks help define education and training requirements.

(2) Examples of approaches to create flexibility [4.2a(2)] in work design might include simplification of job classifications, cross training, job rotation, work layout, and work locations. It might also entail use of technology and changed flow of information to support local decision making.

(3) Compensation and recognition (4.2b) refer to all aspects of pay and reward, including promotion and bonuses. The company might use a variety of reward and recognition approaches — monetary and non-monetary, formal and informal, and individual and group.

Compensation and recognition approaches could include profit sharing and compensation based on skill building, use of new skills, and demonstrations of self-learning. The approaches could take into account the linkage to customer retention or other performance objectives.

Employee evaluations and reward and recognition approaches might include peer evaluations, including peers in teams and networks.

4.3 Employee Education, Training, and Development *(50 pts.)*

Describe how the company's education and training address company plans, including building company capabilities and contributing to employee motivation, progression, and development.

A – D

AREAS TO ADDRESS

a. how the company's education and training serve as a key vehicle in building company and employee capabilities. Describe how education and training address: (1) key performance objectives, including those related to improving customer responsiveness and enhancing high performance work units; and (2) progression and development of all employees.

b. how education and training are designed, delivered, reinforced, evaluated, and improved. Include: (1) how employees and line managers contribute to or are involved in determining specific education and training needs and designing education and training; (2) how education and training are delivered; (3) how knowledge and skills are reinforced through on-the-job application; and (4) how education and training are evaluated and improved.

Notes:

(1) Education and training address the knowledge and skills employees need to meet their overall work objectives. This might include leadership skills, communications, teamwork, problem solving, interpreting and using data, meeting customer requirements, process analysis, process simplification, waste reduction, cycle time reduction, error-proofing, priority setting based upon cost and benefit data, and other training that affects employee effectiveness, efficiency, and safety. It might also include basic skills such as reading, writing, language, and arithmetic.

(2) Training for customer-contact (frontline) employees should address: (a) key knowledge and skills, including knowledge of products and services; (b) listening to customers; (c) soliciting comments from customers; (d) how to anticipate and handle problems or failures ("recovery"); (e) skills in customer retention; and (f) how to manage expectations.

(3) Determining specific education and training needs [4.3b(1)] might include use of company assessment or employee self-assessment to determine and/or compare skill levels for progression within the company or else-where. Needs determination should take into account job analysis — the types and levels of skills required — and the timeliness of training.

(4) Education and training delivery [4.3b(2)] might occur inside or outside the company and involve on-the-job, classroom, computer-based, or other types of delivery. This includes the use of developmental assignments within or outside the company to enhance employees' career opportunities and employability.

(5) How education and training are evaluated [4.3b(4)] could address: effectiveness of delivery of education and training; impact on work unit performance; and cost effectiveness of education and training alternatives.

4.4 Employee Well-Being and Satisfaction *(25 pts.)*

Describe how the company maintains a work environment and a work climate conducive to the well-being and development of all employees.

AREAS TO ADDRESS

a. how the company maintains a safe and healthful work environment. Include: (1) how employee well-being factors such as health, safety, and ergonomics are included in improvement activities; and (2) principal improvement requirements, measures and/or indicators, and targets for each factor relevant and important to the employees' work environment. Note any significant differences based upon differences in work environments among employee groups.

b. what services, facilities, activities, and opportunities the company makes available to employees to support their overall well-being and satisfaction and/or to enhance their work experience and development potential

c. how the company determines employee satisfaction, well-being, and motivation. Include a brief description of methods, frequency, the specific factors used in this determination, and how the information is used to improve satisfaction, well-being, and motivation. Note any important differences in methods or factors used for different categories or types of employees, as appropriate.

Notes:

(1) Examples of services, facilities, activities, and opportunities (4.4b) are: personal and career counseling; career development and employability services; recreational or cultural activities; non-work-related education; day care; special leave for family responsibilities and/or for community service; safety off the job; flexible work hours; outplacement; and retiree benefits, including extended health care. These services also might include career enhancement activities such as skills assessment, helping employees develop learning objectives and plans, and employability assessment.

(2) Examples of specific factors which might affect satisfaction, well-being, and motivation are: effective employee problem or grievance resolution; safety; employee views of leadership and management; employee development and career opportunities; employee preparation for changes in technology or work organization; work environment; workload; cooperation and teamwork; recognition; benefits; communications; job security; compensation; equality of opportunity; and capability to provide required services to customers. An effective determination is one that provides the company with actionable information for use in improvement activities.

(3) Measures and/or indicators of satisfaction, well-being, and motivation (4.4c) might include safety, absenteeism, turnover, turnover rate for customer-contact employees, grievances, strikes, worker compensation, as well as results of surveys.

(4) How satisfaction, well-being, and motivation information is used (4.4c) might involve developing priorities for addressing employee problems based on impact on productivity.

(5) Trends in key measures and/or indicators of well-being and satisfaction should be reported in Item 6.3.

5.0 Process Management (140 pts.)

The *Process Management* Category examines the key aspects of process management, including customer-focused design, product and service delivery processes, support services, and supply management involving all work units, including research and development. The Category examines how key processes are designed, effectively managed, and improved to achieve higher performance.

5.1 Design and Introduction of Products and Services
(40 pts.)

Describe how new and/or modified products and services are designed and introduced and how key production/delivery processes are designed to meet key product and service quality requirements, company operational performance requirements, and market requirements.

(A – D)

AREAS TO ADDRESS

a. how products, services, and production/delivery processes are designed. Describe: (1) how customer requirements are translated into product and service design requirements; (2) how product and service design requirements are translated into efficient and effective production/delivery processes, including an appropriate measurement plan; and (3) how all requirements associated with products, services, and production/delivery processes are addressed early in design by all appropriate company units, suppliers, and partners to ensure integration, coordination, and capability.

b. how product, service, and production/delivery process designs are reviewed and/or tested in detail to ensure trouble-free and rapid introduction

c. how designs and design processes are evaluated and improved to achieve better product and service quality, time to market, and production/delivery process effectiveness

Notes:

(1) Design and introduction might address:
- *modifications and variants of existing products and services, including product and service customization;*
- *new products and services emerging from research and development or other product/service concept development;*
- *new/modified facilities to meet operational performance and/or product and service requirements; and*
- *significant redesigns of processes to improve customer focus, productivity, or both.*

Design approaches could differ appreciably depending upon the nature of the products/services — entirely new, variants, major or minor process changes, etc. If many design projects are carried out in parallel, responses to Item 5.1 should reflect how coordination of resources among projects is carried out.

(2) Applicants' responses should reflect the key require-ments for their products and services. Factors that might need to be considered in design include: health; safety; long-term performance; environmental impact; "green" manufacturing; measurement capability; process capability; manufacturability; maintainability; supplier capability; and documentation.

(3) Service and manufacturing businesses should interpret product and service design requirements to include all product- and service-related requirements at all stages of production, delivery, and use.

(4) A measurement plan [5.1a(2)] should spell out what is to be measured, how and when measurements are to be made, and performance levels or standards to ensure that the results of measurements provide information to guide, monitor, control, or improve the process. This may include service standards used in customer-contact processes. The term, "measurement plan," may also include decisions about key information to collect from customers and/or employees from service encounters, transactions, etc. The actual measurement plan should not be described in Item 5.1. Such information is requested in Item 5.2.

(5) "All appropriate company units" [5.1a(3)] means those units and/or individuals who will take part in production/ delivery and whose performance materially affects overall process outcome. This might include groups such as R&D, marketing, design, and product/process engineering.

15

5.2 Process Management: Product and Service Production and Delivery *(40 pts.)*

Describe how the company's key product and service production/delivery processes are managed to ensure that design requirements are met and that both quality and operational performance are continuously improved.

AREAS TO ADDRESS

a. how the company maintains the performance of key production/delivery processes to ensure that such processes meet design requirements addressed in Item 5.1. Describe: (1) the key processes and their principal requirements; and (2) the measurement plan and how measurements and/or observations are used to maintain process performance.

b. how processes are evaluated and improved to improve products and services and to achieve better performance, including cycle time. Describe how each of the following is used or considered: (1) process analysis and research; (2) benchmarking; (3) use of alternative technology; and (4) information from customers of the processes — within and outside the company.

(A – D)

Notes:

(1) Key production/delivery processes are those most directly involved in fulfilling the principal requirements of customers — those that define the products and services.

(2) Measurement plan [5.2a(2)] is defined in Item 5.1, Note (4). Companies with specialized measurement requirements should describe how they ensure measurement effectiveness. For specialized physical, chemical, and engineering measurements, describe briefly how measurements are made traceable to national standards.

(3) The focus of 5.2a is on <u>maintenance</u> of process performance using measurements and/or observations to decide whether or not corrective action is needed. The nature of the corrective action depends on the process characteristics and the type of variation observed. Responses should reflect the type of process and the type of variation observed. A description should be given of how basic (root) causes of variation are determined and how corrections are made at the earliest point(s) in processes. Such correction should then minimize the likelihood of recurrence of this type of variation anywhere in the company.

(4) The focus of 5.2b is on <u>improvement</u> of processes — making them perform better than the original design. Better performance might include one or more of the following: operational, customer-related, and financial performance. After processes have been improved, process maintenance (5.2a) needs to adjust to the changes. Process improvement methods might utilize financial data to evaluate alternatives and set priorities.

(5) "Process analysis and research" [5.2b(1)] refers to a wide range of possible approaches for improving processes. Examples include process mapping, optimization experiments, basic and applied research, error proofing, and reviewing critical encounters between employees and customers from the point of view of customers and employees.

(6) Information from customers [5.2b(4)] might include information developed as described in Items 7.2, 7.3, and 2.3.

(7) Results of improvements in products and services and in product and service delivery processes should be reported in Items 6.1 and 6.2, as appropriate.

5.3 Process Management: Support Services

(30 pts.)

Describe how the company's key support service processes are designed and managed so that current requirements are met and that operational performance is continuously improved.

(A – D)

AREAS TO ADDRESS

a. how key support service processes are designed. Include: (1) how key requirements are determined or set; (2) how these requirements are translated into efficient and effective processes, including operational requirements and an appropriate measurement plan; and (3) how all requirements are addressed early in design by all appropriate company units to ensure integration, coordination, and capability.

b. how the company maintains the performance of key support service processes to ensure that such processes meet design requirements. Describe: (1) the key processes and their principal requirements; and (2) the measurement plan and how measurements are used to maintain process performance.

c. how processes are evaluated and improved to achieve better performance, including cycle time. Describe how each of the following is used or considered: (1) process analysis and research; (2) benchmarking; (3) use of alternative technology; and (4) information from customers of the processes — within and outside the company.

Notes:

(1) Support services are those that support the company's product and/or service delivery, but are not usually designed in detail with the products and services themselves because their requirements do not usually depend a great deal upon product and service characteristics. Support service design requirements usually depend significantly upon internal requirements. Support services might include finance and accounting, software services, sales, marketing, public relations, information services, supplies, personnel, legal services, plant and facilities management, research and development, and secretarial and other administrative services.

(2) The purpose of Item 5.3 is to permit applicants to highlight separately the design (5.3a), maintenance (5.3b), and improvement (5.3c) activities for processes that support the product and service design, production, and delivery processes addressed in Items 5.1 and 5.2. The support service processes included in Item 5.3 depend on the applicant's type of business and other factors. Thus, this selection should be made by the applicant. Together, Items 5.1, 5.2, 5.3, and 5.4 should cover all key operations, processes, and activities of all work units.

(3) Measurement plan [5.3a(2)] is described in Item 5.1, Note (4). Process maintenance (5.3b) is described in Item 5.2, Note (3). Process improvement (5.3c) is described in Item 5.2, Note (4).

(4) "Process analysis and research" [5.3c(1)] refers to a wide range of possible approaches for improving processes. See Item 5.2, Note (5).

(5) Information from customers [5.3c(4)] might include information developed as described in Items 7.2, 7.3, and 2.3. However, most of the information for improvement [5.3c(4)] is likely to come from "internal customers" — those within the company who use the support services.

(6) Results of improvements in support services should be reported in Item 6.2.

5.4 Management of Supplier Performance (30 pts.)

Describe how the company assures that materials, components, and services furnished by other businesses meet the company's performance requirements. Describe also the company's actions and plans to improve supplier relationships and performance.

AREAS TO ADDRESS

a. summary of the company's requirements and how they are communicated to suppliers. Include: (1) a brief summary of the principal requirements for key suppliers, the measures and/or indicators associated with these requirements, and the expected performance levels; (2) how the company determines whether or not its requirements are met by suppliers; and (3) how performance information is fed back to suppliers.

b. how the company evaluates and improves its management of supplier relationships and performance. Describe current actions and plans: (1) to improve suppliers' abilities to meet requirements; (2) to improve the company's own procurement processes, including feedback sought from suppliers and from other units within the company ("internal customers") and how such feedback is used; and (3) to minimize costs associated with inspection, test, audit, or other approaches used to track and verify supplier performance.

Notes:

(1) The term "supplier" refers to other-company providers of goods and services. The use of these goods and services may occur at any stage in the production, design, delivery, and use of the company's products and services. Thus, suppliers include businesses such as distributors, dealers, warranty repair services, transportation, contractors, and franchises as well as those that provide materials and components.

If the applicant is a unit of a larger company, and other units of that company supply goods/services, this should be included as part of Item 5.4.

The term "supplier" also refers to service suppliers such as health care, training, and education.

(2) Key suppliers [5.4a(1)] are those that provide the most important products and/or services, taking into account the criticality and volume of products and/or services involved.

(3) "Requirements" refers to the principal factors involved in the purchases: quality, delivery, and price.

(4) How requirements are communicated and how performance information is fed back might entail ongoing working relationships or partnerships with key suppliers. Such relationships and/or partnerships should be briefly described in responses.

(5) Processes for determining whether or not requirements are met [5.4a(2)] might include audits, process reviews, receiving inspection, certification, testing, and rating systems.

(6) "Actions and plans" (5.4b) might include one or more of the following: joint planning, rapid information and data exchanges, use of benchmarking and comparative information, customer-supplier teams, partnerships, training, long-term agreements, incentives, and recognition. Actions and plans might also include changes in supplier selection, leading to a reduction in the number of suppliers.

(7) Efforts to minimize costs might be backed by analyses comparing suppliers based on overall cost, taking into account quality and delivery. Analyses might also address transaction costs associated with alternative approaches to supply management.

6.0 Business Results (250 pts.)

The **Business Results** Category examines the company's performance and improvement in key business areas — product and service quality, productivity and operational effectiveness, supply quality, and financial performance indicators linked to these areas. Also examined are performance levels relative to competitors.

6.1 Product and Service Quality Results *(75 pts.)*

Summarize performance results for products and services and/or product and service offerings and results of improvement efforts, using key measures and/or indicators of such performance and improvement.

┌───┐
AREAS TO ADDRESS

a. current levels and trends in key measures and/or indicators of quality of products and services and/or product and service offerings. Graphs and tables should include appropriate comparative data.
└───┘

Notes:

(1) Results reported in Item 6.1 should reflect performance relative to key non-price product and service requirements — those described in the Business Overview and addressed in Items 7.1, 3.1, and 5.1. The measures and/or indicators should address factors that affect customer preference — performance, timeliness, availability, and variety. Examples include defect levels, repeat services, delivery response times, and complaint levels.

(2) Data appropriate for inclusion might be based upon one or more of the following:
• internal (company) measurements;
• field performance;
• data collected by the company or on behalf of the company through follow-ups (7.2c) or surveys of customers on product and service performance; and

• data collected or generated by organizations, including customers.

Although data appropriate for inclusion are primarily based upon internal measurements and field performance, data collected by the company or other organizations through follow-ups might be included for attributes that cannot be accurately assessed through direct measurement (e.g., ease of use) or when variability in customer expectations makes the customer's perception the most meaningful indicator (e.g., courtesy).

(3) Comparative data might include industry best, best competitor, industry average, and appropriate benchmarks. Such data might be derived from independent surveys, studies, laboratory testing, or other sources.

6.2 Company Operational and Financial Results

(110 pts.)

Summarize results of the company's operational and financial performance and performance improvement efforts using key measures and/or indicators of such performance and improvement.

┌───┐
AREAS TO ADDRESS

a. current levels and trends in key measures and/or indicators of company operational and financial performance. Graphs and tables should include appropriate comparative data.
└───┘

Notes:

(1) Key measures and/or indicators of company operational and financial performance include the following areas:
• productivity and other indicators of effective use of manpower, materials, energy, capital, and assets. (Aggregate measures such as total factor productivity, ROI, margin rates, operating profit rates, and working capital productivity are encouraged. Aggregate economic and/or market value measures are also appropriate.);
• company-specific indicators such as innovation rates, innovation effectiveness, cost reductions through innovation, and time to market;

• environmental improvements reflected in emissions levels, waste stream reductions, by-product use and recycling, etc. (See Item 1.3);
• cycle time, lead times, set-up times, and other responsiveness indicators; and
• process assessment results such as customer assessment or third-party assessment (such as ISO 9000).

(2) Comparative data might include industry best, best competitor, industry average, and appropriate benchmarks.

6.3 Human Resource Results *(35 pts.)*

Summarize human resource results, including employee development and indicators of employee well-being and satisfaction.

Ⓡ

AREAS TO ADDRESS

a. current levels and trends in key measures and/or indicators of employee development, well-being, satisfaction, self-directed responsibility, and effectiveness. Graphs and tables should include appropriate comparative data.

Notes:

(1) Measures and/or indicators should include safety, absenteeism, turnover, and satisfaction. Comparative data might include industry best, best competitors, industry average, and appropriate benchmarks. Local or regional data on absenteeism and turnover are also appropriate. Financial measures such as worker compensation cost or turnover cost reductions are appropriate for inclusion.

(2) Measures and/or indicators of development should cover not only extent (for example, percent of employees trained or hours of training per year) but also effectiveness. Financial information such as benefit cost ratios for training is appropriate for inclusion.

(3) Examples of satisfaction factors are given in Item 4.4, Note (2).

(4) The results reported in Item 6.3 derive from activities described in the Items of Category 4.0. Results should address all categories and types of employees.

6.4 Supplier Performance Results *(30 pts.)*

Summarize results of supplier performance and performance improvement efforts using key measures and/or indicators of such performance and improvement.

Ⓡ

AREAS TO ADDRESS

a. current levels and trends in key measures and/or indicators of supplier performance. Graphs and tables should include appropriate comparative data.

Notes:

(1) The results reported in Item 6.4 derive from activities described in Item 5.4. Results should be broken out by key supplies and/or key suppliers, as appropriate. Results should include performance of supply chains and/or results of outsourcing, if these are important to the applicant. Data should be presented using the measures and/or indicators described in 5.4a(1).

(2) Results reported should be relative to all principal requirements: quality, delivery, and price. If the company's supplier management efforts include factors such as building supplier partnerships or reducing the number of suppliers, data related to these efforts should be included in responses.

(3) Comparative data might be of several types: industry best, best competitor(s), industry average, and appropriate benchmarks.

7.0 Customer Focus and Satisfaction (250 pts.)

The *Customer Focus and Satisfaction* Category examines the company's systems for customer learning and for building and maintaining customer relationships. Also examined are levels and trends in key measures of business success — customer satisfaction and retention, market share, and satisfaction relative to competitors.

7.1 Customer and Market Knowledge (30 pts.)

Describe how the company determines near-term and longer-term requirements, expectations, and preferences of customers and markets, and develops listening and learning strategies to understand and anticipate needs.

 (A – D)

AREAS TO ADDRESS

a. how the company determines current and near-term requirements and expectations of customers. Include: (1) how customer groups and/or market segments are determined and/or selected, including how customers of competitors and other potential customers are considered; (2) how information is collected, including what information is sought, frequency and methods of collection, and how objectivity and validity are ensured; (3) how specific product and service features and the relative importance of these features to customer groups or segments are determined; and (4) how other key information and data such as complaints, gains and losses of customers, and product/service performance are used to support the determination.

b. how the company addresses future requirements and expectations of customers and potential customers. Include an outline of key listening and learning strategies used

c. how the company evaluates and improves its processes for determining customer requirements, expectations, and preferences

Notes:

(1) The distinction between near-term and future depends upon many marketplace factors. The applicant's response should reflect these factors for its market(s). Methods used in 7.1a(2) and 7.1b might be the same or similar.

(2) The company's products and services might be sold to end users via other businesses such as retail stores or dealers. Thus, "customer groups" should take into account the requirements and expectations of both the end users and these other businesses.

(3) Some companies might use similar methods to determine customer requirements/expectations and customer satisfaction (Item 7.3). In such cases, cross-references should be included.

(4) Customer groups and market segments [7.1a(1)] might take into account opportunities to select or <u>create</u> groups and segments based upon customer- and market-related information. This might include individual customization.

(5) How information is collected [7.1a(2)] might include periodic methods such as surveys or focus groups and/or ongoing processes such as dialogs with customers.

(6) Product and service features [7.1a(3)] refer to all important characteristics and to the performance of products and services that customers experience or perceive throughout their overall purchase and ownership. The focus should be primarily on features that bear upon customer preference and repurchase loyalty — for example, those features that differentiate products and services from competing offerings. This might include price and value.

(7) Examples of listening and learning strategies (7.1b) are:
* *relationship strategies, including close integration with customers;*
* *rapid innovation and field trials of products and services to better link R&D and design to the market;*
* *close monitoring of technological, competitive, societal, environmental, economic, and demographic factors that may bear upon customer requirements, expectations, preferences, or alternatives;*
* *focus groups with demanding or leading-edge customers;*
* *training of frontline employees in customer listening;*
* *use of critical incidents to understand key service attributes from the point of view of customers and frontline employees;*
* *interviewing lost customers;*
* *won/lost analysis relative to competitors;*
* *post-transaction follow-up (see 7.2c); and*
* *analysis of major factors affecting key customers.*

(8) Examples of evaluation and factors appropriate for 7.1c are:
* *the adequacy and timeliness of the customer-related information;*
* *improvement of survey design;*
* *the best approaches for getting reliable and timely information — surveys, focus groups, customer-contact personnel, etc.;*
* *increasing and decreasing importance of product/service features among customer groups or segments; and*
* *the most effective listening/learning strategies.*

The evaluation might also be supported by company-level analysis addressed in Item 2.3.

7.2 Customer Relationship Management *(30 pts.)*

Describe how the company provides effective management of its responses and follow-ups with customers to preserve and build relationships, to increase knowledge about specific customers and about general customer expectations, to improve company performance, and to generate ideas for new products and services.

AREAS TO ADDRESS

a. how the company provides information and easy access to enable customers to seek information and assistance, to comment, and to complain. Describe how contact management performance is measured. Include key service standards and how these standards are set, deployed, and tracked.

b. how the company ensures that formal and informal complaints and feedback received by all company units are resolved effectively and promptly. Briefly describe the complaint management process, including how it ensures effective recovery of customer confidence, how it meets customer requirements for resolution effectiveness, how it ensures that complaints received by company units are aggregated and analyzed for use throughout the company, and how it seeks to eliminate causes of complaints.

c. how the company follows up with customers on products, services, and recent transactions to determine satisfaction, to resolve problems, to seek feedback for improvement, to build relationships, and to develop ideas for new products and services

d. how the company evaluates and improves its customer relationship management. Include: (1) how service standards, including those related to access and complaint management, are improved based upon customer information; and (2) how knowledge about customers is accumulated.

Notes:

(1) Customer relationship management refers to a process, not to a company unit. However, some companies might have units which address all or most of the requirements included in this Item. Also, some of these requirements might be included among the responsibilities of frontline employees in processes described in Items 5.2 and 5.3.

(2) How the company maintains easy access for customers (7.2a) might involve close integration, electronic networks, etc.

(3) Performance measures and service standards (7.2a) apply not only to employees providing the responses to customers but also to other units within the company that make effective responses possible. Deployment needs to take into account all key points in a response chain. Examples of measures and standards are: telephonic, percentage of resolutions achieved by frontline employees, number of transfers, and resolution response time.

(4) Responses to 7.2b and 7.2c might include company processes for addressing customer complaints or comments based upon expressed or implied guarantees and warranties.

(5) The complaint management process (7.2b) might include analysis and priority setting for improvement projects based upon potential cost impact of complaints, taking into account customer retention related to resolution effectiveness. Some of the analysis requirements of Item 7.2 relate to Item 2.3.

(6) Improvement of customer relationship management (7.2d) might require training. Training for customer-contact (frontline) employees should address: (a) key knowledge and skills, including knowledge of products and services; (b) listening to customers; (c) soliciting comments from customers; (d) how to anticipate and handle problems or failures ("recovery"); (e) skills in customer retention; and (f) how to manage expectations. Such training should be described in Item 4.3.

(7) Information on trends and levels in measures and/or indicators of complaint response time, effective resolution, and percent of complaints resolved on first contact should be reported in Item 6.1.

7.3 Customer Satisfaction Determination (30 pts.)

Describe how the company determines customer satisfaction, customer repurchase intentions, and customer satisfaction relative to competitors; describe how these determination processes are evaluated and improved.

AREAS TO ADDRESS

a. how the company determines customer satisfaction. Include: (1) a brief description of processes and measurement scales used; frequency of determination; and how objectivity and validity are ensured. Indicate significant differences, if any, in processes and measurement scales for different customer groups or segments; and (2) how customer satisfaction measurements capture key information that reflects customers' likely future market behavior.

b. how customer satisfaction relative to that for competitors is determined. Describe: (1) company-based comparative studies; and (2) comparative studies or evaluations made by independent organizations and/or customers. For (1) and (2), describe how objectivity and validity of studies or evaluations are ensured.

c. how the company evaluates and improves its processes and measurement scales for determining customer satisfaction and satisfaction relative to competitors. Include how other indicators (such as gains and losses of customers) and dissatisfaction indicators (such as complaints) are used in this improvement process. Describe also how the evaluation determines the effectiveness of companywide use of customer satisfaction information and data.

Notes:

(1) Customer satisfaction measurement might include both a numerical rating scale and descriptors for each unit in the scale. An effective (actionable) customer satisfaction measurement system provides reliable information about customer ratings of specific product and service features and the relationship between these ratings and the customer's likely future market behavior — repurchase and/or positive referral. Product and service features might include overall value and price.

(2) The company's products and services might be sold to end users via other businesses such as retail stores or dealers. Thus, "customer groups" or segments should take into account these other businesses and the end users.

(3) Customer dissatisfaction indicators include complaints, claims, refunds, recalls, returns, repeat services, litigation, replacements, downgrades, repairs, warranty work, warranty costs, misshipments, and incomplete orders.

(4) Comparative studies (7.3b) might include indicators of customer dissatisfaction as well as satisfaction.

(5) Evaluation (7.3c) might take into account:
- *how well the measurement scale relates to actual customer behavior;*
- *the effectiveness of pre-survey research used in survey design;*
- *how well customer responses link to key business processes and thus provide actionable information for improvement; and*
- *how well customer responses have been translated into cost/revenue implications and thus provide actionable information for improvement priorities.*

(6) Use of data from satisfaction measurement is called for in 5.2b(4) and 5.3c(4). Such data also provide key input to analysis (Item 2.3).

7.4 Customer Satisfaction Results (160 pts.)

Summarize the company's customer satisfaction and dissatisfaction results using key measures and/or indicators of these results. Compare results with competitors' results.

Ⓡ

AREAS TO ADDRESS

a. current levels and trends in key measures and/or indicators of customer satisfaction and dissatisfaction. Results should be segmented by customer groups and product and service types, as appropriate.

b. current levels and trends in key measures and/or indicators of customer satisfaction relative to competitors. Results should be segmented by customer groups and product and service types, as appropriate.

Notes:

(1) Results reported in this Item derive from methods described in Items 7.3 and 7.2.

(2) Measures and/or indicators of satisfaction relative to competitors (7.4b) should include gains and losses of customers and customer accounts to competitors as well as gains and losses in market share.

(3) Measures and/or indicators of satisfaction relative to competitors might include objective information and/or data from independent organizations, including customers. Examples include survey results, competitive awards,

recognition, and ratings. Such information and data should reflect comparative satisfaction (and dissatisfaction), not comparative performance of products and services (called for in Item 6.1).

(4) Customer retention data might be used in both 7.4a and 7.4b. For example, in 7.4a, customer retention might be included as a satisfaction indicator, while in 7.4b, customer retention relative to competitors might be part of a switching analysis to determine competitive position and the factors responsible for it.

SCORING SYSTEM

The system for scoring applicant responses to Criteria Items (Items) and for developing feedback is based upon three evaluation dimensions: (1) Approach; (2) Deployment; and (3) Results. All Items require applicants to furnish information relating to these dimensions. Specific factors associated with the evaluation dimensions are described below. Scoring Guidelines are given on page 25.

Approach

"Approach" refers to how the applicant addresses the Item requirements — the method(s) used. The factors used to evaluate approaches include the following:

- appropriateness of the methods to the requirements
- effectiveness of use of the methods. Degree to which the approach:
  - is systematic, integrated, and consistently applied
  - embodies evaluation/improvement cycles
  - is based upon data and information that are objective and reliable
- evidence of innovation. This includes significant and effective adaptations of approaches used in other types of applications or businesses.

Deployment

"Deployment" refers to the extent to which the applicant's approach is applied to all requirements of the Item. The factors used to evaluate deployment include the following:

- use of the approach in addressing business and Item requirements
- use of the approach by all appropriate work units

Results

"Results" refers to outcomes in achieving the purposes given in the Item. The factors used to evaluate results include the following:

- current performance levels
- performance levels relative to appropriate comparisons and/or benchmarks
- rate, breadth, and importance of performance improvements
- demonstration of sustained improvement and/or sustained high-level performance

Item Classification and Scoring Dimensions

Award Criteria Items are classified according to the kinds of information and/or data applicants are expected to furnish.

The two types of Items and their designations are:

1. Approach/Deployment   (A–D)

2. Results   (R)

Approach and Deployment are linked to emphasize that descriptions of Approach should always convey Deployment — consistent with the specific requirements of the Item. Although Approach and Deployment dimensions are linked, feedback to the applicant reflects strengths and/or areas for improvement in either or both dimensions.

Results Items depend on data demonstrating performance levels and trends. However, the evaluation factor, "breadth and importance of performance improvements", is concerned with how widespread and how significant an applicant's improvement results are. This is directly related to the Deployment dimension. That is, if improvement processes are widely deployed, there should be corresponding results. A score for a Results Item is thus a composite based upon overall performance, taking into account the breadth and importance of improvements.

"Relevance and Importance" as a Scoring Factor

The three evaluation dimensions described above are all critical to assessment and feedback. However, evaluation and feedback must also consider the relevance and importance to the applicant's business of improvements in Approach, Deployment, and Results. The areas of greatest relevance and importance should be addressed in the Business Overview, and are a primary focus of Items such as 3.1, 5.1, 5.2, 6.1, and 7.1. Of particular importance are the key customer requirements and key business drivers.

Assignment of Scores to Applicants' Responses

Baldrige Award Examiners observe the following guidelines in assignment of scores to applicants' responses:

- All relevant Areas to Address should be included in the Item response. Also, responses should reflect what is relevant and important to the applicant's business.
- In assigning a score to an Item, an Examiner first decides which scoring range (e.g., 40% to 60%) best fits the overall Item response. Overall "best fit" does not require total agreement with each of the statements for that scoring range. Actual score within the range depends upon an Examiner's judgment of the closeness of the Item response in relation to the statements in the next higher and next lower scoring ranges.
- An Approach/Deployment Item score of 50% represents an approach that meets the basic objectives of the Item and that is deployed to the principal activities covered in the Item. Higher scores reflect maturity (cycles of improvement), integration, and broader deployment.
- A Results Item score of 50% represents clear indication of improvement trends and/or good levels of performance in the principal results areas covered in the Item. Higher scores reflect better improvement rates and comparative performance as well as broader coverage.

SCORING GUIDELINES

SCORE	APPROACH/DEPLOYMENT
0%	■ no systematic approach evident; anecdotal information
10% to 30%	■ beginning of a systematic approach to the primary purposes of the Item ■ early stages of a transition from reacting to problems to a general improvement orientation ■ major gaps exist in deployment that would inhibit progress in achieving the primary purposes of the Item
40% to 60%	■ a sound, systematic approach, responsive to the primary purposes of the Item ■ a fact-based improvement process in place in key areas; more emphasis is placed on improvement than on reaction to problems ■ no major gaps in deployment, though some areas or work units may be in very early stages of deployment
70% to 90%	■ a sound, systematic approach, responsive to the overall purposes of the Item ■ a fact-based improvement process is a key management tool; clear evidence of refinement and improved integration as a result of improvement cycles and analysis ■ approach is well-deployed, with no major gaps; deployment may vary in some areas or work units
100%	■ a sound, systematic approach, fully responsive to all the requirements of the Item ■ a very strong, fact-based improvement process is a key management tool; strong refinement and integration — backed by excellent analysis ■ approach is fully deployed without any significant weaknesses or gaps in any areas or work units

SCORE	RESULTS
0%	■ no results or poor results in areas reported
10% to 30%	■ early stages of developing trends; some improvements *and/or* early good performance levels in a few areas ■ results not reported for many to most areas of importance to the applicant's key business requirements
40% to 60%	■ improvement trends *and/or* good performance levels reported for many to most areas of importance to the applicant's key business requirements ■ no pattern of adverse trends *and/or* poor performance levels in areas of importance to the applicant's key business requirements ■ some trends *and/or* current performance levels — evaluated against relevant comparisons *and/or* benchmarks — show areas of strength *and/or* good to very good relative performance levels
70% to 90%	■ current performance is good to excellent in most areas of importance to the applicant's key business requirements ■ most improvement trends *and/or* performance levels are sustained ■ many to most trends *and/or* current performance levels — evaluated against relevant comparisons *and/or* benchmarks — show areas of leadership and very good relative performance levels
100%	■ current performance is excellent in most areas of importance to the applicant's key business requirements ■ excellent improvement trends *and/or* sustained excellent performance levels in most areas ■ strong evidence of industry and benchmark leadership demonstrated in many areas

PREPARING THE BUSINESS OVERVIEW

The Business Overview is an outline of the applicant's business, addressing what is most important to the business, the key factors that influence how the business operates, and where the business is headed. In simplest terms, *the Business Overview is intended to help Examiners understand what is relevant and important to the applicant's business.*

The Business Overview is of critical importance to the applicant because:

■ it is the most appropriate starting point for writing and self-assessing the application, helping to ensure focus on key business issues and to achieve consistency in responses, especially in reporting business results; and

■ it is used by the Examiners and Judges in all stages of application review, including the site visit.

Guidelines for Preparing the Business Overview

The Business Overview consists of five sections as follows:

1. **Basic description of the company**
   This section should provide basic information on:
   ■ the nature of the applicant's business: products and services;
   ■ company size, location(s), and whether it is publicly or privately owned;
   ■ the applicant's major markets (local, regional, national, or international) and principal customer types (consumers, other businesses, government, etc.). (Note any special relationships, such as partnerships, with customers or customer groups.);
   ■ a profile of the applicant's employee base, including: number, types, educational level, bargaining units, and special safety requirements; and
   ■ major equipment, facilities, and technologies used.

   If the applicant is a subunit of a larger entity, a brief description of the organizational relationships to the parent company and percent of employees it represents should be given. Briefly describe also relationships of the applicant's products and services to those of the parent company and/or other subunits of the parent company. If the parent company provides key support services, these should be briefly described.

2. **Customer requirements**
   This section should provide information on:
   ■ key customer requirements (for example, on-time delivery, low defect levels, price demands, and after-sales services) for products and services. Briefly describe all important requirements, and note significant differences, if any, in requirements among customer groups.

3. **Supplier relationships**
   This section should provide information on:
   ■ types and numbers of suppliers of goods and services;
   ■ the most important types of suppliers, dealers, and other businesses; and
   ■ any limitations or special relationships that may exist in dealing with some or all suppliers.

4. **Competitive factors**
   This section should provide information on:
   ■ the applicant's position (relative size, growth) in the industry;
   ■ numbers and types of competitors;
   ■ principal factors that determine competitive success such as productivity growth, cost reduction, and product innovation; and
   ■ changes taking place in the industry that affect competition.

5. **Other factors important to the applicant**
   This section should provide information, as appropriate, on:
   ■ major new thrusts for the company such as entry into new markets, or segments;
   ■ new business alliances;
   ■ introduction of new technologies;
   ■ the regulatory environment affecting the applicant, such as occupational health and safety, environmental, financial, and product;
   ■ changes in strategy; and
   ■ unique factors.

Page Limit

The Business Overview is limited to four pages. These four pages are not counted in the overall application page limit. Typing instructions for the Business Overview are the same as for the application. These instructions are given in the *1996 Business Application Forms and Instructions* booklet. Ordering instructions for this booklet are given on page 47.

It is strongly recommended that the Business Overview be prepared first and that it be used to guide the applicant in writing and reviewing the application.

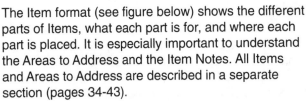

Writing an application for the Baldrige Award involves responding in 70 or fewer pages to the requirements given in the 24 Criteria Items. The guidelines given in this section are offered to assist applicants to respond most effectively to the Item requirements.

The guidelines are presented in three parts: (1) General Guidelines regarding the Award Criteria booklet, including how the Items are formatted; (2) Guidelines for Responding to Approach/Deployment Items; and (3) Guidelines for Responding to Results Items.

General Guidelines

1. Read the entire Award Criteria booklet.

The main sections of the booklet provide an overall orientation to the Criteria, including how applicants' responses are evaluated. Applicants should be thoroughly familiar with the following sections:

- Award Criteria (pages 6-23)
- Scoring information (pages 24-25)
- Glossary of Key Terms (pages 4-5)
- Item Descriptions (pages 34-43)

2. Review the Item format.

The Item format (see figure below) shows the different parts of Items, what each part is for, and where each part is placed. It is especially important to understand the Areas to Address and the Item Notes. All Items and Areas to Address are described in a separate section (pages 34-43).

Each Item is classified either (A – D) or (R), depending on the type of information required. The meaning of these classification symbols is given on page 24. Guidelines for responding to Approach/Deployment Items are given on page 28. Guidelines for responding to Results Items are given on page 29.

3. Start by preparing the Business Overview.

The Business Overview is the most appropriate starting point for writing an application. The Business Overview is intended to help everyone — including the company's application writer(s) and reviewer(s) — to understand what is most relevant and important to the applicant's business. Guidelines for preparing the Business Overview are given on page 26.

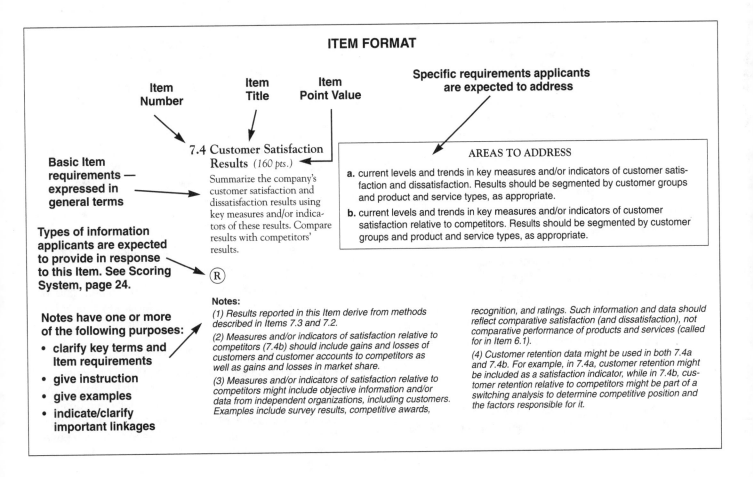

ITEM FORMAT

Item Number

Item Title

Item Point Value

Specific requirements applicants are expected to address

Basic Item requirements — expressed in general terms

7.4 Customer Satisfaction Results *(160 pts.)*

Summarize the company's customer satisfaction and dissatisfaction results using key measures and/or indicators of these results. Compare results with competitors' results.

Types of information applicants are expected to provide in response to this Item. See Scoring System, page 24.

(R)

AREAS TO ADDRESS

a. current levels and trends in key measures and/or indicators of customer satisfaction and dissatisfaction. Results should be segmented by customer groups and product and service types, as appropriate.

b. current levels and trends in key measures and/or indicators of customer satisfaction relative to competitors. Results should be segmented by customer groups and product and service types, as appropriate.

Notes have one or more of the following purposes:

- clarify key terms and Item requirements
- give instruction
- give examples
- indicate/clarify important linkages

Notes:
(1) Results reported in this Item derive from methods described in Items 7.3 and 7.2.

(2) Measures and/or indicators of satisfaction relative to competitors (7.4b) should include gains and losses of customers and customer accounts to competitors as well as gains and losses in market share.

(3) Measures and/or indicators of satisfaction relative to competitors might include objective information and/or data from independent organizations, including customers. Examples include survey results, competitive awards,

recognition, and ratings. Such information and data should reflect comparative satisfaction (and dissatisfaction), not comparative performance of products and services (called for in Item 6.1).

(4) Customer retention data might be used in both 7.4a and 7.4b. For example, in 7.4a, customer retention might be included as a satisfaction indicator, while in 7.4b, customer retention relative to competitors might be part of a switching analysis to determine competitive position and the factors responsible for it.

Guidelines for Responding to Approach/Deployment Items

The Award Criteria focus on performance results. Results Items (6.1, 6.2, 6.3, 6.4, and 7.4) require applicants to summarize results of all kinds, including operational, customer-related, and financial. However, results, by themselves, offer little *diagnostic* value. For example, if results are poor in some areas or improving at rates slower than the competition's, it is important to understand *why* this is so and *what* might be done to accelerate improvement. Approach/Deployment Items permit diagnosis of the applicant's most important systems, activities, and processes — the ones that offer the greatest potential for fast-paced improvement of the applicant's performance. Diagnosis and feedback depend heavily upon the *content and completeness* of Approach/Deployment Item responses. For this reason, it is important to respond to these Items by providing key process information. Guidelines for organizing such information are given below.

1. **Understand the meaning of "how".**

   Items that request information on approach include Areas to Address that begin with the word "how". Responses to such Areas should provide as complete a picture as possible to enable meaningful evaluation and feedback. *Responses should outline key process details such as methods, measures, deployment, and evaluation factors.* Information lacking sufficient detail to permit an evaluation and feedback, or merely providing an example, is referred to in the Criteria booklet as *anecdotal information.*

2. **Write and review response(s) with the following guidelines, questions, and comments in mind:**

   - Show *what* and *how.*

     – Does the response show what is done, and does it give a clear sense of how?

     It is important to give basic information about *what* key processes are and *how* they work. Although it is helpful to include *who* performs the work, merely stating *who* does not permit feedback. For example, stating that "customer satisfaction data are analyzed for improvement by the Customer Service Department" does not set the stage for useful feedback, because from this very limited information, potential strengths and weaknesses in the analysis cannot be identified at all.

   - Show that activities are *systematic.*

     – Does the response show a systematic approach, or does it merely provide an example (anecdote)?

Approaches that are systematic use data and information for cycles of improvement. In other words, the approaches are systematic *over time,* and thus show learning and maturity. Scores above 50% rely upon clear evidence that approaches are systematic.

   - Show deployment.

     – Does the response give clear and sufficient information on deployment? For example, from a response, could one clearly distinguish whether an approach described is used in one part of the company or in a few, most, or all parts?

Deployment can be shown compactly by using summary tables that outline what is done in different parts of the company. This is particularly effective if the basic approach is described in a narrative.

   - Show focus and consistency.

     – Does the response show that the applicant is focused on key processes and on improvements that offer the greatest potential to improve business performance?

There are four important factors to consider regarding setting the stage for focus and consistency: (1) the Business Overview should make clear what is important; (2) the Strategic Planning Category, including the key business drivers, should highlight areas of greatest focus and describe how deployment is accomplished; (3) descriptions of company-level analysis (Item 2.3) should show how the company analyzes performance information to set priorities; and (4) company-level review (1.2b) should show how performance information is tracked and used. Focus and consistency in the Approach/Deployment Items should be accompanied by corresponding results being reported in Items 6.1, 6.2, 6.3, 6.4, and 7.4.

   - Respond fully to Item requirements.

     – Does the response lack information on important parts of an Area to Address?

Missing information will be interpreted as a gap in approach and/or deployment. All Areas should be addressed and checked in final review.

3. **Cross-reference when appropriate.**

Applicants should try to make each Item response self-contained. However, there may be instances when responses to different Items are mutually reinforcing. It is then appropriate to reference responses to other Items, rather than to repeat information. In such cases, applicants should use Area designators (for example, "see 2.3a").

Guidelines for Responding to Results Items

The Award Criteria place greatest emphasis on results. Items 6.1, 6.2, 6.3, 6.4, and 7.4 call for results related to all key requirements, stakeholders, and goals. The following information, guidelines, and example relate to effective and complete presentation of results.

1. **Note the meaning of the five key requirements for effective presentation of results data.**

   ■ trends show directions of results and rates of change;

   ■ performance levels show performance on some meaningful measurement scale;

   ■ comparisons show how trends and/or levels compare with those of other, appropriately selected organizations;

   ■ breadth of results shows completeness of deployment of improvement activities; and

   ■ focus shows that results reported are consistent with and cover the most important requirements for business success, highlighted in the Business Overview and included in responses to other Items.

2. **Include trend data covering actual periods for tracking trends.**

   No minimum period of time is specified for trend data. Time periods might span five years or more for some results. Trends might be much shorter for some of the company's improvement activities. Because of the importance of showing deployment and focus, new data should be included even if trends and comparisons are not yet well established.

3. **Use a compact format.**

   Presenting many results can be done compactly by using graphs and tables. Label graphs and tables for easy interpretation. Results over time or compared with others should be "normalized" — presented in a way (such as use of ratios) that takes into account various size factors. For example, if the company's work force has been growing, reporting safety results in terms of accidents per 100 employees would permit more meaningful trend data than total accidents.

4. **Integrate results into the body of the text.**

   Descriptions of results and the results themselves should be close together in the application. Use figure numbers that correspond to Items. For example, the third figure for Item 6.1 would be 6.1-3. (See example on the figure shown to the right.)

   The following graph illustrates data an applicant might present as part of a response to Item 6.1, Product and

Service Quality Results. In the Business Overview and in Item 7.1, the applicant has indicated on-time delivery as a key customer requirement.

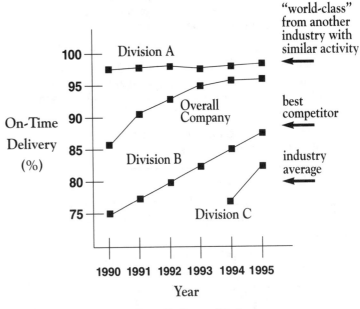

Figure 6.1-3   On-Time Delivery Performance

Using the graph, the following characteristics of clear and effective data presentation are illustrated:

■ A figure number is provided for reference to the graph in the text.

■ Both axes and units of measure are clearly labeled.

■ Trend lines report data for a key business requirement — on-time delivery.

■ Results are presented for several years.

■ Appropriate comparisons are clearly shown.

■ The company shows, using a single graph, that its three divisions separately track on-time delivery.

To help interpret the Scoring Guidelines (page 25), the following comments on the graphed results would be appropriate:

■ The current overall company performance level is excellent. This conclusion is supported by the comparison with competitors and with a "world-class" level.

■ The company exhibits an overall excellent improvement record.

■ Division A is the current performance leader — showing sustained high performance and a slightly positive trend. Division B shows rapid improvement. Its current performance is near that of the best industry competitor, but trails the "world-class" level.

■ Division C — a new division — shows rapid progress. Its current performance is not yet at the level of the best industry competitor.

Award Criteria Purposes

The Malcolm Baldrige National Quality Award Criteria are the basis for making Awards and for giving feedback to applicants. In addition, the Criteria have three important roles in strengthening U.S. competitiveness:

- to help improve performance practices and capabilities;

- to facilitate communication and sharing of best practices information among and within organizations of all types, based upon a common understanding of key performance requirements; and

- to serve as a working tool for managing performance, planning, training, and assessment.

Award Criteria Goals

The Criteria are designed to help companies enhance their competitiveness through focus on dual, results-oriented goals:

- delivery of ever-improving value to customers, resulting in marketplace success; and

- improvement of overall company performance and capabilities.

Core Values and Concepts

The Award Criteria are built upon a set of core values and concepts. These values and concepts are the foundation for integrating customer and company performance requirements within a results-oriented framework. These core values and concepts are:

Customer-Driven Quality

Quality is judged by customers. All product and service features and characteristics that contribute value to customers and lead to customer satisfaction and preference must be a key focus of a company's management system. Value, satisfaction, and preference may be influenced by many factors throughout the customer's overall purchase, ownership, and service experiences. These factors include the company's relationship with customers that helps build trust, confidence, and loyalty. This concept of quality includes not only the product and service characteristics that meet basic customer requirements, but it also includes those features and characteristics that enhance them and differentiate them from competing offerings. Such enhancement and differentiation may be based upon new offerings, combinations of product and service offerings, rapid response, or special relationships.

Customer-driven quality is thus a strategic concept. It is directed toward customer retention, market share gain, and growth. It demands constant sensitivity to emerging customer and market requirements, and measurement of the factors that drive customer satisfaction and retention.

It also demands awareness of developments in technology and of competitors' offerings, and rapid and flexible response to customer and market requirements.

Success requires more than defect and error reduction, merely meeting specifications, and reducing complaints. Nevertheless, defect and error reduction and elimination of causes of dissatisfaction contribute significantly to the customers' view of quality and are thus also important parts of customer-driven quality. In addition, the company's success in recovering from defects and errors ("making things right for the customer") is crucial to building customer relationships and to customer retention.

Leadership

A company's senior leaders need to set directions and create a customer orientation, clear and visible values, and high expectations. Reinforcement of the values and expectations requires personal commitment and involvement. The leaders' basic values and commitment need to address all stakeholders and include areas of public responsibility and corporate citizenship. The leaders need to guide the creation of strategies, systems, and methods for achieving excellence and building capabilities. The systems and methods need to guide all activities and decisions of the company. The senior leaders need to commit to the development of the entire work force and should encourage participation and creativity by all employees. Through their personal involvement in planning, communications, review of company performance, and employee recognition, the senior leaders serve as role models, reinforcing the values and building leadership and initiative throughout the company.

Continuous Improvement and Learning

Achieving the highest levels of performance requires a well-executed approach to continuous improvement. The term "continuous improvement" refers to both incremental and "breakthrough" improvement. Improvement needs to be "embedded" in the way the company functions. Embedded means: (1) improvement is part of the daily work of all work units; (2) improvement processes seek to eliminate problems at their source; and (3) improvement is driven by opportunities to do better, as well as by problems that must be corrected. Sources of improvement include: employee ideas; R&D; customer input; and benchmarking or other comparative performance information.

Improvements may be of several types: (1) enhancing value to customers through new and improved products and services; (2) reducing errors, defects, and waste; (3) improving responsiveness and cycle time performance; (4) improving productivity and effectiveness in the use of all resources; and (5) improving the company's performance in fulfilling its public responsibilities and serving as a corporate citizenship role model. Thus, improvement is intended not only to provide better products and services, but also to be more responsive and efficient — both conferring additional marketplace advantages. To meet these objectives, continuous improvement must contain cycles of planning, execution, and evaluation. This requires a basis — preferably a quantitative basis — for assessing progress and for deriving information for future cycles of improvement. Such information should directly link performance goals and internal operations.

Employee Participation and Development

A company's success in improving performance depends increasingly on the skills and motivation of its work force. Employee success depends increasingly on having opportunities to learn and to practice new skills. Companies need to invest in the development of the work force through education, training, and opportunities for continuing growth. Such opportunities might include classroom and on-the-job training, job rotation, and pay for demonstrated skills. Structured on-the-job training offers a cost effective way to train and to better link training to work processes. Work force education and training programs may need to utilize advanced technologies, such as electronic support systems, computer-based learning, and satellite broadcasts. Increasingly, training, development, and work organizations need to be tailored to a diverse work force and to more flexible, high performance work practices.

Major challenges in the area of work force development include: (1) integration of human resource management — selection, performance, recognition, training, and career advancement; and (2) aligning human resource management with business plans and strategic change processes. Addressing these challenges requires acquisition and use of employee-related data on skills, satisfaction, motivation, safety, and well-being. Such data need to be tied to indicators of company or unit performance, such as customer satisfaction, customer retention, and productivity. Through this approach, human resource management may be better integrated and aligned with business directions.

Fast Response

Success in competitive markets increasingly demands ever-shorter cycles for new or improved product and service introduction. Also, faster and more flexible response to customers is now a more critical requirement. Major improvement in response time often requires simplification of work organizations and work processes. To accomplish such improvement, the time performance of work processes should be among the key process measures. There are other important benefits derived from this focus: response time improvements often drive simultaneous improvements in organization, quality, and productivity. Hence it is beneficial to consider response time, quality, and productivity objectives together.

Design Quality and Prevention

Business management should place strong emphasis on design quality — problem and waste prevention achieved through building quality into products and services and efficiency into production and delivery processes. In general, costs of preventing problems at the design stage are much lower than costs of correcting problems that occur "downstream". Design quality includes the creation of fault-tolerant (robust) or failure-resistant processes and products.

A major issue in competition is the design-to-introduction ("product generation") cycle time. Meeting the demands of rapidly changing markets requires that companies carry out stage-to-stage coordination and integration ("concurrent engineering") of functions and activities from basic research to commercialization. Increasingly, design quality also includes the ability to incorporate information gathered from diverse sources and data bases, that combine factors such as customer preference, competitive offerings, marketplace changes, and external research findings and developments.

From the point of view of public responsibility, the design stage is a critical decision point. Design decisions affect process waste streams and the composition of municipal and industrial wastes. The growing demands for a cleaner environment mean that companies' design strategies need to include environmental factors.

Consistent with the theme of design quality and prevention, improvement needs to emphasize interventions "upstream" — at early stages in processes. This approach yields the maximum overall benefits of improvements and corrections. Such upstream intervention also needs to take into account the company's suppliers.

Long-Range View of the Future

Pursuit of market leadership requires a strong future orientation and a willingness to make long-term commitments to all stakeholders — customers, employees, suppliers, stockholders, the public, and the community. Planning needs to anticipate many types of changes including those that may affect customers' expectations of products and services, technological developments, changing customer segments, evolving regulatory requirements, community/societal expectations, and thrusts by competitors. Plans, strategies, and resource allocations need to reflect these commitments and changes. A major part of the long-term commitment is developing employees and suppliers and fulfilling public responsibilities.

Management by Fact

Modern business management systems depend upon measurement, data, information, and analysis. Measurements must derive from the company's strategy and encompass all key processes and the outputs and results of those processes. Facts and data needed for performance improvement and assessment are of many types, including: customer, product and service performance, operations, market, competitive comparisons, supplier, employee-related, and cost and financial. Analysis refers to extracting larger meaning from data to support evaluation and decision making at all levels within the company. Such analysis may entail using data to reveal information — such as trends, projections, and cause and effect — that might not be evident without analysis. Facts, data, and analysis support a variety of company purposes, such as planning, reviewing company performance, improving operations, and comparing company performance with competitors' or with "best practices" benchmarks.

A major consideration in the use of data and analysis to improve performance involves the creation and use of performance measures or indicators. Performance measures or indicators are measurable characteristics of products, services, processes, and operations the company uses to track and improve performance. *The measures or indicators should be selected to best represent the factors that lead to improved customer, operational, and financial performance. A system of measures or indicators tied to customer and/or company performance requirements represents a clear basis for aligning all activities with the company's goals.* Through the analysis of data from the tracking processes, the measures or indicators themselves may be evaluated and changed. For example, measures selected to track product and service quality may be judged by how well improvement in these measures correlates with improvement in customer satisfaction and customer retention.

Partnership Development

Companies should seek to build internal and external partnerships to better accomplish their overall goals.

Internal partnerships might include those that promote labor-management cooperation, such as agreements with unions. Agreements might entail employee development, cross-training, or new work organizations, such as high performance work teams. Internal partnerships might also involve creating network relationships among company units to improve flexibility and responsiveness.

External partnerships might be with customers, suppliers, and education organizations for a variety of purposes, including education and training. An increasingly important kind of external partnership is the strategic partnership or alliance. Such partnerships might offer a company entry into new markets or a basis for new products or services. A partnership might also permit the blending of a company's core competencies or leadership capabilities with complementary strengths and capabilities of partners, thereby enhancing overall capability, including speed and flexibility. Internal and external partnerships should seek to develop longer-term objectives, thereby creating a

basis for mutual investments. Partners should address the key requirements for success of the partnership, means of regular communication, approaches to evaluating progress, and means for adapting to changing conditions. In some cases, joint education and training could offer a cost-effective means to help ensure success.

Corporate Responsibility and Citizenship

A company's management should stress corporate responsibility and encourage corporate citizenship. Corporate responsibility refers to basic expectations of the company — business ethics and protection of public health, safety, and the environment. Health, safety, and environmental considerations include the company's operations as well as the life cycles of products and services. Companies need to address factors such as resource conservation and waste reduction at their source. Planning related to public health, safety, and the environment should anticipate adverse impacts that may arise in facilities management, production, distribution, transportation, use and disposal of products. Plans should seek to prevent problems, to provide a forthright company response if problems occur, and to make available information needed to maintain public awareness, safety, and confidence. Inclusion of public responsibility areas within a performance system means meeting all local, state, and federal laws and regulatory requirements. It also means treating these and related requirements as areas for continuous improvement "beyond mere compliance." This requires that appropriate measures be created and used in managing performance.

Corporate citizenship refers to leadership and support — within limits of a company's resources — of publicly important purposes, including areas of corporate responsibility. Such purposes might include education improvement, improving health care value, environmental excellence, resource conservation, community services, improving industry and business practices, and sharing of nonproprietary quality-related information. Leadership as a corporate citizen also entails influencing other organizations, private and public, to partner for these purposes. For example, individual companies could lead efforts to help define the obligations of their industry to its communities.

Results Orientation

A company's performance system needs to focus on results. Results should be guided by and balanced by the interests of all stakeholders — customers, employees, stockholders, suppliers and partners, the public, and the community. To meet the sometimes conflicting and changing aims that balance implies, company strategy needs to explicitly address all stakeholder requirements to ensure that actions and plans meet the differing needs and avoid adverse impact on any stakeholders. The use of a balanced composite of performance measures offers an effective means to communicate requirements, to monitor actual performance, and to marshal support for improving results.

Award Criteria Framework

The core values and concepts are embodied in seven Categories, as follows:

1.0 Leadership
2.0 Information and Analysis
3.0 Strategic Planning
4.0 Human Resource Development and Management
5.0 Process Management
6.0 Business Results
7.0 Customer Focus and Satisfaction

The framework connecting and integrating the Categories is given in the figure below.

The framework has three basic elements:

Driver

Senior executive leadership sets directions, creates values, goals, expectations, and systems, and pursues customer and business performance excellence.

System

The system comprises the set of well-defined and well-designed processes for meeting the company's customer and overall performance requirements.

Goal

The basic aims of leadership and the purposes of the system are two-fold:

Customer and Marketplace Performance
Customer and marketplace performance means delivery of ever-improving value to customers, high levels of customer satisfaction, and a strong competitive position.

Business Performance
Business performance is reflected in a wide variety of financial and non-financial results, including human resource development and corporate responsibility.

The seven Criteria Categories shown in the figure are subdivided into Items and Areas to Address:

Items

There are 24 Items, each focusing on a major requirement. Item titles and point values are given on page 3. The Item format is shown on page 27.

Areas to Address

Items consist of one or more Areas to Address (Areas). Information is submitted by applicants in response to specific requirements of these Areas.

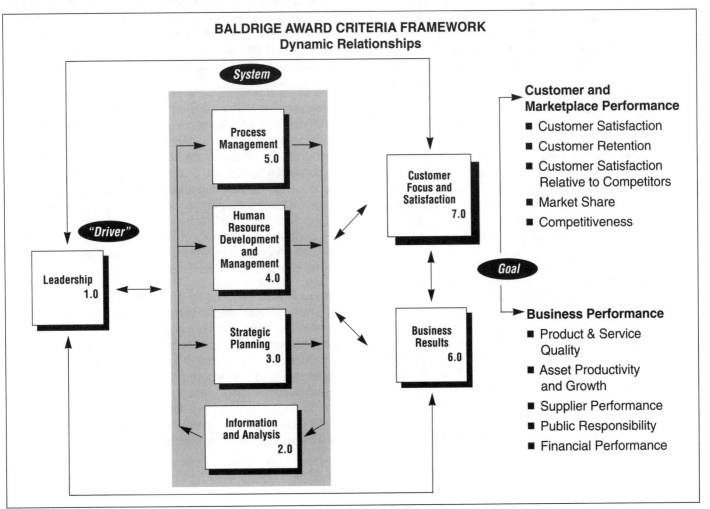

BALDRIGE AWARD CRITERIA FRAMEWORK
Dynamic Relationships

Leadership

Leadership (Category 1.0) is the focal point within the Criteria for the company's leadership system, values, and performance expectations. The performance expectations include those that address the needs of all stakeholders. The Category begins with the key roles of senior executives — those that cannot be delegated to others.

1.1 Senior Executive Leadership

This Item addresses how the company's senior executives set directions and build and maintain a leadership system conducive to high performance, individual development, initiative, and organizational learning. Executive leadership needs to take into account all stakeholders — customers, employees, suppliers, partners, stockholders, the public, and the community.

Area 1.1a calls for information on the major aspects of leadership — creating values and expectations, setting directions, developing and maintaining an effective leadership system, and building company capabilities. Setting directions includes creating future opportunities for the company and its stakeholders.

This Area includes executives' review of company performance, capabilities, and organization. This aspect of leadership is crucial, because of the fast pace of competition. A major aim is to create organizations that are flexible and responsive — changing easily to adapt to new needs and opportunities. Through their roles in strategy development and review of company performance, the senior executives develop leadership and adapt organizations to changing opportunities and requirements.

Area 1.1b calls for information on how senior executives evaluate and improve the effectiveness of the company's leadership system, including their own leadership skills. Such an evaluation is intended to assess the development of leadership throughout the company in order to direct the attention of senior executives to key needs.

1.2 Leadership System and Organization

This Item addresses how the company's leadership system creates an effective organization and management system — focused on overall performance.

Area 1.2a calls for information on how the company's organization, management, and work processes support its customer and performance objectives. This information should include the roles and responsibilities of managers and supervisors. Designs of organizations and management of operations need to eliminate functional and management barriers that could lead to losing sight of customers and cause decision paths to be ineffective

and slow. The Area also calls for information on how the company's values, expectations, and directions are "made real" throughout the company via distributed leadership and effective communications.

Although senior executives' communications are a critical part of overall effective communications, making values, expectations, and directions real demands constant reinforcement and "truth testing", as employees observe whether or not stated values and expectations are actually the basis for the company's key decisions and actions. Communications need to include performance measures and objectives which help provide focus as well as alignment of company units.

Area 1.2b calls for information on how company and work unit performance are reviewed. Reviews are a primary means to communicate and reinforce what is really important, how performance is measured, and how well business objectives are being met. Important considerations in reviews are the content and organization of information to stimulate and make possible concerted action and learning. This means that reviews should include non-financial and financial information. Together, these types of information present a clear picture of status and trends relative to the company's key business drivers, the needs of all stakeholders, progress relative to competitors, and productivity of asset use. These are primary input data for setting improvement priorities.

The value of reviews depends heavily upon creating an integrated information system — one that is complete and is organized for understanding and action. Since a major purpose of reviews is to identify improvements and resource-use priorities, the information for reviews needs to connect financial and operational data. Traditional cost accounting methods usually do not provide an adequate basis for targeting operational improvements that will lead to the most significant financial gains. Alternative accounting approaches such as activity-based costing might offer the best means to understand processes and activities in terms of true financial costs and benefits.

Although labor productivity growth is often a key measure of organizational effectiveness, productivity of use of all resources provides a more complete picture of overall performance. Thus, an integrated information system should include measures of total-factor productivity. Such measures take into account all factors in production: manpower, materials, capital, and assets. Approaches based upon economic indicators also provide useful information as they help determine whether or not performance improvements are contributing to wealth creation.

The many important connections among operational, customer-related, financial, and economic performance are addressed in Item 2.3.

1.3 Public Responsibility and Corporate Citizenship
This Item addresses how the company integrates its values and expectations regarding its public responsibilities and corporate citizenship into its business planning and performance improvement practices.

Area 1.3a calls for information on three basic aspects of public responsibility: (1) making risk factors and legal requirements an integral part of performance improvement; (2) sensitivity in planning facilities, products, services, and operations to issues of societal concern whether or not these issues are currently embodied in law; and (3) emphasizing legal and ethical conduct in the company's values and performance improvement processes.

Fulfilling public responsibilities means not only meeting all local, state, and federal laws and regulatory requirements, but also treating these and related requirements as areas for improvement "beyond mere compliance". This means that the company should maintain constant awareness of potential public impacts related to its products, services, facilities, and operations.

Area 1.3b calls for information on how the company leads as a corporate citizen in its key communities. The issues in this Area relate to the company as a member of different types of communities and as a positive influence upon other organizations. Opportunities for leadership and involvement include assistance by the company to strengthen community services, education, health care, the environment, and practices of trade and business associations. This includes community service by employees, encouraged, supported, and recognized by the company. For example, companies and their employees could help to influence the adoption of higher standards in education by communicating employability requirements to schools and to other education organizations. Companies could also assist schools and students to adopt new learning and communications technologies and systems such as computers and modern communications networks.

Information and Analysis

Information and Analysis (Category 2.0) is the focal point within the Criteria for all key information to drive the improvement of overall performance and company competitiveness. In simplest terms, Category 2.0 is the "brain center" for the alignment of a company's information system with its strategic directions. The Category addresses the information and analysis requirements for performance improvement based upon the improvement of key processes.

However, as information, information technology, and analysis might themselves be primary sources of competitive advantage and productivity growth, the Category also addresses these possibilities.

2.1 Management of Information and Data
This Item addresses the company's selection and management of information and data to support overall business goals with primary emphasis on supporting process management and performance improvement.

Area 2.1a calls for a description of how information and data needed to drive improvement of overall company performance are selected and managed. The Area has three parts. The first part addresses selection and emphasizes key business drivers and business strategy — important areas of performance and competitive advantage. The second part addresses the design of the company's measurement system and how it ensures the alignment of company operations with business priorities. The third part addresses management of data and information, and emphasizes user needs — rapid access and update, and reliability.

Area 2.1b calls for information on how the company evaluates and improves its selection, analysis, and management of information and data. The Area emphasizes alignment with business priorities, support of process management, and feedback from information and data users. The evaluation might take into account factors such as paths of data use, extent and effectiveness of use, gaps, sharing, and organization of information and data. It might also include assessment of the adequacy of the technologies used to meet marketplace or internal requirements.

Overall, Item 2.1 represents a key foundation for a performance-oriented company. This foundation should include non-financial and financial information and data.

Although the main focus of Item 2.1 is on information and data for the effective management of performance, information, data, and information technology often have major strategic significance as well. For example, information technology could be used to build and disseminate unique knowledge about customers and markets and create the ability to "customize" products and services and operate more quickly and more successfully in key markets. Also, information technology and the information and data made available through such technology could be of special advantage in business networks or alliances. Responses to Areas 2.1a and 2.1b should take into account such strategic use of information and data. Accordingly, "users" should then be interpreted as business partners as well as company units.

2.2 Competitive Comparisons and Benchmarking
This Item addresses external drivers of improvement — data and information related to competitive position and to best practices. Such data may have both operational and strategic value.

Area 2.2a calls for information on how competitive comparisons and benchmarking information are selected and used to help drive improvement of overall company performance. The Area addresses four key aspects of effective selection and use of competitive comparisons and benchmarking information and data: (1) determination of needs and priorities; (2) criteria for seeking appropriate information — from within and outside the company's industry and markets; (3) use of information and data to improve understanding of processes and process performance; and (4) use of information and data to promote major improvements in areas most critical to the company's competitive strategy.

Area 2.2b calls for information on how the company evaluates and improves its processes for selecting and using competitive and benchmark information to improve planning and to drive improvement of performance and competitive position.

The major premises underlying this Item are: (1) companies facing tough competition need to "know where they stand" relative to competitors and to best practice performance for similar activities; (2) comparative and benchmarking information often provide impetus for significant ("breakthrough") improvement and alert companies to competitive threats and new practices; and (3) companies need to understand their own processes and the processes of others, before they compare performance levels.

Benchmarking information may also support business analysis and decisions relating to core competencies, alliances, and outsourcing.

2.3 Analysis and Use of Company-Level Data
This Item addresses company-level analysis — the principal basis for guiding a company's process management toward business results. Despite the importance of individual facts and data, they do not usually provide a sound basis for actions or priorities. Action depends upon understanding cause/effect connections among processes and between processes and business results. Process actions may have many resource implications; results may have many cost and revenue implications as well. Given that resources for improvement are limited, and cause/effect connections are often unclear, there is a critical need to provide a sound analytical basis for decisions.

In the Criteria, this role is served by analyses of many types. Item 2.3 is the central analysis point in an integrated data and analysis system. This system is built around financial and non-financial data.

Area 2.3a calls for information on how data and information from all parts of the company are aggregated and analyzed to support reviews, business decisions, and planning. The focus is on three key areas of performance: customers and markets, operational performance, and competitive performance. The analyses in this Area depend upon non-financial and financial data, connected to provide a basis for action.

Area 2.3b calls for analysis linking customer and market data, improvements in product and service quality, and improvements in operational performance to improvement in financial and/or market indicators. The purpose of this linkage is to guide the selection of improvement actions toward significant gains, revenue growth, reduced operating costs, and effective use of all assets. Analysis should utilize indicators of financial and economic performance that permit meaningful comparisons over time and with competitors and other organizations. One such indicator is working capital productivity.

Strategic Planning

Strategic Planning (Category 3.0) addresses strategic and business planning and deployment of plans, with a strong focus on effective translation and deployment of customer and operational performance requirements. The Category stresses that customer-driven quality and operational performance excellence are key strategic business issues that need to be an integral part of company planning. Specifically:

- customer-driven quality is a strategic view of quality. The focus is on the drivers of customer satisfaction, customer retention, and market share — key factors in competitiveness and business success;

- operational performance improvement contributes to short-term and longer-term productivity growth and cost/price competitiveness. The focus on building operational capability — including speed, responsiveness, and flexibility — represents an investment in strengthening competitive fitness.

The Criteria also emphasize that continuous improvement must be an integral part of the daily activity of all work units. The special role of Category 3.0 is to provide an effective focus for daily work, aligning it with the company's strategic directions.

In particular, strategic planning is needed to:

- understand the key customer and operational requirements as input to setting strategic directions. This will help ensure that ongoing process improvements will be aligned with the company's strategic directions.
- optimize the use of resources and ensure bridging between short-term and longer-term requirements that may entail capital expenditures, training, etc.
- ensure that deployment will be effective — that there are mechanisms to transmit requirements and achieve alignment on three basic levels: (1) company/executive level; (2) the key process level; and (3) the work-unit/individual-job level.

The Category requirements are intended to emphasize strategic thinking and acting and do not imply formalized plans, planning systems, departments, or specific planning cycles. Nor does the Strategic Planning Category imply that all improvements could or should be planned in advance. Rather, the Category recognizes that an effective improvement system combines improvements of many types and extents and requires clear strategic guidance, particularly when improvement alternatives compete for scarce resources. In most cases, priority setting depends heavily upon an economic rationale. However, there might also be critical requirements such as public responsibilities which are not driven by financial considerations.

3.1 Strategy Development

This Item addresses how the company develops its view of the future, sets strategic directions, and translates these directions into actionable key business drivers, including customer satisfaction and market leadership requirements. The focus of the Item is on competitive leadership. Such leadership usually depends upon revenue growth as well as on operational effectiveness. Although no specific time horizon is included in the Item, the thrust of the Item is sustained competitive leadership.

Area 3.1a calls for information on the key influences, challenges, and requirements that might affect the company's future opportunities and directions — taking as long a view as possible. The main purpose of the Area is to develop a thorough and realistic context for the development of customer- and market-focused strategy to guide ongoing decision making, resource allocation, and companywide management.

Area 3.1b calls for information on how strategy and plans are translated into actionable key business drivers, that serve as the basis for operationalizing and deploying plan requirements, addressed in Item 3.2. This translation might include a determination of activities the company should perform itself and those for which it might utilize partners or seek partners.

Area 3.1c calls for information on how the company evaluates and improves its strategic planning and plan deployment processes. This might involve input from work units regarding key deployment factors — effective translation and communications of strategy and plans, adequacy of resources, and key new needs. Of particular importance is the evaluation of how well key measures throughout the company are aligned.

Item 3.1 plays a central directional role in the Criteria. It seeks to focus company leadership on developing a competitive strategy and on creating a clear basis (key business drivers) for communicating and operationalizing this strategy. This requires the creation of a view of the future that takes into account not only the markets or segments to compete in but also how to compete. "How to compete" presents many options and requires good understanding of the company's and competitors' strengths and weaknesses. Operationalizing the strategy in the form of key business drivers is intended to highlight the importance of clear and measurable performance objectives. These objectives serve to guide the design and management of key processes. The objectives may also serve to align communications and compensation and recognition systems with performance objectives.

3.2 Strategy Deployment

This Item addresses how the company's key business drivers are deployed. The Item also calls for a projection of the company's performance. The main intent of the Item is to focus on effective operationalizing of the company's directions via key business drivers, incorporating measures that permit the tracking of progress and performance.

Area 3.2a calls for information on the company's key business drivers and how these drivers are translated into an action plan. This includes spelling out key performance requirements, alignment of work unit, supplier, and/or partner plans, how productivity, cycle time, and waste reduction are addressed, and the principal resources committed to the accomplishment of plans. Of central importance in this Area is how alignment and consistency are achieved — for example, via key processes and key measurements. The alignment and consistency are intended also to provide a basis for priorities for ongoing improvement activities — part of the daily work of all work units.

Area 3.2b calls for a two-to-five year projection of key measures and/or indicators of the company's performance. It also calls for comparing projected performance versus competitors and key benchmarks. This projection/comparison is intended to encourage companies to improve their understanding of and tracking of dynamic, competitive performance factors. Through this tracking process, companies should be better prepared to take into account their rates of improvement relative to competitors as a diagnostic management tool.

Human Resource Development and Management

Human Resource Development and Management (Category 4.0) is the focal point within the Criteria for all key human resource practices — those directed toward the creation of a high performance workplace. The Category addresses human resource development and management requirements in an integrated way. This integration is concerned with how well the human resource practices derive from and are aligned with the company's strategic directions. The Category also includes key factors for the assessment of employee well-being and satisfaction so that it can be used as a diagnostic tool.

4.1 Human Resource Planning and Evaluation
This Item is the point of direct linkage between human resource planning and the company's strategic directions. The Item addresses how the company aligns its overall human resource planning and practices with its business directions so that high performance workplace practices become part of a coordinated organizational strategy.

Area 4.1a calls for information on key human resource plans derived from company strategic and business planning. The Area calls for the primary thrusts, broadly defined, of the company's human resource plans — the ones needed to support the company's overall strategic directions. The Area calls for a summary of work design, employee development, recruitment, compensation, and other factors. This is intended to provide a multiyear context and guide for overall human resource planning, management, and evaluation.

Area 4.1b calls for information on how the company evaluates and improves its overall human resource planning and management. This Area is the "brain center" for human resource processes and results, as it relies upon employee-related and company performance data and information, and ties the overall evaluation to company strategy and business results. However, the evaluation also must go beyond broad strategy to the essential

details of human resource effectiveness. The evaluation needs to provide the company's senior executives with information on strengths and weaknesses in human resource practices and development that might bear upon the company's abilities to achieve its short-term and longer-term business objectives. For example, the evaluation should take into account the development and progression of all categories and types of employees, including new employees. The evaluation should also monitor the extent of deployment of education and training throughout the company, and how well education and training support company performance improvement. The overall evaluation needs to rely heavily upon the well-being and satisfaction factors addressed in Item 4.4 and the human resource results presented in Item 6.3.

The linkage between human resource practices and business results is a particularly important and challenging part of the overall evaluation. It is especially important that companies seek to understand the factors in the work climate that contribute to or inhibit high performance. Just as it is important to prioritize customer problems, it is also important to prioritize employee problems based on impacts on revenues and costs. This might require connecting employee satisfaction data and customer satisfaction data.

4.2 High Performance Work Systems
This Item addresses how the company's job design, compensation, and recognition approaches enable and encourage all employees to contribute effectively, operating within high performance work units. The Item emphasizes that achieving high performance requires effective work and job design and meaningful reinforcement.

Area 4.2a calls for information on job design and work organizations. The basic aims of such design and organizations should be to enable employees to exercise more discretion and decision making, leading to greater flexibility and more rapid response to the changing requirements of the marketplace. Effective job design and flexible work organizations are necessary but may not be sufficient to ensure high performance. Job and organization design needs to be backed by information systems, education, and appropriate training to ensure that information flow supports the job and work designs. Also important is effective communication across functions and work units to ensure focus on customer requirements.

Area 4.2b addresses the important alignment of incentives with work systems. The basic thrust of this Area is the consistency between the company's compensation and recognition system and its work structures and processes.

The Area calls for information on employee compensation and recognition — how these reinforce high performance job design, work organizations, and teamwork. To be effective, compensation and recognition might need to be based, wholly or in part, upon demonstrated skills and/or evaluation by peers in teams and networks.

4.3 Employee Education, Training, and Development

This Item addresses how the company develops the work force via education, training, and on-the-job reinforcement of knowledge and skills. Development is intended to meet the needs of a high performance workplace on an ongoing basis. This means that education and training need to be ongoing as well.

Area 4.3a calls for information on how the company's education and training serve as a key vehicle in building company capabilities and employee capabilities. The Area focuses on these two capabilities, treating them as investments the company makes in its long-term future and the long-term future of employees.

Area 4.3b calls for information on how education and training are designed, delivered, reinforced, and evaluated, with special emphasis upon on-the-job application of knowledge and skills. The Area emphasizes the importance of the involvement of employees and line managers in design of training, including clear identification of specific needs. This involves job analysis — understanding the types and levels of the skills required and the timeliness of training. The Area also emphasizes evaluation of education and training. Such evaluation could take into account line managers' evaluation, employee self-evaluation, and peer evaluation of value received through education and training relative to needs identified in design. Evaluation could also address factors such as the effectiveness of education and training delivery, impact on work unit performance, costs of delivery alternatives, and benefit/cost ratios.

4.4 Employee Well-Being and Satisfaction

This Item addresses the work environment, the work motivational climate, and how they are tailored to foster the well-being, satisfaction, and development of all employees.

Area 4.4a calls for information regarding a safe and healthful work environment to determine how the company includes such factors in its planning and improvement activities. Important factors in this area include establishing appropriate measures and recognizing that employee groups might experience very different environments.

Area 4.4b calls for information on the company's approach to enhance employee well-being, satisfaction, and growth potential based upon a holistic view of employees as key stakeholders. The Area emphasizes that the company needs to consider a variety of mechanisms to build well-being and satisfaction. Increasingly, these mechanisms relate to development, progression, employability, and external activities. This might include family or community service activities.

Area 4.4c calls for information on how the company determines employee satisfaction, well-being, and motivation. The Area recognizes that many factors might affect employee motivation. Although satisfaction with pay and promotion potential is important, these factors might not be adequate to assess the overall climate for motivation and high performance. For this reason, the company might need to consider a variety of factors in the work environment to determine the key factors in motivation. Factors inhibiting motivation need to be prioritized and addressed. Further understanding of these factors could be developed through exit interviews with departing employees. The Area also addresses how the information and data on the satisfaction, well-being, and motivation of employees are actually used in improvement activities. Such activities might draw upon human resource results presented in Item 6.3.

Process Management

Process Management (Category 5.0) is the focal point within the Criteria for all key work processes. Built into the Category are the central requirements for efficient and effective process management — effective design, a prevention orientation, evaluation and continuous improvement, linkage to suppliers, and overall high performance.

An increasingly important concept in all aspects of process management and organizational design is flexibility. In simplest terms, flexibility refers to the ability to adapt quickly and effectively to changing requirements. Depending on the nature of the business' strategy and markets, flexibility might mean rapid changeover from one product to another, rapid response to changing demand, or the ability to produce a wide range of products. Flexibility might demand special strategies such as modular designs, sharing of components, and specialized training.

5.1 Design and Introduction of Products and Services

This Item examines how the company designs and introduces products and services. A major focus of the Item is the rapid and effective integration of production and delivery, early in the design phase. This integration is intended to capitalize on windows of opportunity in markets and to minimize downstream problems for customers and/or eliminate the need for design changes that might be costly to the company.

Area 5.1a calls for information on the design of products, services, and their production/delivery processes. Three aspects of this design are examined: (1) the translation of customer requirements into the design requirements for products and services; (2) how the product and service design requirements are translated into efficient and effective production/delivery processes; and (3) how all requirements associated with products, services, and production/delivery processes are addressed early in the design process by all appropriate company units to ensure integration and coordination. Many businesses also need to consider requirements for suppliers and/or business partners at the design stage. Overall, effective design must take into account all stakeholders in the value chain.

It should be noted that although the main focus of Area 5.1a is on the design of products, services, and processes to meet customer requirements, effective design must also consider cycle time and productivity of production and delivery processes. This might entail detailed mapping of manufacturing or service processes and redesigning (reengineering) them to achieve efficiency as well as to meet customer requirements.

Area 5.1b calls for information on how product, service, and production/delivery process designs are reviewed and/or tested in detail prior to full-scale launch. Such review and/or testing is intended to ensure that all parts of the production/delivery system are capable of performing according to design. This stage could be a crucial one — with a positive or negative customer reaction and potentially high cost to the company if pre-launch changes are significant.

Area 5.1c calls for information on how designs and design processes are evaluated and improved to progressively improve quality, productivity, and cycle time. This Area is intended to determine how companies extract lessons learned to build capabilities for future designs. Such evaluation might take into account delays and problems experienced during design, feedback from those involved, and post-launch problems that might have been averted through better design. The evaluation and improvement should strive for a continuous flow of work in the key design and delivery processes.

If many design projects are carried out in parallel, or if the company's products utilize parts, equipment, and facilities used for other products, coordination of resources might be a major concern and might offer means to significantly reduce unit costs and time to market.

5.2 Process Management: Product and Service Production and Delivery
This Item addresses two different but related concerns — how the company maintains and how it improves key production and delivery processes.

Area 5.2a calls for information on the maintenance of process performance to ensure that processes perform according to their design. The information required includes a description of the key processes and their specific requirements, and how performance relative to these requirements is known and maintained. Specific reference is made to a measurement plan. Such a plan requires the identification of critical points in processes for measurement or observation. Implied in this plan is that measurements or observations be made at the earliest points in processes to minimize problems that may result from variations from expected (design) performance. When measurements or observations reveal such variations, a remedy — usually called corrective action — is required to restore the performance of the process to its design performance. Depending on the nature of the process, the correction could involve technical, human, or both factors. Proper correction involves correcting at the source (root cause) of the variation. In some cases, customers may directly witness or take part in the process, and contribute to or be a determinant of process performance. In such cases, variations among customers must be taken into account in evaluating how well the process is performing. This might entail specific or general contingencies depending on customer response. This is especially true of professional and personal services.

Area 5.2b calls for information on how processes are improved to achieve better performance. Better performance means not only better quality from the customers' perspective but also better operational performance — such as productivity — from the company's perspective. Area 5.2b anticipates that companies use a variety of process improvement approaches. Area 5.2b calls for information on how the company uses or considers four key approaches. These are: (1) process analysis and research; (2) benchmarking; (3) use of alternative technology; and (4) information from customers of the processes — within and outside the company. Together, these approaches offer the widest range of possibilities, including complete redesign ("reengineering") of processes.

5.3 Process Management: Support Services
This Item addresses how the company designs, maintains, and improves its support service processes.

Area 5.3a calls for information on the design of key support service processes. Such design needs to be based upon the requirements of the company's customers and of other units ("internal customers") within the company — those within the company who use the output of the process. The requirements of effective design are as outlined in Item 5.1 — coordinated and integrated to ensure efficient and effective performance.

Area 5.3b calls for information on how the company maintains the performance of the key support service processes. This information includes a description of the key processes and their principal requirements and a description of the measurement plan and how it is used. The requirements of Area 5.3b are similar to those described above in Area 5.2a.

Area 5.3c calls for information on how the company evaluates and improves the performance of the key support service processes. The Area calls for information on how the company uses or considers four key approaches. These are: (1) process analysis and research; (2) benchmarking; (3) use of alternative technology; and (4) information from customers of the processes — within and outside the company. Together, these approaches offer the widest range of possibilities, including complete redesign ("reengineering") of processes.

5.4 Management of Supplier Performance
This Item addresses how the company manages performance of external providers of goods and services. Such management might be built around longer-term partnering relationships, particularly with key suppliers.

Area 5.4a calls for basic information on the company's principal requirements for its key suppliers, expected performance and measures used to assess performance, how the company determines whether or not its requirements are being met, and how performance information is fed back to suppliers.

Area 5.4b calls for information on how the company evaluates and improves its supplier management. This includes three main elements: improving supplier abilities to meet requirements; improving its own supplier management processes; and reducing costs associated with the verification of supplier performance.

For many companies, suppliers are an increasingly important part of achieving not only high performance and lower-cost objectives, but also strategic objectives. For example, key suppliers might provide unique design, integration, and marketing capabilities. Exploiting these advantages requires joint planning and partner relationships. Such planning and relationship building might entail the use of longer-term planning horizons and customer-supplier teams. Successful exploitation might also entail special information linkages and rapid data exchanges.

Business Results

Business Results (Category 6.0) provides a results focus for all processes and process improvement activities.

Through this focus, the Criteria's dual purpose — superior value of offerings as viewed by customers and the marketplace, and superior company performance reflected in operational and financial indicators — is maintained. Category 6.0 thus provides "real-time" information (measures of progress) for evaluation and improvement of processes, aligned with overall business strategy. Analysis of business results data and information is called for in Item 2.3. Review of business results is addressed in Item 1.2.

6.1 Product and Service Quality Results
This Item addresses current levels and trends in product and service quality using key measures and/or indicators of such quality. The measures and/or indicators selected should relate to requirements that matter to the customer and to the marketplace. These features are derived from customer-related Items ("listening posts") which make up Category 7.0. If the features have been properly selected, improvements in them should show a clear positive correlation with customer and marketplace improvement indicators — captured in Item 7.4. The correlation between quality and customer indicators is a critical management tool — a device for defining and focusing on key quality requirements. In addition, the correlation might reveal emerging or changing market segments, changing importance of requirements, or even potential obsolescence of products and/or services.

Area 6.1a calls for data on current levels and trends in product and service quality. The levels and trends might reflect changes in existing products and services or include new offerings. The Area also calls for comparative information so that the results reported can be evaluated against competitors or other relevant external measures of performance.

6.2 Company Operational and Financial Results
This Item addresses the operational and financial performance of the company. Paralleling Item 6.1, that focuses on requirements that matter to the customer, Item 6.2 focuses on factors that best reflect company operational and financial performance. Such factors are of two types: (1) generic — common to all companies; and (2) business-specific. Generic factors include financial and economic indicators, cycle time, and productivity, as reflected in use of labor, materials, energy, capital, and assets. Productivity, cycle time, or other operational indicators should reflect **aggregate company performance**. Business- or company-specific effectiveness indicators vary greatly. Examples include rates of invention, environmental quality, export levels, new markets, percent of sales from recently introduced products or services, and shifts toward new segments.

Area 6.2a calls for data on current levels and trends in company operational and financial performance. The Area also calls for comparative information so that results reported can be meaningfully evaluated against competitors or other relevant external measures of performance.

6.3 Human Resource Results
This Item addresses the company's human resource results — those relating to employee development, effectiveness, well-being, and satisfaction.

Results reported could include generic and business- or company-specific factors. Generic factors include safety, absenteeism, turnover, and satisfaction. Business- or company-specific factors include those commonly used in the industry or created by the company for purposes of tracking progress. Results reported might include input data, such as extent of training, but the main emphasis should be placed on measures of effectiveness.

Area 6.3a calls for data on current levels and trends in key human resource areas — development, well-being, satisfaction, self-directed responsibility, and effectiveness. The Area also calls for comparative information so that results can be meaningfully evaluated against competitors or other relevant external measures of performance.

6.4 Supplier Performance Results
This Item addresses current levels and trends in key measures and/or indicators of supplier performance. Suppliers are external providers of materials and services, "upstream" and/or "downstream" from the company. The focus should be on the most critical requirements from the point of view of the company — the buyer of the products and services. Data reported should reflect results by whatever means they occur — via improvements by suppliers within the supply base, through selection of better performing suppliers, or both.

Area 6.4a calls for data on current levels and trends in supplier performance. Measures and indicators of performance should relate to all key requirements — quality, delivery, and price. The Area also calls for comparative information so that results reported can be meaningfully evaluated against competitors or other relevant external measures of performance.

Customer Focus and Satisfaction
Customer Focus and Satisfaction (Category 7.0) is the focal point within the Criteria for understanding in detail the voices of customers and of the marketplace. The Category emphasizes relationship management as a key requirement and calls for a variety of listening and learning strategies as well. However, much of the information needed for understanding the voices of customers and of the marketplace must come from measuring results and

tracking trends. Such results and trends provide hard information not only on customers' views but also on their marketplace behaviors. The results and trends offer a means to determine whether or not priorities for improvement activities are appropriately directed.

7.1 Customer and Market Knowledge
This Item addresses how the company determines current and emerging customer requirements and expectations. The thrust of the Item is that in a rapidly changing competitive environment many factors may affect customer preference and customer loyalty, making it necessary to listen and learn on a continuous basis.

Area 7.1a calls for information on the company's process for determining current and near-term requirements and expectations of customers. The information sought includes the completeness of the customer pool, including recognition of segments and customers of competitors. Other information sought relates to sensitivity to specific product and service requirements and their relative importance to customer groups. The Area is concerned with overall validity of determination methods. The validity should be supported by use of other data and information such as complaints and gains and losses of customers.

Area 7.1b calls for information on how the company addresses future requirements and expectations of customers — its key listening and learning strategies. Such strategies depend a great deal upon the nature of the company's products and services, the competitive environment, and relationships with customers. The listening and learning strategy selected should provide timely and useful information for decision making. The strategy should take into account the company's competitive strategy. For example, if the company customizes its products and services, the listening and learning strategy needs to be backed by a capable information system — one that rapidly accumulates information about customers and makes this information available where needed throughout the company or the overall value chain.

Research-intensive, product-driven companies might rely upon field trials of prototypes with special customers as a key learning strategy.

Area 7.1c calls for information on how the company evaluates and improves its processes for determining customer requirements and expectations. Such evaluation/improvement could entail a variety of approaches — formal and informal — that seek to stay in close touch with customers and with issues that bear upon customer loyalty and customer preference. The purpose of the evaluation called for in Area 7.1c is to find reliable and cost-effective means to understand customer requirements and expectations on a continuous basis.

7.2 Customer Relationship Management

Item 7.2 addresses how the company provides effective management of its responses and follow-ups with customers. Relationship management provides a potentially important means for companies to gain understanding about, and to manage, customer expectations. Also, frontline employees may provide vital information relating to building partnerships and other longer-term relationships with customers.

Area 7.2a calls for information on how the company provides easy access for customers specifically for purposes of seeking information or assistance and/or to comment and complain. This Area also calls for information on service standards and their use.

Area 7.2b focuses on the complaint management process. The principal issue addressed is prompt and effective resolution of complaints, including recovery of customer confidence. However, the Area also addresses how the company learns from complaints and ensures that production/delivery process employees receive information needed to eliminate the causes of complaints. Elimination of the causes of complaints involves aggregation of complaint information from all sources for evaluation and use throughout the company.

Area 7.2c calls for information on how the company follows up with customers regarding products, services, and recent transactions to determine satisfaction, to resolve problems, to build relationships, and to gather information for improvement or for new products and services.

Area 7.2d calls for information on how the company evaluates and improves its overall customer relationship management. Such improvements may be of several types. Examples include improving service standards, such as complaint resolution time and resolution effectiveness, and improving the use of customer feedback to improve production/delivery processes, training, and hiring. The Area also addresses how knowledge about customers is accumulated, an important aspect of relationship building.

7.3 Customer Satisfaction Determination

This Item addresses how the company determines customer satisfaction and satisfaction relative to competitors. Satisfaction relative to competitors and the factors that lead to preference are of critical importance to managing in a competitive environment.

Area 7.3a calls for information on how the company gathers information on customer satisfaction, including any important differences in approaches for different customer groups or segments. The Area highlights the importance of the measurement scale to focus on those factors that best reflect customers' market behaviors — repurchase, new business, and positive referral.

Area 7.3b calls for information on how satisfaction relative to competitors is determined. Such information might be derived from company-based comparative studies or studies made by independent organizations. The purpose of this comparison is to develop information that can be used for improving performance relative to competitors and to better understand the factors that drive markets.

Area 7.3c calls for information on how the company evaluates and improves its processes and measurement scales for determining customer satisfaction and satisfaction relative to competitors. This evaluation/improvement process is expected to draw upon other indicators such as gains and losses of customers and customer dissatisfaction indicators such as complaints. The evaluation should also consider how well customer satisfaction information and data are used throughout the company. Such use is likely to be enhanced if data are presented in an actionable form. To be actionable, survey responses should meet two conditions: (1) responses are tied directly to key business processes, so that what needs to be improved is clear; and (2) responses are translated into cost/revenue implications to support the setting of improvement priorities.

7.4 Customer Satisfaction Results

This Item addresses the principal customer-related results — customer satisfaction and customer satisfaction relative to competitors. The Item calls for the use of all relevant data and information to establish the company's performance. Relevant data and information include: customer satisfaction and dissatisfaction; gains and losses of customers and customer accounts; gains and losses in market share; and competitive awards, ratings, and recognition from independent organizations, including customers.

The reason for including measures of both satisfaction and dissatisfaction is that they usually provide different information. That is, the factors in high levels of satisfaction may not be the same factors as those that relate to high levels of dissatisfaction. In addition, the effect of individual instances of dissatisfaction on overall satisfaction could vary widely depending upon the effectiveness of the company's resolution ("recovery") of a problem.

Area 7.4a calls for information on current levels and trends in key measures and/or indicators of customer satisfaction and dissatisfaction.

Area 7.4b calls for information on current levels and trends in key measures and/or indicators of customer satisfaction relative to competitors. The presentation of results might include information on gains and losses of customers and customer accounts relative to competitors. It might also include market share information.

KEY CHARACTERISTICS OF THE AWARD CRITERIA

1. The Criteria are directed toward business results.
The Criteria focus principally on key areas of business performance, given below.

> Business results are a composite of:
> (1) customer satisfaction/retention;
> (2) market share, new market development;
> (3) product and service quality;
> (4) financial indicators, productivity, operational effectiveness, and responsiveness;
> (5) human resource performance/development;
> (6) supplier performance/development; and
> (7) public responsibility/corporate citizenship.

Improvements in these results areas contribute to overall company performance, including financial performance. The results areas also recognize the importance of suppliers and of community and national well-being.

The use of a composite of indicators helps to ensure that strategies are balanced — that they do not trade off among important stakeholders or objectives. The composite of indicators also helps to ensure that company strategies bridge short-term and long-term goals.

2. The Criteria are nonprescriptive.
The Criteria are a set of interrelated, results-oriented requirements. However, the Criteria imply wide latitude in how requirements are met. Accordingly, the Criteria do not prescribe:

- specific tools, techniques, technologies, systems, measures, or starting points;
- that companies should or should not have departments for quality or planning; or
- how the company itself should be organized.

The Criteria do emphasize that these and other factors be regularly evaluated as part of the company's performance reviews. The factors listed are important and are very likely to change as needs and strategies evolve.

The Criteria are nonprescriptive because:

(1) The focus is on results, not on procedures, tools, or organizations. Companies are encouraged to develop and *demonstrate* creative, adaptive, and flexible approaches for meeting basic requirements. Nonprescriptive requirements are intended to foster incremental and major ("breakthrough") improvement.

(2) Selection of tools, techniques, systems, and organizations usually depends upon many factors such as business size, business type, the company's stage of development, and employee capabilities.

(3) Focus on common requirements within a company, rather than on specific procedures, fosters better understanding, communication, and sharing, while supporting creativity in approaches.

3. The Criteria are comprehensive.
The Criteria address all internal and external requirements of the company, including those related to the needs and expectations of all stakeholders. Accordingly, all company work unit processes are tied to these requirements. New strategies may be readily adapted within the same set of Criteria requirements.

4. The Criteria include interrelated (process→results) improvement/learning cycles.
There is dynamic linkage among the Criteria requirements. Action-oriented learning takes place via feedback among the process and results elements.

The learning cycles have four, clearly defined stages:

(1) planning, including design of processes, selection of measures, and deployment of requirements;

(2) execution of plans;

(3) assessment of progress, taking into account internal and external results indicators; and

(4) revision of plans based upon assessment findings.

5. The Criteria emphasize alignment.
The Criteria call for improvement/learning cycles in all parts of the company. To ensure that cycles carried out in different parts of the company support one another, overall aims need to be consistent or *aligned.* Alignment in the Criteria is achieved via connecting and reinforcing measures, derived from overall company performance requirements. These measures tie directly to customer value and to overall performance. The use of measures thus channels different activities in consistent directions. Their use often avoids the need for detailed procedures or centralization of decision making or process management. Measures thus serve both as a communications tool and a basis for deploying consistent overall performance requirements. Such alignment ensures consistency of purpose while at the same time supporting speed, innovation, and decentralized decision making.

6. The Criteria are part of a diagnostic system.
The Criteria and the Scoring Guidelines make up a two-part diagnostic (assessment) system. The Criteria are a set of 24 results-oriented requirements. The Scoring Guidelines spell out the assessment dimensions — Approach, Deployment, and Results — and the key factors used to assess relative to each dimension. An assessment thus provides a profile of strengths and areas for improvement relative to the 24 basic requirements. In this way, the assessment directs attention to actions that contribute to the results composite described above.

CHANGES FROM THE 1995 AWARD CRITERIA

The Criteria continue to evolve toward comprehensive coverage of performance, addressing the needs and expectations of all stakeholders — customers, employees, stockholders, suppliers, and the public. The Criteria for 1996 further strengthen and integrate the high performance and competitiveness improvement themes emphasized in 1995. The most significant changes made in the Criteria and in the Criteria booklet are summarized as follows:

- Although the number of Items remains at 24, one Item has been added to the Business Results Category, and two Items from the Customer Focus and Satisfaction Category (Items 7.4 and 7.5 in 1995) have been combined.

- The number of Areas to Address (Areas) has been reduced from 54 to 52.

- A Message to Executives has been added to provide a broad perspective on the meaning of performance in the Award Criteria and on the larger benefits from participating in the Award process.

- A Glossary of Key Terms has been added to better define and to help tie together the major performance themes in the Criteria.

- A separate section, Preparing the Business Overview, has been added to highlight the particular importance of this Overview to writing, reviewing, and evaluating an application. Applicants are encouraged to prepare the Business Overview *first*. This recommendation is made for two reasons: (1) to help ensure that responses to the Criteria Items focus on what is relevant and important to the business; and (2) to bring about better consistency among responses to different Items.

- The Award Criteria Response Guidelines have been revised. The purpose of this revision is to help applicants and other users of the Criteria to prepare responses that make possible better feedback. Particular emphasis is placed on helping applicants provide clearer and more complete information on deployment.

- The Criteria Framework diagram has been revised to better reflect the results goals and the meaning of performance.

- The section on Item Descriptions has been revised and updated.

Applicants and other users of the Award Criteria are cautioned to note that some changes in wording have been made in many Items and Item Notes.

Changes, by Category, are:

Leadership
- Item 1.2 now has two Areas compared with three in 1995. Areas 1.2a and 1.2b from 1995 were combined, thus better integrating communications with other related organizational requirements. In addition, the company performance review Area (1.2b in 1996 and 1.2c in 1995) is now much more explicit in its requirements. The Area now calls for nonfinancial and financial data related to the needs of all key stakeholders. It also calls for information on the tracking of progress relative to plans, competitive performance, and productivity in the use of assets.

Information and Analysis
- Item 2.1 (Area 2.1a) now includes a requirement to provide information on the design of the company's performance measurement system. This change is intended to enhance the diagnostic value of the Item and strengthen the feedback to applicants.

Strategic Planning
- Major planning concepts, most notably, "key business drivers," have been included in a Glossary of Key Terms.

Human Resource Development and Management
- The meaning of "high performance work," the focus of Item 4.2, has been included in the Glossary of Key Terms.
- An Item has been created in Category 6.0 (Item 6.3) for reporting all human resource results.

Process Management
- The meaning of "process" has been included in the Glossary of Key Terms.

Business Results
- A new Item, Human Resource Results (Item 6.3), has been created. This Item is intended to provide a better focus on and a more comprehensive treatment of the human resource results required by the Human Resource Development and Management Category and previously included in the Company Operational and Financial Results (Item 6.2 in 1995).

Customer Focus and Satisfaction
- Two Items from 1995 (Customer Satisfaction Results and Customer Satisfaction Comparison) have been combined. The new Item (Customer Satisfaction Results) integrates the requirements included in the two 1995 Items.

ELIGIBILITY CATEGORIES AND RESTRICTIONS

> Companies considering applying for the Award in 1996 will also need the booklet entitled *1996 Business Application Forms and Instructions,* which provides greater detail on eligibility requirements and restrictions. Ordering instructions are given on page 47.

Basic Eligibility

Public Law 100-107 establishes the three eligibility categories of the Award: Manufacturing, Service, and Small Business. Any for-profit business located in the United States or its territories may apply for the Award. Eligibility for the Award is intended to be as open as possible to all U.S. companies. Minor eligibility restrictions and conditions ensure fairness and consistency in definition. For example, publicly or privately owned, domestic or foreign-owned, joint ventures, incorporated firms, sole proprietorships, partnerships, and holding companies may apply. Not eligible are: local, state, and national government agencies; not-for-profit organizations; trade associations; and professional societies.

Award Eligibility Categories

Manufacturing
Companies or subunits of larger entities that produce and sell manufactured products or manufacturing processes, and producers of agricultural, mining, or construction products.

Service
Companies or subunits that sell services.

Small Business
Complete businesses with not more than 500 full-time employees. Business activities may include manufacturing and/or service. A small business must be able to document that it functions independently of any other businesses which are equity owners. If there are equity owners with some management control, at least 50% of the small business' customer base must be other than the equity owners.

Subunits

For purposes of the Award, a subunit means a subsidiary, business unit, division, or like organization. In the Manufacturing and Service categories, subunits of a company might be eligible, but small businesses must apply as a whole. The following application conditions apply for subunits:

- The unit must be in existence for at least one year;

- The unit must have clear definition of organization as reflected in corporate literature, i.e., the unit must function as a business entity;

- The unit must have more than 500 full-time employees, OR
  The unit must have 25% of all company employees; and

- The entire unit must be included in the application.

Restrictions on Eligibility

Four restrictions apply:

1. More than 50% of the applicant unit's employees must be located in the U.S. or its territories, OR

   more than 50% of the applicant unit's physical assets must be located in the U.S. or its territories;

2. At least 50% of a subunit's customer base must be free of direct financial and line organization control by the parent company;

3. Individual units or partial aggregations of units of "chain" organizations (a chain organization is an organization where each unit [e.g., subsidiary or franchise] performs a similar function or manufactures a similar product) are not eligible; and

4. Company units performing any of the business support functions of the company are not eligible.

Multiple-Application Restrictions

1. A subunit and its parent company may not both apply for Awards in the same year; and

2. Only one subunit of a company may apply for an Award in the same year in the same Award category.

Future Eligibility Restrictions

1. If a company receives an Award, the company and all its subunits are ineligible for a period of five years.

2. If a subunit receives an Award, it is ineligible to apply for a period of five years.

3. If a subunit consisting of more than one-half of the total sales of a company receives an Award, neither that company nor any of its other subunits is eligible to apply for a period of five years.

Eligibility Determination

In order to ensure that Award recipients meet all reasonable requirements and expectations in representing the Award throughout the U.S., potential applicants must have their eligibility approved prior to applying for the Award. Potential applicants for the 1996 Award are encouraged to submit their Eligibility Determination Forms as early as possible, but not later than March 1, 1996. This form is contained in the *1996 Business Application Forms and Instructions* booklet.

HOW TO ORDER COPIES OF 1996 AWARD MATERIALS

> **Note:** The *1996 Award Criteria* and the *1996 Business Application Forms and Instructions* are two separate booklets.

Individual Orders

Individual copies of either booklet can be obtained free of charge from:

> Malcolm Baldrige National Quality Award
> National Institute of Standards and Technology
> Route 270 and Quince Orchard Road
> Administration Building, Room A537
> Gaithersburg, MD 20899-0001
> Telephone: 301-975-2036
> Telefax: 301-948-3716

Bulk Orders

Multiple copies of the *1996 Award Criteria* may be ordered in packets of 10 for $29.95 plus shipping and handling from ASQC. Order Item number: T1022.

How to Order

ASQC offers three convenient ways to order:

- For fastest service, call toll free 800-248-1946 USA and Canada (in Mexico, please dial toll free 95-800-248-1946). Have item numbers, your credit card or purchase order number, and (if applicable) ASQC member number ready.

- Or fax your completed order form to ASQC at 414-272-1734.

- Or mail your order to: ASQC Customer Service Department, P.O. Box 3066, Milwaukee, WI 53201-3066.

Payment

Your payment options include: Check, money order, purchase order, VISA, MasterCard, or American Express. Payment must be made in U.S. currency; checks and money orders must be drawn on a U.S. financial institution. All foreign orders must be prepaid. Please make checks payable to ASQC.

Shipping Fees

The following shipping and processing schedule applies to all orders:

Order Amount	U.S. Charges	Canadian Charges
0 – $34.99	$ 4.00	$ 9.00
$35.00 – 99.99	6.25	11.25
Over $100.00	12.50*	17.50

- Orders shipped within the continental U.S. and Canada where UPS service is available will be shipped UPS.

- Please allow one to two weeks for delivery.

- There is a charge of 25% of the total order amount for shipments outside the U.S./Canada. Please allow six to eight weeks for delivery.

- Your credit card will not be charged until your items are shipped. Shipping and processing is charged one time, up front, for the entire order.

* If actual shipping charges exceed $12.50, ASQC will invoice the customer for additional expense.

FEES FOR THE 1996 AWARD CYCLE

Eligibility Determination Fees

The eligibility determination fee is $100 for all potential applicants. This fee is nonrefundable.

Application Fees

- Manufacturing Company Category—$4500
- Service Company Category—$4500
- Small Business Category—$1500
- Supplemental Sections—$1500

These fees cover all expenses associated with distribution and review of applications and development of feedback reports. Detailed information is given in the *1996 Business Application Forms and Instructions* booklet.

Site Visit Review Fees

Site visit review fees will be set when the visits are scheduled. Fees depend upon the number of Examiners assigned and the duration of the visit. Site visit review fees for applicants in the Small Business category will be charged at one-half of the rate charged for companies in the Manufacturing and Service categories.

Site visit fees cover all expenses and travel costs associated with site visit participation and development of site visit reports. These fees are paid only by those applicants reaching the site visit stage.

Eligibility Determination Forms due — March 1, 1996
Award Applications due — April 1, 1996

HOW TO ORDER AWARD EDUCATIONAL MATERIALS

Each year, the Award Program develops materials for use in training members of the Board of Examiners, and for sharing information on the successful quality strategies of the Award winners. The listed materials and information may be obtained from ASQC. To order a 1995 Case Study Packet (Colony Fasteners, Inc., Midstate University, or Mountainview Health System), bulk orders of the 1996 Award Criteria, or the Award Winners Videos, contact:

> ASQC
> Customer Service Department
> P.O. Box 3066
> Milwaukee, WI 53201-3066
> Telephone (800) 248-1946
> Telefax (414) 272-1734

Case Studies

The case studies are used to prepare Examiners for the interpretation of the Award Criteria and the Scoring System. The case studies, when used with the Award Criteria, illustrate the Award application and review process. The case study packet is illustrative of an application for the Baldrige Award and is useful in understanding the benefits of the Baldrige process, as well as for self-assessment, planning, training, and other uses.

1995 Case Study Packet: Colony Fasteners, Inc.

Item Number T996: $49.95 plus shipping and handling

1995 Education Pilot Program Case Study Packet: Midstate University

Item Number T504: $6.11 plus shipping and handling

1995 Health Care Pilot Program Case Study Packet: Mountainview Health System

Item Number T506: $6.11 plus shipping and handling

Award Winners Videos

The Award winners videos are a valuable resource for gaining a better understanding of excellence in quality management and quality achievement. The videos provide background information on the Award Program, highlights from the annual Award ceremony, and interviews with representatives from the winning companies.

1995 – *Available, Feb. 1996*		$20.00
(Item Number T1030)		
1994 – Item Number TA922:		20.00
1993 – Item Number TA515:		20.00
1992 – Item Number TA512:		20.00
1991 – Item Number TA996:		15.00
1990 – Item Number T992:		15.00
1989 – Item Number T502:		10.00
1988 – Item Number T993:		10.00

QUEST FOR EXCELLENCE VIII CONFERENCE

The Annual Quest for Excellence Conference provides a unique opportunity to hear firsthand the Award-winning strategies of the past year's winners. Presentations are made by the CEOs and other key individuals who are transforming their organizations. The annual Quest for Excellence Conference is the principal forum for Award winners to present their overall strategies in detail.

The two and one-half day Quest for Excellence VIII Conference will provide ample opportunities to explore the Award Criteria in depth and to network with executive-level people from around the country.

The Conference dates are February 5-7, 1996. The Conference will be held at the Washington Hilton and Towers, in Washington, D.C. For further information, contact the Malcolm Baldrige National Quality Award, Administration Building, Room A537, Gaithersburg, MD 20899; telephone 301-975-2036 or FAX 301-963-0339.

THE MALCOLM BALDRIGE NATIONAL QUALITY IMPROVEMENT ACT OF 1987 – PUBLIC LAW 100-107

The Malcolm Baldrige National Quality Award was created by Public Law 100-107, signed into law on August 20, 1987. The Award Program, responsive to the purposes of Public Law 100-107, led to the creation of a new public-private partnership. Principal support for the program comes from the Foundation for the Malcolm Baldrige National Quality Award, established in 1988.

The Award is named for Malcolm Baldrige, who served as Secretary of Commerce from 1981 until his tragic death in a rodeo accident in 1987. His managerial excellence contributed to long-term improvement in efficiency and effectiveness of government.

The Findings and Purposes Section of Public Law 100-107 states that:

" 1. the leadership of the United States in product and process quality has been challenged strongly (and sometimes successfully) by foreign competition, and our Nation's productivity growth has improved less than our competitors' over the last two decades.

2. American business and industry are beginning to understand that poor quality costs companies as much as 20 percent of sales revenues nationally and that improved quality of goods and services goes hand in hand with improved productivity, lower costs, and increased profitability.

3. strategic planning for quality and quality improvement programs, through a commitment to excellence in manufacturing and services, are becoming more and more essential to the well-being of our Nation's economy and our ability to compete effectively in the global marketplace.

4. improved management understanding of the factory floor, worker involvement in quality, and greater emphasis on statistical process control can lead to dramatic improvements in the cost and quality of manufactured products.

5. the concept of quality improvement is directly applicable to small companies as well as large, to service industries as well as manufacturing, and to the public sector as well as private enterprise.

6. in order to be successful, quality improvement programs must be management-led and customer-oriented, and this may require fundamental changes in the way companies and agencies do business.

7. several major industrial nations have successfully coupled rigorous private-sector quality audits with national awards giving special recognition to those enterprises the audits identify as the very best; and

8. a national quality award program of this kind in the United States would help improve quality and productivity by:
    A. helping to stimulate American companies to improve quality and productivity for the pride of recognition while obtaining a competitive edge through increased profits;
    B. recognizing the achievements of those companies that improve the quality of their goods and services and providing an example to others;
    C. establishing guidelines and criteria that can be used by business, industrial, governmental, and other organizations in evaluating their own quality improvement efforts; and
    D. providing specific guidance for other American organizations that wish to learn how to manage for high quality by making available detailed information on how winning organizations were able to change their cultures and achieve eminence. "

The Malcolm Baldrige National Quality Award
1996 Education Pilot Program
1996 Health Care Pilot Program

Managed by:

United States Department of Commerce
Technology Administration
National Institute of Standards and Technology
Route 270 and Quince Orchard Road
Administration Building, Room A537
Gaithersburg, MD 20899-0001

Administered by:

ASQC
P.O. Box 3005
Milwaukee, WI 53201-3005

611 East Wisconsin Avenue
Milwaukee, WI 53202

Malcolm Baldrige
National
Quality
Award

1996

Business

Application Forms & Instructions

The Award, composed of two solid crystal prismatic forms, stands 14 inches tall. The crystal is held in a base of black, anodized aluminum with the Award winner's name engraved on the base. A solid bronze, 22-karat, gold-plated, die-struck medallion is captured in the front section of the crystal. The medal bears the inscriptions: "Malcolm Baldrige National Quality Award" and "The Quest for Excellence" on one side and the Presidential Seal on the other.

Awards traditionally are presented by the President of the United States at a special ceremony in Washington, D.C.

Awards are made annually to recognize U.S. companies that excel in quality management and quality achievement. Awards may be given in each of three eligibility categories:

- Manufacturing companies
- Service companies
- Small businesses

Award recipients may publicize and advertise receipt of the Award. Award recipients are expected to share information about their successful quality strategies with other U.S. organizations.

Crystal by Steuben
Medal by The Protocol Group

CONTENTS

**If you plan to apply for the Award in 1996, you will also need the booklet entitled
1996 Award Criteria. Ordering instructions are given on page 28.**

Eligibility Determination Package due — March 1, 1996
Award Application Package due — April 1, 1996

INFORMATION ON THE BALDRIGE AWARD AND THE AWARD PROCESS

What is the purpose of this booklet?

The purpose of this booklet is to provide Award Program information sufficient for interested businesses to decide whether to apply for the Award **and** to provide eligibility and application instructions and forms.

What is the Malcolm Baldrige National Quality Award?

The Malcolm Baldrige National Quality Award (MBNQA), created by public law in 1987, is the highest level of national recognition for quality performance and practices that a U.S. company can receive.

The major focus of the Award is on results and customer satisfaction. It is **not** given for specific products or services. To be an Award recipient, a company must have a system which ensures continuous improvement in the delivery of products and/or services and provides a way of satisfying and responding to customers.

Awards may be given annually in each of three eligibility categories: manufacturing companies, service companies, and small businesses.

Why was the Award established?

The Award was established to promote the awareness of quality as an increasingly important element in competitiveness. Not only does it recognize excellent businesses, the Award also exists to increase the understanding of the requirements for performance excellence. To accomplish this, the Award promotes a sharing of information on successful performance strategies and the benefits derived from implementation of these strategies.

Who may participate?

Privately or publicly owned for-profit businesses located in the United States are eligible to apply for the Award. Subunits of companies may apply if they are discrete, largely self-sufficient entities, and if they meet certain size requirements.

Who is involved with the Award process?

The process is a public-private partnership involving:

Private or publicly owned businesses: These businesses are the applicants for the Award. Additionally, businesses are integral to the development of the Award Criteria.

National Institute of Standards and Technology (NIST): Responsibility for the Award is assigned to the Department of Commerce. NIST, an agency within the Department's Technology Administration, manages the Award Program.

American Society for Quality Control (ASQC): ASQC assists in administering the Award Program under contract to NIST.

Board of Examiners: The Board of Examiners evaluates Award applications and prepares feedback reports for the applicants. Examiners are volunteers primarily from the private sector, who are selected on the basis of their business and quality expertise; expertise in assessing to Baldrige and Baldrige-like Criteria; length, breadth, and type of experience; communication skills; education and training; and achievement and recognition.

Judges: Judges select Award applicants that will undergo site visits and recommend Award recipients. Judges are appointed by the Secretary of Commerce from all sectors of the U.S. economy.

Board of Overseers: The Board is appointed by the Secretary of Commerce and is the advisory organization on the Award to the Department of Commerce. Board members are distinguished leaders from all sectors of the U.S. economy.

The Foundation for the Malcolm Baldrige National Quality Award: The Foundation was created to raise funds to permanently endow the Award Program and to manage that endowment.

What are the Award Criteria?

The Award Criteria provide organizations with an integrated, results-oriented framework for implementing and assessing processes for managing all operations. These Criteria are also the basis for making Awards and providing feedback to applicants. The Criteria consist of seven Categories:

Leadership: The company's leadership system, values, expectations, and public responsibilities.

Information and Analysis: The effectiveness of information collection and analysis to support customer-driven performance excellence and marketplace success.

Strategic Planning: The effectiveness of strategic and business planning and deployment of plans, with a strong focus on customer and operational performance requirements.

Human Resource Development and Management: The success of efforts to realize the full potential of the work force to create a high performance organization.

Process Management: The effectiveness of systems and processes for assuring the quality of products and services.

Business Results: The company's performance and improvement in key business areas — product and service quality, productivity and operational effectiveness, supply quality, and financial performance indicators linked to these areas.

Customer Focus and Satisfaction: The effectiveness of systems to determine customer requirements and satisfaction and the demonstrated success in meeting customers' expectations.

What is the basis for the Criteria?

Criteria are developed from the state-of-the-art learnings of private and public sector organizations that are working to achieve organizational quality and performance excellence. The Criteria represent validated, leading-edge practices for achieving business excellence.

What does a company receive for applying?

All applicants receive a feedback report, outlining their strengths and areas for improvement based on the Baldrige Award Criteria. Feedback reports are often used by companies as part of their strategic planning processes to focus on their customers and to improve productivity, as well as to help guide their organizational improvement programs.

How are Award recipients selected?

Award applications are reviewed by a team from the Board of Examiners. High-scoring applicants receive site visits. Award recipients are recommended from among the site-visited companies by a Panel of Judges. The Secretary of Commerce makes the final selection of Award recipients.

What does a company receive if it is an Award recipient?

Award recipients receive a crystal trophy bearing a gold-plated, die-struck medallion with the inscriptions "Malcolm Baldrige National Quality Award" and "The Quest for Excellence." Awards are traditionally presented by the President of the United States at a special ceremony in Washington D.C.

Award recipients may publicize and advertise receipt of the Award.

What is expected of Award recipients?

Award recipients are required to share information on their successful performance and quality strategies with other U.S. organizations. However, recipients are not required to share proprietary information, even if such information was part of their Award application. The principal mechanism for sharing information is the annual Quest for Excellence Conference, highlighted on the inside back cover.

How do companies apply?

Applying for the Award is a two-step process. The first step is eligibility determination which involves establishing that the company meets eligibility requirements. Instructions and forms for establishing eligibility are located on pages 7-16 of this booklet.

Once eligibility has been determined, the second step consists of preparing and completing an application form and an application report. The application report must summarize the company's practices and results in response to the requirements in the Items of the Award Criteria. The instructions and forms needed to apply are contained in this booklet, pages 19-27.

What is the cost to apply?

There is a nonrefundable $100 fee for all potential applicants seeking formal eligibility determination.

The basic application fees for 1996 are: $4500 for Manufacturing and Service categories and $1500 for Small Business. Site visit fees are also paid by applicants reaching the site visit stage.

How do I acquire the 1996 Award Criteria and related educational materials?

A copy of the 1996 Award Criteria may be obtained by contacting:

Malcolm Baldrige National Quality Award
National Institute of Standards and Technology
Route 270 and Quince Orchard Road
Administration Building, Room A537
Gaithersburg, MD 20899-0001
Telephone: (301) 975-2036
Telefax: (301) 948-3716
E-mail: oqp@nist.gov

Educational materials, including a case study featuring a sample Award application and feedback report, may be ordered from ASQC. Page 28 of this booklet contains information on ordering Award educational materials.

1996 APPLICATION STEPS AND KEY DATES

Step 1: Eligibility Determination

Deliverable: Eligibility Determination Package postmarked to ASQC by **March 1, 1996**.

Step 1:

Prepare and submit the Eligibility Determination Package as early as possible, but no later than March 1, 1996, to establish eligibility in one of three Award categories: Manufacturing, Service, and Small Business. Details are found on pages 7-16.

Step 2: Award Application

Deliverable: Award Application Package postmarked to ASQC by **April 1, 1996**.

Step 2:

Prepare and submit 20 copies of the application report, with the application fee(s) by April 1, 1996. Details are found on pages 19-27.

FEES FOR THE 1996 AWARD CYCLE

Eligibility Determination Fee

Postmarked to ASQC with the Eligibility Determination Package by **March 1, 1996**.

There is a nonrefundable $100 fee for submitting an Eligibility Determination Package, which must be included as part of the submission.

Application Fee

Postmarked to ASQC with the Award Application Package by **April 1, 1996**.

The fee, which must be included as part of the Award Application Package, covers expenses associated with the review of applications and development of feedback reports.

Manufacturing Category - $4500

Service Category - $4500

Small Business Category - $1500

Supplemental Sections - $1500 each (See page 19.)

Site Visit Review Fee

Due at ASQC two weeks after site visit.

The site visit review fee is paid only by applicants receiving a site visit.

The fee is set when visits are scheduled and covers expenses associated with site visit participation and the development of site visit reports.

The fee depends upon the number of sites to be visited, the number of Examiners assigned, and the duration of the visit.

The fee for small business applicants is one-half the rate for applicants in the manufacturing and service categories.

1996 AWARD PROGRAM PROCESSES AND TIME FRAMES

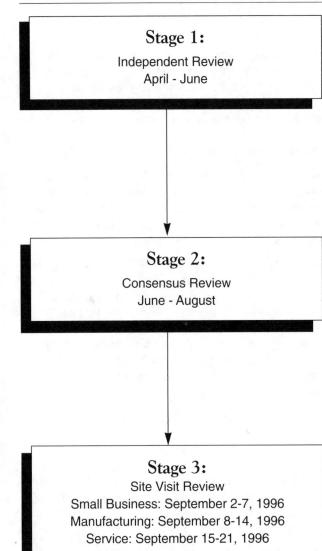

Stage 1:

Independent Review
April - June

Stage 2:

Consensus Review
June - August

Stage 3:

Site Visit Review
Small Business: September 2-7, 1996
Manufacturing: September 8-14, 1996
Service: September 15-21, 1996

Stage 1:

The application report is reviewed independently by at least five members of the Board of Examiners.

At the conclusion of this review, the Panel of Judges determines which applications should be forwarded for consensus review. At each stage, applicants receive every reasonable consideration to advance to the next stage.

Stage 2:

The application report is reviewed jointly by at least five members of the Board of Examiners led by a Senior Examiner.

At the conclusion of this review, the Panel of Judges determines which applicants should receive site visits.

Stage 3:

Site visit verification and clarification of the application report is conducted for the highest scoring candidates by at least five members of the Board of Examiners led by a Senior Examiner.

Site visits consist primarily of a review of pertinent records and data and interviews with executives and employees. Applicants selected for site visits receive the names of Examiners scheduled to participate. No site visits are conducted at sites outside of the United States or its territories.

A report by the site visit review team is submitted to the Panel of Judges.

Stage 4:
Judges' Final Review
October 1996

Award Ceremony
Fall 1996

Feedback Reports
Feedback Reports Distributed
July - December

Stage 4:

The Panel of Judges conducts final reviews and presents a set of Award recipient recommendations to the Director of NIST who conveys the recommendations to the Secretary of Commerce. The Secretary of Commerce makes the final determination of Award recipients.

Role Model Determination:

The Secretary of Commerce and the Director of NIST are responsible for determining that an applicant would be an appropriate role model and therefore should be approved as a Baldrige Award recipient. The purpose of this determination is to help ensure that the Award's integrity is preserved.

For the role model determination, NIST conducts records checks on potential Award recipients to ensure compliance with legal and regulatory requirements. These include records of the Internal Revenue Service, the Federal Bureau of Investigation, the Bureau of Export Administration, the General Services Administration, and local police and judicial offices in the headquarters' jurisdiction of the applicant. No new or independent investigations are conducted.

The Ceremony:

The Awards are traditionally presented by the President of the United States at a special ceremony in Washington, D.C.

Feedback Reports:

Each applicant receives a feedback report after it is determined that the applicant will not move to the next stage of consideration for the Award.

Feedback reports are prepared by members of the Board of Examiners based on the applicant's responses to the Award Criteria.

STEP 1 - 1996 ELIGIBILITY DETERMINATION PACKAGE INSTRUCTIONS

I. Purpose

The purpose of this section is to provide applicants with instructions for preparing the 1996 Eligibility Determination Package, the first step in applying for the Malcolm Baldrige National Quality Award (MBNQA). These instructions describe the considerations that are used to determine eligibility and how to fill out the Eligibility Determination Form.

II. Objective

The objective of the Eligibility Determination Package is to provide sufficient information to establish if the applicant is eligible to apply for the MBNQA. In addition, the completed Eligibility Determination Package represents a useful profile of the applicant. For this reason, it is included in the application report under Step 2 and is often the first part Examiners read in the application.

III. Content Requirements

A. Eligibility Determination Form and Attachments
(See pages 11-16)

1. The form must be filled out completely and signed.

2. A line and box organization chart for the applying organization must be attached.

3. If the applying organization is a subunit of a larger organization, the following must also be attached:

   – Line and box organization charts showing the relationship of the applicant to the highest management level of the parent organization, including all intervening levels, and

   – a copy of the relevant section/pages of an official company publication supporting the subunit designation.

B. Letter of Transmittal

A transmittal letter on company stationery signed by the Authorizing Official or designee must cover the Eligibility Determination Package.

C. Fee

A check or money order must be attached for the nonrefundable fee of $100. The fee must be payable to "The Malcolm Baldrige National Quality Award."

D. Submission

Potential applicants for the 1996 Award are encouraged to submit the Eligibility Determination Package as soon as possible after November 1, 1995, **but must do so no later than March 1, 1996.**

IV. 1996 Eligibility Determination

The Eligibility Determination Package will be reviewed. If clarification is required, the designated Eligibility Inquiry Point will be contacted. Applicants will be notified of their eligibility status within fourteen days of receipt by ASQC of the package, or additional information will be requested. The form showing the eligibility determination decision will be returned.

V. 1996 Eligibility Categories and Restrictions

A. Basic Eligibility

Public Law 100-107 establishes three eligibility categories of the Award: Manufacturing, Service, and Small Business. Any for-profit business located in the United States or its territories may apply for the Award. Eligibility for the Award is intended to be as open as possible to all U.S. companies. Publicly or privately-owned, domestic or foreign-owned, joint ventures, incorporated firms, sole proprietorships, partnerships, and holding companies may apply. The three categories are defined as follows:

1. **Manufacturing**
   Companies or subunits (discussed below) that produce and sell manufactured products or manufacturing processes, and those companies that produce agricultural, mining, or construction products. (See SIC Codes on page 18.)

2. **Service**
   Companies or subunits (discussed below) that sell services. (See SIC Codes on page 18.)

   Note: *Proper classification of companies that perform both manufacturing and service is determined by the larger percentage of sales.*

3. **Small Business**
   Complete businesses with not more than 500 full-time employees. Business activities may include manufacturing and/or service.

B. Restrictions on Eligibility

The following restrictions and conditions ensure fairness and consistency in definition:

1. **Excluded Organizations**
   Local, state, and national government agencies, not-for-profit organizations, trade associations, and professional societies are not eligible.

2. **Subunits**
   For purposes of the 1996 Award application, a subunit will be taken to mean a subsidiary of a larger business; a business owned by a holding company; or a business unit, division, or like unit of a larger

organization. In the Manufacturing and Service categories, subunits of a company may be eligible for the Award. Small businesses must apply as a whole; subunits of small businesses are not eligible.

The following application conditions apply for subunits:

a. The subunit must be a discrete, largely self-sufficient entity. That is, the unit must function as a business entity, not as a collection of activities aggregated for purposes of writing an Award application.

b. The entire subunit must be included in the application.

c. At least 50 percent of the subunit's customer base (dollar volume for products and services) must be free of direct financial and line organization control by the parent company. For example, a subunit is not eligible if its parent company and/or other subunits of the parent company are the customers for more than one-half of its total products and services.

("Parent company" refers to the company that owns or controls subunits through the ownership of voting stock.)

d. The subunit must be in existence for at least one year.

e. Individual units or partial aggregations of units of "chain" or "franchise" organizations (such as hotels, retail stores, banks, restaurants, or different plants manufacturing the same product) are not eligible.

For eligibility purposes, a chain or franchise organization is defined as an organization where each unit performs a similar function or manufactures a similar product. Accordingly, a potential applicant is not eligible if the parent company or another unit of the parent company provides the same products or services. Similarly, an individual unit is not eligible if customers would be unable to distinguish easily which unit of the company provides the products or services to them.

f. Subunits performing solely business support functions of the company are not eligible. Examples of business support functions include: Sales, Marketing, Distribution, Customer Service, Finance and Accounting, Human Resources, Environmental-Health-Safety of Employees, Purchasing, Legal Services, and Research and Development.

g. The subunit must satisfy at least one of the following conditions:

– The subunit must have more than 500 full-time employees, OR

– It must have at least 25 percent of all employees in the worldwide operations of the parent company, OR

– The subunit owned by a holding company was independent prior to being acquired.

h. A small business must be able to document that it functions independently of any other businesses which are equity owners. If there are equity owners with some management control, at least 50 percent of the small business' customer base (dollar volume for products and services) must be from other than the equity owners, or other businesses owned by the equity owners.

A small business owned by a holding company is eligible if it can document its independent operation and that other units of the holding company are in different businesses.

3. Location
A company or its subunit is eligible only if the operational practices associated with all major business functions of the applicant are inspectable in the United States or its territories. Also, one or both of the following conditions must apply:

a. more than 50 percent of the applicant's employees must be located in the U.S. or its territories, OR

b. more than 50 percent of the applicant's physical assets must be located in the U.S. or its territories.

4. Multiple-Application Restrictions

a. A subunit and its parent company may not both apply for Awards in the same year.

b. Only one subunit of a company may apply for an Award in the same year in the same Award category.

5. Future Eligibility Restrictions

a. If a company receives an Award, the company and all its subunits are ineligible to apply for another Award for a period of five years.

b. If a subunit receives an Award, that subunit and all its subunits are ineligible to apply for another Award for a period of five years.

c. If a subunit consisting of more than one-half of the total sales of a company receives an Award, neither that company nor any of its other subunits is eligible to apply for another Award for a period of five years.

ELIGIBILITY DETERMINATION FORM - INSTRUCTIONS

Item Instructions

Item 1. Applicant
Provide the official name and mailing address of the applicant. Check whether or not the applicant has existed for at least one year, or prior to April 1, 1995. If the answer is "No," briefly explain.

Attach line and box organizational chart for the applying organization.

Item 2. Highest-Ranking Official
Provide the name, title, mailing address, and telephone number of the applicant's highest-ranking official.

Item 3. For-Profit Designation
Check the appropriate response. Only for-profit organizations are eligible for an Award.

Item 4. Size of Applicant
a. Give an estimate of the number of employees of the applicant as of the date the 1996 Eligibility Determination Form is submitted. Where there is a significant proportion of part-time employees, count employees in proportion to the time they work (e.g., 75 employees who work one-third time would count as 25 full-time equivalents).

b. State the approximate percent (to the nearest whole number) of employees of the applicant located in the United States or its territories.

c. State the approximate percent (to the nearest whole number) of physical assets of the applicant located in the United States or its territories.

d. Give the number of different sites of all units of the applicant. Separate sites need not be counted for offices or other work areas located near each other if the applicant considers them as one location for business and personnel purposes.

e. Check the appropriate range for sales of the applicant for the preceding fiscal year.

Item 5. Industrial Classification
From page 18 choose up to three two-digit SIC Codes that best describe the applicant's products and/or services. Three- or four-digit SIC Codes may be used, if such information is available.

Item 6. Award Category
Based on the information given on page 7, indicate in which one of the three Award categories the applicant is planning to apply.

Item 7. Percent Customer Base
Check the appropriate response. If the answer is "No," briefly describe these customers and their relationship to the applicant.

Item 8. Site Listing and Descriptors
a. Provide the complete address of each site. In cases where the applicant has many sites performing the same function, these sites may be aggregated under one listing. Instead of the addresses for each, a summary statement about the locations may be made. If the applicant has foreign sites, these sites must be included. The Site Listing and Descriptors page should be duplicated if all sites cannot be listed on a single page. The 1996 Application Report must address activities in foreign sites in the appropriate Items. No site visits will be conducted at sites outside the United States or its territories. If a site visit is to be conducted, a more detailed listing will be requested when the visit is planned.

b. Provide the approximate **percent** of the applicant's employees at each site. Provide the approximate **percent** of the applicant's sales accounted for by the output of each site. Use "Not Applicable" (N/A) for percent sales of headquarters or similar offices, when appropriate.

c. Describe the types of all major products or services that are the output of the site. It may be necessary to state the relationship between the output of the site and the applicant's final products and services. It is not necessary to list every product or service.

Item 9. Business Factors
Provide a brief description of the following key business factors:
a. Nature of the applicant's business (products, services, and technology). A list of major competitors must be included;

b. Nature of major markets (local, regional, national, and international). A list of **major** customers must be included; and

c. Importance of suppliers, dealers, distributors, and franchises. A list of **major** suppliers and an indication of the type of product or service provided must be included.

Item 10. Subunit Designation
If the applicant is a subunit of a larger organization, then responses to Item 10a through 10j are required; otherwise, go to Item 11.

a. Provide the name and address of the parent company and the name and title of the highest official of the highest level of ownership of the parent company. Provide the number of worldwide employees of the parent company including all its subunits. Do not include joint ventures.

b. Check the appropriate response.

c. Check the appropriate response.

d. Check the appropriate response.

e. Check the appropriate response.

f. Check the appropriate response. If two or more subunits from the parent company are planning to apply, provide a brief explanation. Only one can be accepted per Award category.

g. Submit a short document, such as an annual report or the appropriate page(s) from a company publication, showing the organization of the parent company and its relationship to the applying unit. This publication must show that the applying unit has existed for at least one year. Indicate the title of this document.

h. Briefly describe the organizational structure and management links to the parent company.

   Attach line and box organization chart(s) showing the relationship of the applicant to the highest management level of the parent organization, including all intervening levels.

i. Check the appropriate response. If "Yes" is checked, provide a brief description of the market and product or service similarity and the organizational relationships of all units providing the same or similar products and services and the approximate sales for each of those units.

j. Briefly describe the major business support functions provided to the applicant by the parent company or by other units of the parent company.

Item 11. Supplemental Sections
Check the appropriate response. If "No" is checked, the Eligibility Inquiry Point will be contacted. Applicants that have two or more diverse product and/or service lines (i.e., in different two-digit SIC Codes) with customers, types of employees, technology, planning, and quality that are so different that the application report alone does not allow sufficient detail for a fair examination may be required to submit one or more supplemental sections in addition to the application report (see page 19). The use of supplemental sections must be approved during the eligibility determination process and is mandatory once approved.

Item 12. Eligibility Inquiry Point
During the review of the 1996 Eligibility Determination Form and associated materials, the applicant may need to be contacted for additional information. Please designate a person who is knowledgeable about the organization and its structure to answer such inquiries.

Item 13. Signature, Authorizing Official
The signature of the applicant's highest-ranking official or designee is required.

1996 Eligibility Determination
ASQC will return your form with the official determination checked in the box. An approved 1996 Eligibility Determination Form must accompany each of the twenty copies of the 1996 Application Report.

Eligibility Determination Package Preparation Instructions

The 1996 Eligibility Determination Form may be duplicated. In addition, page 2 of the 1996 Eligibility Determination Form (Item 8, Site Listing and Descriptors) should be duplicated if all sites cannot be listed on a single page.

Send a letter of transmittal on company stationery along with the completed form and fee to:

Malcolm Baldrige National Quality Award
c/o ASQC
P.O. Box 3005
Milwaukee, WI 53201-3005

Overnight Mailing Address:
Malcolm Baldrige National Quality Award
c/o ASQC
611 East Wisconsin Avenue
Milwaukee, WI 53202
(414) 272-8575

To avoid delay, applicants are encouraged to submit their completed Eligibility Determination Package as soon as possible after November 1, 1995, **but must do so no later than March 1, 1996.** All items should be answered. Incomplete forms will cause a delay in determination. All information is considered confidential.

The 1996 Eligibility Determination Package submission must be postmarked on or before March 1, 1996, to be considered for the 1996 Award. If a question arises about the deadline having been met, a dated receipt from the postal or overnight carrier will be required. However, applicants are encouraged to submit the form well ahead of the deadline to avoid delays.

Malcolm Baldrige National Quality Award

1 **Applicant**

Name _____

Address _____

_____

_____

Has the applicant officially or legally existed for at least one year?
(Check one.) ___Yes ___No (Briefly explain.)

_____

_____

Attach a line and box organizational chart for the applying organization.

2 **Highest-Ranking Official**

Name Mr.
Mrs.
Ms.
Dr. _____

Title _____

Applicant Name _____

Address _____

_____

_____

Telephone No. _____

3 **For-Profit Designation**

Is the applicant a for-profit business?
(Check one.) ___Yes ___No

4 **Size of Applicant**

a. Total number of employees _____

b. Percent employees in the U.S. and/or territories _____

c. Percent physical assets in U.S. and/or territories _____

d. Total number of sites _____

e. Sales preceding fiscal year *(Check one.)*

___ 0-$1M   ___ $10M-$100M   ___ $500M-$1B

___ $1M-$10M   ___ $100M-$500M   ___ Over $1B

5 **Industrial Classification**

List up to three most descriptive two-digit SIC Codes.
(See page 18.)

_____ _____ _____

6 **Award Category**
(Check one.)

___ Manufacturing   ___ Service   ___ Small Business

7 **Percent Customer Base**

Is over 50% of the sales of the applicant to customers outside of the applicant's organization, its parent company, and other companies with financial or organizational control of the applicant or parent company?
(Check one.) ___Yes ___No (Briefly explain.)

OMB Clearance #0693-0006
Expiration Date: June 30, 1997

This form may be copied and attached to, or bound with, other application materials.

Malcolm Baldrige National Quality Award

8 Site Listing and Descriptors

a. Address of Site	b. Relative Size — *Percent* of Applicant's		c. Description of Products or Services
	Employees	Sales	

This page may be copied and attached to, or bound with, other application materials.

Provide all the information for each site except where multiple sites produce similar products or services. For such multiple site cases, see page 9.

9 **Business Factors**

Provide a brief description of the following key business factors:

a. Nature of the applicant's business (products, services, and technologies); conclude with a list of ***major*** competitors

b. Nature of major markets (local, regional, national, and international); conclude with a list of ***major*** customers

Malcolm Baldrige National Quality Award

9 ### Business Factors (Continued)

c. Importance of suppliers, dealers, distributors, and franchises; conclude with a list of *major* suppliers

10 ### Subunit Designation

Is applicant a subsidiary, business unit, division, or like organization of a larger organization or holding company? (Check one.)

___Yes (Continue)   ___ No (Go to Item 11.)

a. Parent Company

Name

_____

Address

_____

_____

_____

Highest Official

_____

Title

_____

Number of worldwide employees of the

parent company _____

b. Does the applicant have more than 500 employees? (Check one.)   ___Yes ___No

c. Does the applicant comprise over 25 percent of the worldwide employees of the parent company? (Check one.)   ___Yes ___No

d. If the parent organization is a holding company, did the applicant operate as an independent company prior to acquisition? (Check one.)   ___Yes ___No

e. Does the applicant consist of more than 50 percent of the worldwide sales of the parent company? (Check one.)   ___Yes ___No

f. Is the applicant's parent company or another subunit of the parent company intending to apply? (Check one.)

___Yes (Briefly explain.)   ___ No   ___Don't know

10 **Subunit Designation** (Continued)

g. Name the document supporting the subunit designation.

_____

_____

Include a copy of the document with this form.

h. Briefly describe the organizational structure and management links to the parent company.

Attach line and box organizational chart(s) showing the relationship of the applicant to the highest management level of the parent organization, including all intervening levels.

i. Do other units within the parent company provide similar products or services?

(Check one.) ___Yes (Briefly explain.) ___No

j. Briefly describe the major business support functions provided to the applicant by the parent company or by other units of the parent company.

Malcolm Baldrige National Quality Award

11 Supplemental Sections

Does the applicant have: (a) a single performance system that supports all of its product and/or service lines, and (b) products or services essentially similar in terms of customers, technology, types of employees, planning, and quality?

(Check one.) ____ Yes (Go to item 12.)

____ No (Briefly describe the differences in the products and/or services covered in terms of differences in customers, technology, types of employees, planning, and quality. You will be contacted.)

12 Eligibility Inquiry Point

Mr.
Mrs.
Ms.
Name Dr. _____

Title _____

Applicant Name _____

Mailing Address _____

_____

Overnight
Mailing Address _____

Telephone No. _____

Telefax No. _____

13 Signature, Authorizing Official

Date _____

X

Mr.
Mrs.
Ms.
Name Dr. _____

Title _____

Applicant Name _____

Address _____

_____

_____

Telephone No. _____

DO NOT WRITE BELOW THIS LINE

1996 Eligibility Determination

☐ Manufacturing

☐ Service

☐ Small Business   ☐ Ineligible

_____

Award Administration

For Official Use Only

1996 ELIGIBILITY DETERMINATION PACKAGE CHECKLIST

1. **Eligibility Determination Form:**
   a. Have all questions been answered completely?

   ___Yes   ___No

   b. Is a line and box organization chart included which shows all components of the applicant organization?

   ___Yes   ___No

   c. If the applicant is a subunit of a larger organization:

   • Are line and box organization charts included which show the relationship of the applicant to the highest management level of the parent organization, including all intervening levels?

   ___Yes   ___No

   • Are relevant sections/pages of an official company publication supporting the subunit designation included?

   ___Yes   ___No

   d. Is the Eligibility Determination Form signed by the Authorizing Official or designee?

   ___Yes   ___No

2. **Letter of Transmittal:**
   Is the Eligibility Determination Package covered by a letter on company stationery and signed by the Authorizing Official or designee?

   ___Yes   ___No

3. **Fee:**
   Is a check for the nonrefundable eligibility determination fee of $100 included?

   ___Yes   ___No

If you have checked "No" to ANY question on this list, please recheck the Instructions before submitting your Eligibility Determination Package.

STANDARD INDUSTRIAL CLASSIFICATION (SIC) CODES

Manufacturing and Products

Code	Sector
01	Agriculture – crops
02	Agriculture – livestock
08	Forestry
09	Fishing, hunting, and trapping
10	Metal mining
12	Coal mining
13	Oil and gas extraction
14	Mineral quarrying
15	General building contractors
16	Heavy construction contractors
17	Special trade contractors
20	Food products
21	Tobacco products
22	Textile mill products
23	Apparel
24	Lumber and wood products
25	Furniture and fixtures
26	Paper and allied products
27	Printing and publishing
28	Chemicals
29	Petroleum refining
30	Rubber and plastics
31	Leather and leather products
32	Stone/clay/glass/concrete products
33	Primary metal industries
34	Fabricated metal products
35	Machinery/computer equipment
36	Electrical/electronic equipment
37	Transportation equipment
38	Instruments/watches and clocks/optical goods
39	Miscellaneous manufacturing

Services

Code	Sector
07	Agricultural services
40	Railroad transportation
41	Local & interurban transport
42	Trucking and warehousing
44	Water transportation
45	Air transportation
46	Pipelines, except natural gas
47	Transportation services
48	Communications
49	Electric/gas/sanitary services
50	Wholesale trade/durable goods
51	Wholesale trade/nondurable goods
52	Retail building materials
53	General merchandise stores
54	Food stores
55	Automotive dealers & service stations
56	Apparel and accessory stores
57	Furniture stores
58	Eating and drinking places
59	Miscellaneous retail
60	Banking
61	Credit agencies
62	Security & commodity brokers
63	Insurance carriers
64	Insurance agents
65	Real estate
67	Holding & other investment offices
70	Hotels and lodging places
72	Personal services
73	Business services
75	Automotive repair and services
76	Miscellaneous repair services
78	Motion pictures
79	Amusement and recreation
80	Health services
81	Legal services
82	Educational services
83	Social services
84	Museums and art galleries
86	Membership organizations
87	Professional services
89	Miscellaneous services

STEP 2 - 1996 AWARD APPLICATION PACKAGE INSTRUCTIONS

I. Purpose

The purpose of this section is to provide applicants determined eligible under Step 1 with instructions for preparing the 1996 Award Application Package. These instructions describe content, format, assembly, and submission requirements and give guidelines for responding to the Criteria Items.

II. Objective

The objective of the 1996 Award Application Package is to allow the applicant to provide sufficient information to permit a rigorous evaluation by the Board of Examiners. Information is required on its performance management system and on results of its improvement processes.

III. Content Requirements

A. Application Report - All Applicants

Only a 1996 Application Report is required if an applicant has a single performance system that supports all of its product and/or service lines and if the products or services are essentially similar in terms of customers, technology, types of employees, planning, and quality. *This is the case with most applicants*.

A 1996 Application Report must contain:

■ Front Cover

■ Title Page

■ Table of Contents

■ Approved 1996 Eligibility Determination Form

■ Organization Chart(s)

■ 1996 Application Form

■ Business Overview (4 pages or less)

■ Glossary of Terms and Abbreviations

■ Response Addressing the Criteria Items (Item 1.1 through 7.4) (70 pages or less).

■ Summary of Supplemental Sections, if applicable (2 pages or less). (See "Supplemental Sections" below.)

■ Back Cover

All units/subunits of the applicant must be included in the 1996 Application Report [and/or Supplemental Section(s)].

Note: More explanation of the content and writing of these report parts is contained below in the sections entitled "Description of 1996 Application Report Parts" and "Guidelines for Writing a 1996 Application Report."

B. Supplemental Sections

In order to maintain an equivalent level of detail for all sizes and types of applicants, certain complex applicants may also need to provide supplemental sections. Supplemental sections are intended to permit applicants with the most complex organizations and performance systems to describe them in sufficient detail to permit a rigorous examination. Supplemental sections may be required if the applicant has two or more diverse product and/or service lines (i.e., in different two-digit SIC Codes) with customers, technology, types of employees, planning, and quality that are so different that the application report alone will not allow sufficient detail for a fair examination.

The use of supplemental sections must be approved during eligibility determination. Once supplemental sections are approved, they must be submitted by the applicant. If both an application report and supplemental section(s) are submitted, the application report should cover the largest aggregation of similar product or service lines that are supported by a single performance system.

Together, the application report and the supplemental section(s) must cover all products and/or services and all performance systems of the applicant.

Each 1996 Supplemental Section must contain:

■ Front Cover

■ Title Page

■ Table of Contents

■ Organization Chart

■ Summary of Supplemental Section(s) (2 pages or less)

■ Business Overview (4 pages or less)

■ Glossary of Terms and Abbreviations

■ Response Addressing the Criteria Items (Items 1.1 through 7.4) (50 pages or less).

■ Back Cover

IV. Format Requirements

The application report and supplemental section(s), if any, must meet the page limit, typing, and format requirements below.

A. Page Limits and Exclusions

1. The Business Overview for the application report and each supplemental section is limited to four single-sided pages. If the Business Overview exceeds the four-page limit, the excess pages will be counted as part of the page count for the response addressing the Criteria Items.

2. The response addressing the Criteria Items is limited to 70 single-sided pages including pictures, graphs, figures, tables, and appendices. The response must contain the same Category and Item numerical designations (Item 1.1 through Item 7.4) as the 1996 Criteria. Applicants should denote the Areas to Address with letters a, b, c, etc., corresponding to each Area. Applicants should denote responses to Areas by underlining the Item/Area (e.g., 4.2b).

3. The covers, dividers, tab separators, Title Page, Table of Contents, Organization Chart(s), Eligibility Determination Form, Application Form, and Glossary of Terms and Abbreviations which contain only the subject material will not be counted as part of the page limit in either the application report or supplemental section. However, if these pages contain **any** additional material, e.g., text, quotes, graphs, figures, data tables, or pictures, they will be considered part of the response addressing the Criteria Items and counted as part of the page count for it.

4. The Summary of Supplemental Section(s), if applicable, is limited to two single-sided pages. If the summary exceeds the two-page limit, the excess will be counted as part of the page count for the response addressing the Criteria Items.

5. In supplemental sections, the response addressing the Criteria Items is limited to 50 single-sided pages.

B. Paper size: standard 8 1/2 by 11 inch

C. Typing

1. Font Size

   - fixed pitch font of 12 or fewer characters per inch OR

   - proportional spacing font of point size 10 or larger

2. Line Spacing – Equivalent of two points of lead between lines

   Note: *One point of lead equals 1/72, or 0.0138, inch.*

3. Font Style – Any font style may be used that meets the font size and line spacing requirements, but Helvetica and Times or equivalent styles are preferred.

4. Type used in picture captions, graphs, figures, data tables, and appendices must also meet the requirements for font size and line spacing. If the table or graph is reduced from its original size for inclusion, applicants must use larger type sizes in preparing the original so that the reduced material in the application meets the font size requirements.

D. Format

1. The number of lines per page must not exceed 60, including the page headings and page number.

2. A margin of at least 3/4 inch on the side of the page which is bound or fastened and at least 1/2 inch on the opposite side of the page is preferred.

3. Pages set up in a two-column format are preferred. Pages may be printed on both sides.

E. Page Numbering – The pages of the application report must be numbered consecutively from start to finish (e.g., 1, ..., 70).

F. Tabs or Dividers – Sections of the report should be separated using labeled section tabs or dividers which contain only the title of the section.

V. Assembly Requirements

A. All components of the 1996 Application Report and 1996 Supplemental Section(s) must be securely fastened to prevent separation during handling. The use of clips or binders with easily opened pressure-sensitive clips is discouraged. Supplemental section(s) must be bound separately from the application report.

B. The use of bulky binders or similar heavy covers is discouraged.

C. Copies of video or audio tape or other information aids are not acceptable.

VI. Submission Requirements

A. Applicants must submit a 1996 Award Application Package containing:

1. Twenty bound copies of the complete application report and, if appropriate, twenty bound copies of each supplemental section.

2. A check or money order covering the application fees for the application report and, if appropriate, each supplemental section.

   The 1996 application fees are:

   - Manufacturing Company Category – $4500
   - Service Company Category – $4500
   - Small Business Category – $1500
   - Supplemental Sections – $1500

   The check or money order should be made payable to **The Malcolm Baldrige National Quality Award.**

B. The 1996 Award Application Package must be postmarked or consigned to an overnight delivery service **no later than April 1, 1996**, to be eligible for a 1996 Award. If a question arises about the deadline having been met, the applicant will be asked to supply a dated receipt from the postal or overnight carrier.

Incomplete submissions or those which do not meet the requirements given in the sections entitled "Content Requirements" and "Format Requirements" will be returned along with the fee payment.

Send the complete 1996 Award Application Package to:

Malcolm Baldrige National Quality Award
c/o ASQC
611 East Wisconsin Avenue
Milwaukee, WI 53202
414-272-8575

VII. Description of 1996 Application Report Parts

Each copy of the 1996 Application Report contains:

A. Front Cover

B. Title Page with the name of the applicant.

C. Table of Contents with the page number of each Category and Item. Areas to Address need not be included in the Table of Contents.

D. A complete copy of the **1996 Eligibility Determination Form** approved by ASQC, including all Site Listing and Descriptors pages, and if the applicant is a subunit of a larger organization or is owned by a holding company, a line and box organization chart of the parent/holding company showing where the applicant fits into the overall organization.

E. A line and box **organization chart of the applicant** with sufficient detail for Examiners to understand the relationships between subunits of the applicant mentioned in the 1996 Application Report.

F. A copy of the completed and signed **1996 Application Form** (see page 27 of this booklet). A signed 1996 Application Form indicates that the applicant agrees to the terms and conditions of the Award process and, if chosen, agrees to host a site visit, to facilitate an open and unbiased examination, to pay reasonable costs associated with the site visit, and, if selected as an Award recipient, to share information on successful performance and quality strategies with other U.S. organizations.

G. The **Business Overview** is an outline of the applicant's business, addressing what is most important to the business and the key factors that influence how the business operates and where it is headed. It is a vital part of the overall application and is used by the Examiners in all stages of the application review. (See the sections below on writing the Business Overview, pages 22-23.)

H. A **Glossary of Terms and Abbreviations** used in the application report and each supplemental section.

I. The **Response Addressing the Criteria Items** must respond separately to each of the Items of the 1996 Award Criteria. (See the section below entitled **"Guidelines for Writing a 1996 Application Report."**)

- Respond to each Item as a whole. Address the set of Areas with an emphasis that reflects the applicant's business and performance system. To facilitate review by the Board of Examiners, applicants are encouraged to respond to the Areas in the order given in the Items. The applicant must address activities in foreign sites in the appropriate Items.

- If an Area to Address does not pertain to an applicant's business or performance system, the applicant must provide a statement of one or two sentences explaining why the Area is not applicable. This statement should be given at the end of the overall response to the Item. The Item/Area designator should be used as described under format requirements.

J. If applicable, a **Summary of Supplemental Sections** — a brief description of each supplemental section, including the products, services, and SIC Codes.

K. Back Cover

VIII. Guidelines for Writing a 1996 Application Report

Writing an application for the Baldrige Award involves responding in 70 or fewer pages to the requirements given in the 24 Award Criteria Items. The guidelines given in this section are offered to assist applicants to respond most effectively to the Item requirements.

The guidelines are presented in four parts:
(A) General Guidelines regarding the Award Criteria booklet, including how the Items are formatted; (B) How to Prepare the Business Overview; (C) Guidelines for Responding to Approach/Deployment Items; and (D) Guidelines for Responding to Results Items.

A. General Guidelines

1. Read the entire Award Criteria booklet.
The main sections of the booklet provide an overall orientation to the Criteria and how applicants' responses are evaluated. Applicants should be thoroughly familiar with the following sections of the 1996 Award Criteria booklet:

- Award Criteria (pages 6-23)

- Scoring Information (pages 24-25)

- Glossary of Key Terms (pages 4-5)

- Item Descriptions (pages 34-43)

2. Review the Item format.
The Item format (see figure below) shows the different parts of Items, what each part is for, and where each part is placed. It is especially important to understand the Areas to Address and the Item Notes. All Items and Areas to Address are described in a separate section of the 1996 Award Criteria booklet (pages 34-43).

Each Item is classified either (A – D) or (R), depending on the type of information required. The meaning of these classification symbols is given on page 24 of the 1996 Award Criteria booklet. Guidelines for responding to Approach/Deployment Items and guidelines for responding to Results Items are given on pages 24 and 25, respectively, of this booklet.

3. Start by preparing the Business Overview.
The Business Overview is the most appropriate starting point for writing an application. The Business Overview is intended to help everyone — including the company's application writer(s) and reviewer(s) — to understand what is most relevant and important to the applicant's business.

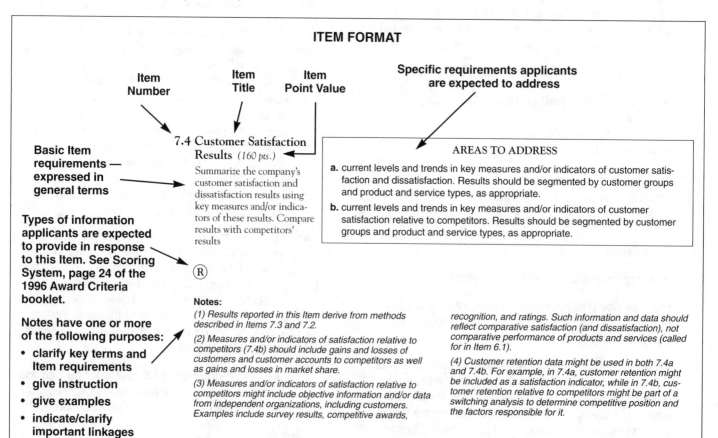

ITEM FORMAT

Item Number · Item Title · Item Point Value · Specific requirements applicants are expected to address

7.4 Customer Satisfaction Results *(160 pts.)*

Summarize the company's customer satisfaction and dissatisfaction results using key measures and/or indicators of these results. Compare results with competitors' results

(R)

Basic Item requirements — expressed in general terms

Types of information applicants are expected to provide in response to this Item. See Scoring System, page 24 of the 1996 Award Criteria booklet.

Notes have one or more of the following purposes:
- clarify key terms and Item requirements
- give instruction
- give examples
- indicate/clarify important linkages

AREAS TO ADDRESS

a. current levels and trends in key measures and/or indicators of customer satisfaction and dissatisfaction. Results should be segmented by customer groups and product and service types, as appropriate.

b. current levels and trends in key measures and/or indicators of customer satisfaction relative to competitors. Results should be segmented by customer groups and product and service types, as appropriate.

Notes:

(1) Results reported in this Item derive from methods described in Items 7.3 and 7.2.

(2) Measures and/or indicators of satisfaction relative to competitors (7.4b) should include gains and losses of customers and customer accounts to competitors as well as gains and losses in market share.

(3) Measures and/or indicators of satisfaction relative to competitors might include objective information and/or data from independent organizations, including customers. Examples include survey results, competitive awards, recognition, and ratings. Such information and data should reflect comparative satisfaction (and dissatisfaction), not comparative performance of products and services (called for in Item 6.1).

(4) Customer retention data might be used in both 7.4a and 7.4b. For example, in 7.4a, customer retention might be included as a satisfaction indicator, while in 7.4b, customer retention relative to competitors might be part of a switching analysis to determine competitive position and the factors responsible for it.

B. How to Prepare the Business Overview

1. Description of the Business Overview

The Business Overview is an outline of the applicant's business, addressing what is most important to the business, the key factors that influence how the business operates, and where the business is headed. In simplest terms, *the Business Overview is intended to help Examiners understand what is relevant and important to the applicant's business.*

The Business Overview is of critical importance to the applicant because:

- it is the most appropriate starting point for writing and self-assessing the application, helping to ensure focus on key business issues and to achieve consistency in responses, especially in reporting business results; and

- it is used by the Examiners and Judges in all stages of application review, including the site visit.

2. Guidelines for Preparing the Business Overview

The Business Overview consists of five sections as follows:

(a) Basic description of the company
This section should provide basic information on:

- the nature of the applicant's business: products and services;

- company size, location(s), and whether it is publicly or privately owned;

- the applicant's major markets (local, regional, national, or international) and principal customer types (consumers, other businesses, government, etc.). (Note any special relationships, such as partnerships, with customers or customer groups.);

- a profile of the applicant's employee base, including: number, types, educational level, bargaining units, and special safety requirements; and

- major equipment, facilities, and technologies used.

If the applicant is a subunit of a larger entity, a brief description of the organizational relationships to the parent company and percent of employees it represents should be given. Briefly describe also relationships of the applicant's products and services to those of the parent company and/or other subunits of the parent company. If the parent company provides key support services, this should be briefly described.

(b) Customer requirements
This section should provide information on:

- key customer requirements (for example, on-time delivery, low defect levels, price demands, and after-sales services) for products and services. Briefly describe all important requirements, and note significant differences, if any, in requirements among customer groups.

(c) Supplier relationships
This section should provide information on:

- types and numbers of suppliers of goods and services;

- the most important types of suppliers, dealers, and other businesses; and

- any limitations or special relationships that may exist in dealing with some or all suppliers.

(d) Competitive factors
This section should provide information on:

- the applicant's position (relative size, growth) in the industry;

- numbers and types of competitors;

- principal factors that determine competitive success such as productivity growth, cost reduction, and product innovation; and

- changes taking place in the industry that affect competition.

(e) Other factors important to the applicant
This section should provide information, as appropriate, on:

- major new thrusts for the company such as entry into new markets or segments;

- new business alliances;

- introduction of new technologies;

- the regulatory environment affecting the applicant, such as occupational health and safety, environmental, financial, and product;

- changes in strategy; and

- unique factors.

3. Page Limit

The Business Overview is limited to four pages. These four pages are not counted in the overall application page limit. Typing instructions for the Business Overview are the same as for the application and are given on page 20.

> *It is strongly recommended that the Business Overview be prepared first and that it be used to guide the applicant in writing and reviewing the application.*

C. Guidelines for Responding to Approach/ Deployment Items

The Award Criteria focus on performance results. Results Items (6.1, 6.2, 6.3, 6.4, and 7.4) require applicants to summarize results of all kinds, including operational, customer-related, and financial. However, results, by themselves, offer little *diagnostic* value. For example, if results are poor in some areas or improving at rates slower than the competition's, it is important to understand *why* this is so and *what* might be done to accelerate improvement. Approach/Deployment Items permit diagnosis of the applicant's most important systems, activities, and processes — the ones that offer the greatest potential for fast-paced improvement of the applicant's performance. Diagnosis and feedback depend heavily upon the *content and completeness* of Approach/Deployment Item responses. For this reason, it is important to respond to these Items by providing key process information. Guidelines for organizing such information are given below.

1. Understand the meaning of "how".

Items that request information on approach include Areas to Address that begin with the word "how". Responses to such Areas should provide as complete a picture as possible to enable meaningful evaluation and feedback. *Responses should outline key process details such as methods, measures, deployment, and evaluation factors.* Information lacking sufficient detail to permit an evaluation and feedback, or merely providing an example, is referred to in the Criteria booklet as *anecdotal information.*

2. Write and review response(s) with the following guidelines, questions, and comments in mind:

■ Show *what* and *how.*

- Does the response show what is done and does it give a clear sense of how?

It is important to give basic information about what key processes are and how they work. Although it is helpful to include who performs the work, merely stating who does not permit feedback. For example, stating that "customer satisfaction data are analyzed for improvement by the Customer Service Department" does not set the stage for useful feedback, because from this very limited information, potential strengths and weaknesses in the analysis cannot be identified at all.

■ Show that activities are *systematic.*

- Does the response show a systematic approach, or does it merely provide an example (anecdote)?

Approaches that are systematic use data and information for cycles of improvement. In other words, the approaches are systematic *over time,* and thus show learning and maturity. Scores above 50 percent rely upon clear evidence that approaches are systematic.

■ Show deployment.

- Does the response give clear and sufficient information on deployment? For example, from a response, could one clearly distinguish whether an approach described is used in one part of the company or in a few, most, or all parts?

Deployment can be shown compactly by using summary tables that outline what is done in different parts of the company. This is particularly effective if the basic approach is described in a narrative.

■ Show focus and consistency.

- Does the response show that the applicant is focused on key processes and on improvements that offer the greatest potential to improve business performance?

There are four important factors to consider regarding setting the stage for focus and consistency: (1) the Business Overview should make clear what is important; (2) the Strategic Planning Category, including the key business drivers, should highlight areas of greatest focus and describe how deployment is accomplished; (3) descriptions of company-level analysis (Item 2.3) should show how the company analyzes performance information to set priorities; and (4) company-level review (1.2b) should show how performance information is tracked and used. Focus and consistency in the Approach/Deployment Items should be accompanied by corresponding results being reported in Items 6.1, 6.2, 6.3, 6.4, and 7.4.

■ Respond fully to Item requirements.

- Does the response lack information on important parts of an Area to Address?

Missing information will be interpreted as a gap in approach and/or deployment. All Areas should be addressed and checked in final review.

3. Cross-reference when appropriate.

Applicants should try to make each Item response self-contained. However, there may be instances when responses to different Items are mutually reinforcing. It is then appropriate to reference responses to other Items, rather than to repeat information. In such cases, applicants should use Area designators (for example, "see 2.3a").